ON JUSTIFICATION

PRINCETON STUDIES IN CULTURAL SOCIOLOGY

Paul J. DiMaggio, Michèle Lamont,

Robert J. Wuthnow, Viviana A. Zelizer

A LIST OF TITLES IN THIS SERIES
APPEARS AT THE BACK OF THE BOOK.

Luc Boltanski
Laurent Thévenot

ON JUSTIFICATION

ECONOMIES OF WORTH

Translated by Catherine Porter

PRINCETON UNIVERSITY PRESS

PRINCETON AND OXFORD

© EDITIONS GALLIMARD, PARIS, 1991

ENGLISH TRANSLATION © 2006 BY PRINCETON UNIVERSITY PRESS

PUBLISHED IN FRANCE AS *DE LA JUSTIFICATION:*
LES ÉCONOMIES DE LA GRANDEUR, 1991

PUBLISHED BY PRINCETON UNIVERSITY PRESS, 41 WILLIAM STREET,
PRINCETON, NEW JERSEY 08540

IN THE UNITED KINGDOM: PRINCETON UNIVERSITY PRESS,
3 MARKET PLACE, WOODSTOCK, OXFORDSHIRE OX20 1SY

ALL RIGHTS RESERVED

OUVRAGE PUBLIÉ AVEC LE CONCOURS DU MINISTÈRE FRANÇAIS CHARGÉ DE LA
CULTURE—CENTRE NATIONAL DU LIVRE [WORK PUBLISHED WITH THE HELP OF
FRENCH MINISTRY OF CULTURE—NATIONAL CENTER FOR BOOKS]

LIBRARY OF CONGRESS CATALOGING-IN-PUBLICATION DATA

BOLTANSKI, LUC.

[DE LA JUSTIFICATION. ENGLISH]

ON JUSTIFICATION : ECONOMIES OF WORTH / LUC BOLTANSKI, LAURENT
THÉVENOT ; TRANSLATED BY CATHERINE PORTER.

P.   CM.

INCLUDES BIBLIOGRAPHICAL REFERENCES AND INDEX.

ISBN-13: 978-0-691-11837-6 (HARDCOVER : ALK. PAPER)

ISBN-10: 0-691-11837-X (HARDCOVER : ALK. PAPER)

ISBN-13: 978-0-691-12516-9 (PBK.: ALK. PAPER)

ISBN-10: 0-691-12516-3 (PBK.: ALK. PAPER)

1. SOCIAL SCIENCES—PHILOSOPHY.   2. ECONOMICS—MORAL AND ETHICAL
ASPECTS.   3. JUSTIFICATION (THEORY OF KNOWLEDGE)   4. COMMON GOOD.
I. THÉVENOT, LAURENT.   II. TITLE.

H61.B622   2006

300'.1—DC22   2005020884

BRITISH LIBRARY CATALOGING-IN-PUBLICATION DATA IS AVAILABLE

THIS BOOK HAS BEEN COMPOSED IN JANSON

PRINTED ON ACID-FREE PAPER. ∞

PUP.PRINCETON.EDU

PRINTED IN THE UNITED STATES OF AMERICA

1 3 5 7 9 10 8 6 4 2

CONTENTS

ON JUSTIFICATION

PREFACE

How We Wrote This Book

READERS OF THIS BOOK may find it somewhat discomfiting not to encounter a familiar cast of characters: none of the groups—social classes, blue-collar workers, white-collar workers, youth, women, voters, and so on—with which we have become acquainted thanks to the social sciences and the quantitative sociological data that proliferate today; none of the "men without qualities" whom economists call "individuals" and who serve to buttress analyses of rational choices and preferences. Nor are there any of the life-size characters who have been appropriated for the realm of scientific knowledge by sociology, history, or anthropology in their most literary forms, much the way similar figures are highlighted by journalists or novelists. Short on groups, individuals, and persons, our book nevertheless abounds in beings, some of them human, some of them things. Whenever these beings appear, the state in which they operate is always qualified[1] at the same time. The relation between these person-states and thing-states (which constitutes what we define as a *situation*) is the object of our study.

Still, we have not forgotten the beings with which the social sciences have familiarized us. Our investigation of the problems posed by the juxtaposition of those beings within a single discursive framework, and even within individual utterances, has led us to focus our research on the questions raised by the very act of qualifying not only things but also those beings particularly resistant to qualification that we call persons. It was important to us to center our study on operations of qualification, because this position allowed us to shift back and forth between the type of inquiry that usually falls under epistemology and the sort of questioning typical of sociology or anthropology. Indeed, operations of qualification can be grasped as elementary components of scientific activity in general, which presupposes that a relation of equivalence has been established among the objects under study. But operations of qualification also constitute the basic cognitive operations of social interaction; social coordination requires a continuous effort of comparison, agreement on common terms, and identification.

Generalizing Field Observations and Producing Statistical Equivalency

Our way of working made us mindful of different approaches—scientific and everyday—to qualification, and also of the problems that arise when a relation is established between those ways of qualifying. In fact, in our own past experience—Laurent Thévenot as an economist and statistician, Luc Boltanski as a sociologist—we have constantly had to manipulate the large collective beings that need to be evoked in order to deal almost cartographically with what has conventionally been called society since the first half of the nineteenth century. But one of us is a producer and user of statistical nomenclatures and the other a sociologist working in the field with methods of observation derived from ethnology; as such, we could not be completely blind to the tension between the necessity for qualification prior to any classification and the resistance to qualification of the material to be classified. Regardless of how we might process it, that material consisted of statements gathered from persons—many of whom challenged the taxonomic enterprise with unforeseen and thus unclassifiable qualifications. When they had the opportunity, some even spoke up against the efforts of experts and scholars to classify them in a way that would relate them to other persons by forcing them into a single category.

The problem of the relation between category and item in descriptions in the social sciences became strikingly clear to us, and in a form that was particularly hard to justify in terms of epistemological requirements, in those instances where a researcher had attempted to make a statement about macrobeings (social classes, for example) more vivid by tacking on an interview excerpt, obscuring the problematic relation between a general statement and a concrete example by presenting the latter as illustrative or typical. The same tension is immediately present in any discourse (the discourse of descriptive statistics, for instance) that draws on numerical data from matrixes formed by the intersection of analytical categories and observations about human behavior, while reducing the challenge of interweaving these two descriptive languages into a single commentary to a problem of rhetoric, writing, or style. The same remark applies to a procedure used in many forms of content analysis: a researcher assigns someone's response to a category, on the grounds that it is a typical response, in order to justify setting it up as a linguistic phenomenon that can be subjected to scientific analysis. The analysis makes no mention of the sense of discomfort that often arises in a simple face-to-face encounter between an investigator, questionnaire in hand, and a person being questioned in his own home, surrounded by familiar objects; the investigator's very presence, quite as much as her statements, constantly threatens to turn an enterprise aimed at pinning down the truth of a situation within the standardized grid of a questionnaire into a disconcerting, futile, and possibly offensive exercise.

A naive interpretation of this tension would suggest that it is created by an excessive disparity between a given reality and categories deemed either inadequate or else too general to conform to the contours of that reality. Here we run into the usual criticisms directed at statistics and, more generally, at any globalizing approach. In fact, our very first steps entailed looking more closely than researchers usually do at the operations involved in compiling raw data in terms of established categories. These primary research operations, which precede any attempt to explain or even to process the material collected, are at once the most fundamental operations of all and the least often problematized or explored.

Prompted by the light Pierre Bourdieu's anthropological research shed on the relation between classifying operations and practical interventions (1977), we first directed our attention to the methods that statisticians, sociologists, and legal scholars use to codify and more generally to shape data. We paid particular heed to connections being made with other generally accepted forms of qualification that help consolidate and stabilize the categories that researchers are attempting to construct or apply.

We pursued two different but parallel approaches. In one set of studies, using Alain Desrosières's work on socioprofessional categories as a starting point (1987), we sought to produce a history of the construction of the category of cadres, people at the managerial level in business—the new middle class; we wanted to show how the class came to be established by drawing on earlier already-stabilized groupings (such as those formed around collective agreements) (Boltanski 1987). To do this, we had to reconstitute earlier attempts by spokespersons for political parties and unions to define the content and limits of the category. Before it came to designate a taken-for-granted "official" group, the existence of the category itself remained problematic; it had to be constructed the way social or political causes are put together, that is, with the declared intention of correcting an injustice by gaining recognition for a social group that had previously gone unnoticed. But our study of the group of people who identify themselves as cadres today showed that when they are questioned about their professional identity, the actors themselves tend to bring the process of representation back into play,[2] and thus to act as representatives in their turn. Moreover, statistical processing of data, which works in principle by combining variables, does not succeed in wholly eliminating the presence of persons. Human beings resurface in difficult cases where the conventional treatment of variables does not suffice. In such cases, in order to assign the respondents to a category, the agent responsible for processing the material has to imagine persons by comparing them to people he knows.

Ordinary Identification and Scientific Qualification

Our second set of parallel studies consists in observing and analyzing both categories with indistinct boundaries, such as young people (Thévenot 1979), and the procedures used in large statistical agencies to codify data, often by lower-level staff. This is usually treated as a routine, unproblematic task (Thévenot 1983). We paid special attention to instances in which the normal course of the statistical chain is interrupted because the codifiers sense that the instructions they have been given are inadequate. These moments of doubt arise in particular when the codifiers have to decide how to categorize cases that seem questionable to them and arouse their suspicions. When the codification has to do with a person's profession, the codifiers can quell their doubts and proceed with categorization by looking at other information in the questionnaire, such as educational level or income. But this association of characteristics often leads a codifier to question a title or professional category indicated by the respondent. The latter may be "demoted," assigned to a category of lower status than the one that first seemed to be indicated in the responses. In such a case, we observe a correction of the interviewee's statement, or, to use a term with a statistical flavor, an imputation, which the operator—codifier or researcher—made with conviction and sometimes with an element of moral reprobation, just as if she had been involved in an imaginary dispute with the individual who was the object of her classification. In this process, operators who made such imputations thus tended to displace the individual within a given order, acting as if he had usurped a status to which he was not entitled—in short, the operator lowered the respondent's worth.

In one of its principal findings, this study revealed the similarity between the way a person accounts for his behavior through associations with other persons he views as equivalent and the way a researcher assigns disparate individuals to a single category so as to explain their behavior by a single law. This observation prompted us to be as attentive to the qualifications provided by respondents as to the category assignments made by the survey directors. As a result, we ended up shifting the problematic from the opposition between the level of generality of a category and the singularity of a particular case to the conflict among different ways of qualifying people.

We had to give up the more economical approach to resolving this conflict, which consists in privileging the qualifications assigned during the survey analysis in preference to those proposed by the actors, and which in some respects resembles an everyday way of formulating criticisms in disputes. In fact, although in principle researchers and statisticians are expected to remain neutral, the ones we observed were unable to qualify responses without passing judgment; this was clear from the way they categorized marginal or doubtful cases.

From Comparison to Judgment

Expanding on our observations of coding operations and our historical study of the development of sociooccupational categories, we undertook experimental research aimed at a deeper analysis of the comparative cognitive operations performed by nonspecialists assessing profession or social class (Boltanski and Thévenot 1983). This research confirmed the existence of a relation between classification and judgment, a relation that emerged clearly in one of the exercises we proposed to groups of about a dozen people. The participants had to negotiate collectively in order to agree on a single nomenclature, drawing on the various comparisons each had made independently in a preceding phase. During the exercise, which was presented as a game, the participants critiqued one another's proposals not only in terms of logical coherence but also in terms of justice; for example, they thought it was unfair to a female factory worker to equate her with a cleaning woman, even though the two may have had the same level of education and income. In another exercise, the participants competed to identify the social class of an unknown (but real) person on the basis of indices of various types that they could obtain for a price. These clues were disclosed one by one, and only to the purchaser. The players were enthusiastic about the game because it produced a winner (the one who made the most accurate identification at the lowest cost). The exercise showed that variations in qualification were accompanied by explicit judgments in the form of comments such as "I'm going to move him up a notch" or, after finding out what the unknown person liked to read, "I didn't have that one pegged properly." The link between cognitive activity and evaluation was obvious in the excitement the players showed in the process of making a judgment.

But this exercise also taught us something else. The information it offered the players was intentionally of different types. One type took the form of criteria, variables that are a matter of public record (and seen as being in the national interest), information found in vital statistics, national economic indices, and conventional collective categories such as age, educational level, and company size. Other types of information involved a more personal approach to the individual through her tastes or private behavior. Thus the exercise entailed the very tension between category and item that we had set out to study. The instructions given to the players did not resolve this tension. Told to discover the profession or social class of the unknown person, some players came up with a statistical approximation ("there's an 80 percent chance that this one's a cadre"); others interpreted their task as unveiling the identity of the person concealed behind the questionnaire. Thus the exercise made it possible to bring out multiple relationships within which many incompatible comparisons and judgments could be made. Some of the players turned out to resemble statisticians or researchers; equipped with the laws of society, they sought to assign the unknown individual to a category through a series of specifications based on intersecting variables. These players in effect constructed proofs in the form of correlations; their solutions thus had the nature of statistical proof. Conversely, other players were caught up in the intrigue of the investigation and tried to ferret out the mystery person using highly indirect signs (like those in Carlo Ginzburg's [1980] index paradigm) such as literary tastes, favorite sports, or the age and model of the person's car.

As this last example implies, the players' associative operations seemed quite closely linked to the successive arrangements of objects into which the players were thrust by the questions to which answers were being suggested. So long as the objects were organized in coherent arrangements, the appearance of a small number of objects, one by one, as information was being dispensed, sufficed to conjure up quite compelling images that led the players to reinterpret or to reject new information, and thus led them to a stabilized assessment, often at an early stage of the exercise.

Finally, our research also brought to light an unexpected effect of engaging in the task of identification. When one of the members managed to "capture" the mystery person, as the players put it, in the double sense of tracking down and unmasking, that success was often accompanied by a sense of discomfort. When the players were reminded that there was a real person behind the exercise, they could no longer see what they were doing merely as a game; they were uncomfortable with their own efforts to pin the person down. The players who were most skilled at interpreting indirect indices, information that might be called personal or even intimate— and these were the ones who got the highest scores, as a rule—also often turned out to be the most ill at ease, even ashamed, when they had to explain their methods publicly, in front of other players who had relied on more "legitimate" criteria. They would have been less uncomfortable if they had made their inferences in private conversation, where nothing precludes taking personal information about someone into account in order to gauge his intentions. In short, it was because the arrangement included statistical questionnaires, reference to official information, and a public discussion requiring that the associations made be broadly generalizable, that the evaluation of another person—a perfectly ordinary undertaking— appeared unacceptable.

Our research brought to light the problematic nature of the process through which personal traits are related to categories of classification, and it led us to embark on a more systematic exploration of sociooccupational classifications (Desrosières and Thévenot 1988). But the analysis of the way singularity is subsumed within general forms cannot be reduced to statistical questions or even to problems of classification. We thus extended our study of the constraints that bear on the treatment of singularity in two research projects that seem quite unrelated at first glance, since one dealt with the conditions under which complaints of injustice are valid and the other with forms of adjustment among disparate resources in businesses.

Construction of Proofs and Tension between
the General and the Particular

We were able to elucidate the constraints that govern attempts to generalize a situation: participants are required to eliminate all personal references
in order to behave acceptably in the process of generalizing. We identified
these constraints by analyzing the way in which ordinary individuals attempt to seek redress for personal grievances by arguing that these concern
the collectivity as a whole and that reparation requires public recognition
of the wrong that has been done them (Boltanski 1990b). One of the principal results of this research was to show that lawsuits that are dismissed for
lack of evidence and in some cases deemed entirely delusional are characterized by an inadequate or unsuccessful representation of the general nature of the injustice suffered. This flaw became particularly apparent in
cases where no institution stepped in to broaden the scope of the victim's
complaint and turn it into an exemplary case in a collective cause. A panel
of "judges" made up of ordinary citizens rejected documents comprising
letters, or, rather, voluminous files sent to newspapers but never published,
on the grounds that the objects offered as evidence were extremely disparate in nature. Some of these were personal (an unfaithful spouse), or
even private (a feeling of anxiety), while others were of the broadest generality (for example, misconduct on the part of labor union leaders, the prevailing mood of a nation, or even international stability).

By analyzing the process of generalizing about pieces of evidence according to their form and the congruence of their association (and congruence is essential if they are to be credible in the course of litigation),
one can gain access to the idea of justice in uncustomary ways. Instead of
applying a transcendental rule, as is traditionally done, one follows pragmatic dictates that determine the appropriateness, or what we might call
the fitness, of a set of arrangements. This approach was reinforced by research into technical arrangements in which objects play an important
role, as is the case in business enterprises. We found that the need to rely
on general forms pertains not only to efforts to bring human beings together in groups or in support of causes, but also, although even less no-
ticeably, to efforts to hold the world of industry together: in order to function satisfactorily and fit together properly, technological objects have to
be able to draw on resources that are already set up in a form that lends itself to linking their local and global contexts.

Our approach to the question of efficiency from the point of view of adjustment requirements led us to study the kinds of investments that give
objects some form of generality. These investments of form endow the objects with capabilities and thus ensure predictable behavior (Thévenot

1984; Eymard-Duvernay 1986).[3] They expand the objects' presence in space and time by legitimizing the comparison of their operations in different situations. The need for investments of form was particularly apparent at the dawning of big business, when tools such as measurements, schedules, standards, and regulations helped productive organizations become stable over time and helped them expand their extension in space. Although costly, these tools repaid the investment by reducing uncertainty about the objects' capacities and their compatibility.

The Tension between Different Forms of Generality

By treating the operations of qualification and generalization within a single analytical framework in our diverse research projects, we were able to grasp both the type of case that can constitute a cause in which justice is demanded and the type of investment that can ensure the adjustment of diverse resources within a common form. Our approach, which relied on establishing parallels between the demand for justice among human beings and the need for adjustment of fit among things, gave us a way to treat entities that seem very different using a common set of conceptual tools. In a later stage, it led us to explore the possibility of multiple forms of investment and the multiple forms of generality that characterize these entities.

In studying the way organizations and businesses function, we focused on resources and arrangements based on personal ties, proximity among persons and among things, and the role of personal attachments to persons and things in maintaining lasting bonds; this gave us a new perspective on features that are usually viewed negatively, as outdated impediments to market growth or technological progress. It led us to recognize the existence of an alternative form of generality that we call "domestic" to distinguish it from an "industrial" form characterized by standardization, stability over time, and the anonymity of its functional entities. Domestic generality does not translate into technical efficiency; instead, it is expressed in terms of trust, and it is based on established traditions and precedents. Domestic resources are implemented in a mode of personnel management that valorizes the specific experience acquired by staff members in a firm through seniority. Economists speak of *internal* markets to designate this type of management, which is differentiated from a market order in which human beings must be mobile, without attachments or past histories. But the goal of our systematic analysis of a particular form of generality was to apprehend diverse elements of an organization's operation within a single framework, and to show that a single economy of domestic forms makes it possible to grasp rules for managing the labor force, types of relations with suppliers or regular clients, various sorts of know-how, specific types of equipment, and different learning styles (Thévenot 1989a). The reference to a form of generality also led us to relate a way of treating persons in general to a way of treating things in general. By highlighting the congruence between the qualification of people and the qualification of objects, this approach made it possible to link questions that are often approached from different perspectives and in different disciplines—disciplines that specialize in the study of social relations or contracts on the one hand, in technological constraints or product quality (Eymard-Duvernay 1989a) on the other.

But this opening toward alternative forms of generality also brought to the surface the critical tensions that result from the juxtaposition of several different ways of establishing equivalencies among beings, and thus of generalizing. Since the critique of the archaic aspects of tradition constitutes only one of the prevailing expressions of these tensions, it was necessary to deal symmetrically with each form of generality if we wanted to account for the entire set of critical tensions, with each form serving as a platform for the critical devaluation of another. A symmetrical approach of this sort is particularly necessary in the analysis of organizations that can be called complex in that their operation obeys imperatives stemming from different forms of generality; their confrontation produces tensions and leads to more or less precarious compromises. Our analysis allowed us, most importantly, to bring to light the internal tensions found at the heart of what constitutes the economy. Market arrangements are not conducive to the integration of a temporal perspective; by contrast, industrial arrangements allow for the possibility of projection into the future and displacement in space, while domestic arrangements make it possible to establish links with the past and allow specific assets to put down local roots.

The goal of symmetry led to methodological decisions that governed both our field observations and the way we constructed models aiming to reveal the coherence of these observations. It became clear that the constraints attached to the various modes of generalization applied not only to the actors' practices of justification but also to the various analytical frameworks for understanding the social world. Thus statistical frequency does not allow the production of proofs except on the basis of calculations made about already-standardized objects that belong to a form of industrial generality (Thévenot 1987, 1990b). Conversely, knowledge based on examples, a type of knowledge that is often at work in monographic surveys, draws upon the memory of past experiences—experiences whose validation is based on the testimony of trustworthy informants and thus relies on a form of domestic generality.

Our research on justice enabled us to bring to light yet another form of generality, one that can be called civic in the sense that it replaces the world of domestic relations with a world in which all relations, if they are to be legitimate, must be made publicly known with reference to the collective entities—voluntary associations, democratic institutions, and so on—that ground their general interest. At the same time, these analyses highlighted another tension in which domestic relations engaging people personally are contrasted with relations that can be called desingularized, in the sense that, in order to act appropriately, the actors can be present only insofar as they belong to collectivities. They shed their own names and bodies in order to take on the qualifiers that mark their membership in institutions or groups, as a spokesman does, for example, when he signs a document with the title he has won by being elected to the presidency of an organization. The same process enabled us to understand other platforms for critical operations. The support provided by forms of civic life allows someone caught up in an affair to denounce the scandals that arouse her indignation.[4] The analysis of affairs judged scandalous showed that such critiques could always be reduced, schematically, to the exposing of personal bonds and consequently of interests that, from the civic standpoint, necessarily appeared to be selfish; these personal ties brought together behind the scenes persons ostensibly seeking the public good (for example, judges and defendants, mayors and real estate developers). However, these same personal bonds are sources of trust and loyalty, and thus cannot be called into question when all the actors are immersed in a domestic world. Moreover, it also became clear that the tension between the domestic world and the civic world did not involve persons alone. This tension was no less a source of discomfort when objects belonging to a domestic form and others belonging to a civic form turned out to be involved in a composite arrangement, as is the case when a victim, determined to procure public acknowledgment of the harm of which he complains, mixes together intimate or personal details about his own body or household objects with entities that are civic in nature when he is presenting his case.

Attention to Critical Operations

To describe each of these orders of generality—domestic, industrial, and civic—and the intersecting criticisms that the participants, or actors, bring to bear on actions stemming from one or another of these orders while grounding their criticisms in an arrangement of a different nature, we had to be particularly attentive to our descriptive language. We had to avoid bringing in references to unrelated forms of generality; the use of such references would have transformed an observation into a critique, as often happens in the social sciences. This restriction was not merely a quirk of our method, nor did it result from an ethical bias. It arose from our observation of a relationship between the explanatory principles used in the social sciences and the interpretive principles brought to bear by the actors whom the social sciences take as their object while often stressing the gap they see between the observer and the observed. To illustrate the difficulties to which this situation gives rise, let us consider a notion that is often used in the social sciences to attribute motives to actors, namely, the quest for visibility and for credit in the eyes of others (sociologists of science speak, for instance, of scientific credit). Now, recourse to this seemingly neutral notion introduces into descriptive language a way of constructing generality—and thus of supporting justifications and critiques—that is not unfamiliar to the actors themselves. For actors, in their disputes, do not hesitate to appeal to celebrity to shore up their claims, as we see, for example, when demands are supported by a petition bearing the names of famous people. This same form of generality is also at stake when actors stigmatize the pursuit of recognition in the critical unveiling of a hidden motive, as happens when participation in a petition is denounced as a self-centered quest for publicity or, more generally, when the tyranny of public opinion is criticized. Likewise, the introduction of interests into descriptive language and, even more tellingly, the introduction of offers and demands that are presumed to converge in a marketplace raise problems of the same type by bringing in the market order of generality.

This reflection on the symmetry between the descriptive languages or explanatory principles used by the social sciences, on the one hand, and the modes of justification or criticism used by actors, on the other hand, made us particularly attentive to the tensions that permeate sociology when it claims to be reconciling a positivist conception of scientific neutrality with a requirement that it engage in social criticism. For critical sociology then confronts the impossibility of capturing the necessarily normative dimensions that support its contribution to the denunciation of social injustices; this impossibility leads it inevitably to place undue emphasis on the externality of science in order to establish the legitimacy of its own practice.

Thus drawing attention to interests—which are revealed behind arguments aiming at disinterestedness or the common good and pegged as "rationalizations" (this is one of the mainsprings of sociology when it purports to be unmasking shams or ideologies)—can be observed as well in the ordinary undertakings of actors when they seek to devalue one form of justification in order to enhance the value of another. However, there is one fundamental difference: in the case of the social sciences, the normative supporting arguments put forward in the critiques that actors direct at one another during their disputes constitute a blind spot, allowing social scientists to exempt themselves from the demands for justification that ordinary actors have to confront.

The approach we adopted thus led us to be attentive to the relationships between the qualifications produced by researchers and those produced by actors. As soon as a researcher can no longer base the validity of her affirmations on her stance of radical exteriority, the definitiveness of the description comes into question. In such cases the researcher is obliged, in her description, to adhere as closely as possible to the procedure the actors themselves use in establishing proof in a given situation; this approach entails paying careful attention to the diversity of forms of justification. By following the actors, researchers are thus led to make explicit a greater variety of forms of justification than the ones evoked above—the civic, domestic, industrial, and market forms, or that of fame. The same type of attention to the relevance of the objects introduced in a proof, particularly when the proof is developed in the course of ongoing controversies, makes it possible to recognize the generality of personal or intimate expressions that are often described in terms of enthusiasm or inspiration. These modes of expression, tending toward authenticity, seem to be exempt from the requirements of generality of which we have found various specifications. However, closer examination leads us to identify a form of worth predicated on inspiration that makes it possible, as the other forms do, to associate actors in an agreement that is valid for all.[5]

Our attempt to treat these various forms of generality symmetrically led to the construction of a common framework in which the requirements of justice among human beings and the requirements of fitness among things could be treated with a single set of instruments. The establishment of an acceptable proof, whether we are dealing with proofs in law, science, or technology, in fact presupposes that one can rely on resources that have already been subject to generalization. Why not examine, within a single framework, trials demanding justice together with technological testing or scientific proofs?[6] Proofs oriented toward the sense of what is just have in common with scientific proofs the fact that they both rely not only on mental states, in the form of convictions or beliefs, but also on stable and coherent arrangements, and thus on objects subject to general assessment. This approach makes it possible to get around the split between what is just, which can be brought to light only through argumentation validated by reason, and what is properly "adjusted," whose glaring self-evidence depends entirely on the natural or instrumental fit between things.

Generality and the Common Good: Concepts of Worth in Political Philosophy

Concepts of worth become particularly salient in disputes, and can be observed in many everyday situations. Characterized by uncertainty about the evaluation of persons, such situations are propitious for discerning modes of qualification. Still, disputes do not lead to a systematic demonstration that would make it possible to uncover the principles of worth on which the evaluation is based. Yet such demands for systematization and exposure of underlying principles are precisely the ones that must be met by political philosophies, which are expected, if they are to be convincing, to show that the definitions of the common good associated with these concepts of worth are well founded. Comparing a set of constructions produced by political philosophies may thus make it possible to bring various principles into focus in order to establish a model of the way in which they can sustain their claims to justice.

Our detour by way of political philosophy allowed us to advance, then, in our understanding of the capacities that actors bring into play when they have to justify their actions or their criticisms. When one is attentive to the unfolding of disputes, one sees that they are limited neither to a direct expression of interests nor to an anarchic and endless confrontation between heterogeneous worldviews clashing in a dialogue of the deaf. On the contrary, the way disputes develop, when violence is avoided, brings to light powerful constraints in the search for well-founded arguments based on solid proofs, a search that thus manifests efforts toward convergence at the very heart of a disagreement. The constructions of political philosophy constitute privileged instruments for clarifying these constraints and for making fully explicit the foundations that most often remain implicit in the course of arguments exchanged in the heat of action.

The fact remains that the sections of our work that present analyses of canonical texts of political philosophy must not be read in isolation, independently of the overall objective. If such were our intent, our enterprise would be very presumptuous indeed, and a single lifetime would not suffice to establish parallels between the works upon which we draw here in order to establish model polities and to survey all the commentaries devoted to these works. As will be clearer in what follows, we have not dealt with any of these texts in and for itself, or in terms of the history from which it derives; we have treated each one as a work written to elucidate the grammar of political bonds. We sought to subject all the texts we studied to a common set of questions, the way one does in undertaking to encode a given body of information.

This use of political philosophy led us to set aside philosophies of either a realist or a critical bent that regard social order as emanating from power and domination in favor of constructions whose goal is to build equilibrium within the polity; such constructions all depict a world in which human beings are sharply distinguished from other entities and are brought together among themselves, furthermore, by their fundamental equality. These political philosophies can thus be defined by their goal of constructing a common humanity. That is what allowed us, first of all, to treat these different theoretical constructions collectively, drawing out the principles of legitimate order that they contain: inspiration in Augustine's *City of God*, the domestic principle in Bossuet's *Politics*, the signs of glory and the value of fame in Hobbes's *Leviathan*, the general will in Rousseau's *Social Contract*, wealth in Adam Smith's *Wealth of Nations*, and industrial efficiency in Saint-Simon's *Du système industriel*. In this way we sought to show that even a political philosophy that had embodied individualism by designing an order based on market transactions could be assimilated to the model of the common good. This is easier to see in Adam Smith's construction than in later economic theory, especially because in his *Theory of Moral Sentiments* Smith gives an explicit account of the anthropology that corresponds to the human capabilities assumed in a market world.

Not only does a comparison of these texts bring recurring references to a common humanity to light, but it also shows clearly that each of these philosophies proposes a different principle of order, allowing us to spell out in what the worth of the worthy consists and how a justifiable order among persons is established. It is on such an ordering process that individuals rely when they have to justify their actions or support their criticisms. To be sure, most members of our society have not read the original works that inspired us to construct models of the competence that is brought to bear in disputes. But the ordering principles that are formalized in these political philosophies are also inscribed in the arrangements of objects that make up the situations of daily life.

The Search for a Common Model

By moving back and forth between classical constructions of political philosophy and justifications produced by actors in disputes, we were able to construct a solid link between political philosophy and sociology. Thus we managed to bypass the often polemical opposition between these two disciplines, between a transcendental aim oriented toward the statement of principles on the one hand and on the other hand an attention to disparities that is often labeled relativism and that converges with a more general opposition—one that is also seen at work in arguments contrasting law with social science—between reference to rules and reference to practices. We pay sustained attention, in our work, to differences in the way the sense of fitness or rightness is expressed, by recognizing a number of different forms of generality, each of which is a form of worth that can be used to justify an action. This pluralism brings our position close to the one developed by Michael Walzer and, as it did for Walzer in his *Spheres of Justice* (1983), it led to our interest in a theory of justice that would take into account the diversity of ways to specify the common good. This path led us to encounter the sense of injustice that is aroused when different orders of justice are confused, and especially when justifications of a market order are extended beyond their legitimate boundaries.

But our effort seeks to overcome the problems of cultural relativism that an opening toward diversity necessarily entails. To achieve this end, we had to commit ourselves more deeply to analyzing the sense of injustice felt by actors when certain forms of justification impinge on situations to which they do not apply. In order to understand the actors' capacity for criticizing, we had to construe them as endowed with the possibility of shifting from one form of justification to another while remaining true to a consistent set of requirements. These requirements are common to all the orders of worth we identified; we sought to make them explicit, and to show how they can be integrated into a model of the polity. This model can be viewed in two ways: as a theory of justice compatible with various constructions of political philosophy and as a capability whose existence must be presupposed if we are to account for the way the members of a complex society criticize, challenge institutions, argue with one another, or converge toward agreement. One way to verify the validity of this model is to show that it also accounts for problems that arise when arguments are based on illegitimate values—illegitimate in the sense that they are not compatible with justifiable principles; arguments in favor of eugenics are a case in point.

That which, in the model of the polity, justifies inequalities between person-states converges with certain requirements made explicit by Rawls (1973): first, the requirement that these inequalities offer some benefit to the least-favored members of society, a benefit that corresponds, for us, to an idea of the common good; second, the requirement that unequal positions and offices be open to all members, a requirement that corresponds to our contention that states of worth, which must not be attached to persons, must be put to a test. But in the model presented here, one of whose objectives is to integrate political philosophy with a pragmatics of judgment, the distinction between person-states and persons themselves occupies a key position, as does the operation by means of which these states are attributed and a situational judgment is made. By focusing on the moment when states are attributed to persons, we can move from a formal principle of democratic openness to the uncertainty of the critical moment. The analysis of this moment bears upon the way the uncertainty is reduced in a test that, if it is to be acceptable, must simultaneously take into account the circumstances of the particular situation and be justifiable in general terms. Now, a central feature of our model of the polity is that it precludes assigning worth to persons on a definitive basis. This restriction introduces anxiety into the process of attributing states of worth and generates recurrent questioning of their distribution.

This anxiety is not made explicit in political philosophy, and it led us to be particularly attentive to the pragmatic conditions of the attribution of worth; it led us to leave the sphere of foundations and principles that belongs to political philosophy so as to enter the sphere of action. This is the sphere in which one encounters the question of objects and the issue of the relation between human persons and things. For the analysis of the questioning of worth in a given situation, on the basis of the actions that occur in that situation, brings to light the place of the objects that must be involved if a test is to be realistic. By paying attention to the connections between the reasons given and the objects drawn on for support, the connections between the models of justice involved and the modalities of action, one can avoid putting the burden of coordinating behaviors either solely on unified beliefs or representations or else on systems or laws that put all potentialities for order on the side of the regularity of things, in line with a recurrent opposition in the social sciences between culture and society, representation and morphology, or—in the Habermasian synthesis—communication and system.

The Social Bond Put to the Test of Things

This approach thus led us to distance ourselves from some of sociology's most common presuppositions. These are especially evident, first of all, in the way sociology treats beliefs, values, or representations, and, secondly, in the way it treats objects. The forms of generality and worth whose economy we describe here are in fact not attached to collectivities but to situations; this observation led us to turn away from the set of scientific instruments that is firmly entrenched in the notions of culture and social group. The persons whom we follow in their tests are obliged by the situation in which they are involved to shift from one mode of adjustment to another, from one measure of worth to another. That this plasticity constitutes a defining feature of normalcy is attested by numerous attributions of pathology, especially of paranoia, claims that stigmatize those who resist the adjustments required when passing from one situation to another. As for objects, our aim is to grant them the place they deserve, within the constraints of what constitutes a realistic judgment, by refusing to allow ourselves to see them merely as arbitrary supports offered to the symbolic investments of persons, for whom objects would represent nothing but a way of expressing their belonging to groups or (and according to this logic it would amount to the same thing) a way of manifesting their distinction.

Nevertheless, we do not align ourselves with a form of realism that is particularly well developed in economics, a realism that sees objects—defined either by their capacity to be exchanged and to provide a natural support for a price or by their functional capacity to be efficient—as the only power imposing order on persons. Rejecting both realist fetishization and symbolist deconstruction, we seek to show how persons confront uncertainty by making use of objects to establish orders and, conversely, how they consolidate objects by attaching them to the orders constructed. In this sense, our undertaking aims at a dynamic realism, in that it seeks to bring the work of construction to light yet without reducing reality to a purely labile and local agreement about meaning. This theoretical orientation, which seeks to grasp action in its relation to uncertainty, implied a method of observation that required us to focus our research on moments of questioning and criticism, and these constitute the principal scenes presented in this work. Moreover, the decision to give priority to the study of such moments struck us as particularly well adapted to the study of a society in which criticism occupies a central position and constitutes a major instrument available to actors for testing the relation between the particular and the general, the local and the global.

To illuminate the worlds of objects that allow the test of worth to be implemented, we used behavioral handbooks designed for businesses (in order to have a sample of closely related situations corresponding to the various forms of generality), and we carried out an eminently unrespectful operation that consisted in juxtaposing these modest compilations of highly perishable practical advice with timeless works of political philosophy. Still, our encounter with these practical modes of reasoning did not limit us to the economic sphere; as we shall see when we read the repertoires drawn from them, they deal by and large with daily activities in spaces of very different kinds.

Finally, since these handbooks—unlike the political philosophies we examined—are not designed to contribute to the debate over justice but rather to guide action, and thus must contend with existing realities, they have to confront the practical problem of shifting from one world to another. Thus they allowed us to identify operations of compromise that are designed to accommodate various forms of generality by pointing toward possible ways of getting beyond their contradictions, thereby heading off disputes and avoiding the risk of escalating criticism.

Our decision to center our analysis on handbooks intended for business use may appear biased and limited, given the object of our research, which extends to all kinds of justifications and not just those that concern economic life. Undertaken as an initial survey, intended primarily to hone our analytical tools for dealing with the information gathered in the field, our analysis of the handbooks turned out to yield more benefit than we originally anticipated. While our numerous field investigations using the analytic framework of orders of worth made it possible to lengthen the list of beings involved in justifiable actions, they did not lead us to call into question the core elements of each of the worlds that had been extracted from the handbooks, that is, the form of coherence characterizing each one and the beings most apt to bring that coherence to the forefront. The fact that the portrayals of the various worlds that we sketched from these published handbooks could be sustained undistorted as we shifted from one empirical terrain to another provides evidence supporting the general character of the matrix extracted from this limited and specialized corpus.

The evidence we accumulated opened the way to a new and systematic approach to organizations, construed not as unified entities characterized in terms of spheres of activity, systems of actors, or fields, but as composite assemblages that include arrangements deriving from different worlds (Boltanski and Thévenot 1989). This systematic approach allowed us to use a single framework for the purpose of comparison, and to adopt a register that was not limited to the language of competition and technical efficiency as we accumulated observations bearing upon quite diverse organizations—businesses in the industrial or service sector, territorial collectivities, public administrations or academic establishments, and cultural configurations or innovative arrangements. The diversity in question is not projected onto differences in activity or milieu; instead, it is dispersed throughout an organization. No organization can survive, however industrial it may be, if it does not tolerate situations of differing natures. It is precisely the plurality of the mechanisms deriving from the various worlds that accounts for the tensions that pervade these organizations. The same approach led us to pay attention not only to operations of criticism but also to those of compromise that make it possible to keep together beings whose justification would entail their separation into different worlds subscribing to different orders of generality. An additional advantage of this approach is that it allowed us to compare the various methods of compromise presented by different organizations and thus to respect the uniqueness of local configurations even while enriching the general framework.

The Line of Argument

Our argument unfolds as follows. The first chapter is devoted to the examination of some of the classic answers offered by the social sciences to the question of agreement. Starting from the controversy between Durkheimian sociology and laissez-faire economics, we show how, beyond their differences, these two opposing views regard agreement as based on the relation between particular persons and a form of generality that we call the higher common principle. This bilevel construction is the basic architecture of a political metaphysics. Our observation is not a critical one, for such a framework allows the human sciences to be true to their subject—that is, persons whose agreement presupposes a reference to a principle that extends beyond themselves—and to advance toward legitimate generalizations. Chapter 2 is devoted to an initial examination of this political metaphysics in market political philosophy.

Chapter 3 deals with the constraints that bear upon the constitution of forms of agreement aimed at generality. Our analyses rely on classic works of political philosophy understood as works by grammarians of the political bond, and they lead to the construction of a model of legitimate order in the polity. The polity model spells out the requirements that must be met by a higher common principle in order to support justifications. It allows us to clarify the distinction between legitimate forms of the common good, which we call forms of "worth," and other, illegitimate values (such as those of eugenics). The polity model is presented as a model of competence that may be compared with the practical capabilities put into play by persons when the latter have to justify their judgments in response to criticism. Chapter 4 is devoted to the analysis of political philosophies chosen because the expressions of the common good on which they rely are present today, in our own society.

In chapter 5, we look at the principles of order we identified earlier and analyze their role in tests that help people reach agreement on the distribution of states of worth among persons. In the polity model, states of worth cannot be attached to persons in a fixed way. Agreement thus has to be brought about in practice, in real-world tests involving objects in relation to which persons measure themselves and determine their own relative worth. Each of the sets of objects associated with the various orders constitutes a coherent world. Chapter 6 offers a schematic description of these worlds on the basis of an analysis of handbooks that seek to teach people how to behave appropriately in situations governed by each of the forms of the common good we have identified.

Chapter 7 deals with the relation among the various worlds we have depicted. We examine this relation by studying disputed situations in which beings of several different natures are valued simultaneously. We analyze the sense of injustice that arises when a test is corrupted by an unwarranted transfer of worth, and we examine criticisms in which there is disagreement not only over the result of the test but also over the principle that governs its implementation. The disagreement over worth may be resolved by resorting to another test, which may either be carried out in the world originally at issue or, through a reversal of the situation, be brought into play in the alternative world as a result of the disagreement. Chapter 8 focuses on the development of criticisms derived from the handbooks we drew upon earlier to present the different worlds used for proof.

In chapter 9, we examine composite situations that include beings from several worlds, situations in which disagreement is set aside through compromise, thereby avoiding recourse to a test. We show how a compromise, in order to be acceptable, must be based on the quest for a common good of a higher order than the ones the compromise attempts to reconcile. But because this common good remains unspecified as long as it has not been made explicit and established in a polity, compromises remain fragile. It is always possible, in the name of one of the principles in contention, to denounce a compromise as a sacrifice of principle. Compromises are less fragile when the groundwork for them is laid by embedding them in specific arrangements. The analysis of the way a compromise is prepared offers an overview of the way new forms of the polity are used to build new polities. In Chapter 10, we draw on the corpus of handbooks to delineate the figures of compromise, as we did for criticisms in chapter 8. In the final chapter, we examine other ways of bringing a dispute to a close, approaches that involve suspending the constraint of justification. Thus, in relativization, persons may avoid testing and escape disagreement over what really matters by agreeing that nothing matters. This figure leads us to examine the way in which the social sciences make the shift from relativization, which presents a necessarily unstable character, to relativism, which resorts to explanations based on power relations and treats power as a general equivalent without reference to the common good.

This project could not have been carried out without the contributions of many people. The work of Bruno Latour (1988, 1989; Latour and Woolgar 1988), along with that of Michel Callon (Callon and Latour 1981; Callon and Law 1989), has been helpful from the outset, all the more so in that it has gone hand in hand with attentive readings of our own work. Stimulating in its audacity, the research done by Latour and Callon deserves much credit, both for showing the relationship between the weaving of social bonds and the fabrication of objects and for building a bridge between modern social science and political philosophy. We are thinking in particular of the way they use Hobbes's political theory to extend and rework certain contributions of ethnomethodology.

Our reading of Albert Hirschmann's *The Passions and the Interests* (1977), along with his critiques of our own early work devoted to social identification, encouraged us personally, while his work has served as an exceptional example of scholarly investigation of the relations between political and moral philosophy and the social sciences, especially economics.

Louis Dumont's writings (1970, 1994, 1986) have also profoundly marked our own work. His analysis of subordination to the whole has proved very enlightening, as has his reworking of the notion of ideology. Paul Ricoeur's work (1974, 1991) has also made a major contribution to a renewed analysis of that notion, by juxtaposing it with practical reason. Similarly, François Furet's work on the French Revolution and its historiography (1981a) has been of significant help in our effort to overcome the opposition, so well entrenched in French intellectual traditions, between the history of philosophical or political ideas and the sociological or historical analysis of the ordinary behavior of persons.

The construction of the analytic framework presented here went hand in hand with the establishment of an empirical research program carried out by a network of scholars brought together in a series of seminars we gave at the École de Hautes Études en Sciences Sociales, connected with the Groupe de Sociologie Politique et Morale (Group for the study of political and moral sociology) and with the Centre d'Études de l'Emploi (Center for the study of employment), which contributed to the development of the Proteus program as well as to a first publication of the framework of the economies of worth, which was intended to serve as a working instrument for our research. This network owes a great deal to François Eymard-Duvernay, Jean-Louis Derouet, and Alain Desrosières. Their work on organizational economics, on the sociology of education, and on the history of statistics has been of great value to us; we owe them a debt of gratitude for their patience in following our own work step by step and for the confidence they manifested during difficult periods when the seeming incongruity of some of the avenues our research was pursuing might have discouraged others. We are particularly grateful to Alain Desrosières for his generosity, his goodwill, his unfailingly pertinent and constructive comments, and his skill in bringing people together. Without him, our work would quite simply never have seen the light of day.

The chance to present the various stages of development of this work and submit them for discussion was an invaluable advantage. We made progress when we faced objections raised by students and researchers and when we looked into problems they had encountered in their own work, especially when they were preparing advanced degrees. Our research thus benefited from the contributions of many people: Pierre Boisard; Agnès Camus; Francis Chateauraynaud, whose trenchant remarks enlivened our discussions and stimulated our reflection; Philippe Corcuff, with his interest in synthesizing; Vinoli Delamourd; Nicolas Dodier, who was informed in his interest and generous with his time; Francis Kramarz; Claudette Lafaye, whose field experience gave rise to questions that called for clarification; Marie-Thérèse Letablier; and André Wissler, who examined our hypotheses attentively and tested them empirically. The secretarial services provided by Danièle Burre and Annette Dubret kept our prolonged undertaking in good order.

We should also like to thank the following people for their careful reading at various stages of our work and for the insights they have offered us from their various disciplines: Monique Djokic, Olivier Favereau, Pierre Livet, Patrick Fridenson, Steven Kaplan, Serge Moscovici, Jacques Revel, David Stark, and Heinz Wisman. Finally, we avoided the often-painful moments that precede publication thanks to the understanding of Eric Vigne, who succeeded in combining the efficiency of a professional with the passion of an inspired editor.

Joëlle Affichard and Elisabeth Claverie are also in our thoughts: throughout the entire process of producing this book, we profited from their helpful observations and their moral support, which made us appreciate all the more their worth in various worlds.

PART ONE

THE IMPERATIVE TO JUSTIFY

One

THE SOCIAL SCIENCES AND THE
LEGITIMACY OF AGREEMENT

THIS BOOK DEALS WITH the relation between agreement and discord. Its primary aim is to build a framework within which a single set of theoretical instruments and methods can be used to analyze the critical operations that people carry out when they want to show their disagreement without resorting to violence, and the ways they construct, display, and conclude more or less lasting agreements.

The issue of how agreements are reached is one of the fundamental issues that the social sciences have taken over from political philosophy, appropriating it in the languages of order, equilibrium, norms, culture, and so forth (Habermas 1984–87). But the study of the agreement-reaching process should not exclude an examination of instances in which order breaks down, as evidenced by some moment of crisis, disequilibrium, critique, dispute, or contestation. For example, there is no reason to maintain a radical opposition between sociologies of consensus and sociologies of conflict, although they derive from quite different traditions. Our intent here, on the contrary, is to treat instances of agreement reaching and critique as intimately linked occurrences within a single continuum of action.

Contemporary social scientists often seek to minimize the diversity of their constructs by situating them within a single basic opposition. In one tradition, rooted in Durkheimian sociology, the ordering principle rests in the notion of the collective. In another tradition, any sort of order or equilibrium is construed as the unintended result of individual choices; this principle informs approaches that borrow the rational choice model from economics. Our own perspective offers a third approach: we seek to embrace the various constructs within a more general model, and to show how each one integrates, in its own way, the relation between moments of agreement reaching and moments of critical questioning.

The opposition between what belongs to the collective and what belongs to the individual has been reinforced through a series of crosscutting critiques that often pit sociologists and economists against one another. For example, the sociologist Alessandro Pizzorno points out that utilitarian presuppositions do not suffice to account for voter confidence; some specific explanatory factor such as identification with a political party—which is totally irrelevant from a utilitarian standpoint—must be added

(1990, 305). The opposition between explanations based on groups and explanations based on individuals not only marks the boundary between sociology and economics, it can also arise within each of these disciplines; the opposition between the two approaches appears so radical that, more often than not, it defines the basic methodological choice made by contemporary social scientific researchers.

It is possible, of course, to bridge the gap and develop arguments that recognize the reality of social phenomena (collective determinations) while drawing on rational calculations normally attributed to individuals (personal strategies), as when we speak of collective strategies. The kinds of explanations produced by political science in particular encourage such accommodations: this is the case with analyses that seek to address the "negotiation" (an interpersonal relationship described with reference to a market modality) of interests that are deemed "collective" in nature (a designation presupposing the establishment of a general interest). But a reaffirmation of the opposition between individualism and collectivism threatens to break these explanatory assemblages apart by foregrounding their internal contradictions.

Must all developments in the social sciences conform to this dichotomy? How can we deal with empirical materials and results produced by disciplines that appeal alternately to one or the other of these explanatory modes? How might we imagine bringing them together and coming to terms with their contradictions in a way that goes beyond the unsatisfying juxtaposition of common references to the economic and social realms, to individual interests and collective forces?

The Critique of Sociology's Lack of Realism

Scholars who account for human behavior in terms of individual choice challenge the first approach by showing that its "holism" is untenable and that it remains too tainted by metaphysics to satisfy the requirements of science. They hold that one cannot base an explanation on the reality of so-called collective phenomena; on the contrary, what one has to show is how these phenomena can result from the behavior of the only beings pertinent to the analysis, the individuals involved. From this standpoint, it would be more fitting conceptually to treat persons as individuals than as agents, for we would be positing individuals free from all normative constraints who can follow the dictates of their personal appetites. This line of argument, crystallized in the opposition between collectivist and individualist disciplines, implies that sociology takes people in groups as its only empirical subjects, whereas economics, a more realist discipline, concerns itself only with individuals.

F. A. Hayek's *Scientism and the Study of Society* offers a particularly trenchant formulation of these critiques. The author contrasts "methodological individualism" with a "scientistic approach treating as facts those collectives which are no more than popular generalizations"—or, as he puts it later on, "vague popular theories" (1952, 38, 54). To dismantle the totalist (collectivist) prejudice, he borrows the terms in which Charles Victor Langlois and Charles Seignobos formulated their critique of sociology: "[I]n the imagination as in direct observation, [collective acts] always reduce to a sum of individual actions. The 'social fact,' as recognized by certain sociologists, is a philosophical construction, not a historical fact" (210–11 n. 29).

Individualism: A Different Social Metaphysics

Our work seeks to bring to light certain elements of similarity underlying the apparently irreconcilable methodological opposition we have described (an opposition that becomes particularly pronounced when it is expressed as an antinomy: "individual" vs. "collective"). To this end, we shall focus on those aspects of the competing modes of explanation that remain obscured when this antinomy is used to elucidate their differences.

First of all, let us note that an explanation based on social factors can also recognize persons. Indeed, this dual constraint accounts for the importance granted by such explanations to the internalization of collective determinations, in the form of a quasi unconscious lying deep within every human being. In parallel fashion, and contrary to what the term "individual" generally implies, whether it is used by economists who vaunt "individualism" or by sociologists who critique it while denouncing the anomic character of risky trade among competitors (Durkheim 1997 [1893], xxxi–xxxviii), individuals as viewed by economists—individuals who enter into relationships in a marketplace—function as qualified persons. We shall seek to show that, on the contrary, the conception of the individual required by economists to make their argument imposes constraints on the social actor that make him a moral being. We are not using the term "moral" here as it is used by certain theoreticians of liberalism, in the limited sense of having a benevolent disposition that would compensate for self-interested greed. We shall try to show that moral capacity is presupposed in the construction of an order of market exchanges among persons, who must be capable of distancing themselves from their own particularities in order to reach agreement about external goods that are enumerated and defined in general terms. The fact that the goods are private property often obscures the hypothesized common knowledge that the universality of their definition implies. The conventions defining common knowledge allow acquisitive desires to compete and adapt to one another, but these conventions generally remain implicit (natural) in economic theory. We shall relate them to Adam Smith's efforts to define persons who display this moral capacity in terms of the notions of "sympathy" and "impartial spectator" that he develops in his *Theory of Moral Sentiments* (1976 [1759]).

As soon as one can show persons acting "under" the group, or point to the convention of market competition that weighs "on" individuals, the opposition begins to fade, suggesting that the collective/individual dichotomy is not the appropriate way to account for the differences between the two models. The models cannot address their common object, human commerce, without making a twofold reference, on the one hand to the singular status of these persons, and on the other hand to the possibility of transcending the particular traits of persons and laying a foundation for agreement in what we shall call a *higher common principle*. This principle can be spelled out in quite different ways, depending on whether it is expressed through the collective will or through the universality of market goods. The tension between reliance on general forms and reference to particular persons does not result, then, from a confrontation between the two explanatory systems; rather, it is intrinsic to each system. A bilevel configuration, incorporating both the level of particular persons and a level of higher generality, forms a common theoretical framework that constitutes the two systems as a political metaphysics.

Political Metaphysics as a Social Science

Our effort to bring out common elements in seemingly contrasting explanatory methodologies—one based on "individual" behavior and one based on "collective" behavior—will allow us to sketch a new object for the social sciences, an object that can tie together the requirements for agreement and the conditions for discord.

To do this, we shall have to pay much more attention than is customary to the structure of each of the two methodological constructs. These are reduced to cursory outlines by oppositionalist accounts, and they are ignored altogether by crosscutting critiques. However, to simplify the exercise and to make our own approach easier to grasp, we shall consider only two of the theoretical developments offered by the social sciences; we shall not attempt to cover all the disciplines they include, or everything the terms "sociology" or "economics" may ordinarily designate. We have chosen to work with the sociology of collective phenomena and the economy of the marketplace because the explanatory schemas that underlie these theoretical constructs are coherent and can be integrated in a variety of ways.

Because each of these disciplines seeks to formulate laws according to which human beings enter into relationships, whether they come to terms in an expression of the collective will or negotiate their acquisitive desires in a marketplace, each relies on a rule for reaching agreement (on collective identity or market goods); each refers to a universal form that extends beyond the idiosyncratic characteristics of particular persons. Our effort to bring to light the political metaphysics underlying both economics and sociology is complicated by the break with philosophy that allowed each of these fields to be constituted as a scientific discipline. Nevertheless, we should like to suggest that each one is a product of the political philosophy that served as its matrix and in which the underlying metaphysics is clearly discernible.

Our investigation of the origins of these disciplines reveals that in each case a normative higher common principle was transformed into a positive scientific law. This reductive operation, which is characteristic of naturalism in the social sciences, is the price paid by economics and sociology for becoming associated with the natural sciences, with a political physics. But such a reduction profoundly modifies the meaning of the rule adopted for reaching agreement and the way it relates to particular persons. In political philosophy, a rule is a convention, a support that can ensure collective agreement among persons familiar with the convention. Later on, we shall see how a political philosophy is elaborated in an effort to justify such a convention. In the political physics that the social sciences are helping to develop, a rule is a scientific law that applies to persons and things alike. There is no longer any place for collective agreement about a form of generality. The two levels of political metaphysics are projected onto a single plane, one on which beings can no longer be distinguished except by the extent to which their behavior conforms to a common pattern, and this will depend on the degree to which they comply more or less scrupulously with the law.

Thus, in Durkheim's sociology, the collective being is not only a moral being (it becomes a moral being when Durkheim writes not as a sociologist but as a political philosopher) but also an object that is as real as a specific person, and even more "objective." The reductive conflation of the two levels—that of the collective moral being and that of individual persons—that is implied by the sociological realism of collective phenomena is accompanied by the metamorphosis of a principle of agreement (the general will) into a law that applies to persons. Durkheim shunts aside the resulting theoretical difficulties by developing an explanatory system based on the assumption that people will (more or less consciously) internalize—as a compelling or determining factor—the principle of political philosophy that allows them to enter into relationships with others and to reach collective agreement.

Economists are confident that they can expose the metaphysics underlying the sociological approach, and they challenge the claim that sociology is a science. Economists question the reality of collective phenomena, which they view as human constructs. Like all institutions, such constructs have to be explained in terms of the interests of individuals, which are the only realities economists are willing to recognize. This line of argument is crystallized in the opposition between disciplines focusing on the collective and disciplines focusing on the individual: the implication is that sociology recognizes only people in groups as empirical subjects, while economics, more grounded in reality, deals only with particular individuals.

However, economists feel free to condemn the social metaphysics of sociologists only because they are not aware of the higher common principle that is also embedded in the positive laws their own discipline brings to light. One can look for this principle in the property that economic actors share: they are driven by interest or needs. We shall probably be able to articulate the principle most clearly if we begin with market goods, which play precisely the same role in economic law that collective beings play in Durkheim's sociology. Individuals as seen by economists, individuals who interact in a marketplace, are not particular persons; they are moral beings capable of distancing themselves from their own particularity and coming to terms over commonly identified goods on which their acquisitive desires have converged and reached agreement. Market goods, which are commonly evaluated in terms of price, provide the framework for the political metaphysics embedded in economics.

We should highlight, here, an important difference in the way the reductive conflation of the two levels of metaphysics is achieved in each of the two explanatory systems we have mentioned, a difference that may account for the persistence of the collective/individual opposition in efforts to relate the two explanations. As we have seen, sociological realism achieves reduction through the internalization of collective reality, a process that takes on the aspect of an unconscious. In economics, a comparable reduction is achieved by differentiation between goods and persons. The fact that the goods in question acquire value only if they are appropriated by persons masks the fact that they need to be qualified in terms of a common definition. This commonality is the condition for reaching agreement by means of competition, and it offers persons a way to transcend their own particularities. However, the common good deriving from market competition cannot be reduced and transformed into a positive law without leaving traces on the proposed model of human understanding or of the psychology of human actors themselves. For economists, individuals are not riven by tension between their internalized collective representations and their own personal motivations, as persons are for sociologists;

nevertheless, they carry within themselves the trace of a desire transformed into interest, that is, they have a direct relation with market goods that overrides all other forms of desire.

The Question of Agreement

At the heart of the argument between two social sciences that are generally presumed to be in mutual opposition in every respect, we can thus recognize the same basic structure (a conventional higher common principle bringing together particular persons), the same naturalism relying on the same fundamental transformation (of a higher common principle into a positive law), whether the explanatory system is based on social phenomena or market individualism. This demonstration leads us to challenge the prevailing dichotomy and to draw two conclusions from the infiltration of a metaphysical construct into disciplines conceived on the basis of a break with philosophical approaches.

The first conclusion, a positive one, stems from the observation that each of the scientific explanatory systems we are considering demonstrates the reality of a possible form of agreement reaching among persons (by means of the group in the one case, by means of the marketplace in the other). To be sure, the social sciences in question treat collective agreement as if it were subject to a positive law that governs interpersonal interactions universally, independently of the will of individuals. It can be shown, however, that each of the disparate forms for reaching agreement corresponds to a general principle proposed by an earlier political philosophy in order to provide a basis for the common good and to ensure agreement by harmonizing individual wills. The positive data contributed by each of our two disciplines—and which we have no intention of rejecting—thus provide proof of the effectiveness of the various principles, and suggest that we should take them seriously when they are invoked as justifications.

The second conclusion, a negative one, complicates the approach suggested by the first. At a minimum, two incommensurable principles of agreement exist: consequently, neither of the two disciplines that transform these principles into positive laws can address the relation between the two forms of law. This inability is particularly troublesome in the treatment of objects that cross boundaries—organizations, for example. Such objects owe their appearance entirely to "good neighbor" concessions granted by adherents to one or the other of the two approaches: economic actors entering into exchanges in a competitive marketplace or social actors subjected to norms. These concessions are fragile, and they can easily be denounced if one of the protagonists breaks the pact by insisting on the universality of his own system for explaining human behavior.

Our undertaking is grounded in these conclusions. How can it be that economics and sociology both translate a metaphysical principle into a positive law, when each discipline subscribes to a definition of reality that is radically opposed to metaphysics? Our response is that neither can deal with the interactions of people in society, which is what both aim to do, unless they take the forms of agreement that people have fashioned into account. And yet each treats agreement reaching as if it were a natural law, so that the way agreement is constructed becomes by that very token exempt from analysis. The construction of agreement is the object we propose to study, in a project that presupposes taking seriously the requirements for reaching agreement and for resolving disputes in general. For the time being, then, we shall set aside all behaviors that are not subject to these requirements; we shall consider them again only at the end of our study.

Association and Forms of Generality

Our approach to the coordination of human behavior led us to pay attention to the cognitive ability that allows human beings to establish associations among things that count, to identify beings independently of circumstances, and to reach agreement on forms of generality. Associations are based on a relation—one that can be made explicit, if only by a single word—to something that is more general, something common to all the objects brought together. Association is distinguished here from simple spatial or temporal contiguity, even if proximity can support a form of similarity (Foucault 1973, 18). The fact remains that persons are not always obliged to make their associations explicit, and, a fortiori, they are not obliged to provide grounds for establishing them; we also have to allow for the possibility of ill-founded associations.

We shall not study the human capacity to establish associations for its own sake, and we shall not explore the universe—a limitless one, moreover—that includes all the systems of classification (taxonomies, nomenclatures, and the like) that have already been put into service or that remain to be developed. Among the infinite number of possible associations, we shall be concerned only with those that are not only common, and thus communicable, but that can be supported through *justifications*.

In the absence of other persons, the obligation to establish common associations does not arise, and we shall show that when others are present, one of the ways to avoid making comparisons in order to shift one's focus back to the circumstances (an operation we shall call *relativizing*) consists precisely in setting aside the presence of the others (as human beings) or, if that cannot be done, in ignoring it. However, if persons are not to remain confined within relativization, they must have a means of reaching agreement about their associations.

Despite disagreement about associations, people may be able to come to terms, that is, to reach an understanding—a momentary, local understanding—in such a way that the disagreement is smoothed over even though it is not resolved by reference to a common association. A settlement of this type may be described as not being completely defensible in "logical" terms.

If the parties to a dispute cannot come to terms, the associations cannot remain at the discretion of the persons involved. Tensions rise, and so does the level at which agreement is sought and in view of which disagreements are formulated. It is no longer a question of choosing between the colors brown and green, for instance, or of settling on greenish brown. What the protagonists are demanding is a meeting of the minds on the classification in terms of which the colors in question are only particular classes. To provide a basis for association, the parties involved thus need to have access to a principle that determines relations of equivalence. This process of shifting to a higher level of generality, which in classificatory orderings takes the form of referring to more abstract categories, could be pursued indefinitely in the quest for an ever higher principle of agreement.

However, instead of proceeding through an interminable regression of this sort, disputes most often end in convergence on a higher common principle, or in the confrontation of several such principles. Very quickly, in fact, a question of the following sort tends to be raised: "On what basis are we choosing the color?" This question manifests a shift from a simple association to a judgment aiming at generality; the answer will lead to the formulation of the principle that justifies the associations being made, and it will make it possible to specify the nature of the test that will allow the parties to reach agreement about the adequacy of these associations to the particular things to which they apply. To designate these forms of association, people generally refer either to a technical definition implying a standard measure implemented by means of scientific devices, to a subjective belief influenced by common opinion, to a prevailing usage that perpetuates an entrenched tradition, to an ineffable aesthetic sentiment, or even to an ethical or political requirement, if it so happens, for example, that the color under consideration is to serve as an emblem.

An attempt to confront such varied principles of judgment with one another cannot fail to appear incongruous, given how incommensurable and incompatible they seem to be. This appearance of incompatibility is made manifest by the plurality of oppositions that traverse them: material/symbolic, positive/normative, reality/values, subjective/objective, singular/collective, and so on. And yet our aim is to treat these different modalities of identification ("technical constraint," "argument of an aesthetic nature," or "moral viewpoint") within a single analytic framework. Focusing on associations capable of bringing about agreement and of being incorporated into judgments, we shall argue that the foregoing modalities refer to principles of *justice* (or of *justness*, a less incongruous term when a technical mode of justification is in question) that presuppose the presence of other persons. As Henri Lévy-Bruhl (1964) points out, justice has the property of bringing disputes to an end; we shall treat that property as a distinctive feature of justice. From this standpoint, we shall try to subject associations that are normally kept separate to the same requirements, whether these associations emerge from the singularities of the individual psyche addressed by psychology, engage the collective interests studied by sociology, belong to an economic or political order, or arise from a technical judgment based on one of the natural sciences. Thus the disagreements we shall examine may take the form of discord among people considered in their singular relationships or personal disputes under the sway of some passion, as well as collective conflicts, political struggles, even economic hardships or technological malfunctions.

The perspective we have in view is in many respects disconcerting. It may seem excessive to suggest a direct link between a cognitive operation of association and the foundation of a form of justice. Is there not a primordial gap between the human exercise of identifying objects and the establishment of laws that apply to persons by governing their mutual understanding? If we do not maintain this gap, do we not regress toward a prescientific state of knowledge, in which values and facts would be confused at the heart of a natural order? And will not this providential confusion necessarily lead to the "self-evidence" of a perennial order that excludes the question of agreement and contradicts our earlier remarks on the plurality of forms of agreement?

At the point where we are about to begin examining these questions in greater depth, let us note that there are many instances in which associations are not subject to an imperative of justification but are instead perceived as fortuitous. In such cases, we deem the attendant circumstances *contingent*; these include things and persons related by contiguity that need not be taken into account. Immersed in circumstances, one yields to the particular without seeking to establish equivalencies and consequently without seeking to specify the importance of the persons and things involved. The passerby one bumps into may be anyone at all—a judge or a celebrity, for instance; if the encounter goes no further, it hardly matters. The circumstances are not important because the true nature of the beings that come into contact in such cases need not be at issue. Beings that can be qualified according to incompatible modalities may cross paths or bump into one another without recognizing one another. Thus, on some fall afternoon in a forest, persons who are unacquainted with one another may be walking in the same wooded glen: strollers, lovers, hunters, mushroom gatherers, woodcutters, Boy Scouts, and so on. Their presence in the same space is a matter of circumstance and does not produce a situation with which they have to deal in common. Bringing these strangers together within the field of an objectivizing gaze, placing them on the same stage, making them present in the same space, each one carrying on his own activity according to his own nature: this device is a mainspring of comedy, especially vaudeville. But in everyday life, unlike the theater, there is no framework to circumscribe the stage and offer it to the spectator's gaze; in our everyday experience, coexistence does not always produce a situation. The beings whose paths cross by chance do not ordinarily share a common involvement in the circumstances. If they do become involved—for example, if an accident occurs—the question of justification comes to the fore: does the forest belong to the strollers or to the people who are working to maintain it?

Although the study of these sorts of circumstances does not fall within our purview, to the extent that no constraint of agreement applies to them, the fact remains that the attempt to return to a state of contingent circumstance after a disagreement over the value of making associations has arisen can be understood only in relation to an imperative to justify that this effort seeks to suspend. At the end of our study, we shall look again at the operation of *relativizing*, which is a way of seeking to remain within contingent circumstances by setting aside or ignoring those beings whose prominence tends to recast a situation of contingency as a situation of a defined nature.

The Order of the General and the Particular

Even when the capacity or propensity for association that persons use to coordinate their behavior has been recognized, it does not automatically follow that the forms in which associations are made will have the same type of generality. In order to imagine a world in which a common type of generality has been acquired, let us imagine situations—we call them *natural* situations—in which agreement over associations is perfectly established. A company manager shows some foreign industrialists the most modern assembly line in the factory in which he holds a position of responsibility. Everything goes smoothly, and every being he points out to his visitors is a wholly typical member of the class to which it belongs. The visitors see objects devoid of any irregularities: no particular feature stands out to catch anyone's attention. Both the words of the host's commentary and the casings of the new machines reflect the infinite series of similar things that they bring together under a single technical term. Even the factory and office workers carrying out their duties are qualified according to the same form of generality. The visitors and their guide are certain to understand what they are seeing—that is, the efficient functioning of the assembly line—in the same way. If all parties were asked to produce reports at the end of the visit, the results would not necessarily be identical, but reading them side by side would not produce any troubling contradictions; the accounts would complement one another harmoniously.

It is easy to recognize here the sanctity of an Eden-like world in which such scenes would be repeated in the course of a long ceremony that follows a firmly established protocol to the letter. It would take a very astute observer indeed to detect the difference between the protocol and the enactment, between a report and what really happened. Yet in the societies we are studying, natural situations in which everything holds together, in which there are no exceptional beings, cannot last. How is the harmonious arrangement of things and persons in a state of common generality likely to be disrupted? Most simply, by a breakdown. Let us imagine a visitor whose attention has been drawn to a motionless machine with waiting parts piled up in front of it, or to a vacant work station, or to a heap of rubbish in the bottom of a packing case. Puzzled, the visitor asks questions about these awkward things that invite doubts about the smooth operation of the assembly line. We should stress here and now the way the visitor fastens onto these things in support of some doubt of his own. The looming disagreement cannot be expressed in a pure debate over ideas; arguments have to be substantiated by things. In order to ease the discomfort produced by the visitor's questions, the host has to "go into detail" and cut back on the requirement of generality that kept his commentary at a high level and brought agreement in its wake. The machine, he explains, has a defect resulting from a particular problem with the manufacturing process; the worker is absent for a particular personal reason; the parts are flawed because of a particular impurity in the raw materials. The clamor of particular details that invade the situation and threaten to upset its harmony brings out, a contrario, the accommodations that are needed to disentangle from discrete circumstances things and persons that have been assembled by associations and to involve these things and persons in a situation that holds together.

The example makes it clear that after the fall from Eden illustrated by the failings described above, the operation of association entails a hierarchical ordering that distributes the classes of beings in question according to their level of generality, thus attributing relative values to those classes. A machine that functions normally is situated at a higher level of generality than a defective machine, which is endowed with a lower capacity than the former to do its job—to ensure regular production—in the future; the defective machine will be termed less "reliable." Even in the extreme case in which the scale from the highest level of generality to the lowest is compressed as tightly as possible, at least two states remain, the state defined by the association and the state of the particular element that falls outside the more general state. Now, instead of being related in the way a whole is related to its parts, as the logic of set theory would have it, these states are related by an order that treats the general as superior to the particular. The order thus constituted leads to the qualification of persons in just the same way as it determines the qualification of objects, on the basis of their associations.

The Requirement of General Agreement and the Legitimacy of Order

Under what conditions can a form of equivalence be common?—that is, under what conditions can it allow a qualification of persons and objects capable of framing an agreement or substantiating arguments in a disagreement? In answering this question, we propose to take seriously the imperative to justify that underlies the possibility of coordinating human behavior, and to examine the constraints that weigh on agreement concerning a common good. We are not satisfied, for example, with the use of the notion of "legitimization," which, in the wake of Max Weber's work, tends to confuse justification with deceit by rejecting the constraints of coordination and resorting to a relativism of values. Justifiable acts are our focus: we shall draw out all the possible consequences from the fact that people need to justify their actions. In other words, people do not ordinarily seek to invent false pretexts after the fact so as to cover up some secret motive, the way one comes up with an alibi; rather, they seek to carry out their actions in such a way that these can withstand the test of justification.

How can a social science hope to succeed if it deliberately neglects a fundamental property of its object and ignores the fact that persons face an obligation to answer for their behavior, evidence in hand, to other persons with whom they interact? It suffices to be attentive, as we try to be in the pages that follow, to the justifications that people develop, in speech and in action, to see that the social sciences must begin to take this phenomenon into account, must reckon with the fact that the ordinary course of life demands nearly constant efforts to maintain or salvage situations that are falling into disarray by restoring them to order. In everyday life, people never completely suppress their anxieties, and, like scientists, ordinary people never stop suspecting, wondering, and submitting the world to tests.

The act of bypassing justice and behaving only as one pleases, without being burdened by the requirement to explain, is the defining act of violence. But by the same token, such acts fall outside the scope of our research. Without denying the possibility of such acts or the role that they may play in human affairs, we shall thus exclude civil war from our study, along with tyranny (which bases the order of the polity on force and fear); more generally, we shall rule out situations that are submerged by violence and in which the process of justification has been completely set aside.

Some situations of discord may well turn out to be temporarily suspended between justification and violence, poised on a watershed where they may still shift toward the search for a resolution or, on the contrary, sink into violence. But the moment they degenerate into violence they escape us, and we abandon them. In contrast, we refuse to assert that flyers distributed by strikers to denounce the injustice of low salaries, or declarations by management ordering the strikers to go back to work, are forms of violence (qualified in such cases as symbolic), or that we are dealing here with false appearances concealing an underlying violence, or that such appearances would draw all their force and reality from the violence that has preceded them or that threatens to follow.

Thus we shall ask under what conditions a principle of agreement is held to be legitimate. From the foregoing remarks, we draw what we take to be two major difficulties in the construction of legitimacy. The first has to do with order. We have suggested the way the requirement of reaching agreement might lead to the constitution of an order. Order is needed for disputes to end—for example, when two persons are "sizing one another up" and challenging one another over the unequal importance of two facts that are being compared. But do the inequalities that result from this process not enter into tension with what may appear to be a principle governing the entire set of legitimate forms of justification that we have taken as our object, a principle we shall call the *principle of common humanity*? In the light of this principle, cannot the application to humanity of any ordering principle at all be viewed as an unjustifiable act of "domination" that only serves the "personal interests" of those who would benefit from it?

Let us note that the theory of sublimation (to which Freud failed to give any systematic form) is one of the most fully developed attempts ever made to address this question; it offers an explicit theoretical formulation of the way our society understands worth and of the arguments sometimes invoked to justify the existence of the worthy. This theory accounts for the possibility that men and women can be great (that is, worthy), and it therefore accounts for the possibility of an acceptable form of inequality. In this sense, it is the theory of the legitimacy of a social order. It implies an internal economy of the individual (the economy of the libido and of the displacement of psychological investments), an economy of relations among persons within society, an economy of the inequalities that prevail in the distribution of worth (between sexes, classes, and so on), and an economy of the relation between cultures. Furthermore, Freud also uses the term "sublimation" to refer to a form of generalization. The libido, a mysterious energy that unifies the seemingly disparate ways in which persons attract one another and relate to one another, allows for displacements along the axis connecting the particular with the general. Thus, if one takes to heart the "general interests of humanity," worries about them, speaks in their name, one is transforming a private desire associated with an embodied attachment (to a member of one's family) into a disembodied generic relation that can no longer be the object of individual bodily satisfaction. However, the analytic construction and its methodological apparatus are riddled with powerful tensions. One approach is to take seriously the process by which a person increases in worth, and to demonstrate the place of this process in the foundation of a society. A different approach entails a critical unmasking of discourse: when a subject speaks in the name of the "general interests of humanity," "science," or "art," his or her particular interests, drives, and passions come to light. In this second case, as Paul Ricoeur points out (1974, 99–159), interpretation grounded in suspicion then shifts from the general to the particular, and more especially from the general interest to the particular interests of persons. Each person is endowed with a biological identity and a libido that claims its due, in conformity with a generic instinct, of course, but to the benefit of the person's own body. This tension between the constitution of an order and the critical move that calls it into question lies at the heart of our investigation.

The second major difficulty is related to our observation of the seeming plurality of forms of agreement. How is that plurality possible when, as many have noted, universality seems to be a necessary condition of legitimacy? How can persons act and reach agreement even when multiple modalities for agreement seem to obtain?

In our view, these two difficulties cannot be resolved separately; analyzing the way the two questions are linked is our best hope for reaching an understanding of the notion of legitimacy. Thus we devote part 2 to this analysis, and to the development of a common model of the *polity*, to which we relate the legitimate forms of agreement that serve as the ultimate recourse for clarifying and resolving disputes. We seek to identify the way these forms of agreement are constructed by examining the way they are treated in political philosophy. Conceived as a grammatical enterprise intended to pin down these forms and make them explicit, our undertaking allows us to spell out the constraints with which a higher common principle must comply in order to be acceptable and consequently to be applied in justifications.

An initial study of market political philosophy allows us to identify constraints that we can then systematize in a model of political grammar tested against other examples of political philosophy. This grammar is clearly dependent on the definition of the whole to which it applies. We do not claim that this whole covers all the social orders that have ever been constructed, and we leave open, provisionally, the question of what is encompassed in it. Given the range of political philosophies that have allowed us to illustrate the model and to derive examples of primary forms of the common good, readers will be able to judge the adequacy of our selection for themselves. The primary forms we have extracted are not the only ones compatible with the grammar, moreover, and we shall have occasion to suggest a way in which new formulations of the common good may be constituted.

Once we have posited the model as a system of constraints with which the constitution of a legitimate order (that is, an order capable of encompassing disagreement) must comply, we shall be able to expand it by specifying a competence with which persons must be endowed if they are to be capable of justifying their judgments in response to criticism, or of adjusting situations in such a way as to forestall criticism.

The Reality Test and Prudent Judgment

The possibility of resorting to several different principles of agreement, which is suggested when we face the facts established by economic and sociological approaches to human actions, opens the door to additional difficulties. In this respect, we can speak of a *complex* society, for the reference to a culture, which might account for the community of associations in terms of a shared symbolism, does not provide a way to resolve the problem of reaching agreement. The recognition of a plurality of cultures or value systems shared by communities or groups of persons still does not remove the difficulty resulting from their problematic juxtaposition. Thus, despite these contradictions, in order to explain the absence of discord, we would have to move toward the hypothesis of systematic deception that would conceal the domination of some parties by others.

In our view, people need to involve things in *tests* in order to handle disagreements. In order to carry out such tests, it is not enough to make use of principles of equivalence. When such principles are invoked, they are understood to be accompanied by objects that the persons involved can use to measure themselves against one another. Indeed, the greater or lesser capacity of persons to endow these objects with *value* is what gives rise to a justified order. Each of the sets of objects associated with the various higher common principles forms a coherent and self-sufficient world, a *nature* for which we suggest representations in part 3.

A test leads the persons involved to agree on the relative importance of the beings that turn out to be implicated in the situation, whether the issue is, for example, the relative usefulness of two machines or two investments, the relative merits of two students, the competence of two business executives, or the tokens of respect that two local dignitaries owe one another. Very diverse beings—persons, institutions, tools, machines, rule-governed arrangements, methods of payment, acronyms and names, and so forth—turn out to be connected and arranged in relation to one another in groupings that are sufficiently coherent for their involvement to be judged effective, for the expected processes to be carried out, and for the situations to unfold correctly (as opposed to disrupted situations that are qualified, depending on the applicable discipline, as pathological, dysfunctional, or conflictual, for example). In order for the system to be open to judgment with reference to a higher common principle, each being (person or thing) has to be adjusted to it. When these conditions are fulfilled, we can say that the situation "holds together." A situation of this type, which holds together in a coherent way and which includes no questionable objects, is a *natural* situation. The simplest way to construct a situation conducive to natural behavior is to include in it beings that share the same nature, and to exclude from it beings of different natures. If some of the beings involved in the situation have the same general extension while others remain contingent or possess a different type of generality, the situation does not hold together.

Our approach differs from others, even from those that leave open the possibility of several forms of "legitimacy" or "rationality," in that we have opted to treat scientific and technical justness in the same way as other forms of justification (forms that are usually distinguished from scientific and technological forms by their ethical character), yet we do not reduce all these forms of generality to a single equivalent (for example belief, or force). In our construct, the nature studied by scientists and technologists—which is viewed by some as having the privilege of reality and objectivity—is not the only one in which objects can be found. Every nature has its objects, and all objects can be used for testing.

Thus we are led to short-circuit the distinction between the two definitions of what is *adjusted*, oriented respectively toward *justness* and *fitness*, and to use a single set of conceptual instruments to deal with situations in which maladjustment will be qualified either in the register of injustice or else, for example, in that of dysfunctionality. Maladjustment may thus result from human failure, for instance when what is at stake in a dispute—as in a crisis involving honor—is the proper distribution of the respect with which the persons involved regard one another; or it may result from a failure on the part of persons and objects—as in a disagreement involving the distribution of goods (income, jobs, material objects, diplomas, and so on) among persons. But maladjustment may also have to do with the very ordering of objects among themselves, for instance, when it is necessary to bundle together the technical characteristics of a machine, the modalities of its financing, and the mechanisms that govern its use.

The requirement of testing modifies the scope of our inquiry, which moves from the study of the constructs of political philosophy to the study of practical reason, or, to go further back in the tradition, to the study of prudent behavior. Just as we shall seek to understand the way the polity model is structured by the requirement that the plurality of principles of agreement must be reduced, we shall attempt to show that the model is similarly informed by the way the tensions inherent in a universe embracing multiple natures—tensions between reason and practice, between generality and contingency, and between justice and equity—constrain judgment while allowing it a certain latitude. Part 5 of our work will thus be devoted to the study of the procedures that make it possible to bring disputes to a close.

Two

THE FOUNDATION OF AGREEMENT IN
POLITICAL PHILOSOPHY: THE EXAMPLE
OF THE MARKET POLITY

RECENT DEVELOPMENTS in economic theory, which have helped distinguish the question of equilibrium from that of social welfare, have tended to obscure the fact that political economics sets out to address the issue of social concord. Hypothesizing persons in a state of primitive disorder, in keeping with the passions that move them and that lead them into conflict, political economic theory presents the possibility of general agreement by showing how reference to a single principle can transform the furious heat of interpersonal confrontations into a general welfare that guarantees a peaceful society. The interests of particular individuals are thus tied to the interests of all. The resolution of disagreements comes about as part of a coordinated process that relies on two supports: a common identification of market goods, whose exchange defines the course of action, and a common evaluation of these objects in terms of prices that make it possible to adjust various actions. The behavior of persons can thus be viewed as reasonable, coherent, and *justifiable* according to a principle that is known and acknowledged by all, as opposed to unconscious motivations or hidden or inadmissible interests. Furthermore, as in other political philosophies, the possibility of reaching agreement is tied to a version of human nature that is adapted to it and that gives the structure a solid foundation. Thus Adam Smith's political philosophy includes a *Theory of Moral Sentiments* (1976 [1759]); we shall seek to show that this text describes the workings of a human understanding that conforms to the requirements of a principle of competition. This specification of human nature is more fully developed in Smith's work than in later economic treatises, in which it is generally merged with optimizing rationality.

Our quest to understand the principles according to which actions are subjected to justification implies a need to reexamine the way in which political economics satisfies the foregoing requirements so as to resolve the question of order. We shall thus attempt to draw from Smith's work—while recalling the earlier constructs on which it relies—a definition of a principle of agreement and an analysis of human nature intended to explain how any person can adjust to this principle. We do not intend to add yet another exegesis to the long list of commentaries on Smith's work, and our analysis will remain intentionally selective. We seek to show how a higher common market principle can make it possible to establish an order that is, on this basis, as "holistic" as others. In the process, we shall review the various expressions of the opposition between individualism and holism, or between the individual and the collective, or between the private and the public spheres, so as to relate them—going against the grain of current approaches—to a common model. This model will help us discern clearly the difference between a particular person and an "individual" in a market state: "individuals" are as metaphysical as the collective beings of sociology, and just as "collective," in their own way, since they constitute part of the definition of the common good.

A Social Bond Based on an Inclination toward Exchange in One's Own Interest

The elements ensuring the foundation of a *polity* that rests on the establishment of a market bond can be drawn from Adam Smith's writings. The market bond unites persons through the intermediary of rare goods offered to the appetites of all, and competition among acquisitive desires makes the price attached to the possession of an object less important than the fact that others desire it. A number of elements of this grammar (the term is Smith's own: he suggests that "the rules of justice may be compared to the rules of grammar" 1976 [1759], 175) had already been formulated. For example, Smith's discussion of the value of goods is grounded in a long series of treatises on fair price; in the scholastic tradition, the prominence of these glosses extending Aristotle's writings stems from the fact that they are part of the construction of general systems of equity.

The Law of Nature and Nations, a treatise by Samuel Pufendorf that Smith had in his library, provides a particularly rigorous formulation of this question, in which the value of things and the value of persons are encompassed in a single species of "moral being," termed a "moral quantity" and understood as a moral "mode of estimation." "Now *Moral Quantity*," Pufendorf writes, "is met with first in *Things*, where it is called *Price*; secondly in *Persons*, where we term it *Esteem*; both which were included in the Notion of *Value*; and thirdly, in *Actions*, where it has not yet acquired a peculiar name" (1749 [1672], 12). Jean Barbeyrac, Pufendorf's French translator (from the Latin), points out that "the Author remarks here, that the first and second Sort of moral Quantities are express'd by the Word *Valor*, to which our *English* word *Value* is equivalent" (n. 4). Pufendorf makes it quite obvious (more clearly than Smith, in some respects) that the scarcity of a good is an important factor in its market value: "That which chiefly raises the Price, is Scarcity" (462). Moreover, he construes price as a form of expression for the desires of others, a form we analyze as a way to comprehend those others:[1] "For the Ambition of Mortals esteems those things most, which few Men have in common with them; and on the other side, thinks meanly of those which are seen in the hands of every one" (462). But here Pufendorf's construct is accompanied by a critical questioning: "Tho' indeed it proceeds from the Corruption and Pravity of Human Nature, that we value real Goods more or less, according as few or many possess them in common with us. For my Goods are never the worse, because others possess the like; nor the better, because others want them" (462). Because Adam Smith's project is explicitly informed by a perspective similar to that of a jurist, and because Smith seeks to propose a foundation for principles of agreement that have to govern relations among people, his work includes the basic elements of a market political grammar, systematically arranged. It differs in this respect from later texts on economics, whose authors are intent on disentangling a set of instruments specific to their discipline from the original dross, which they deemed excessively moralistic.

Smith's initial project as presented at the end of *Theory of Moral Sentiments* (1976 [1759], hereafter *TMS*), is in fact an attempt to construct a theory of justice, and to account for "the general principles of law and government," not restricting himself to "laws of police" as he thought Cicero and Plato had done, but rather following Grotius's example in attempting to establish "a system of what might properly be called natural jurisprudence, or a theory of the general principles which ought to run through and be the foundation of the laws of all nations" (341). After the publication of *Research into the Nature and Causes of the Wealth of Nations* (1991 [1776], hereafter *WN*), the author judged that he had fulfilled his promise "in what concerns police, revenue, and arms" (1880 [1795], 3). He made this explicit thirty years after *The Theory of Moral Sentiments* was first published, in a preface to the significantly revised and expanded sixth edition; his only regret was his failure to complete his *Lectures in Jurisprudence*.

The attention focused on *The Wealth of Nations*, while it consolidated the underpinnings of economics as a discipline, helped keep Smith's two works separate, although the author had viewed them originally as part of a single project; moreover, of the two, he placed higher value on *Theory of Moral Sentiments* (according to Samuel Romilly, cited in Raphael 1975, 85). We need to take the opposite tack and reconnect the two works, if we are to consider Smith's project not in relation to later economic theory but as an effort—in the wake of other such endeavors—to establish a new sort of social bond that could connect persons to a common good. Such a bond is achieved through the arrangement of a marketplace in which individuals well disposed to one another but governed by their own personal interests enter into competition in order to acquire rare goods, in such a way that their wealth endows them with worth, since it is the expression of the unsatisfied desires of the others.

It is because of the deliberately systematic character of Smith's project[2] that these two works are appropriate for describing the elements of a political philosophy, even though, as we shall have occasion to recall later on, many earlier attempts to construct an order based on a market bond can be identified, and even though Smith's texts include discordant elements in relation to the earlier construction, as for example in his occasional references to other definitions of worth, definitions that the author sometimes uses in order to denounce the very type of social bond that he himself had helped establish.

Given the point of view we have adopted here, we shall not review all of Smith's work; indeed, even in *The Wealth of Nations* we shall focus chiefly on one small section in the early chapters, the discussion of the way a market works. From an economist's standpoint, this section might be deemed the least original; for our purposes, however, it is important to see how Smith's discussion of markets is related to the views on sympathy and the impartial spectator that he develops in *Theory of Moral Sentiments*, in order to understand the way this political grammar was constructed. Smith's views on the division of labor, on what is to be included in a theory of work value, or on investment—none of which will be considered here—can be related rather to the development of what we shall later call *industrial* worth, with reference to texts by Saint-Simon. At present we shall focus chiefly on the market arrangement and the moral states Smith associates with it, even though one could emphasize equally well, on the contrary, the passages in *Wealth of Nations* that point to a different principle of worth. Indeed, this has been done by economists determined to demonstrate the lag in economic theory that could be attributed to the role Smith assigned to the cost of work, at the expense of a worth resulting from market competition (Kauder 1953), or, in a different spirit, by historians eager to demonstrate Smith's originality with respect to the Aristotelian fair price tradition, a tradition that reached Smith by way of Pufendorf, Carmichael, and his own teacher, Hutcheson (Robertson and Taylor 1957).

Unlike the writers who sought to base worth on work and its utility, and despite the emphasis he placed in his work on the division of labor, which probably reflects Mandeville's influence (1924 [1714], cxxxiv), Smith did not construe the division of labor as the principle of "general opulence," and it is not what underlies market reciprocity, as it is for Hume (Deleule 1979, 51). "This division of labour, from which so many advantages are derived, is not originally the effect of any human wisdom" (*WN*, 13). Rather, "it is the necessary, though very slow and gradual, consequence of a certain propensity in human nature which has in view no such extensive utility; the propensity to truck, barter, and exchange one thing for another" (13). This human propensity presupposes that the parties involved are endowed with the capacity to reach agreement on a deal, to make contracts with one another in a conventional manner.

> It is common to all men, and to be found in no other race of animals, which seem to know neither this nor any other species of contracts. Two greyhounds, in running down the same hare, have sometimes the appearance of acting in some sort of concert. . . . This, however, is not the effect of any contract, but of the accidental concurrence of their passions in the same object at that particular time. Nobody ever saw a dog make a fair and deliberate exchange of one bone for another with another dog. Nobody ever saw one animal by its gesture and natural cries signify to another, this is mine, this is yours; I am willing to give this for that. (13)

As we shall observe systematically in part 2, the development of a higher common principle on the basis of a new form of social bond always goes hand in hand with a critique of bonds constructed in conformity with other principles. Smith thus denounces bonds of personal dependence as part of the same argument in which he spells out the benefits to be derived from the market bond; he presents the latter as an instrument of liberation from servitude and from the long chain of subordination that connects the various beings whose potential worth we shall see when we look at the *domestic* polity. "Commerce and manufactures gradually introduced order and good government, and with them, the liberty and security of individuals, among the inhabitants of the country, who had before lived almost in a continual state of war with their neighbours, and of servile dependency upon their superiors" (*WN*, 385). By extending the network of persons they bring into contact with one another, market exchanges remove any tinge of personal dependence from interpersonal relations. In particular, market exchanges lead to a denunciation of the domestic bonds between master and worker, a principal target of Turgot's edicts. "Each tradesman or artificer derives his subsistence from the employment, not of one, but of a hundred or a thousand different customers. Though in some measure obliged to them all, therefore, he is not absolutely dependent upon any one of them" (*Édits de Turgot*, cited in *WN*, 390). As initially depicted by Smith, the chain of domestic bonds that is broken by market relations extends even to household pets. "A spaniel endeavours by a thousand attractions to engage the attention of its master who is at dinner, when it wants to be fed by him. Man sometimes uses the same arts with his brethren, and when he has no other means of engaging them to act according to his inclinations, endeavours by every servile and fawning attention to obtain their good will" (*WN*, 14). As for charitable giving, which expresses *domestic* worth, as we shall see, a man in need of assistance is well advised not to count too much on it. Rather than appealing to the "benevolence" of "well-disposed people," he "will be more likely to prevail if he can interest their self-love in his favour, and shew them that it is for their own advantage to do for him what he requires of them." Mutual "good offices" are thus acquired "by treaty, by barter, and by purchase" (14).

The way Smith contrasts the market bond with the *domestic* bond is very similar to the way Pascal and his Jansenist contemporaries Jean Domat and Pierre Nicole represented the relative benefits of "concupiscence" and "benevolence." In his *Pensées*, Pascal refers to "[m]an's greatness³ even in his concupiscence. He has managed to produce such a remarkable system from it and make it the image of true charity" (*Pensées* 1966, 60 [Brunschwig no. 402]). As Nicole observes in an essay on "grandeur" and in a later text on charity and self-love:

> To comprehend more fully how great our Obligation is to State-government, we must consider, that Men being void of Charity by the disorder of Sin, nevertheless remain full of wants, and in an infinite number of ways depend one upon another. Concupiscence therefore hath taken the place of Charity that it may supply these wants, and the means it uses are such that one cannot enough admire them; vulgar Charity cannot reach so far. . . . What a piece of Charity would it be, to built for another an intire [*sic*] House, furnish it with all necessary Houshold-stuff; and after that to deliver him up the Key? Concupiscence does this cheerfully. (Nicole 1696 2:97–98)

> Thus one may say truly, that absolutely to reform the World, that's to say, to banish all the Vices, and all the gross Disorders therein, and to make Mankind happy even in this Life, there needs only instead of Charity, to give every one a harmless Self-Love, which may be able to discern its true Interests, and to incline thereto by the ways which true Reason shall discover to it. . . . [Even if society were] absolutely void of Charity, we should see every where nothing but the Form and Characters of Charity. (3:105)

Individuals in Concert in Their Lust for Goods

Not only does the establishment of the market bond presuppose that individuals are subject in a concerted way to a common penchant for exchange; it is also sustained by the common identification of external goods. Objects of desire that are fully detachable from the human body and thus suited for use in exchanges, these goods provide the underpinnings for interpersonal relations. The requirement that such goods be rare influences their distribution: it informs the competition among desires that is enacted in the marketplace, and it makes possession of the desired goods a way of expressing others.

The orchestration of acquisitive desires was the keystone of Smith's political philosophy, but it was by no means his own invention. In the scholastic texts, Aristotelian commutative justice governs the exchange of goods and services among individuals, and "fair price" theories imply at least community participation in price-setting (*"communis aestimatio"*), and even, among the later scholastics, market competition as such (de Roover 1955). In the Jansenist tradition, man is portrayed as replacing a "unique good" with "apparent goods" whose "division" nevertheless helps "unite men in a thousand ways" (Domat, *Traité des lois*, 1828, 25, cited in Faccarello 1984).

As Gilbert Faccarello has shown (1984, 1999), Pierre de Boisguilbert starts with elements of the Jansenist construct mentioned above, but he replaces the underlying art of politics (Nicole 1696, 2:167–68) with references to the "balance," "equilibrium," or "justice" of "competition." As the "spirit of all markets," the "desire for profit" suffices to create an "equilibrium" or "balance" between buyer and seller (Faccarello 1984, 52), and "it is in the interest of every buyer to have a large number of merchants, as well as a great deal of merchandise, so that competition will induce each seller to offer his goods for less, in order to increase sales" (3:105).

We are indebted to Albert O. Hirschman (1977) for his analysis of the historical development of such ideas as desire, fame, self-love, vanity, appetite, and virtue, which allows him to show how the notions of passion and interest had been treated prior to Smith's work, and, more generally, to reconstitute the arguments that had been produced on the topic of liberalism (1977, 1982a). Following Hirschman but confining ourselves here to the most explicit statements in which a balance of passions is represented as the principle underlying the fabrication of an order that transcends the confusion of private interests, we shall look briefly at the formulations offered by Vico, Montesquieu, and Steuart.

In *The New Science of Giambattista Vico*, first published in 1725, the author describes a balance that depends not on avarice alone but on three distinct vices. "Out of ferocity, avarice, and ambition, the three vices which run throughout the human race, [legislation] creates the military, merchant, and governing classes [*la corte*], and thus the strength, riches and wisdom of commonwealths. Out of these three great vices, which could certainly destroy all mankind on the face of the earth, it makes civil happiness." Thanks to divine Providence, a veritable "divine legislative mind" for the world, "the passions of men each bent on his private advantage, for the sake of which they would live like wild beasts in the wilderness, made the civil institutions by which they may live in human society" (Vico

1984 [1725], 62). And while "it is true that men have themselves made this world of nations," Vico construes the legislating intelligence as capable of transcending "particular ends that men had proposed to themselves" in favor of "wider ends," which "[a superior mind] has always employed to preserve the human race upon this earth" (425).

In *The Spirit of the Laws*, Montesquieu also calls into question the power of reason to govern human behavior. In his view, stirred-up passions are more likely to contribute to a state of equilibrium. "This nation, always heated, could more easily be led by its passions than by reason, which never produces great effects on the spirits of men" (1989 [1748], 327). Commerce and competition "that puts a just price on goods and establishes the true relations between them" (344) ensure peace: "It is an almost general rule that everywhere there are gentle mores, there is commerce and that everywhere there is commerce, there are gentle mores" (338). The image of commerce as a restraint on the passions, studied by Hirschman in its various embodiments, is summed up in the following statement: "And, happily, men are in a situation such that, though their passions inspire in them the thought of being wicked, they nevertheless have an interest in not being so" (389–90).

In his *Inquiry into the Principles of Political Oeconomy* of 1767, James Steuart lays out the outline of a "political oeconomy" in which despotic power is restrained by a complex interplay of commercial and industrial mechanisms that can be compared to clockwork. "When once a state begins to subsist by the consequences of industry, there is less danger to be apprehended from the power of the sovereign. The mechanism of his admiration becomes more complex, and . . . he finds himself so bound up by the laws of his political oeconomy, that every transgression of them runs him into new difficulties" (Steuart 1767, 1:215–17, cited in Hirschman 1977, 83–84).

David Hume's approach warrants more detailed attention, given its influence on the development of Smith's system. In his *Treatise of Human Nature* (1739–40), Hume rejects the idea that reason is a means of keeping the passions in balance. According to him, reason favors "judgment concerning causes and effects" in arithmetic or mechanics, but, beyond these limits, reason alone "never influences any of our actions." Hume illustrates this postulate with the example of market calculation, distinguishing it from passion, which spurs to action: "abstract or demonstrative reasoning . . . never influences any of our actions, but only as it directs our judgment concerning causes and effects" (1978 [1739–40], 414). Reason can act only as a "slave" to the passions (415) and, "['t]is certain, that no affection of the human mind has both a sufficient force, and a proper direction to counter-balance the love of gain. . . . Benevolence to strangers is too weak for this purpose" (492). The balance needed to maintain order in society can be achieved only by putting this passion into play against itself, so that "itself alone restrains it" (492).

Hume highlights the role played by goods unattached to the body in the instrumentation of this balance; this third type of goods is distinguished both from "the internal satisfaction of our minds"—for we are "perfectly secure in the enjoyment" of the latter—and from the "external advantages of our body," which can be taken away from us, but which "can be of no advantage to him who deprives us of them." In this gradation of properties, which range from the quality of personhood to unattached, appropriable goods, only the latter "are both expos'd to the violence of others, and may be transferr'd without suffering any loss or alteration; while at the same time, there is not a sufficient quantity of them to supply every one's desires and necessities" (487–88). Conventions concerning the ownership of goods and the conditions of their alienation complete this instrumentation of the market bond and help "bestow stability on the possession of those external goods"; indeed, "it is by that means we maintain society" (489). Moreover, Hume seeks to provide an endogenous account of how conventions are established, whether they concern property, language, or "common measures of exchange": such conventions arise "gradually," "by our repeated experience of the inconveniences of transgressing [them]," and "without any promise" (490).

The organization of the various elements that figure in the construction of a form of general agreement depending on market bonds is brought to light in a passage in which Hume explains how the elements work together and analyzes what happens when certain human mind-sets confront situations in which rare and transmissible external goods—common objects of human desires—are presented. "Justice takes its rise from human conventions; and . . . these are intended as a remedy to some inconveniences, which proceed from the concurrence of certain *qualities* of the human mind with the *situation* of external objects. The qualities of the mind are *selfishness* and *limited generosity*: And the situation of external objects is their *easy change*, join'd to their *scarcity* in comparison of the wants and desires of men" (494, Hume's italics). Exchange arrangements presuppose that all the persons involved are in the same state, that they are all *individuals* free of any personal dependence: "and 'tis to restrain this selfishness, that men have been oblig'd to separate themselves from the community, and to distinguish betwixt their own goods and those of others" (495). Once placed in this state that gives them access to the market, individuals redirect their vanity toward goods, and the constraint of scarcity that presides over the distribution of these goods is the basis for a new type of worth. The possession of the most precious goods is a form of expression of the desire of others, and it therefore determines the way an original subordination is expressed.

The plurality of higher common principles gives rise to a *critique* that we shall examine in detail later on; it is important to note here that both Hume and Smith, even as they work toward the establishment of a market polity, allude to prior critiques of the market bond in the name of vainglory. Their reminders fall within a long tradition of critiques of this type of worth going back to the Stoics' propositions about the vanity of ownership and the wise man's detachment with respect to wealth. Seneca took the opposite tack from Hume and Smith: in distinguishing between goods and other qualities persons may have, he denied that goods could express those other qualities in any way; thus, for him, goods could not be used to justify any sort of worth. In "De Vita Beata," Seneca calls the relationship between persons and goods into question:

> In my case, if riches slip away, they will take from me nothing but themselves, while if they leave you, you will be dumbfounded, and you will feel that you have been robbed of your real self; in my eyes riches have a certain place, in yours they have the highest; in fine, I own my riches, yours own you. . . . Place me in a house that is most sumptuous, place me where I may have gold and silver plate for common use; I shall not look up to myself on account of these things, which, even though they belong to me, are nevertheless no part of me. (157 [22.5], 165 [25.1])

Hume's undertaking, like Smith's, contributes to the construction of a coherent polity in which human nature entails certain affective dispositions toward other people and toward things, but is not based on a capacity for rational calculation. In this respect, the two philosophers' formulations differ fundamentally from later ones, produced after economics had become an autonomous science, that stabilize the opposition between the "subjective" and the "objective," as Schumpeter describes it. "[S]ubjective valuation creates the objective value—We know that this had been taught, in the case of commodities, by the scholastic doctors—and not the other way round: a thing is beautiful because it pleases, it does not please because it is 'objectively' beautiful" (Schumpeter 1954, 127). If the market bond is to be used to construct a form of agreement, persons must be subject to a governing passion that orients them toward the possession of goods; they must thus be closely attached to their particular interests, which is not at all the case in the *civic* form of generality. But at the same time persons have to be detached enough from themselves and from *domestic* subordinations to get along with all the other individuals in a marketplace that serves as the higher common principle, and to agree about the goods exchanged, which express their desires. This is the attitude toward goods that Barbeyrac describes in his commentary on Pufendorf, referring to Thomasius's distinction between a "thing of the same kind" and a "thing which is capable of an equivalent" (Thomasius, *Jurisprudentia Divina*, cited in Pufendorf 1749 [1672] 464 n. 2).

> For only the first [a thing of the same kind] can be priced as high as we please. As for the other, if in a Loan, or Exchange, for Example, one pretends to value his Wine or Corn at an higher Rate, although in reality they are of the same Nature and Goodness as that of the other Bargainer, Mr. *Thomasius* says, "That he offends against the natural Equality of Mankind, which doth not allow us to weigh our own and other Mens Interests in an unequal Balance, and judge differently of them, or of what appertains to them, without a just Cause." We may, also, add, That the Nature of Commerce, by which Value is settled, requires Equality.

Because *Theory of Moral Sentiments* presents a description of this state in which human beings are suited for the market bond, owing to "that imaginary change of situations . . . [which produces] the most perfect harmony of sentiments and affections" (*TMS*, 19), a state that is built on the basis of a "sympathetic" disposition and a moral being called an "impartial spectator," Smith's text is an essential element for our understanding of the way a market polity is constructed.

The Sympathetic Disposition and
the Position of Impartial Spectator

Hume had already depicted a common sympathetic disposition, a quasi-psychological sentiment, shared by all parties, on which the social bond can be based without any need to invoke reason or benevolence; as we have seen, Hume deemed the latter too weak a passion to curb the attraction toward profit. All men's minds are so similar that "[no one can] be actuated by any affection, of which all others are not, in some degree, susceptible," and "when I see the *effects* of passion in the voice and gesture of any person, my mind immediately passes from these effects to their causes, and forms such a lively idea of the passion, as is presently converted into the passion itself." Any object that pleases its possessor "is sure to please the spectator, by a delicate sympathy with the possessor" (1978, [1739–40] 575–77).

Smith's thinking runs along the same lines. In his view, judgments are not shaped directly by the idea of the usefulness of certain behaviors; rather, they are modeled on the tastes and passions of others: "The idea of the utility of all qualities of this kind, is plainly an after-thought, and not what first recommends them to our approbation" (*TMS*, 20). Taking up Hume's earlier positions ("the utility of any object, according to him, pleases the master by perpetually suggesting to him the pleasure or conveniency which it is fitted to promote" [179]), Smith seeks to carry the line of argument further by noting that pleasure may not even have any relation to utility. To illustrate this remark, he presents a series of examples, critiques denouncing the illusory nature of reference to needs and to utility; thus he calls into question what we shall later call *industrial* worth. The first of these examples shows a man more tormented by the idea of setting his home up impeccably than he is attracted by the idea of living comfortably in it:

> To attain this conveniency [setting all of the chairs in their places with their backs against the wall] he voluntarily puts himself to more trouble than all he could have suffered from the want of it. . . . What he wanted therefore, it seems, was not so much this conveniency, as that arrangement of things which promotes it. Yet it is this conveniency which ultimately recommends the arrangement, and bestows upon it the whole of its propriety and beauty. (180)

The second example features someone obsessed with acquiring a watch that keeps perfect time, no matter the price. "But the person so nice with regard to this machine, will not always be found either more scrupulously punctual than other men, or more anxiously concerned upon any other account, to know precisely what time of day it is. What interests him is not so much the attainment of this piece of knowledge, as the perfection of the machine which serves to attain it" (180). In each case, Smith discloses the madness, or at the very least the unreasonableness, of behavior directed toward order and precision. Each of these behaviors could be described today in psychiatric terms as "compulsive"; each manifests symptoms found on charts of obsessional neurosis.

Indeed, Freud's libidinal economy exhibits forces or entities such as the unconscious capable of accounting for the equilibrium of such situations that are out of kilter. The example Smith uses to question the importance of a principle of efficacity is interesting in that it introduces the idea, one we shall pursue later in this work, that principles have to be adapted to situations; if they are not, fixation on a particular principle without regard for the situation will be viewed as a sign of abnormality or even of madness. Indeed, there would be nothing strange at all about the modes of behavior described above if the room to be furnished were a large industrial workshop or if the watch were going to be used to time coordinated technological activities. It is because the situations under consideration are *domestic* and do not lend themselves to meticulous ordering that it is hard to justify the sacrifices participants have been willing to make. Thus meticulousness is all the more easily unveiled by a psychiatrist as manic obsessional behavior when it is manifested in nonprofessional activities.

Smith uses another set of examples to denounce the vanity of those who seek goods that are more costly than they are useful, "trinkets" or "baubles" (180): "Wealth and greatness are mere trinkets of frivolous utility" (181). Condemning "that love of distinction so natural to man" (182), Smith weighs what is precious against what is necessary: "To one who was to live alone in a desolate island it might be a matter of doubt, perhaps, whether a palace, or a collection of such small conveniencies as are commonly contained in a tweezer-case, would contribute most to his happiness and enjoyment" (182). Vanity and the desire for the approval of others—which, as we shall see, can ground a different form of agreement by way of *fame*—are expressed, in Smith's construct, by way of goods. Worth is no longer measured in terms of esteem but in terms of wealth. "It is the vanity, not the ease or the pleasure, which interests us. But vanity is always founded upon the belief of our being the object of attention and approbation. The rich man glories in his riches, because he feels that they naturally draw upon him the attention of the world" (50–51). Vanity becomes "that great purpose of human life which we call bettering our condition" (50). Although Smith rejects this equivalence between worth and wealth as illusory, it nevertheless underlies the formula according to which the more worthy express the desires of the less worthy in the market polity. "The pleasures of wealth and greatness, when considered in this complex view, strike the imagination as something grand and beautiful and noble, of which the attainment is well worth the toil and anxiety which we are so apt to bestow upon it. And it is well that nature imposes upon us in this manner. It is this deception which rouses and keeps in continual motion the industry of mankind" (183).

Smith sets the feeling of sympathy at the heart of his construct, to sustain the bond between ourselves and another that causes us, as we contemplate "our brother upon the rack," to "enter as it were into his body, and become in some measure the same person with him" (9). He makes this feeling the mode of approval that underlies a process of agreement reaching that he refuses to ground in self-love or personal interest alone, or on reason and calculations of utility: "Sympathy, however, cannot, in any sense, be regarded as a selfish principle";[4] moreover, "it was not the thought of what we had gained or suffered which prompted our applause or indignation" (317). It is also true that "a man may sympathize with a woman in childbed; though it is impossible that he should conceive himself as suffering her pains in his own proper person and character" (9). This inclination toward sympathy thus lies midway, in a sense, between the state in which persons give themselves over entirely to their own particular interests and the state in which they have access to "the general subjects of science and taste" "which . . . are considered without any particular relation either to ourselves or to the person whose sentiments we judge of" (19). "[A]ll the general subjects of science and taste, are what we and our companion regard as having no particular relation to either of us. We both look at them from the same point of view, and we have no occasion for sympathy, or for that imaginary change of situations from which it arises, in order to produce, with regard to these, the most perfect harmony of sentiments and affections" (19). Smith describes the result of this "mutual sympathy" in terms of shared pain, which is reminiscent of the shared benefits that bind individuals in competition.

> How are the unfortunate relieved when they have found out a person to whom they can communicate the cause of their sorrow? Upon his sympathy they seem to disburthen themselves of a part of their distress: he is not improperly said to share it with them. He not only feels a sorrow of the same kind with that which they feel, but as if he had derived a part of it to himself, what he feels seems to alleviate the weight of what they feel. (15)

Criticizing Hutcheson for his reference to a specific power of perception, a "moral sense," Smith posits that one must follow nature, which "acts here, as in all other cases, with the strictest oeconomy, and produces a multitude of effects from one and the same cause" (321); that cause is sympathy, a faculty possessed by all persons. Sympathy is therefore a fundamental component of Smith's construct, because—like the definition of the state of impartial spectator, which we shall examine later—it helps transform persons subject to passions into individuals who can identify with one another and thus come to terms over a market of external goods.

The role of sympathy was also discussed by Cabanis, and his approach makes it possible to understand the shift between the use of sympathy to construct individuals in market political philosophy and the role of the physiological determination of that instinct in the organicist constitution of society proposed in the *industrial polity* and reworked by Durkheim. In *On the Relations between the Physical and Moral Aspects of Man*), the memoirs Cabanis published in 1802 (1981), the author depicted the sympathetic disposition within the human body as a basic instinct (598). His overall project was designed to bring the moral sciences into the realm of the physical (13), and to constitute a single overarching science, the "science of man," which the Germans called "anthropologie" (33). Opposing metaphysics, he proposed a theory based on physiology that later influenced Saint-Simon's positivism, as we shall see in part 2.

> Moral sympathy, too, offers effects that merit attention. By the power of their signs alone, the impressions can be communicated from a sensible being, or one considered as such, to other beings which, to share them, seem to identify with him. We see individuals attracted to or repelled by one another. At times their ideas and feelings respond to one another by a secret language as quick as the impressions and fall into perfect harmony. (12)

And Cabanis reminds us that "[t]hese effects [of moral sympathy], and many others that are related to them, have been very carefully analyzed. Scottish philosophy considers them to be the principle of all ethical relations" (12). For Cabanis, sympathy clearly helps man acquire worth. "It is soon recognized that the only side on which [man's] pleasures can be extended indefinitely is that of his relations with those that are like him—that his existence becomes broader in the measure in which he becomes involved in their emotions and makes them share those that move him" (17). Pantomimic signs

> are the first of all, the only ones that are common to the entire human race. This is the true universal language. Before the knowledge of any spoken language, these signs make child run to child, make him smile at those who smile at him. . . . Other languages are formed, and soon we exist scarcely less in others than in ourselves. . . . [It is this faculty] that many philosophers have believed to depend on a sixth sense. They have called it by the name SYMPA-THY. (69)

According to Cabanis, moral sympathy depends on deep-seated organic tendencies. "In the entire organic system, the resemblance or analogy of matters makes them gravitate particularly toward one another" (583), as can be observed in the case of scars or transplants (584).

The reference to the "spectator" state is already present in Hutcheson, who was Smith's teacher, and in Hume, who greatly influenced Smith. For Hutcheson, this reference serves, like the staging of the reaction of "observers," to appeal to the judgment of others to justify, through the reinforcement of public opinion, a conduct inspired by benevolence, whose foundations Hutcheson seeks to establish. "Virtue is then called amiable or lovely, from its raising goodwill or love in *spectators* toward the agent" (Hutcheson, *Inquiry concerning Virtue*, 1:viii, cited in Raphael 1975, 86).

Hume also refers to a spectator state in which persons have access to a common viewpoint. "Every particular person's pleasure and interest being different, 'tis impossible men cou'd ever agree in their sentiments and judgments, unless they chose some common point of view, from which they might survey the object, and which might cause it to appear the same to all of them" (Hume 1978 [1739–40], 641). The spectator is sometimes described as a "judicious spectator" (632), sometimes as "every spectator" (641), to justify access to a viewpoint shared with others, and to establish independence from the influence that domestic bonds can exercise on sympathy by favoring "persons close to us" and persons "of our acquaintance" over "strangers" (631–32).

Smith first mentions the "impartial spectator" when he praises self-control—a virtue in the Stoic and Christian traditions—in people who do not yield to anger or rage but rather feel "the indignation which they naturally call forth in that of the impartial spectator" (*TMS*, 24). "As to love our neighbor as we love ourselves is the great law of Christianity, so it is the great precept of nature to love ourselves only as we love our neighbor, or what comes to the same thing, as our neighbor is capable of loving us" (25). The appeal to a spectator can be seen as a way of staging the viewpoint of others, and this impression is confirmed in the example of the mirror, which we need for self-observation. A human creature who has had no communication with his own species

> could no more think of his own character, of the propriety or demerit of his own sentiments and conduct, of the beauty or deformity of his own mind, than of the beauty or deformity of his own face. All these are objects which he cannot easily see, which naturally he does not look at, and with regard to which he is provided with no mirror which can present them to his view. Bring him into society, and he is immediately provided with the mirror which he wanted before. (110)

However, Smith wanted to establish his distance from a measure of agreement based on the approval of others, that is, on fame, as we present it in part 2. In the second edition of *Theory of Moral Sentiments*, Smith introduced some modifications into his text; he explained the changes in a response to a letter from Gilbert Elliot that must have raised this point (Raphael 1975, 90–91). The modifications were intended "both to confirm my Doctrine that our judgements concerning our own conduct have always a reference to the sentiment of some other being, and to show that, notwithstanding this, real magnanimity and conscious virtue can support itselfe under the disapprobation of all mankind" (October 1759, Smith 1977, 49). Smith's mistrust of opinion can be traced back to the Calas affair, in which Voltaire pleaded in favor of Calas's innocence. Smith, who spent time in Toulouse two years later, in 1764 and 1765 (Raphael 1975, 92), was struck by the affair, and he mentions it in *Theory of Moral Sentiments* (217).

The "sentiment of others" is reworked to become jurisdiction over the inner self and an internal division of the person that is not unlike Rousseau's figure of the sovereign. "When I endeavour to examine my own conduct, when I endeavour to pass sentence upon it, and either to approve or condemn it, it is evident that, in all such cases, I divide myself, as it were, into two persons; and that I, the examiner and judge, represent a different character from that other I, the person whose conduct is examined into and judged of" (*TMS*, 113). This argument is developed further in the sixth edition, where it leads to the distinction between a love of praise, which causes people to yield to "the sentiment of others," to give themselves over to flattery and untruth, to "look upon themselves, not in the light which, they know, they ought to appear to their companions, but in that in which they believe their companions actually look upon them"

(115), and a desire for praiseworthiness founded on self-approbation that, far from the roar of applause, "stands in need of no confirmation from the approbation of other men" (117) nor of "appeal . . . to a much higher tribunal" (130). The impartial spectator appears here as an internal agency of appeal (and it is in this respect that it resembles Rousseau's figure) that can be invoked to override the weight of fame. "But though man has, in this manner, been rendered the immediate judge of mankind, he has been rendered so only in the first instance; and an appeal lies from his sentence to a much higher tribunal, to the tribunal of their own consciences, to that of the supposed impartial spectator, to that of the man within the breast, the great judge and arbiter of their conduct" (130).

The spatial metaphor of perspective provides a perfect illustration of the relation between the spectator's observational framework and the measure of "real worth."

> [I]t is only by consulting this judge within, that we can ever see what relates to ourselves in its proper shape and dimensions; or that we can ever make any proper comparison between our own interests and those of other people. As to the eye of the body, objects appear great or small, not so much according to their *real dimensions,* as according to the nearness of their situation; so do they likewise to what may be called the natural eye of the mind: and we remedy the defects of both of these organs pretty much in the same manner. . . . I can form a just comparison between those great objects and the little objects around me, in no other way, than by transporting myself, at least in fancy, to a different station, from whence I can survey both at nearly equal distances, and thereby *form some judgment of their real proportions.* (134–35, emphasis added)

As we shall have occasion to note later on, when we examine the critical opening that results from the plurality of higher common principles, *market* worth, although frequently challenged in everyday life, is often criticized in the name of some other worth. Veblen (1953 [1899]) was operating in a critical mode when he produced a detailed depiction of the mechanisms of market worth in American society, denouncing *market* worth in the name of the *industrial* worth that we shall analyze later. We should note that this constant reference to industrial worth did not keep Veblen from calling it into question in his own existence, by rejecting its trappings, whether technological (for example, telephones) or conventional (for example, a uniform procedure for grading students). Veblen's sketch of situations constructed according to the market polity is informed by his anthropological skill; he offers precise renderings of beings who can serve in the calculation of market worth (even including non-"productive" domestic animals [102]). And he is led to distinguish between situations that conform to the principles of industrial worth (which he calls *industrial efficiency*] and bonds based on the acquisition of market goods, which disturb the application of his principles when they come into play. The distinction thus developed throughout his book leads him to denounce a number of *compromises* between these two principles of worth, like those through which an engineer and a businessman reach agreement within one of the large new "corporations." And as C. Wright Mills notes in his introduction, Veblen devoted his entire career to clarifying the difference between the efficiency of an honest engineer and the businessman's fanatical love of profit (x–xi). Veblen associates the "conspicuousness" of accumulating goods with detachment from personal dependence (72), while stressing the characteristic features of the market bond explicitly construed as a way of encompassing and expressing others: "possessions then come to be valued not so much as evidence of a successful foray, but rather as evidence of the prepotence of the possessor of these goods over other individuals in the community" (36). In contemporary economic literature, the reference to "conspicuous consumption," considered as a degraded expression of consumer desires that are not directed toward useful goods, is a very discreet trace of the fundamental tension between *market* worth and *industrial* worth that is found at the heart of economic theory.

Just as we rediscover elements stemming from *civic* worth and *industrial* worth in Durkheim's definition of an organicist sociology, and just as the worth of *fame* is used as a critical springboard in the sociology of the sciences, in the same way the construction of the market bond, and particularly the development of the spectator position, mark not only the sociology that is directly inspired by economics, but also less explicitly, George Herbert Mead's construction, and consequently the sociology that places interpersonal interactions at the heart of its problematics.

Indeed, in *Mind, Self, and Society* (1962 [1934]), Mead reworks the notions of sympathy and spectatorship whose centrality we have seen in the form of market agreement; moreover, Mead is charged with "individualism" on this account by Georges Gurvitch in the preface that precedes the French edition of Mead's work. In a chapter entitled "The Nature of Sympathy," Mead posits that "sympathy comes, in the human form, in the arousing in one's self of the attitude of the individual whom one is assisting, the taking the attitude of the other when one is assisting the other" (299). Through play (and Mead's analyses of role playing, game playing, and dramatization have been highly influential), whether it is the "free play" of a child who plays all the roles or "rule-governed games," individuals learn to "take the attitude of everyone else involved" (151).

> The individual experiences himself as such, not directly, but only indirectly, from the particular standpoints of other individual members of the same social group, or from the generalized standpoint of the social groups as a whole

to which he belongs [which Mead calls the "generalized-other"]. For he enters his own experience as a self or individual, not directly or immediately, not by becoming a subject to himself, but only in so far as he first becomes an object to himself just as other individuals are objects to him or in his experience. . . . When it [the self] has arisen we can think of a person in solitary confinement for the rest of his life, but who still has himself as a companion. (138, 140)

As in the writings to which we have referred earlier, the relationship between this construction of human states and exchanges specific to the marketplace is explicit in Mead's work, for he stresses the importance of agreement on the externality and the nature of the goods being exchanged. "If we can recognize that an individual does achieve himself, his own consciousness, in the identification of himself with the other, then we can say that the economic process must be one in which the individual does identify himself with the possible customers with whom he exchanges things [like a "representative," as Mead adds later]; he must be continually building up means of communication with these individuals to make this process successful" (298). "[The representative] advocate[s] putting one's self in the attitude of the other so as to trick him." Mead accounts for trade by the character of the goods exchanged and the ability of individuals to distance themselves from those goods.

> But what makes [the object of an exchange] a universal thing is that it does not pass into the individual's own direct use. . . . The setting-up, then, of the media of exchange is something that is highly abstract. It depends upon the ability of the individual to put himself in the place of the other to see that the other needs what he does not himself need, and to see that what he himself does not need is something that another does need. The whole process depends on an identification of one's self with the other. (301–2)

Mead is thus led to outline the ideal society as follows: "The ideal of human society is one which does bring people so closely together in their interrelationship, so fully develops the necessary system of communication, that the individuals who exercise their own peculiar function can take the attitude of those whom they affect" (327).

PART TWO

THE POLITIES

Three

POLITICAL ORDERS AND

A MODEL OF JUSTICE

I N THE PREVIOUS CHAPTER we sought to show, in broad outlines, how a market order is constructed; in part 2 we shall attempt to
juxtapose the market order with other orders that are presented in
various works of political philosophy. We hypothesize that all these orders
stem from a common model, and that each embodies the model in a specific way, depending on whether the order of worth is based, for example,
on wealth, esteem, the general will, or competence. Why have we chosen
this approach? As soon as one begins to examine the constraints that bear
upon disagreements and efforts at coordination, one discovers the central
importance of the equivalencies and ordering principles people establish
for the purpose of assessing themselves and one another. We need to understand how people actually do this—how they decide to trust someone's
reputation, for example, or to challenge it instead. Our project is thus different from that of political philosophy, which is limited to the investigation of principles of agreement. Still, we propose to explore the relations
between the kinds of coordinating efforts people make in ordinary situations, on the one hand, and philosophical constructions of a principle of
order and of a common good, on the other. We seek to show that the constraints brought to bear on constructions of order among human beings
have just as much to do with political philosophies as with persons who are
trying to reach agreement on the practical level, and that the abstract and
systematic solutions proposed by the former correspond to the solutions
actually adopted by the latter.

We do not intend to return to the project that gave rise to these philosophical constructs and argue that human beings reach agreement because
their reason leads them unfailingly to adopt one particular principle or another. The simple recognition that there are many such principles already
raises a question to which no political philosophy can offer a satisfactory
answer. But this difficulty is not the only one that separates us from the
project from which the principles of political philosophy arose. As we shift
from discussing principles to examining situations of discord or understanding, we do not simply face an empirical test, a confrontation between
a model and its application. The uncertain moment in which coordination occurs in a given situation opens up new pragmatic problems and

raises questions that political philosophers have not addressed. What is
the nature of the test that a justification must undergo? How do the things
involved in an action serve as proofs? How is a judgment reached, and
what dynamic is at work when that judgment is challenged?

As we seek answers to these questions, our attention will shift, in part 3,
from the order established among persons who are duly qualified and ordered in terms of principles to the circumstantial situations and the uncertain moments in which people and things become involved. At that point
we shall turn to a corpus that is a priori quite unlike the one we shall focus
on here. We shall look at practical handbooks, how-to manuals that propose ways of acting justly and that describe the instruments best suited to
such action.

But first, in part 2, we shall look beyond the specifications of the market principle—and of a human nature compatible with it—that can be
drawn from the work of Adam Smith, in an attempt to uncover a model
that some otherwise quite dissimilar political philosophies have in common. We treat the works we have selected as grammatical enterprises
intended to clarify and fix rules for reaching agreement, that is, both as
bodies of prescriptive rules that make it possible to build a harmonious
polity and as models of the shared *competence* required of persons in order
for agreement to be possible. We use these works to develop a model of legitimate order—termed the *polity* model—that spells out the requirements
a *higher common principle* must satisfy in order to sustain *justifications*. After
explaining why we have chosen these particular works, and after reviewing
the tradition to which they belong, we shall analyze the various hypotheses
that support the formal polity model by comparing it to other models of
communities. Then we shall show how the market polity meets the requirements of the polity model and is thus one of its legitimate specifications. Finally, we shall describe a political construction that does not satisfy
the hypotheses of the polity model, the attempt to develop a "eugenic" social value.

Political Philosophies of the Common Good

We have chosen classic works of political philosophy that offer systematic
expressions of the forms of the common good that are commonly invoked
in today's society. These systems, which we can construe as grammars of
the political bond, serve to justify evaluations of the degree of justness of a
situation in which the concerned parties can no longer compromise, so
that the possibility of reaching agreement is no longer available to them.
Agreement must then be established at a higher level so that equivalence
will be general. An "acceptable" argument, in Ricoeur's terms (1991), is one

that brings this upward movement to a halt "by exhausting the series of 'because,' at least in the particular situation of questioning and interlocution in which these questions are asked" (1991, 189). In other words, the parties feel a need to refer to general rules that will change the nature of their relationship: from an amorphous juxtaposition of incommensurable persons, they become an organized unit and establish the reference of the parts to the whole (to borrow an expression from Louis Dumont [1970, 65]). This reference makes it possible to assess the relative worth of the parties, leading the persons involved either to agree or to judge themselves wronged, lodge a protest, and demand justice.

The underlying foundation of these principles is only rarely made explicit in ordinary contexts. This is why we turn to philosophical constructs that have helped elucidate and formalize each of the systems of worth that can be identified in disagreements today. We extract these constructs from canonical texts that have made them commonplaces of political theory. In other words, we seek to identify the forms of equivalence on which legitimate agreement is based by using classic political treatises, each of which presents, with reference to an equilibrium oriented toward justice, a universal principle intended to govern the polity.

While each of these canonical texts constitutes the systematization of a form of agreement that is routinely used in ordinary situations, it is also the case that an attempt to clarify an agreement allows the parties involved to move back up to a form of justice only if that form has been the object of a systematic construction within the political tradition. In the absence of such a construction, the lineaments of an agreement retain the nature of a simple *correspondence* that can be disqualified by being labeled fortuitous.

The Commonplace Tradition.   Our enterprise might be said to be linked, in a way, with the tradition of studying "topics" or commonplace arguments, a tradition included within the instruction in rhetoric that made up the core of the classical humanities. Lingering for a moment to look at this tradition, we shall need to go further back than Descartes's critique of rhetoric, which is fully incorporated in today's pejorative use of the term and which is expressed in particular in a well-known formula from the *Discourse on Method*: "Those who are in possession of the most forceful power of reasoning and who best order their thoughts so as to render them clear and intelligible can always best persuade one of what they are proposing, even if they speak only the dialect of Lower Brittany and have never learned rhetoric" (1993 [1637], 4). Let us recall the role the Ancients attributed to rhetoric in the foundation of the political order, a role summed up by Cicero in *De Oratore*: "[W]hat other power [but eloquence] could have been strong enough either to gather scattered humanity into one place, or to lead it out of its brutish existence in the wilderness up to our present condition of civilization as men and as citizens, or, after the establishment of social communities, to give shape to laws, tribunals, and civic rights?" (1.8.33).

Does rhetoric include politics, or is it simply a technique available for use by politics? Plato's critique of rhetoric, particularly as expressed through the rhetorician Gorgias, focuses directly on the relation linking rhetoric to truth and justice. In *Phaedrus*, Socrates says of Tisias and Gorgias that they "saw that probabilities are more to be esteemed than truths, [they] who make small things seem great and great things small by the power of their words" (267a–b). In *Gorgias*, Socrates endeavors to show Gorgias the contradiction underlying the relation between rhetoric, "a producer of persuasion" (453a), and justice. If the orator does not speak without knowledge (459b) and if "there is no subject on which the rhetorician could not speak more persuasively than a member of any other profession whatsoever, before a multitude" (456c), he must know what is just and must therefore be a just man (460a–b). How, then, can we account for the fact that he may use his art to do harm (457c, 460d)?

For Plato, this *techne* was to justice what cookery is to medicine (465c), that is, "a semblance of a branch of politics" (463e), "a branch of flattery" (466a); for Aristotle, it is freed of its dependence on morality, as Médéric Dufour explains in his introduction to the French edition of *Rhetoric* (Aristotle 1967, pp. 7, 13): "the orator should be able to provide opposites, as in logical arguments" (*Rhetoric*, 1355a.12), for rhetoric applies in equal measure to opposing theses. Its function, however, is not simply to persuade, as Plato has it, but rather "to find out in each case the existing means of persuasion" (1355b.14). In another difference with Plato, "the true or apparently true" is said to spring from the same faculty and to be established from "the means of persuasion applicable to each individual subject" (1356a.6). Rhetoric focuses on the second term, apparent truth, in order to facilitate "conversations": Aristotle assigns it this objective at the beginning of *Topics* (1.2.25 [101a]). In this work, Aristotle examines "the sources from which the commonplaces should be derived" (8.1.18–19 [155b]): "for if we could grasp to how many and to what kind of objects our arguments are directed and on what bases they rest, and how we are to be well provided with these, we should sufficiently attain the end which is set before us" (1.4.11–14 [101b]).

Cicero makes abundant use of the metaphor of "commonplaces" from which an orator can "dig out" his proofs (*De oratore*, 2.34.146) and draw his arguments after placing them methodically "in readiness" (2.30.130), conveniently labeled, like "gold that was hidden" (2.41.174). He even goes so far as to show the arguments that flow from these sources of proof, and "instantly present themselves for setting forth the case, as the letters do for writing the word" (2.30.130): "It is easy to find things that are hidden if the hiding place is pointed out and marked; similarly if we wish to track down some argument we ought to know the places or topics: for that is the name given by Aristotle to the 'regions,' as it were, from which arguments are drawn" (Cicero, *Topica*, 2.7).

Cicero challenges those who tend to judge truth by means of dialectics and who neglect the oratorical inventiveness that draws on commonplaces and focuses on apparent truths: "[The Stoics] have totally neglected the art which is called τοπιχή (topics), an art which is both more useful and certainly prior in the order of nature" (2.6). This opposition is formulated in a similar way in *De oratore*, where Cicero aims his critiques at Diogenes: "[D]o you observe that . . . it was Diogenes who claimed to be teaching an art of speaking well, and of *distinguishing truth* from error, which art he called by the Greek name of dialectic? This art, if indeed it be an art, contains no directions for discovering the truth, but only for *testing* it" (2.38.157, emphasis added). In Arnauld and Nicole's *Logic or the Art of Thinking*, the chapter entitled "Topics, or the method of finding arguments. How useless this method is" cites Cicero's criticism and levels it against Cartesian criticism: "So it is fairly useless to worry about the order for treating the topics, since it is rather unimportant. But it might be more useful to examine whether it may not be more appropriate not to discuss them at all" (1996 [1683], 181).

Vico's *On the Study Methods of Our Time* is largely devoted to this same opposition, which is once again overturned: Vico advocates the *ars topica*, opposing both Descartes's critical positions and those of Arnauld and Nicole, which are exclusively oriented toward distinguishing truths from falsehoods (Vico 1990 [1709], 17). In the process, he offers a formulation that is very close to Cicero's, but in which Descartes is attacked instead of Diogenes: "[T]he invention of arguments is by nature prior to the judgment of their validity, so that, in teaching, that invention should be given priority over philosophical criticism" (14). In *The New Science*, he asserts that "topics . . . is an art of regulating well the primary operation of our mind by noting the commonplaces that must all be run over in order to know all there is in a thing that one desires to know well; that is, completely" (1984 [1725], 166). Vico glorifies the class of "men of ingenuity [*ingegnosi*] and depth, who, thanks to the one [*ingegno*], are quick as lightning in perception [*acutezze*]" (1963 [1744], 109; on the relationship between *ingenium*, *ingenio*, *acumen*, and *agudeza*, see Alain Pons's note in Vico 1981 [1744], 131).

The description of this topical "ingenuity" that relies on "commonplaces" ties in quite well with the strong cohesiveness and the multiple redundancies that we observe in reading the works we have used to extract *polities*, as well as the works examined in part 3 from which we have drawn the samples of *worlds* that correspond to these polities. "The human mind is naturally impelled to take delight in uniformity," Vico writes in *New Science.* "This axiom, as applied to the fables, is confirmed by the custom the vulgar have when creating fables of men famous for this or that, and placed in these or those circumstances, of making the fable fit the character and condition. These fables are ideal truths suited to the merit of those of whom the vulgar tell them; and such falseness to fact as they contain consists simply in failure to give subjects their due" (Vico 1984 [1725], 73–74 [1.2.47]).

Another opposition that occurs throughout *New Science*, comparable to the first, is of interest to us because it has to do with the relationship between law and jurisprudence, or, in Vico's terms, between what is "certain" and what is "true." What is "certain in the laws" draws upon authority to support an inflexible application of statutory legislation (93 [1.2.111]). What is true, on the other hand, is elucidated by "natural reason." The "natural equity of fully developed human reason," which stems from natural reason, is "a practice of wisdom in affairs of utility, since wisdom in its broad sense is nothing but the science of making such use of things as their nature dictates" (94–95 [1.2.113–14]). This relation between "certitude" and "truth" (Croce highlights Vico's varied use of the terms in *The Philosophy of Giambattista Vico* [1913 (1911), 99]) must be considered, moreover, in the light of the influence of Grotius, whom Vico hails as a "jurisconsult of mankind" (although he criticizes his ahistorical stance). Guido Fasso (1972, 47) sees Grotius's influence in Vico's distinction between what is certain and what is true. Dario Faucci, on the other hand, points out that "Grotius failed to illustrate the relation between reason and authority, which is an aspect of the relationship between certitude and truth (*certum* and *verum*)" (1969, 67).

To end our detour through a tradition that offers a rich array of conceptual categories well suited to the question at hand, we should note that the delicate balance Vico sought was not always maintained by his commentators. While Schumpeter deems Vico one of the three greatest sociologists of all time, along with Galton and Marx (1954, 790–91 [4.3]), others have come up with totally idealistic readings of his work (Grassi 1969, 50) that run along the same lines as Croce's *Philosophy of Giambattista Vico.*

Our own project departs from this tradition, however, in its concern for dealing with justification in a single framework, whether a technical act of production or moral behavior is at stake. This choice finds solid support in the possibility of constructing an *industrial polity* on the same model as the other polities. Let us note that rhetoric, as a *techne* relative to production, is for Aristotle, in contrast, quite distinct from prudence, the latter being a form of practical wisdom having to do with behavior.

We have thus looked for expressions of the *common good* both in the disputes or disagreements that arise in the course of personal interactions (differences that are normally described in the language of politeness, civility, or character) and also in the tensions between what are usually called the public and the private spheres (in situations involving the State), in workplace conflicts (ranging from quarrels between particular employees to conflicts handled collectively), or, more generally, in breakdowns in economic relations (which may be expressed during a market exchange or in relation to a technological investment).

In the process, we have been able to observe the operation of six *higher common principles* to which, in France today, people resort most often in order to finalize an agreement or pursue a contention. These principles may thus be said to constitute the basic political equipment needed to fabricate a social bond. Still, our list of *principles* is not exhaustive; we can discern the shape of other *polities* that might be constructed in conformity with our proposed model.

Criteria for Choosing the Canonical Texts.   Let us now examine the rules that guided us in the choice of the political texts we are using to bring to light the foundations of these higher common principles.

(a) We began by seeking the earliest text, or one of the earliest, in which the polity is presented in systematic form. Such texts, as we have seen, can be compared to works by grammarians: they propose a general formulation—applicable to everyone and in all situations—that validates the play of customs, procedures, settlements, or rules applied locally. There were of course markets, merchants, and arguments based on profit long before Adam Smith. But it is in Smith's work that market relations make it possible, for the first time, to establish a universal principle of justification and to construct a polity based on this principle. Thus we have not sought to distinguish a theoretical market principle from its actual realization, which would be at some remove from the principle and might exist prior to the formulation of the principle, nor have we sought to distinguish an isolated person from a social being, as in the *formal/substantive* opposition proposed by Polanyi. We have viewed Smith's work as that of a political philosopher. The construction of this political grammar gives a general impact, a legitimacy (in the specific sense in which we use this term) to beings and relations engaged in market bonds.

For our purposes, the historical genesis of the texts we are using is not a critical issue, and we shall not address it systematically; to do so would require a degree of analytic work that cannot be undertaken in the framework of the project at hand. The fact remains that polities have been constituted throughout history. Their number cannot be determined a priori. The worths that are called upon today to organize just situations have been stabilized in very different historical periods. Furthermore, they are very unequally inscribed within what we know as the State. Thus what we shall call *civic worth* presents a constitutional character today that associates it with the very definition of the State, while domestic worth, in which generality is constructed on the basis of ties of dependence among persons, is in our day no longer directly tied to the definition of the French state, as was the case with absolute monarchy.

The composition, with reference to various worths, of a state that can never be identified with a single *polity* presupposes, in particular, arrangements of *compromise* among different worths. On the one hand, the obvious disparities among states result from the modulations that are possible in the composition of the various worths. On the other hand, we hypothesize that the constitution of polities has a much more general scope: it is valid, in our view, not for all societies but for all those marked by modern political philosophy.

(b) To serve our purposes, a text has to contain the higher common principle within a construction of worth showing an equilibrium between a form of *sacrifice* and a form of *common good* possessing universal validity. We have rejected texts in which arguments deriving from a polity are scattered, present in an allusive, incidental, or unsystematic manner (texts that precede the foundation of a polity often have these features). Similarly, we have rejected texts in which several worths are closely interwoven.[1] Nor can we use *critical* presentations of a worth. Thus we shall see that worth constructed around the principle of recognition in the eyes of others is present in the texts of the seventeenth-century French moralists, but only to be condemned, which is not the case in the text by Hobbes from which we extracted the *polity of fame*. The text cannot be limited to criticism, but it must depict the world as it is and as it should be; it must indicate how beings in conformity with the natural order ought to be arrayed. Unlike critical texts whose aim is to deconstruct a political order by denouncing the false worths on which it is based, the commonplace constructions (Ansart 1969) on which we shall rely to establish the political grammars that are in use in daily life base the worths they establish on a principle of economy that balances access to the state of worthiness against sacrifice for the common good.

(c) Exposing a harmonious order and its underlying economy of worth, these texts present themselves explicitly as political: they articulate the principles of justice that govern the polity. This is one of the reasons why we turned to St. Augustine, for example, in order to construct *inspired worth*. As a theoretician who uses the notion of grace to construct an indissociably political and mystical conception of the polity and of History, Augustine distinguishes himself from St. John of the Cross or St. Theresa of Avila, in whom the experience of inspiration is expressed in a more striking and purer form but is not tied to the building of a polity (although these latter authors were also builders of religious institutions). The most exemplary case would be that of a mystic who wrote little, if at all, but whose experience of inspiration was the most complete.

Similarly, *domestic worth*, based on personal dependence and on hierarchy, has to be discerned within political treatises that see in the home a higher common principle of universal validity and not, for example, a principle valid only in family relations. Works that make the domestic community the very principle of the State are distinguishable from works such as Aristotle's, which present the domestic community as part of the polity, since "the city-state is prior in nature to the household and to each of us individually. For the whole must necessarily be prior to the part" (*Politics*, 1253a.20).

(d) To the extent that their object is to establish a natural order so as to institute situations that are stabilized by recourse to a higher common principle, the texts used have to have a practical thrust. They must not depict a utopia, the "idea of a republic," as Bodin says about the constructs of Plato and Thomas More (1606 [1576]). They are guides for action, written for the use of those who govern.

A common origin for these works may be sought in the rhetorical tradition whose historical background we have recalled briefly. Quentin Skinner, in his examination of the foundations of modern political thought, has called our attention to the encounter between two different approaches to rhetoric, prior to the Renaissance. In the Italian polities of the twelfth and thirteenth centuries, he showed the continuity between purely technical rhetorical treatises that had an exclusively practical aim, *ars dictaminis* intended to help in the drafting of official documents, and works bringing together recommendations for the proper direction of juridical or political affairs, collections of advice directly intended for rulers, the *podesta*, a genre to which *The Prince* can also be attached (1978, 1:28–35). Furthermore, beginning in the second half of the thirteenth century, the influence of a French approach to teaching rhetoric with direct reference to the classical authors, Cicero in particular, led scholars to take the questions addressed by these authors more seriously. Skinner cites the example of the mid-thirteenth-century writer Brunetto Latini, whose work is at once a practical guide including model letters and speeches, and a treatise on rhetoric and political and moral philosophy incorporating numerous references to Aristotle and Cicero; Latini stresses the fact that the principal science of the government of polities is rhetoric (40). These works thus include a systematic questioning directed at the constitution of the common good and the surpassing of private interests that threaten the survival of republics, a questioning that is characteristic of the canonical texts in which we have sought specifications of polities; they also resemble the practical guides that we shall examine in part 3.

(e) Finally, we have given priority to works that are widely known, and more particularly to texts that have been used for the fabrication of political technologies, that is, for the construction of instruments for establishing equivalence that are of highly general validity, or for the justification of such instruments (this is the case, for example, with Rousseau's *Social Contract*, which was used under the French Revolution to justify juridical structures). This constraint is necessary to make intelligible the relation between the canonical texts, in which worth is established in full generality, and the arrangements or arguments in which people are engaged when they situate themselves with respect to one form of worth or another.

The Polity Model

In this section, we shall try to make increasingly explicit the play of hypotheses that makes it possible to define the common model of a polity. Built around an order of worth, it sustains various constructions of political philosophy and gives direction to the ordinary sense of what is just. As we move ahead step by step, we shall be able to evoke some weaker models of political communities along the way.

The first axiom (a1) is the principle according to which the members of a *polity* share a *common humanity*. The model in fact presupposes an identification of the set of persons capable of reaching agreement, the *members* of the polity, and it posits a form of fundamental equivalence among these members, all of whom belong to humanity on the same basis. Furthermore, the various political metaphysics that we shall study all acknowledge the same definition of humanity; thus they all agree on the way the set of human beings is to be circumscribed, and on the principle according to which, within this set, every human being is as human as every other. This *principle of common humanity* excludes political constructs that incorporate slaves or subhumans. The principle is thus not satisfied by all political metaphysics, and it limits the field of the constructs that we propose to include.

This single constraint, in the absence of any differentiation, determines only a trivial political metaphysics, at a single logical level, which we shall call *Eden* (H1). The set of its members may be combined in a single equivalence class; in this case, common humanity recognizes just one Man, an Adam. Such constructions define perennial worlds in which there reigns perpetual agreement of all with all (as in certain utopias). Although trivial, this model is useful to keep in mind as a limit case for polities.

The constructs that we shall examine assume supplementary constraints. The second axiom of the model, called the *principle of differentiation* (a2), is intended to exclude *Edens*, by assuming at least two possible *states* for the members of the polity. Supposing that behaviors can be adapted to these states (according to modalities that we shall leave aside for the time being), their differentiation already allows for forms of *justification* of actions as well as *tests* designed to attribute the states.

This second principle, operating in isolation, makes it possible to generate another trivial political construct in which personal particularities are preserved to such an extent that there are as many states as there are persons. Under this hypothesis, the principle of common humanity can no longer be respected, and this precludes any possible association of persons in states. Although trivial, this construct is also interesting, for it marks another limit of the polity model, a limit toward which a challenge to any qualification, to any representation, in the name of personal particularities, may lead.

To construct a model polity, it is necessary to determine under what conditions the members of the polity have access to the various *states*, and the first constraint of common humanity influences this determination. Thus the case in which states would be permanently attributed to persons is excluded by the first principle. A political metaphysics that could be described as based on *castes* (or on sexual difference, for example) is incompatible with the principle of common humanity.[2] If the model is to remain based on the principle of *humanity* and if that first constraint and the second are to be compatible, the model must assume for all its members an identical *power* of access to all the states that we shall designate by their common *dignity* (a3). The model of a multistate *humanity* thus opens up the possibility of nontrivial agreements, as well as the possibility of disagreements that would remain limited to *disputes* over the attribution of a state to a person, without leading immediately to deeper *disagreement* over the definition of these states. Such agreements are produced experimentally in situations set up by social psychologists; on the basis of their observations, these researchers attempt to demonstrate the minimal conditions required for the constitution of a group identity that allows the actors to explain behaviors. We shall describe these justifications as weak whenever they are not based on some model of multistate humanity. They contrast with the strong justifications that we have taken as our own research object and that are consistent with the complete *polity* model that includes complementary hypotheses.

Many agreements presuppose not only the explanation of behaviors, or their anticipation (as in model H2), but also their rank ordering, as is the case every time arranging or distributing is at issue. Under these conditions, disputes can be ended only if the states are *ordered* (a4). This order among states, which is necessary to coordinate actions and justify distributions, is expressed by a *scale of values* for the goods or happiness attached to these states; at the same time, it creates a tension with the axiom of *common humanity* (a1). Thus when the power of access to all the states (a3) is not guaranteed, the order constituted may degenerate into a splintering apart of humanities, without any possibility of relations among them.

The political philosophies that we shall examine propose constructions that all contain the tension resulting from this dual constraint (the tension between a1 and a4), and they all include persons who share the property of being human even though they are ordered according to a principle of worth. They provide an account of a humanity that is confronted with unequal worths and that manages nonetheless to avoid civil war.

Given that, by virtue of their common humanity (a1) that identifies them as human beings, all human beings have an equal power of access (a3) to the *higher* states (to which the greatest degrees of happiness are attached), there is no way to understand, without calling upon additional hypotheses, why all members of the polity are not in the supreme state (thus forming an *Eden*). To explain why this is not the case, we have to refer to an *investment formula* (a5) that links the benefits of a *higher* state to a *cost* or a *sacrifice* that is required for access to that state. The formula of sacrifice or economy is the regulator that suppresses the tension between a common humanity and an ordering of states.

The model of *ordered humanity* (H3) makes it possible to justify a larger range of agreements than the previous model. However, the likelihood of a broadly acceptable agreement is still not very well assured, because persons holding the *lower state*, necessarily eager to profit from the benefits attached to the *higher state* (here we are arguing in terms of a simple two-state model, but this property is not at all a necessary one), will be inclined not to support but rather to challenge the cost that implies access to the higher state (a5). This formula, which functions as the keystone of the construction and which has to be able to support the full weight of the dual constraint of the *polity*, thus risks lacking solidity unless it is reinforced by a supplementary hypothesis.

This supplementary axiom plays a central role in the polity model (H4) in that it ties the various states together by means of a hypothesis about the *goods* or *happiness* attached to each. It posits that happiness, which increases as one moves toward the *higher states*, is beneficial to the polity as a whole, that it is a *common good* (a6). It is only under this supplementary condition, added to the rank ordering of the states (a4), that we shall speak of an *order of worth*. The *common good* is opposed to the self-centered pleasure that has to be sacrificed to reach a higher state of *worth*.

In this axiom, we find again the ordinary meaning of the term *polity*, which implies a reference to a common good in an ordered society. In the complete model polity, *common dignity* (a3) becomes an equal capacity to act in terms of the common good. Each order of political philosophy is thus a metaphysics, to the extent that it defines humanities that are linked by a common good surpassing the particular happiness of each person.

The orders thus established are very strongly marked by this last axiom. The state of worthiness is not only differentiated from the state of deficiency in that it dispenses more well-being to those who accede to it, but also in that it has a positive impact on the well-being of the deficient. Their self-centered pleasure is complemented by the benefits of the worth of the worthy. We can better understand the structure of this construction if, instead of immersing it immediately in moral specifications (which will be the task of the political philosophies, moreover), we remain as close as possible to the axiomatic level by identifying the *common good* with a form of generality. As the earlier illustration of a factory visit suggested, legitimate agreement, if it is not Edenic, is based on the constitution of an *order of generality*. What is most important is what is most general, and the generality of the worthy contributes not only to their own well-being (which is thus characterized by a manner of extension of their being) but also to that of the deficient. The state of worthiness gives the measure of the polity, and one cannot attribute worth, that is, one cannot constitute classes of states and order them, except by starting with knowledge of the state of worthiness. The polity is identified by the state of worthiness, and to reach that state is to be identified with the polity. In a model *polity* of this sort (H4), the notions of worth (a4) and of the common good (a6) are merged, combined in the *higher common principle*. The higher common principle makes it possible to contain disagreements within the limits of the acceptable without letting them degenerate into a challenge to the principle of agreement, that is, the definition of states of worthiness and thus the foundations of the polity. Disagreements over the attribution of a state to a person are situated at a lower logical level than the convention applying to these states and to the benefits attached to them.

After bringing to light the constitutive elements of the model polity (the *principle of common humanity* [a1], the *principle of differentiation* [a2], *common dignity* [a3], the *order of worth* [a4], the *investment formula* [a5], and the *common good* [a6]), we shall seek to clarify its formal structure by examining the problems it has to resolve. This clarification requires us to distance ourselves from the works of the political philosophers we have studied, so as to grasp their task as an attempt to integrate two requirements whose compatibility is problematic. The structure of the model supports two basic requirements that are strongly antagonistic: (1) a requirement of common humanity that presupposes a form of identity shared by all persons and (2) a requirement of order governing this humanity. The definition of the *common good* is the keystone of the construction that has to ensure compatibility between these two requirements.

A second perspective requires further distancing, since it involves encompassing the plurality of principles of agreement, instead of remaining inside the framework of just one of these and seeking to establish its uniqueness. As we shall indicate more fully later on when we discuss the coexistence of several polities, we suggest that the polity model is a response to the problem raised by the plurality of available principles of agreement, a response that excludes at the outset the utopia of an Eden. By building an order around a common good, the polity model must allow the number of other principles to be reduced. Although the polity model refers only to a single principle of justification, it is a response to the multiplicity of principles without which the world would be an Eden, and it leaves open the possibility of this multiplicity even while assuring the primacy of a single principle. The reduction of the plurality of common goods is achieved through the construction of an order among them, the lowest being treated as a private good. The *principle of differentiation* (a2) and the *order of worth* (a4) sustain an order according to which one of the forms of generality is endowed with the legitimacy of the *common good* of the polity, whereas all the others are reduced to private goods to which only self-centered pleasures are attached. The other common goods are not completely eliminated; traces of them are found in the description of the happiness of the deficient. They are reduced to personal pleasures, to self-satisfactions. This reduction of a common good to a private good, which governs the relation among polities, will be examined in detail in part 4, devoted to critiques. The reductive power of the polity model and the critical figure that expresses it are absent from an *Eden* in which private goods have no place, no reason for being, even though they are dealt with in general, as in "epideictic" rhetoric. "[A]mplification is most suitable for epideictic speakers, whose subject is actions which are not disputed, so that all that remains to be done is to attribute beauty and importance to them" (Aristotle, *Rhetoric*, 1368a.40). The reduction of the plurality of forms of generality that is achieved by the polity model also sheds light on the *investment formula*: the sacrifice required to accede to a state of worth then appears linked to the setting aside of the other polities. The particular happiness of the lowly, sacrificed in the state of worthiness, is thus the trace of the other common goods that cannot be recognized as such within the polity.

The Case of the Market Polity.   We shall now attempt to test the application of the polity model by returning to some elements brought out in our earlier analysis of market political philosophy. The idea of using political economics to illustrate the polity model we have just presented may seem risky on more than one account. The market has indeed constantly served to challenge the possibility of deliberate general agreement. Moreover, sociology has been developed on the basis of an analysis of the destructive effects of market bonds on the construction of a society. The very notion of individualism that is attached to this type of relation stands in such opposition to the notions of culture, community, collectivity, or society that it is hard to understand, today, how a polity can be built around a market bond in the same way that it might be built with reference to a general collective interest. This similarity is difficult to reestablish on the basis of contemporary texts by economists or sociologists; however, the model polity allows us to bring it to light, either by returning to Adam Smith's work in political philosophy, as we have just done, or by examining contemporary texts that present market worth, as we shall do in chapter 6.

The first requirement, the *common humanity* (a1) that makes it possible to identify human beings, is fundamental in political economics, since it serves to distinguish persons from the external goods they compete to obtain: in the market polity, persons cannot be exchanged like goods. Distinctions of *state* (a2) are defined by differences in wealth, and these states are clearly *ordered* (a4). The hypothesis according to which the possibility of becoming wealthy is open to all (a3) is frequently advanced to support the claim that the market principle can establish justice. The *cost* attached to this form of worth (a5) is the cost of opportunism, which presupposes that human beings are always doing business, seeking to strike a bargain, without ever falling back on traditions, personal attachments, rules, projects, and so forth. The last requirement, that of a *common good* (a6), is the hardest to establish; its most polished formulation, found in Smith's work, justifies our decision to look in that work for the expression of the market political philosophy. If we are to make the claim that the wealth of the wealthy is beneficial to all, we shall have to demonstrate the harmony of a distribution of states of worth that is nonetheless unequal, a distribution that results from a competition among appetites that is governed by access to rare goods ("the invisible hand"). As in all specifications of polities, the worthy are the ones who, by means of their worth, maintain the possibility of a reference to the *higher common principle*. In striking their bargains, the wealthy maintain competition in a marketplace. It is in this sense that luxury benefits everyone, rather than by virtue of the industry it spawns. Unlike patrimonies, wealth that supports market exchanges is profitable to the polity.

Political economics thus establishes a polity by showing how, in order to avoid perpetual disagreement, persons can appeal to a principle of coherence, in their behavior and in the arguments they use to justify that behavior. In the market polity, every disagreement can become a formal dispute to be settled in a market test that the persons involved agree to undergo. The violent encounter between antagonistic appetites is thus calmed in a market to which persons can refer, as a higher common principle, in the search for agreement.

An Illegitimate Order: Eugenics

In our discussion of the polity model, we mentioned the possibility of constructing scales of value leading to the establishment of an order that does not satisfy all the constraints for constituting a polity, and that therefore does not allow the foundation of legitimate justifications. There are modes of evaluation, of qualifying people in a hierarchy of states, that, unlike worths, are not compatible with the requirement of *common dignity*. A major consequence of the absence of common dignity is the questioning of the distinction between human beings and nonhuman beings. An order supported by an *illegitimate value* is thus not established in full generality, insofar as its compatibility with the principle of common humanity has not been established. This is precisely the task assigned to political philosophy, when it is used to distinguish, from among the entire set of prevailing values relative to persons and their tastes, the justified worths on which judgments in the polity can converge.

As an example of an *illegitimate value*, we shall take a moment to look at hierarchies relying on racial inequalities, and on biological inequalities in general. The development of eugenics has led to the formulation of such a "social value" (*civic worth*, in Francis Galton's own terminology), one intended to assess the state of *serviceable citizen*. The axiom of common humanity is not attested, since the endowments of particular persons are irremediably unequal at the moment of birth. The eugenic value has to be distinguished from worths that, in one respect or another, may be viewed as adjacent (Thévenot 1990b). As we do among the philosophers who have contributed to establishing an order of worth, we also find challenges to other possible ways of qualifying people among eugenicists. In the second edition of *Hereditary Genius* (Galton 1972 [1869], 25–26), Galton warns readers against possible confusion between the value he is attempting to constitute and genius, in Gina Lombroso's "technical sense." Lombroso, in associating insane persons with exceptional persons, is led to equate persons of the highest eugenic value with others who would be ranked at a very low level according to this scale, if we refer to Galton's projection (MacKenzie 1981, 18) of the levels of "social value" onto the social categories used in Charles Booth's investigation (1886). While Galton recognizes that "there is a large residuum of evidence which points to a painfully close relation between the two [genius and insanity]" (1972 [1869], 27), he formulates a very clear critique of what we shall analyze later under the head *inspired worth*, justifying such an equivalence by referring to the spirit possessing an inspired person: "If genius means a sense of inspiration, or of rushes of ideas from apparently supernatural sources, or of an inordinate burning desire to accomplish any particular end, it is perilously near to the voices heard by the insane" (27). This critique is based on a reference to "healthy persons," which is found in all attempts to construct a biological "worth."

While eugenic "worth," taken at face value, may resemble the worths established via "engendering," it must nevertheless not be confused with what we shall call *domestic worth*, a worth that includes a mode of association through filiation. The legacy of eminent men is not the prosperity of a great "house," and Karl Pearson explicitly challenges the transmission of lordship, which he deems eugenically inadequate and suited only for maintaining a line of "vulgar plutocrats," people who have not taken care to create and preserve good "stock." Let us note that the reference to "stock," used as the basis for an association, is nevertheless apt to shift between *domestic* worth, biological values, and also *industrial* worth with its productive capital (Sahlins 1976, 104–5). The eugenic order can in fact be viewed as a degenerate industrial order to the extent that human reproduction and the productivity associated with it are judged in the same terms as the production of manufactured objects.[3]

In the various avatars of eugenic value, we can find attempts to constitute a type of common good as well as a form of sacrifice. Carrel writes about building a "new city," and he places "the needs of the public" ahead of personal interest (1935, 292). "No financial or moral rewards," he argues, "should be too great for those who, through the wisdom of their marriage, would engender geniuses" (302). However, this sacrifice, which is judged by whether a person does or does not produce progeny, assumes a calculation bearing on a multigeneration universe.[4] Owing to the temporal asymmetry it entails, this association among several generations precludes maintaining reciprocity in relations among persons. In his theory of justice, John Rawls excludes this form of common good benefiting future generations, emphasizing the temporal asymmetry it produces: "There is no way for later generations to improve the situation of the least fortunate first generation" (1973, 291). But most importantly, the fact that the very delimitation of this humanity becomes an endogenous variable—the sacrifice then being, as it were, that of persons who would fail to exist—is completely incompatible with the constraints that are constitutive of a polity.

Let us emphasize, to conclude our discussion of this illegitimate value, that the Nazis, who went to extremes in the suspension of the constraint of common humanity by excluding from it Jews and Gypsies in particular, were nevertheless unable to maintain that suspension in all situations, for it would have meant constituting two classes of human beings: a class of persons and a class of nonpersons. The hierarchization of those the Nazis deemed nonpersons could not help but contribute to calling that division into question: how can one make some nonpersons play the violin while acknowledging that violin playing is a prerogative of persons?

The associations constituted by judgments of *illegitimate value* are all the less acceptable when one moves toward a situation in which a disagreement must be cleared up through reference to justice, given that the more serious the disagreement is, the higher the requirement of generality of the principles invoked must be. When major crimes, and blood crimes in particular, are being adjudicated, courtrooms are by this token situations in which the distinction between justified arguments and unjustifiable associations is particularly manifest. The former can be used to highlight "attenuating circumstances," which is not the case for the latter. A court trial constitutes a test, and during such a test the arguments advanced for the purpose of justification cannot consist in simple associations. In order to be convincing, they must be developed in such a way that they bring clearly to light the principle of worth, the sacrifice, or the dignity suited to the polity from which they stem. The test is in this respect an opportunity to make worth manifest, along with its infrastructure and its equilibrium.

Four

POLITICAL FORMS OF WORTH

The Inspired Polity

IN *THE CITY OF GOD*, St. Augustine imagines a city whose members base their agreement on total acceptance of God's grace, which they would not resist in any way. It could be argued that Augustine uses the term "city" in a metaphorical sense: not only is the city of God not of this world, but it is in radical contrast with any earthly city.[1] The city of God may be associated in this respect with the eschatological literature that announces the coming of the Kingdom of God as the fulfillment of the history of salvation. In this sense, Augustine's construction stems from a theology and not from a political philosophy. But the history of salvation is also a political history because, in both the Old Testament and the New, the history of humanity's relationship with God can be read in the history of the relationships that human beings forge with one another. What is more, in the New Testament, the term "Kingdom" no longer designates merely the horizon marking the final stage in the history of salvation; for, although it can be fully achieved only by *parousia*, the Second Coming, it is nevertheless already present in the hearts of those who have been touched by grace and who have faith, that is, those who accept without resistance the effects of grace within themselves. In this sense, the Kingdom already exists in the human world, even though it certainly does not constitute this world in its entirety; far from it. *The City of God*, a historical work, like most of the books of the Old Testament, has rightly been called one of the first great edifices of a philosophy of history. Its aim is to trace the history of the struggle between two possible worlds that has been played out since the coming of the Messiah: one of these worlds is imbued with grace, while the other one is deprived of it. This means that for Augustine, the two cities are indeed *models*, neither of which is fully realized in the earthly sphere. In this world, the grace of God is not wholly absent, because not everyone rejects it with equal force. However, this world is not wholly imbued with God's grace, either, because most people reject it. The "nations," "republics," and "peoples" of this world therefore engage in "temporary blends" in which both of the cities, which will be separated by the Last Judgment, are more or less present in varying proportions. The use of the term "city" and the metaphor of the two cities serve to reveal this tension between the two worlds and to show how it has unfolded over the course of history. The parallel between the Kingdom of Heaven and the (earthly) world that is established when they are reduced to two comparable cities—comparable at least in certain respects—allows Augustine to link the history of salvation to political history within a philosophy of history. Transposed to the theological register, the concept of the city, as Augustine uses it, retains some of the properties it has in the political register. Thus the opposition between the two cities cannot be entirely reduced to a clear-cut opposition between the Kingdom and the world, or between good and evil.

The two cities stand in a hierarchical relationship determined by the degree to which each achieves the "common good" and ensures happiness and agreement among beings. Beings are not limited to humans: "we may speak of two cities or communities . . . consisting of . . . angels as well as men," for angels, like men, can be "good and bad."[2] The people among whom the earthly city has the upper hand constitute a "multitude of rational beings united by a common agreement on the objects of their love" (*CG* 890 [19.24]). Indeed, "so also the earthly city . . . aims at an earthly peace, and it limits the harmonious agreement of citizens concerning the giving and obeying of orders to the establishment of a kind of compromise between human wills about the things relevant to mortal life" (877 [19.17]). But the degree of perfection of this concord depends upon the value of that which is loved, and "the better the objects of this agreement, the better the people" (890 [19.24]). The way the cities are ordered therefore depends on the way the common goods they know are ordered. The earthly city, which "has its good in this world, and rejoices to participate in it with such gladness as can be derived from things of such a kind," (599 [15.4]), is "generally divided against itself by litigation, by wars, by battles, by the pursuit of victories that bring death with them or at best are doomed to death" (599 [15.4]). The "lowest goods" it desires "are goods and undoubtedly they are gifts of God. But if the higher goods are neglected, which belong to the City on high, where victory will be serene in the enjoyment of eternal peace—if these goods are neglected and those other goods are so desired as to be considered the only goods, or are loved more than the goods which are believed to be higher, the inevitable consequence is fresh misery, and an increase of the wretchedness already there" (599–600 [15.4]).

Only the city of God merits the name of *polity* according to our definition, for of the two it alone can lead beings to transcend their particularity in the pursuit of a common good. As St. Augustine writes in a passage of *The Literal Meaning of Genesis* that precedes and heralds *The City of God*,[3] owing to its "universal" vocation, that is, the way "which . . . has been divinely imparted to be the common property of all the nations" (420–21 [10.32]), the city of God is founded on "charity," a love that "*seeks not her own*, that is, does not rejoice in her own (*private*) excellence" as opposed to "love of self": "One [is] looking toward the common good, keeping in view the society of saints in heaven, the other bringing the common good under its own power, arrogantly looking to domination; one subject to God, the other rivaling Him; . . . one wishing for its neighbor what it wishes for itself, the other seeking to subject its neighbor to itself" (*LMG* 2, 147; author's emphasis). These two cities present opposing forms of deficiency and worth. While the earthly city is imbued with "pride" (which is responsible for the Fall and original sin), the city of God is founded on "humility," which is the true measure of worth. Indeed, the "proud" are possessed by "self-worship" and are "self-complacent" (*CG* 571–72 [14.13]). They are low in worth because their desires are oriented toward self-satisfaction, which reduces them to solitude. In contrast, the "humble" submit "to what is superior," and their submission leaves them open to worth. "Thus . . . there is something in humility to exalt the mind, and something in exaltation to abase it. . . . [E]xaltation abases and humility exalts" (*CG* 571–72 [14.13]). The earthly city that was born of Cain is based on a crime of fratricide, the "archetype of crime," as Augustine calls it, quoting Lucan: "Those walls were dripping with a brother's blood" (Lucan, *Pharsalus* I, 95, cited in *CG* 600 15.5]); this crime presides over the foundation of all the nations of this world and especially of Rome, while the city of God is based on sacrifice and selflessness.

The chances that the city of God will make a "pilgrimage" to this earthly world (*CG* 635 [15.21]) depend wholly on grace (928 [20.17]). Without redemption by grace, people would give themselves over wholly to the earthly city; thus all real worth in this world depends on the benefit of grace. For example, the inner vision of the prophets depends on an outpouring of grace (1082–83 [22.29). Now, this grace is not humanity's due; it is "undeserved" (635 [15.21]): it is a pure "gift," and human beings cannot buy the favor of the giver (604 [15.7]). Access to a state of grace does not result from human manifestations of virtue, for "God's merciful grace," which belongs to all in principle, although it benefits only a few, is "undeserved" (989 [21.13]). "[I]n this life purification from sins is not effected by our merit, but by the compassion of God" (403 [10.22]). Hence, compassion—grace—is the true foundation of the city of God, which alone can remove men from the eternal wretchedness of the earthly city. Grace is granted most often to the humble. Thus in the earthly city even the hearts of the wisest are clouded, because, " 'in asserting their wisdom'— that is, exalting themselves in their wisdom, under the domination of pride—'they became foolish,'" (593 [14.28]). The reference to foolishness must be taken in the strong sense here. In each of the worlds we are analyzing, belief in one's own worth is treated as folly, as madness whenever it rests on a principle other than the one that establishes worth in the polity;

we shall see this later on in the domestic polity, where madness consists in not knowing who one is, or in the polity of fame, in which people who believe themselves to be inspired are viewed as mad.

Augustine's conception of grace is made clearer in the writings he devoted to the polemic with Pelagius. Pelagius, a Briton by birth, had considerable influence over the new movement of asceticism that was taking hold, particularly among well-educated lay Christians in Rome, during the time Augustine was writing *The City of God.* Pelagius taught that it was possible to attain perfection, and that human nature had been created precisely for this purpose: "Whenever I have to speak of laying down the rules for behaviour and the conduct of a holy life, I always point out, first of all, the power and functioning of human nature, and show what it is capable of doing . . . lest I should seem to be wasting my time, by calling on people to embark on a course which they consider impossible to achieve" (Brown 2000 [1967], 342). To refute Pelagius, who endows man with a grace that is inherent in his nature and always sufficient, Augustine underscores the way that, from the standpoint of grace, the human condition was changed by the Fall. After the Fall, free will does not lead to salvation, although will is not alienated by grace, since a person who implores God for His grace is manifesting free will (Augustine 1990a [414–15], 21 [2.10]). But imploring is not enough, for grace is a free gift (Augustine 1990b [415], 226 [4.4]). Attributing to virtue what belongs to grace, as Pelagius does, is therefore tantamount to perpetuating the sin of pride that led to the Fall.

The principle of grace sets inspired worth apart from the other forms of worth—which are denounced as worldly interests that lead to folly and discord when they are pursued—and thereby creates a hierarchy among the different sorts of goods that attract people and thus create interconnections among them. The most frequently denounced and the most markedly unworthy of these goods is "vainglory," for it is the most directly attached to pride. Excellence is indifferent to fame, and virtue itself is worthless when it sets "too much store by the praises of men" (*CG* 39 [1.28]). In its proclivity for the humble, grace also discredits avarice—which is of the same nature as pride—and the love of riches, for "anyone who refuses to enjoy . . . possession in partnership will not enjoy it at all" (*CG* 601 [15.5]). The influence of grace is also, finally, what brings about a new birth in the city of God, "regeneration," as opposed to "generation," which is the principle of domestic engendering. Hence "Isaac . . . [is] the son of the promise, in whom grace, rather than nature is symbolized, because he is promised as the son of an old man and a barren old woman." In this miraculous birth, "grace is more clearly recognizable" in that "nature is decayed and failing," for grace acts "not by way of generation but by regeneration. . . . The names of the parents are also changed. 'Newness' is the note struck in every detail; and the new covenant is presented in a veiled manner, in the old" (687 [16.26]). Abandoning oneself to grace leads to detachment with respect to domestic values: for example, Abraham the Chaldaean "was bidden to leave his country, his family, and his father's house" to follow the "universal way for the soul's liberation"[4] (422 [10.32]).

The model of inspired worth promised to the meek, who are indifferent to the goods of the worldly city, was put into practice by the saints of late Antiquity (Brown 1978, 8–13); by means of detachment and asceticism, these holy men and women sought to establish a "relationship with the supernatural that was personal to them" (12). These "tangible links between heaven and earth" were achieved in a "carefully maintained tension between distance and proximity" that guaranteed "*praesentia*, the physical presence of the holy" (Brown 1981, 88). This experience of worth is incompatible with the state of "devices [that measure] what men are expected to do in this life," and with the attendant "sense of separateness" (Brown 1978, 43); these lead to a disengagement from other social bonds, as for example in *anachoresis*, which "left the ascetics shorn of the normal social supports of identity" (16, 89). It is precisely by means of detachment from domestic bonds based on kinship, proximity, or linguistic community that the call of grace is heard: Gregory Thaumaturgus speaks of an angelic presence that "has nourished me, has formed me, and led me by the hand. Above all, he joined me to that great man—to a man who had no previous relationship with me; to a man who was no kinsman and no neighbor; to a man who had not come from my province, and was unacquainted with my home" (*Speech of Thanksgiving and Praise of Origen*, cited in Brown 1981, 53). The flesh must be subdued, for it is through the flesh that worths stemming from other "cities"—worths treated here as forms of deficiency—are most irrevocably established, implanting themselves in a person's body and habits: "The woman stood for all that was most stable and enveloping in the life of men" (Brown 1978, 87). In *The Interpretation of Dreams*, Artemidorus of Daldis writes that when a man dreams of his wife, he is usually thinking of his work: "The woman stands either for the profession of the dreamer or for his business obligations" (*Oneirocriticon*, I, 78, 86.23, cited in Brown 1978, 87). In a commentary on Artemidorus, Michel Foucault remarks that the wife "is in a relationship of natural analogy to the dreamer's craft or profession" (1990, 18). Forsaking the pleasures of the flesh is therefore a precondition to forsaking "worldly affairs," the vanity of honors and responsibilities, "the art of public speaking," and the temptation to "become known to important people," because "sexual desire" is the "chain" that reduces people to "the slavery of worldly affairs" (CO 141–42).

Breaking the carnal bonds that attach one to the world through physical lust is thus also a precondition for using the body as an instrument for gaining access to the higher truths, and in that way for using it as a basic instrument of worth. Inspired worth is in fact indissociable from the person; it is attached to his or her very body, whose inspired manifestations are its privileged mode of expression and whose sacrifice constitutes the most complete form of realization.[5] Inspiration is lost when it encounters something that might objectivize it and detach it from the body itself—the inscription that fixes and transports, or even the inner speech that already assumes a reference to a third party: "We first invoke God Himself, not in loud words, but in that way of prayer which is always within our power, leaning in soul towards Him by aspiration, alone towards the alone" (Plotinus, *Enneads*, cited in Brown 2000, 166).

Although sainthood may not be a typical way of fulfilling oneself today, and thus not particularly sought after by a large number of individuals, the reference to this polity remains indispensable whenever persons attain worth without needing recognition from others and without concern for other people's opinions. This is indeed one of the principal features of inspired worth: it valorizes self-abnegation in favor of others (hermits in the desert "pray and do penitence for all" [Chiavaro 1987) without placing any stock at all in recognition by others. "No prophet has ever regarded his quality as dependent on the attitudes of the masses toward him" (Weber 1968 [1922], 242). This is the case, for example, with artists who do not necessarily reject public esteem or money (these are accepted in a compromise that is always difficult to bring about between the worth of fame and market worth), but who do not make these goods the very basis for the value of their work and for their worth; from another angle, it is also the case with those who, in what is conventionally called the "political avant-garde," engage—sometimes to the point of martyrdom—in an action that does not need the support of an organization or even the comprehension of those for whose salvation it is carried out, to be justified. The same thing can be said of those whose inspired gestures make them appear to be innovators, originals, desperate souls, or vandals (Boltanski 1990b).

We have seen that the quest for inspiration is expressed indirectly by the critique of other ways of establishing worth, whether it is a matter of personal dependence with respect to the worthy of this world or of the quest for fame and glory. But this position entails a fundamental ambiguity that has often been noted and discussed, from St. Augustine to Rousseau in his *Confessions*. In fact, if a project directed toward glory, or simply toward other people inasmuch as the recognition of others establishes a person's worth, is sufficient to abolish grace (which does not manifest itself simply because someone believes he or she possesses it, and still less when someone makes a visible display of belief in its possession), why abandon contemplation for expression, why give up silence (*CO* 171) for discourse, why relinquish spiritual passivity in the experience of truth for the "theorization" of that experience?

St. Augustine exposes himself neither to God, in whose eyes "the abyss of human consciousness is naked," nor to men, for "[t]he human race is inquisitive about other people's lives, but negligent to correct their own!" (179–80); he seeks God in the depth of his own "inner space," and praises him to "those whose ears are opened by love" (180) in order to unite their acts of grace with his own—not in order to set himself up as an example, or to challenge their judgment, or to seek their blame or praise. Public confession of sins is suspect, because the denunciation of "vainglory" may still be an indirect way of drawing the admiration of others to oneself:

> [T]he word proceeding out of the mouth and the actions which become known to people contain a most hazardous temptation in the love of praise. This likes to gather and beg for support to bolster a kind of private superiority. This is a temptation to me even when I reject it, because of the very fact that I am rejecting it. Often the contempt of vainglory becomes a source of even more vainglory. For it is not being scorned when the contempt is something one is proud of. (216–17)

The inspired polity, whose establishment requires the renunciation of glory, as we have just seen with Augustine, is the site of permanent tension with the worth of fame. In fact the break with the world, which is necessary to create an opening for inspiration, comes about through the use of ascetic practices whose implementation may be more or less radical. But when the ascetic individual accomplishes extraordinary exploits, he draws crowds to himself and has to flee to escape fame. We owe some of the most rigorous practices of separation from the world to the hermits, the desert Fathers who wanted to be alone with God and who, like Abba Arsenius and Abba Theodore of Pherme, "hated the esteem of other men" (Ward 1967, 14–15) and constantly fled the fame that their ascetic exploits brought them—their contemporaries compared them to "inspired athletes" (Palladius 1965, 18). Abba Arsenius banished the "virgin of senatorial rank" who "came from Rome to see him" (" 'How dare you make such a journey? . . . [I]s it so that on returning to Rome you can say to other women: I have seen Arsenius? Then they will turn the sea into a thoroughfare with women coming to see me' " [13–14]). Abba Theodore refused the office of deacon and fled (73). Abba Poemen, "the Shepherd," shunned his mother's eyes as she wept at his door (177–78). Abba Longinus hid his identity from a woman who, drawn by his fame, asked to see him in order to be healed: "When she met him, she said to him, 'Abba, where does Abba Longinus, the servant of God, live?' not knowing that it was he. He said, 'Why are you looking for that old impostor?'" (123). Abba Moses retreated into the marsh when he learned that the magistrate had heard of him and had set out to meet him; there, he met the people who were looking for him and they asked him: " 'Old man, tell us where the cell of Abba Moses is.' He said to them, 'What do you want with him? He is a fool.' " When he learned later that the old man was Moses, "the magistrate went away greatly edified" (140).[6]

The Domestic Polity

In the classical constructions of the *domestic polity*, people's worth depends on their hierarchical position in a chain of personal dependencies within "a universe ruled and arranged by the mind of God, all in ranks and degrees" (Mousnier 1979–1984, vol. 1, 5). Under this model, the individual person can no longer be dissociated from his or her belonging to a corporate body, for this body is itself conceived as a person characterized by its rank. The individual person is similarly defined by his or her belonging to a lineage endowed with its own identity, superior to that of the persons who embody it over time, in such a way that a testator and an heir may be considered before the law as one and the same (Kantorowicz 1957, 330). The individual person is a link in the "great chain of beings," and each one is positioned between a superior from whom he or she receives, through the intermediary of a personal relation, a power of access to worth and inferiors whom he or she encompasses and embodies.

In this domestic polity, every bond between beings is conceived as generating a familial bond: each man is a father to his subordinates and a son to his superiors. But the familial analogy refers less to blood ties, here, than to the fact of belonging to the same household, as a territory in which the relation of domestic dependence is inscribed. Thus in descriptions of traditional peasant society that conform to this model (here, in the Margeride region in France in the eighteenth and nineteenth centuries), "each one moves around under a halo constituted by the history of his rank, his family, his patrimonial lineage, the space, time, and memory occupied in the village by his *ousta*, his household. His house is a second skin, and even if he has the opportunity to prove his strength as an individual, he ultimately remains defined by his rank or his family status. Without his family, he is nothing" (Claverie and Lamaison 1982, 84). Beings are distributed according to the relation they maintain to a house (as is evidenced by the distinction—a very pertinent one in this polity—between domestic animals and wild animals) and, inside the household, according to the role they play in the reproduction of the family line. This mode of distribution neutralizes age divisions, for the distinction between children and adults is less important (indeed, the particular nature of childhood is not recognized) than the distinction among children within a single domestic unit, depending on whether they are in the position of the eldest (either in biological terms or by virtue of designation by the father: one can "make an eldest son") or among the youngest, condemned to seek their fortune far from home (60). As this example suggests, in a formula of subordination established according to a domestic model, worth is a state that can only be evaluated appropriately if it is linked to the relations of dependence from which persons derive the authority that they can in turn exercise on others. To know one's rank is to know one's worth, and to know oneself: the "*honnête homme*," in Auerbach's terms (1953 [1946], 316–26), is esteemed for never "[pretending] to be what he is not" (316–26; in the logic of this polity, such pretense is a mark of madness), that is, for the precision with which he is able to evaluate his own worth by relating it to the place he occupies in the chain of bonds of personal dependence. Even domestic servants, within the bounds of their own deficient state, share in the worth of their master and his goods.

La Bruyère develops this theme at length:

> A Swiss hall-porter, a *valet-de-chambre*, a footman, if they have no more sense than belongs to their station in life, do no longer estimate themselves by the meanness of their condition, but by the rank and fortune of those whom they serve, and without discrimination think that all people who enter by the door or ascend the staircase where they are in waiting are inferior to them and their master; so true is it that we are doomed to suffer from the great and from all [that belongs] to them. (1929 [1688], 232)

Tocqueville pursues the same idea a century later in *Democracy in America*, in the chapter entitled "How Democracy Affects the Relations of Masters and Servants" (1988 [1835], 572–80). But he presents the idea from a new perspective, drawn from comparatism, that makes critical distancing possible, along with the wholly modern relativism of Tocqueville's "anthropological gaze" on modernity (Furet 1981b, 41):

> In aristocracies the master comes to think of his servants as an inferior and secondary part of himself, and he often takes an interest in their fate by extending the scope of his self-centeredness.
>
> The servants, for their part, see themselves in almost the same way, and they sometimes identify themselves so much with the master personally that they become an appendage to him in their own eyes as well as in his. . . . In this extreme case the servant ends by losing his own sense of self-interest; he becomes detached from it; he deserts himself, as it were, or rather he transports the whole of himself into his master's character, where he creates an imaginary personality for himself. He takes pleasure in identifying himself with the wealth of those whom he obeys; he glories in their fame, exalts himself through their nobility, and constantly feeds on borrowed grandeur to which he often attaches more value than do those who possess it fully and in truth. (1988 [1835], 575)

Bossuet develops one possible demonstration of the domestic polity model for the benefit of the Dauphin (1990 [1709]). His *Politics Drawn from the Very Words of Holy Scripture*, like Augustine's *City of God*, seeks to derive forms of the legitimate bond between beings from an exegesis of the sacred texts. But while Augustine pursues his interpretation in such a way as to highlight what can serve as a basis for the inspired character of the city of God to the detriment of domestic values, which he generally ignores when he is not denouncing them, Bossuet sets out to ground the legitimacy of the kingdom of France in the forms of domestic relations that are so widely exemplified in Scripture (and in the Old Testament in particular). He returns to the ancient idea that the king occupies the same position in the kingdom that God occupies in the universe, expressing it in the modern language of absolutism and borrowing a formula from French translations of Hobbes's *De Cive*: "tout l'Etat est compris dans la personne du roi" (for Hobbes's "a city is contained in the person of a king" [Keohane 1980, 252]).

Bossuet is not the first to have generalized the principle of kinship into a politics, and numerous examples of constructions representing the State as an extension of the family can be found in historical literature (for example, in Andrew Lewis's *Royal Succession in Capetian France* [1986 (1981)], which analyzes the evolution of dynastic forms from the tenth to the fourteenth centuries. But it is precisely Bossuet's status as a latecomer to the topic (and he has essentially no influence on writers who came after him) that makes his work exceptionally interesting. Informed by the constructions of the political philosophy of his day (which it implicitly refutes), Bossuet's text is presented as an axiomatics drawing the consequences from a series of theorems in order to deduce a code of prudent conduct for the Dauphin's benefit, and its systematic character makes it especially useful for our own demonstration. In Bossuet's *Politics*, the domestic model is applied to the construction of a polity that is quite distinct from the family in the limited sense; this was not the case, for example, in earlier texts that sought to establish the dynastic legitimacy of the Capetians. Thus the principle of inheritance by blood, which reinforces the particular nature of the royal person and which implicitly undergirds Bossuet's demonstration, nevertheless does not play a major role in the argument, which is shaped by an intention to base royal authority on the economics of the relation between subjects, the State, and the Prince.

It is in this respect in particular that Bossuet's praise of the absolute Sovereign, which Rousseau will use as a foil (see *The Social Contract*, bk. I, chap. II, where he critiques genealogical theories of the authority of Princes), presents the model of a polity, in the sense in which we are using the term here. And we shall attempt to show further on how the originality of the polity that can be built according to the principles of Rousseau's social contract, the *civic polity*, is distinct from the absolutist variant of the model polity found in Bossuet, by virtue of its intention to use the same human beings to construct three entities, the Sovereign, the State, and individuals, thus dispensing with the delegation of divine authority to the Prince's person, and with the incarnation of the State in the king's own body. But this also means that Bossuet's demonstration helps to lay out the path that will lead to the disembodiment of the sovereign in the civic polity, thus making it possible to escape the difficulties raised by the process of the "transubstantiation" of an individual into a monarch (Marin 1988, 6–7), at the price, to be sure, of constructing the no less paradoxical metaphysics needed to account for the transubstantiation of the people into a Sovereign. In fact, for Bossuet, the king is not only "holy" or even "virtuous," as he is in the genealogical conceptions of ancient France (Lewis 1986, 122–33); above all, he is solitary and responsible, and he exists only for the State, with which he is one. His worth is equal to his sacrifice. In this sacrificial conception of the Prince's worth, the celebration of his virtues consists in putting on display, in all its dimensions, the amplitude of the sacrifice he agrees to make for the happiness of all, a goal to which he subordinates all of his own personal satisfactions.

The topics of the domestic polity and, in particular, the themes of royal solitude and the royal burden, are developed extensively by La Bruyère, whose *Characters* is of sociological interest in that it collects and organizes the principal commonplaces of his time around a social typology. Thus in the chapter titled "Of the Sovereign and the State," we read that "to call a king the father of his people is not so much to eulogise him as to call him by his name and to define what he is" (1929 [1688], 264). La Bruyère emphasizes the prince's sacrifice, and the economy of the relationship he maintains with his subjects:

> There exists a sort of interchange or permutation of duties between a sovereign and his subjects, and between them and him; and I shall not decide which are most obligatory and most difficult. On the one hand, we have to determine what are the bounden duties of reverence, assistance, service, obedience, and dependence, and on the other what are the indispensable obligations of goodness, justice, and protection. (265)

He goes on to ask: "Which condition seems to you the most delicious and the most unfettered, that of the sheep or of the shepherd? Was the flock made for the shepherd or the shepherd for the flock? This is an artless representation of a nation and its prince, but then the prince must be good" (265), and he repeatedly emphasizes the burden under which royalty labors: "If the care of a single family be so burdensome, if a man has enough to do to answer for himself, what a weight, what a heavy load must be the charge of a whole realm!" (266–67).

In a body politic whose cohesion depends on upholding the divine laws, the "sanctity of the oath" is the foundation for bonds among beings. Individuals can only keep discord at bay by making mutual commitments. But such promises will be kept only if the commitment is made in the presence of a superior being who can guarantee that it will be respected. Therefore "the only way to make matters certain" is to swear before something "greater than oneself"; hence, "peoples without religion are, at the same time, without organization, without genuine subordination, and are entirely primitive," for "men who are not bound in conscience cannot protect one another" (Bossuet 1990 [1709], 194). If men cannot reach even an inferior form of agreement except by referring to a transcendent principle, then any instance of submission to a divinity, even an illusory one, has at least the virtue of "strengthen[ing] treaties": "For this it is not absolutely necessary to swear by the true God: it is enough that each swear by the God he recognizes" (194). Yet only "the true religion" which is "founded upon sure principles" can make "state constitutions more stable and solid" (194). Indeed, only the Holy Scriptures, which contain humanity's true genealogy, allow men to establish a political bond and to strengthen its legitimacy by basing it on the principle of generation: "In this way, at whatever given time, going back step by step, one comes to Adam and the beginning of the universe by a manifest series" (198). Breaking the political bond consists, then, in interrupting the chain of generations that unites and classifies beings according to tradition, in such a way that "innovation" becomes an intrinsic source of discord: "the mark of innovation is indelible"; it bears the "blemish" of "schism" and "heresy," of the "revolt" that "separates" families and "breaks" community attachments (201–2).

In this hierarchical political conception of the cosmos, the sovereign is the "minister" of God, who is designated by the term "King of kings" in Bossuet's address to the Dauphin. As such, the sovereign is the repository of "oaths" and the guarantor of "subordination," which in this polity establishes the bond among all the beings that are ordered within the state in the same way as descendants in a bloodline are subordinate to ascendants, children to the father, and the younger to the older. The sovereign has the preeminence of a father, and, depending on the context, the title "father of all" can refer either to the king or to God. The power of judgment is therefore his: "when the prince has decided, there can be no other decision" (82). Love of the father unites the subjects like brothers in their subordination: "We must therefore love one another, because we must all love the same God, who is our common father, and his unity is our bond" (3). The king is one with the land of the nation as the father is one with the mother, and love of "the same country," which produces the "unity of nations" (11) when combined with a common language, is comparable to love for a "common mother," who is the "nurse of all men" (25). More-

over, "peoples" are considered to be "composed of many particular families, having each their rights" (37) and constituting "civil society" or "the
State" (8). The State's authority is an extension of paternal authority.
"Kings were fashioned on the model of fathers" and "the name king is a
father's name" (62). Their power, "coming from on high" (61), "is conferred [upon them] from without" (162). They are the "ministers" of God,
who "has put something divine into kings" (60). Princes, the guarantors
of the polity, therefore hold "the place of God, who is the true father of
the human race" (62). By the same token, "men are all born subjects" and
the "paternal empire, which accustoms them to obey, accustoms them at the
same time to have only one leader" (47).

Exercising this natural authority would not require any special arrangements were it not for the influence of the passions, which divide men and
make it necessary to transform paternal love into a political art form. Men
having become "untractable by the violence of their passions, and incompatible by their different humors, they could not be united, at least to submit altogether to one government, which regulates all" (14). Submission
to the prince makes "one man" of the "multitudes" when, "each renouncing his own will, [he] transfers and reunites it to that of the prince and the
magistrate" (15). Such submission constitutes the foundation of justice
and the social bond, because subordination to power constrains the limitless expression of selfish desires. This is why one must "always respect and
always serve" the king, whether he is "good or bad" (176). In this formulation, "subordination" (174) is divided up by degrees according to hierarchical proximity to God and to his minister, the prince: "Obedience is due
to each according to his rank, and the governor must never be obeyed if
his orders are prejudicial to the prince's" (175).

But the only justification for the existence of the great—the worthy—
lies in their determination to "protect the small" (63). By way of the "government," each subject becomes stronger, because "in the person of the
Prince" he has an "invincible defender" who holds "in his hands all the
strength of the nation." Bossuet repeatedly underscores the relationship
between worth and the protection of the weak: "All strength is transferred
to the sovereign magistrate: every one strengthens him to the prejudice of
his own, and renounces his own life in case of disobedience. The people
gain by this; for they recover in the person of the supreme magistrate
more strength than they yielded for his authority, since they recover in
him all the strength of the nature reunited to assist them" (16–17). The
father-prince is the champion of the weak: "The whole of the Scriptures
charges them to do justice to the poor, to the weak, to the widow, the or-
phan, and to the ward" (17). In this polity, where exchange takes the form
of a "broad circulation of necessary acts of generosity" (Duby 1964, 63),
the division of labor is designed like a mode of mutual assistance within

each domestic unit. As the "supreme victualer" (Kaplan 1976, 5) and as the principle by which exchanges are organized, the "fatherly monarch" (5) must "provide for the people," and "the obligation to take care of the people is the basis of all rights that sovereigns have over subjects" (Bossuet 1990 [1709], 65): "The famished people asked for bread from their king, as from a shepherd, or rather as from their father" (65).

The prince's legitimacy does not depend solely on the protection he grants those who are dependent upon him; it also rests on selflessness and a concomitant renunciation of self-indulgence. The prince displays his dignity in his self-control and in the "firmness" with which he commands his "passions" and masters his "desires" (98). He does not succumb to the unparalleled "temptations connected to power" (394). He compensates for his privileges by sacrificing his person to others: he "is not born for himself" and is made to "[forget] himself" (64). He is a "public good" who gives himself "equally to all" (78). This is indeed how he distinguishes himself from a "tyrant" whose "true character . . . is to think only of himself" (68). In return, all owe him "gratitude" (69) and the love that makes "obedience pleasant" (78). As a public good who unites all others in his own person, he thinks in general terms such as the following: "Be silent, base thoughts: yield to royal thoughts. Thoughts worthy of royalty are those which concern the general good" (163). The prince "should think of great things" (163). "By his greatness he is above small interests" (84), "petty thoughts and narrow views" (163); he is above individual concerns, "mocking words," and "scandal-mongering" (80). "Far above resentment and doing harm" (164), above "intrigue" and "chicanery" (315), he lowers himself only when justice requires that he "go down" to "see what is going on" (276) among the people: "[princes] must descend from this high peak of greatness, which no one approaches but trembling, and mix in some fashion with the people, in order to see things close up, and collect, here and there, the dispersed traces of the truth" (277). The "magnificence" that could be interpreted as a selfish manifestation of his attachment to earthly goods and power is also the result of sacrifice and the gift of himself. For the prince must join "great expenditures to great plans" (165). He expresses his worth through "magnificent gifts" (165). Expenses "of splendor and of dignity," which "in their way [are] no less necessary for the sustaining of majesty," are added to "expenses of necessity" (345).

As an embodiment of the general good, the prince is the "chief judge" (270). He hears individual pleas that are addressed to him personally, for each can bring forth "with respect, [his] just complaints by permitted means" (181). He combines "clemency" with "firmness" (273), but subjects may protest against "the violence of princes" with "respectful remonstrances" (181). In such petitions, accusations of private debauchery are considered in the same light as denunciations of public scandal. For, in a domestic polity, the "personalization of the relationship . . . allows for no distinction between 'family affairs' and 'affairs of state,' between 'marital conflicts' and 'public issues' " (Farge and Foucault 1982, 44–45). In a formula of subordination in which the body politic is incorporated in the "person of the prince" and "inequality [is] radically personal in a nature" (Walzer 1974, 12), "political activity is restricted to [the king's] immediate vicinity," so that in ordinary times "he does not mobilize [the nation's] members if he can help it" beyond the court, because mobilization requires the king's personal presence (27). Although they are separate in theory, the king's two bodies (Kantorowicz 1957) tend to contaminate each other, because "the body corporate is the body natural" (Walzer 1974, 27). As the "royal person" is a "particular man" as well, "the private life of the king becomes synonymous with the public life of the kingdom" (27–28). Similarly, in the king's case and in the case of worthy persons in general, "whispering" is indistinct from "public speaking," individual speech is indistinct from general discourse, the "intensely personal" is indistinct from "issues . . . of the greatest national significance," and "personal favor" is indistinct from "public agreement." As Walzer writes, "whispering is to royal courts what public speaking is to democratic assemblies," and he adds that it was this state of permanent confusion between the personal and the political, the "private" and the "public," that was interpreted in the language of "conspiracy" during the French Revolution, that is, precisely when these two categories had become clearly distinguishable: the royal court was viewed as a monstrous site of "private intrigues with public effects" (27–28).

The legitimists, de Bonald in particular, set out to reestablish a domestic polity in the first half of the nineteenth century. But the reactionary nature of their project sets it apart in the context of political philosophy. The legitimists were attempting to reinstitute a polity whose legitimacy had been damaged by the French Revolution and the development of liberalism, and which, given the growing extension of the "public"/" private" opposition, tended to be excluded from the public domain and confined to the realm of personal relations. To combat the exclusion of the domestic polity from the field of political constructions, de Bonald undertook to demonstrate scientifically (he compared himself to a geometer) the logical possibility of rebuilding society and the State according to the principle of paternal power. He bases the political order on the distinction between three beings: father, mother, and child. He is careful to note that these three beings are "similar, since they are all part of humanity, but not equal, since they have different functions" (1985 [1830], 449). The tension highlighted here between a principle of common humanity and a principle of order inscribes de Bonald's problematics unambiguously within the framework of the axiomatics of the polity that gives rise to the set of political metaphysics we are analyzing in this work. De Bonald seeks to detach these three persons from the framework of the nuclear family, which is based on blood ties, in order to construct them in a general sense, that is, as moral beings representing the actors in a political drama:

> For the individual physical denominations of father, mother, and child, which are common even to the families of animals, let us substitute the general moral expressions of power, minister, and subject, terms that designate intelligent beings, that are applicable to society—indeed to any society—and can apply only to society. . . . We can therefore now operate with these general expressions, which represent all persons in all societies, and solve all the problems that these expressions present. (450–51)

Anthropological literature, too, could surely provide us with additional variants of this effort to generalize the domestic bond, an effort that seems, in the few examples available to us, to accompany the search for a principle of cohesion capable of sustaining political arrays that are too large and culturally too heterogeneous to be based directly on a mythical common genealogy. We are thinking in particular of Maurice Bloch's work on the history of the circumcision ritual in the Merina kingdom of Madagascar, a ritual that, during the late-eighteenth-century reign of Queen Andrianampoinimerina, shifted from being a strictly family ritual, carried out on an irregular basis depending on the rhythms of births in each family, to being a state ritual, carried out by everyone at the same time, once every seven years, in such a way that the circumcision of all subjects was coordinated with the circumcision ceremonies of the royal family (Bloch 1986). During the festival period that accompanied the royal circumcision, the whole kingdom then became an extension of the ruler's domestic space. These circumcision rites provided the opportunity for all, brought together by their participation in the totality of an ordered world, to demonstrate their unity as "senior and junior siblings" alike (119); Bloch's analysis suggests that ritual may play the role attributed to political philosophy in the examples on which our own analyses are based.

The Polity of Fame

Whereas in the domestic polity, worth is inscribed in a hierarchical chain and is defined as the capacity to "encompass" the "will" of subordinates in "one's person," in a formula of subordination based on fame, worth depends only on the opinion of others. For an initial approach to characterizing this polity, we shall turn to the passages in Hobbes's work that focus on the definition of honor. Hobbes's notion of honor may seem peripheral in relation to the core of his political construction; however, it stems from the same set of concepts, and in particular from the same theory of conventional signs. In the polity of fame, the construction of worth is tied to the constitution of conventional signs that condense and display the power generated by the esteem people have for one another, and thus make it possible to weigh persons against one another and to calculate their respective value.

> The signs by which we know our own power are those actions which proceed from the same; and the signs by which other men know it, are such actions, gesture, countenance and speech, as usually such powers produce: and the acknowledgment of power is called HONOUR; and to honour a man (inwardly in the mind) is to conceive or acknowledge, that that man hath the odds or excess of power above him that contendeth or compareth himself . . . and according to the signs of honour and dishonour, so we estimate and make the value or WORTH of a man. (1969 [1640], 34–35)

The nominalist definition of the arbitrariness of signs developed in *The Elements of Law* is inseparable from the way a sovereign is constituted. Elsewhere in the same work, Hobbes characterizes this latter process as arising from the "UNION" of "many wills" or from the "involving of many wills in one or more" (63); he deals with it more fully in *Leviathan* in terms of "personification," artificial persons and authors; here he emphasizes the arbitrary nature of the actor, whose power is derived solely from the authorization of the contracting parties.

Hobbes very often uses a vocabulary borrowed from the world of mercantile trade when he writes about the civic value of persons, and he frequently manages to give the terms he uses a somewhat altered meaning (his notion of "personification" is an example). Some authors, referring in particular to his repeated mention of the "price" of persons, see him as one of the founders of market political philosophy (Macpherson 1964, 9–106). By analyzing the market polity and the polity of fame in turn, it is our intention, on the contrary, to highlight the differences between the two forms of worth on which these polities are based. In the polity of fame, there are no goods external to persons that can, if they are subjected to the condition of scarcity, govern the competition of desires. The recognition of a person's reputation bears directly on the person, and people's attributes, whose definition is arbitrary, are the signs of their fame.[7]

The theory of persons links the construction of the worth of "natural persons," inasmuch as this construction derives from the attribution of signs of honor to the construction of the "fictive person" of the sovereign. The construction of the person, in Hobbes, requires an arrangement in which "signs" (words or deeds) performed by an "actor" are related back or "attributed" to an "author," just as effects can be traced back to a cause. This arrangement, which makes it possible to construct the relative worth of persons with respect to one another in the theory of honor (the most worthy being those to whom the greatest number of others attribute signs of honor), is also central to the construction of the "fictive person" of the sovereign. In the theory of the fictive person, the sovereign's representation of the people, or the actor's representation of the author, is also necessarily a projection of the author into the actor. The sovereign, a "fictive person," is the "actor" who personifies or "personates" ("person" here having the etymological sense of a mask) and "represents" the multitude of subjects that is the author of his acting. This representation of a fictive person may be thought of as presupposing a third party who judges and attributes signs. The third party cannot be distinguished from the author, who is himself identified with the sovereign through the mechanism of attribution (Jaume 1983).

In the *polity of fame*, worth depends solely on the number of persons who award their esteem; by virtue of this formula of equivalence, the polity is thus exempt from all forms of personal dependence. Indeed, if the esteem of the worthy is more valuable than the esteem of the lowly, it is only to the extent that the worthy already concentrate the recognition of others in their own person: to be "honourable" is to be "Honoured, loved, or feared of many" (Hobbes 1997 [1651], 52). Hobbes thereby reduces "all the foundations of honor or of the esteem of distinction to a single term, power" (Goldschmidt 1974, 723), and the degree of one's power depends on the number of persons who contribute to it through their recognition: "The Greatest of humane Powers, is that which is compounded of the Powers of most men, united by consent in one person, Naturall or Civill. . . . Therefore to have servants, is Power; To have friends, is Power: for they are strengths united" (Hobbes 1997 [1651], 48). Power in this sense can be likened to "Fame, increasing as it proceeds" (48). Since a person's value or worth depends on his fame and the opinion of others, "Reputation of power, is Power," and "Good successe is Power," by virtue of the "reputation" it creates (48–50).

Because a person's worth is established by the opinion of others, worth is independent of self-esteem: "For let a man (as most men do) rate themselves as the highest Value they can; yet their true Value is no more than it is esteemed by others" (50). A person's worth or, as Hobbes puts it, his "publique worth," depends solely on public opinion: "The *Value*, or Worth of a man, is as of all other things, his Price; that is to say, so much as would be given for the use of his Power: and therefore is not absolute; but a thing dependent on the need and judgement of another" (50). Hence, "an able conductor of Souldiers, is of great Price in time of War present, or imminent; but in Peace not so. A learned and uncorrupt Judge, is much Worth in time of Peace; but not so much in War" (50). Similarly, the worth of men whose eminence is recognized by only a small number of persons, as is the case for members of the scholarly community, is small, and such men enjoy little power: "The Sciences, are small Power; because not eminent; and therefore, not acknowledged in any man; nor are at all, but in a few; and in them, but of a few things. For Science is of that nature, as none can understand it to be, but such as in a good measure have attayned it" (50).

As a product of recognition, worth is measured by visibility, the degree to which a person is available to the gaze of others: "To be Conspicuous, that is to say, to be known, for Wealth, Office, great Actions, or any eminent Good, is Honourable. . . . On the contrary, Obscurity, is Dishonourable" (53). Honor can therefore be reduced to fame. What Hobbes calls "Civill Honour" (52) depends on gaining the sovereign's regard, but only inasmuch as the sovereign is recognized by the majority, for this is what gives him the power to embody and constitute public opinion: "The manifestation of the Value we set on one another, is that which is commonly called Honouring, and Dishonouring. To Value a man at a high rate, is to *Honour* him; at a low rate, is to *Dishonour* him" (50). Thus, "to shew any sign of love, or feare of another, is to Honour; for both to love, and to feare, is to value" (51). For this reason it would be futile to try to distinguish true honor from a "signe of Honour," because "[t]o do those things to another, which he takes for signes of Honour, or which the Law or Custome makes so, is to Honour; because in approving the Honour done by others, he acknowledgeth the power which others acknowledge" (51). Similarly, the qualities that manifest worth, such as "Magnanimity," "Liberality," and "Courage," are honorable only to the extent that they "proceed from the conscience of Power" (152). Finally, the poor opinion that the lowly have of themselves, which is based on the lack of respect others have for them, is at the origin of their degraded condition, of their "Pusillanimity, Parsimony, Fear, Diffidence" (51).

Hobbes's construction, which equates honor with trustworthiness, singles out one component of the phenomena examined by history and anthropology under the heading of honor. Anthropologists have depicted honor in Mediterranean societies as an unstable compromise among domestic worth (securing the most advantageous positions for a lineage [Favret 1968]), worth through fame (the tribunal of public opinion [Bourdieu 1977]), inspired worth (evident for example in the opposition between the exuberant, irresponsible honor of youth and the calmer, more prudent honor that comes with age [Jamous 1977]), and market values: although traditional Mediterranean societies do not recognize any form of market worth as fully legitimate, most other societies emphasize the presence of underlying "interests" (this aspect was first developed specifically in a theory of "symbolic capital" by Pierre Bourdieu in *The Logic of Practice* [1990, 112–21]). Other works offer a definition of honor as the quality that, by guaranteeing "fidelity to one's word, was the very foundation for sworn oaths, that is, for contracts" (Farès, *L'Honneur chez les Arabes avant l'Islam*, cited in Di Bella 1981). Hobbes himself defines injustice as the absurd breach of a contract: "*Injury*, or *Injustice*, in the controversies of the world, is somewhat like to that, which in the disputations of Scholers is called *Absurdity*. For as it is there called an Absurdity, to contradict what one maintained in the Beginning: so in the world, it is called Injustice, and Injury, voluntarily to undo that, which from the beginning he had voluntarily done" (1997 [1651], 73). Yet in Hobbes's construct, honor is indifferent to "Justice" as defined above: "Nor does it alter the case of Honour, whether an action (so it be great and difficult, and consequently a signe of much power,) be just or unjust: for Honour consisteth onely in the opinion of Power" (53). Thus the *balance* that characterizes the polity of public opinion shifts away from commitments in the form of contracts. For this polity to be established, nothing in the arrangement of the test setting must stand in the way of modifications in worth that reflect fluctuations in public opinion. Such fluidity is not guaranteed if a person's worth depends on contracts or on fidelity to prior commitments.

In the polity of fame, disputes arise when a gap develops between an individual's self-esteem and the esteem in which others hold him or her, the latter being the reality. A person's honor may thus be maintained or threatened, raised or lowered, but the marks of honor and dishonor are always relative, for "high, and low, in this case, is to be understood by comparison to the rate that each man setteth on himselfe" (50). Since a person's "true Value" depends solely on the esteem of others, a person who displays indignation and seeks redress is necessarily resting his case on an error of evaluation, a false or exaggerated estimation of his own importance. Disputes are therefore not a cause for conflict between opinion and conscience, where conscience is defined, as in the inspired polity's condemnation of earthly glory, as immanent knowledge of a higher worth; for, in this model of subordination, where "private Consciences" are identified with "private opinions" (164), "Conscience, [Hobbes] held, was nothing but a subjective belief, a private view" (Koselleck 1988, 26–27).

"It hath been also commonly taught, *That Faith and Sanctity, are not to be attained by Study and Reason, but by supernaturall Inspiration, or Infusion*, which granted, I see not why any man should render a reason of his Faith; or why every Christian should not be also a Prophet; or why any man should take the Law of his Country, rather than his own Inspiration, for the rule of his action" (Hobbes 1997 [1651], 164). It is the public manifestation of a behavior dictated by the inner soul, and by the belief—blind to the opinion of others—that one is the sole possessor of an inspired truth, that is the mark of folly, comparable to a disturbance in a worth whose limits are no longer known:

Another, and a principal defect of the mind, is that which men call MADNESS, which appeareth to be nothing else but some imagination of such predominance above all the rest, that we have no passion but from it. And this conception is nothing else but excessive vain glory, or vain dejection. . . . As first, we have had the example of one that preached in Cheapside from a cart there, instead of a pulpit, that he himself was Christ, which was spiritual pride or madness . . . so also are there examples too many of the degrees, which may therefore be well accounted follies. As it is a degree of the first, for a man, without certain evidence, to think himself inspired, or to have any other effect in himself of God's holy spirit than other godly men have. (1969 (1640), 51–52)

Folly, disguised as inspiration, explodes in full view of the crowd:

Though the effect of folly, in them that are possessed of an opinion of being inspired, be not visible alwayes in one man, by any very extravagant action, that proceedeth from such Passion; yet when many of them conspire together, the Rage of the whole multitude is visible enough. For what argument of Madnesse can there be greater, than to clamour, strike, and throw stones at our best friends? . . . And if there were nothing else that betrayed their madnesse; yet that very arrogating such inspiration to themselves, is argument enough. (1997 [1651], 43–44)

This refusal to recognize the political dimension of inspiration, which is relegated to the sphere of subjectivity and thus deemed arbitrary, and the intent to expose the power of the passions and partisan appetites that lie behind the invocation of inner certainties are what make it possible to establish the equivalence between worth and fame without casting the powers of public opinion in a negative light, as the seventeenth-century French moralists did, and, later, Rousseau ("consideration").[8] Moralists in the Jansenist tradition (La Rochefoucauld, Nicole, Pascal) developed analyses of honor in which the worth of persons, and in particular the worth of the worthy, was presented as merely the product of the opinion of others; but this reduction always takes the form of a critical unveiling: "Man is not great. His desire to become great does not make him so" (Bénichou 1971 [1948]). Thus, the honor of "conscience" (honor "*in foro interno*," to return to Koselleck's terms [1988 [1959], 26]) is contrasted with honor in the eyes of the Court, that is, with false worths. This distinction, which is a more radical form of the denunciation of earthly glory characteristic of the Stoic tradition and of Christianity, reveals the hidden truth of worldly worth, which is dependent on the gaze of others, and in so doing it underscores the characteristics by which true worth is recognized: true worth, unconcerned with public opinion, focuses exclusively on signs that one is among the elect, among those chosen by God.

This thematics was developed by Augustine in his *Confessions* and also in the parts of *The City of God* that set out to refute classical concepts of glory put to the secular use of enhancing the worth of a polity (Lida de Malkiel 1968, 89–92); later, in struggles between the Church and political societies, jurists used the same thematics to defeat the claims—particularly the spiritual claims—of the lay powers (de Lagarde 1956). In a similar way, the Italian Renaissance developed the Ciceronian concept of *virtus* in response to the Christian concept of human deficiency. *Vir virtutis*, which is part of the Renaissance ideal of a gentleman, assumes that it is possible, in this world, to achieve a form of dramatic and heroic excellence that is opposed to the representation of "man's deficiency" and to the condemnation of glory and heroic deeds in the name of divine providence and grace (Skinner 1978, 1:90–101). Like Hobbes, the seventeenth-century French moralists associate heroic feats of strength with interest and self-love (Hirschman 1977, 11), but they do not subject these phenomena to the same moral treatment. Hobbes acquiesces to the reality of their worth when they are recognized as worthy by others, without attempting to diminish them in the name of some other principle of justice. The moralists take a different tack. Rather than directly challenging the established worths that are recognized at court, they relativize them by thrusting them into a world of multiple worths, ordered hierarchically or even treated as incommensurable, as in Pascal's text on tyranny.

> Tyranny consists in the desire to dominate everything regardless of order.
>
> In the various departments for men of strength, beauty, sense and piety, each man is master in his own house but nowhere else. Sometimes they meet and the strong and the handsome contend for mastery, but this is idiotic because their mastery is of different kinds. They do not understand each other, and their mistake lies in wanting to rule everywhere. Nothing can do that, not even strength: it is of no effect in the learned world and only governs external actions. . . .
>
> *Tyranny.* Tyranny is wanting to have by one means what can only be had by another. We pay different dues to different kinds of merit; we must love charm, fear strength, believe in knowledge.
>
> These dues must be paid. It is wrong to refuse them and wrong to demand any others. So these arguments are false and tyrannical. "I am handsome, so you must fear me. I am strong, so you must love me. I am . . ." In the same way it is false and tyrannical to say: "He is not strong, so I will not respect him; he is not clever, so I will not fear him." (Pascal 1966, 45 [Brunschwig no. 332])

(Michael Walzer draws upon this *pensée* to develop his configuration of autonomous spheres of justice [1983, 17–20].)

Jansenist-inspired works offer other ways of conceptualizing the plurality of worths, treating them not as if they were attached to different persons who occupy different places or "chambers," but as if they were brought together in a single person, who can thus be qualified in different ways according to the light in which the person is being considered in the relationship. The paradigm of the man who was king in spite of himself provides one example. This text was designed for the instruction of a "child of high estate"; Nicole, in his *Moral Essays*, attributes it to Pascal (Nicole 1696, 3:129–36):

> A Man by tempest is thrown on an unknown island, whose Inhabitants were in great perplexity to find their King who was lost. This Man resembling, in shape of Body and lineaments of Face, the King, is taken for him, and as such is acknowledg'd by the People. At the first he knows not what to do, but at last resolves not to be wanting to his good fortune. He accepts of all the Homage they render him, and suffers him self to be respected as King.
>
> But as he could not forget his natural condition, at the same time that he receiv'd all these honours, he was conscious to himself that he was not that King the People fought for, and that the Kingdom he govern'd belong'd not to him. Thus he had two sets of thoughts, one by which he acted as King, another by which he knew his own true condition; as also that it was only chance which plac'd him where he was. These latter thoughts he kept secret, and discover'd the other. The first were those he treated his People with, with the latter he manag'd himself. (Nicole 1696, vol. 2, "Of the Condition of the Great," discourse I, p. 131)

Pascal goes on to explain that "there are in the World two sorts of Grandeur, one of establishment, the other natural." Greatness of establishment depends on "the Wills of Men"; it calls for "established forms of respect," "certain exterior Ceremonies," not esteem. Conversely, "natural Grandeur" is independent of "the fancies and humour of Men, because it consists in certain real and positive qualities of the soul and Body": these have the "preference of esteem" (134–35). A child of high birth thus resembles the shipwrecked man who becomes king:

> that wherein you perfectly agree with him, is, that your right, no more than his, is not grounded on any quality or desert of yours, whereby you become worthy thereof. Your Soul and your Body, of themselves, are indifferently made for the condition of a Plowman, and for that of a Duke; and there is no natural tye which fastens them rather to the one condition, than to the other. (132)

Once worth has been divided up into various types, not all equally natural (or real), an individual who is "of two minds" can distance himself from himself and consider his own situation:

> What follows hence? That you ought to have, as the Man we spoke of, two Sets of thoughts; and if exteriorly amongst Men, you act according to your

rank and quality, you must by the other thoughts, more secret but yet more true, acknowledge, that naturally you have nothing above them. If your open publick thoughts raise you above the rest of Mankind, let the secret ones bring you down again, and keep you in a perfect equality with them, that is, in your own natural being. (132–33)

An individual, then, can withdraw into himself or step outside of himself, and this ability gives him a critical faculty, which he may use to denounce worldly vanities in the name of inner truths, for example, or to open his heart and reveal to the public that in some respects he is still a slave to the opinion of others (134–35).

The construction of a market of esteem and of a worth of fame that is not accompanied by renunciation of the Christian hope for worth in itself thus opens up a space for free play such as we find in Rousseau on the various meanings of the term *consideration*: one's consideration for oneself, the consideration of others for oneself, one's consideration for others while keeping one's eye on the gaze of others on oneself. A tradition can then be established (there are vestiges of it today in certain approaches to social psychology) in which the political bond is primarily a matter of gazes. At the same time, we witness the development of a satirical rhetoric and a casuistry of suspicion that serves to identify the state of worth that underlies the artifices of people "of two minds," either by unmasking the claims to natural worth of those whose stature in fact rests on an artificially established worth or else (as is the case today for example with a holder of an academic title who is anxious to have his own value recognized) by establishing in the person's inner self the reality of a worth in which others are determined to see only the result of an external intervention. Suspicion looks for the meanness present in everyone, alert for a chance to unmask the pettiness each individual conceals under the false appearances of a superficial worth; as we see clearly in La Bruyère's texts on human worth, suspicion unfolds in a tension between the worth of the sovereign and the pettiness of the people.

La Bruyère speaks about the sovereign in the same terms as does Bossuet. But he contrasts the king's responsibility with the meanness of the courtier, who is petty because he is freed from the bonds that constitute domestic worth. A favorite "is a chameleon or a Proteus" (La Bruyère 1929 [1688], 254). "No ties of friendship or consanguinity affect a favourite; he may be surrounded on all sides by relatives and friends, but he does not mind them; he is detached from everything, and, as it were, isolated" (259). This detachment is the condition for access to the worth of fame (as it will be the condition for market worth), and the man of the court, where "social opinion . . . [is] identical to [one's] social existence" according to Elias (1983, 91), exists only in the regard others have for him:

"A man who leaves the court for a single moment renounces it for ever; the courtier who was there in the morning must be there at night, and know it again next day, in order that he himself may be known there" (La Bruyère 1929 [1688], 184). But he can only be diminished by this, because worth based on fame is denounced as a delusion: "A man must appear small at court, and let him be never so vain, it is impossible to prevent it; but it is the common lot, and the highest of nobles themselves are there of no consequence" (184). The position of the worthy is therefore filled with ambiguity and uncertainty. One cannot fail to see what it is that attaches the worthy to the universe of domestic worth, and their stature fills the entire space to which the critique applies. But as courtiers and objects of favor and disfavor, they are equated with those who serve them. Their worth, therefore, is no longer a matter of course: "There are some persons who, if they did know their inferiors and themselves, would be ashamed to be above them" (227).

The tension between domestic worth and the worth of fame, unrecognized as such, pervades moralist denunciations of the court, disrupts the order among persons, and frees up a space in which other worths, civic worth and industrial worth, can take hold:

> While the great . . . [who] ignore how to govern a household or a family, boast of their very ignorance . . . some citizens instruct themselves in what is going on within and without the kingdom, study the art of government, become shrewd politicians, are acquainted in the strength and weakness of an entire state, think of bettering their position, obtain a place, rise, become powerful, and relieve their princes of a portion of the cares of the state. (229–30)

In this way, by separating the worth of the worthy from the worth of the sovereign, courtly society creates uncertainty and raises a question whose answer may lie in a return to the inspired authenticity of the inner soul or, as in Hobbes, in the construction of worth on a foundation of arbitrary signs.

The Civic Polity

Rousseau's *Social Contract* sets forth a formula for subordination in which access to worth does not depend on inspiration conceived in the mode of grace, or on the position one occupies in a hierarchical chain of dependencies, or on the opinion of others. We shall use the pleonasm *civic polity* to refer to this formula. Like Bossuet's domestic polity, the civic polity bases civil peace and the common good on the authority of a majestic and impartial Sovereign placed above private interests. But this Sovereign is now disembodied. His political body can come into being without being incarnated in the physical body of a Prince legitimated by his bloodlines. The Sovereign of the civic polity is created by the convergence of human wills that comes about when citizens give up their singularity and distance themselves from their private interests to take only the common good into account.

The formula for subordination presented in *The Social Contract* establishes sovereignty by transcending the problems that the embodiment of the common good in a person raises in the domestic polity. By disembodying sovereignty, which is transferred from the king's body into the general will, and by making the king a citizen like other people, as capable as the others of manifesting virtues and vices, greater or lesser worthiness, this formula relaxes the tensions created by the incarnation of the political body in a natural body. We see this, for example, in the case of "public regicide" (as opposed to secret assassination by a pretender to the throne). According to Michael Walzer's analysis, public regicide manifests the tension between the domestic and civic spheres in the king's body in a particularly problematic way. The king, as body politic, is inviolable, and he cannot be judged because no being exists, in civil society, who is superior to him. But crimes committed by the king in particular nevertheless have the power to destroy the State. Thus Marie Stuart was put on trial and brought before her judges in "the name of parricide only, for [she was] not in court on any question respecting [her] government, but only as respects parricide" (George Buchanan cited in Walzer 1974, 50)—as if parricide were not the "political crime *par excellence*" in a hereditary monarchy, Walzer adds. The political properties of royal sovereignty justify regicide while accounting for its difficulty. It is because the king's body and the body politic are one that the old regime can be killed "in the king's person." But, for the same reasons, public judgment and the execution of the king, in his capacity as king, constitute unprecedented acts that cannot be justified in terms of any existing legal or moral rule. "The king is brought to trial in violation of the laws that he acknowledges; he is judged in the name of political or legal principles to which he never consented. He is judged, moreover, by a court whose authority he does not recognize" (70).

The establishment of a civic worth capable of constituting a principle of legitimate order in the polity can thus be posited as a reasonable alternative either to recognizing the charismatic authority of an inspired leader, or to remaining loyal to relations of personal dependence inscribed in hierarchies treated as if they were natural, or, finally, to submitting to the verdicts of a market of esteem. Indeed, according to Rousseau, it is not enough to free men from the bonds of dependence that subject them to the person of a superior, in order to reveal their true worth and consequently to ensure the conditions for an authentic judgment. For even if they are detached from hierarchical relations, men can still fall under the sway of public opinion. Their pursuit of "consideration" and their penchant for "self-love" put them in a form of dependence that may not place direct physical constraints on their bodies, as was the case in the forms of personal dependence that were in effect under the Old Regime, but it is no less tyrannical, because it subjects them all to the opinion of others and thus places a "price" on "public esteem" (*SD*, 166).[9] In Rousseau's writings, self-love does not have the paradoxical virtues of the "false honor" that Montesquieu discusses (1989 [1748], 27). However egotistical and illusory this passion may be, it takes actions that were initially aimed at satisfying the interest of a particular person and redirects them to serve the "public good" (Pappas 1982); the importance of this mechanism in eighteenth-century political and moral thought is demonstrated by Albert O. Hirschman (1977).[10] Conversely, in Rousseau, vainglory never serves the "common good," and "worldly honor" is opposed to "real honor," as it was for the seventeenth-century French moralists, just as the inauthentic externality of appearance is opposed to the inner authenticity of conscience (for example, see *NH* 69: "Let us leave aside the multitude and look into ourselves"). Liberated in this way from relations of personal dependence, men are nevertheless still not free, for they remain slaves to opinion, which is based not on reality but on power relations among factions and coteries, and conflicts of interest that pit men against one another in temporary groupings formed for selfish ends.

In Rousseau's *Social Contract*, legitimate political relations cannot be established directly on the basis of concrete interactions among persons who are qualified in terms of their affiliations and interests. Indeed, no negotiation or arbitrage is possible at this level, which is wholly subject to the reign of force. If just relations are to be established among persons, human interactions have to be mediated by a relationship to a totality situated at a second level. This detour and the sacrifices it requires are the conditions for civic peace in which no party dominates any other—in other words, a just civic peace. The principal objective of the *Social Contract* is to lay a rational foundation for this second-level totality. Rousseau cannot fall back on supernatural transcendence, as Bossuet did in adopting the easy solution of divine will as the ultimate foundation for paternal authority or royal authority, which amount to the same thing. Nor can he wholly identify the totality with statistical summations of empirical subjects who are qualified by their entire array of affiliations and interests; he cannot identify it either, in a dynamic way, with a composite formed by the subjects' entire array of interactions. As we know, the solution—which will later serve as a model for most nineteenth-century social constructs, Durkheim's in particular, so that it also constitutes one of the foundations of sociology as a scientific discipline—consists in establishing the possibility of a natural transcendence by defining two possible states for persons and thus two possible ways of conceiving the whole that is formed by their union. The union of persons qualified according to the first state is a totality of individuals defined by multiple affiliations and interests and thrust into antagonistic relations.

But persons are endowed with the ability to escape this selfish, deficient state and to reach a second state in which they are concerned not with their own interest but with the interest of all; the possibility of establishing a just civil peace depends on the extent to which they implement this ability, which they are free to cultivate or leave dormant. The second-level formation is in fact the one in which the general will is formed. It comprises the same particular human beings as the first-level formation, but they are in another state in which each person leaves his own cares and interests aside and focuses on the common good. As Patrick Riley has shown (1986, 184–89), this way of constructing a totality is largely derived from Jansenist theology.[11] While Rousseau sets aside the theory of predestination, treating it as an unacceptable form of "favoritism," he adopts the Jansenist use of the term "general" to refer not to the entire set of human beings, or to citizens, but to the *state* reached by each person when, shedding his or her singularity and sacrificing all particular interests, he or she comes to know what is good in general, and succeeds in desiring the common good. In this sense, the idea of the general will is not opposed to individualism: each individual can accede to the general state and recognize the general will, which is first manifested in one's inner self when one renounces the dictates of personal will (249). This is the sense in which Rousseau can set up a radical opposition between the "general will" and the "will of everyone": the "will of everyone" is oppressive, because it expresses the opinion of others taken in their "particular" state: the "will of everyone . . . is concerned with private interests, and is the sum of individual wants." In contrast, the general will, which "is concerned only with the common interest," is the will of the same individuals, but taken in their general state, that is to say, as citizens (*SC* 66).[12]

In *The Social Contract*, the general will cannot be reduced to a sum of individual wills. Private individuals do not commit themselves either through a pact of submission to those whom they have chosen as their leaders or through a series of mutual agreements as in Hobbes, but through a "reciprocal commitment between public and private persons" (*SC* 56). Thus, as Robert Derathé observes, the "same men" constitute "the two contracting parties, but they are perceived from different angles: as members of the sovereign and as individuals," so that "it is as if each one were contracting with himself" (1970, 222–26). Maurice Halbwachs uses his understanding of this bilevel configuration to reinterpret Rousseau's construction—without distorting it—in Durkheimian terms. In his commentary on the 1943 edition of the *Social Contract*, published shortly before his death, he writes: "the general will . . . is not a sum of individual wills, [but] a reality of another order without any common measure between them"; however, the body politic "is more than the sum of these units. It is of another nature" (1976, 95). The law is the expression of the will of this disembodied sovereign. It is exempt from the influence of individual interests when it is laid down by men who are capable of distancing themselves from individual cases and rising above their private existence to embrace things in general. According to Rousseau, "the law considers the subjects of the state as a collectivity and actions in the abstract, but never a man as an individual, nor any particular action. Thus the law can rule that privileges will exist, but it cannot bestow them on any person by name; the law can create different classes of citizen, or even define the qualifications for membership of these classes, but it cannot name this man or that man as members" (*SC* 74). As Robert Derathé points out in his edition of *Du Contract Social*, this natural groundwork provided for political laws guarantees individual liberty, which is conceived as an emancipation from personal dependence on others (Rousseau 1964 [1762], 1449).

The political body instituted by the *Contract* owes its stability to the principle of economy that balances the gains and losses involved in any association. The basic pact acts in two different ways on individuals; indeed, its two actions are not only presented as opposites, but they are also connected with one another in an inverse relation through what Rousseau calls "the balance of gains and losses" (*SC* 59), that is, through a sacrifice that is for the benefit of all and that establishes and justifies worth. Man's "entire soul [is] raised so much higher," but at the cost of renouncing the immediate satisfaction of private interests, the abandonment of desires and the body's primal instincts: when "the voice of duty succeeds to physical impulse and right to appetite, . . . man, who had previously thought of nothing but himself, is compelled to act on other principles, and to consult his reason before he attends to his inclinations" (59). Virtue in this way constitutes the balancing principle of the body politic, in that virtue alone can ensure reciprocity in practice, or, to use the language of *The Social Contract*, "mutuality." Citizens do not become worthy through "the distinction of talents" (*FD*, 18) but through virtue, that is, through the zeal with which they sacrifice whatever distinguishes them in relation to other worths, which are qualified as personal. Unlike distinctions of rank, which are marked by titles, or the benefits of distinction that are accrued through fame, that is, through recognition by others, distinctions that are acquired through civic merit are associated with persons to the extent that these persons serve causes that transcend them. Interpersonal relations are meritorious when they occur in settings arranged in such a way as to desingularize them.

Characterized by means of a mathematical analogy as the "sum" of a "large number of small differences" (66), the general will, which may be expressed by a vote, nevertheless requires quite specific conditions to make itself heard: if their general will is to manifest itself through voting, persons must be free from the hierarchical chains and bonds of dependence to which they were formerly subjected; they must be detached from one another, that is, they must be constituted as individuals (Dumont 1986), "without any communication" among themselves (66), so that "each citizen should decide according to his own opinion" (67). During the French Revolution, for example, we know that this principle of independence was applied in very concrete terms in order to deny domestic servants the right to vote: since they were dependent upon their masters, they did not have the autonomy they would have needed to accede to the state in which they could act for the common good. The same principle accounts, at least in part, for the reluctance to include women in the electoral body, since, as daughters, wives, and mothers, they had for many years been viewed as having a sort of natural purpose that was too strongly tied to the domestic polity to allow them to be recognized as having independent judgment. An internal necessity in the logic of this construction brings a suspicion of conspiracy to bear on the universe of personal relations as a whole. All person-to-person relations that are not mediated by a relation to the totality of the body politic infringe on and degrade the expression of the general will, inflecting it toward individuality, and in this way they constitute a plot that must be denounced:

> But when there are intrigues, and partial associations arise at the expense of the greater one, the will of each of these associations becomes general in relation to its members and particular in relation to the state: it can then be said that the number of voters is no longer the same as the number of men, but only the same as the number of associations. The differences become fewer and give a less general result. (66)

In terms of his or her own participation in the body politic, therefore, each individual is a multiple being, a composite person who can exist in different states. The concrete persons one encounters in the ordinary world, where they are identified by the uniqueness and persistence of their bodily frame, are capable of acting in some cases as particular persons, and in other cases as citizens, as we have seen: "For each individual can have, as a man, a personal will that is contrary or dissimilar to the general will that he has as a citizen" (58). But as political beings and members of a polity, people can also exist in a third state, which is that of magistrate, for the polity must be governed. A different form of will is attached to this third state of magistrate or governor, which is open to all citizens in Rousseau's polity. As a legal entity, the "body of the government" has a specific identity and self-awareness, and its members must be united in a common "sensibility" that they need in order to "act in concert": "in order that the body composing the government should have its own existence, a genuine life of its own, making it distinct from the body of the state, in order that all its members may act in concert and fulfill the purpose for which it is established, it needs to possess an individual self, a common sensibility among its members, its own will and force tending to self-conservation" (95).

But this shared "sensibility," based on affinities, is also a malevolent power that can turn magistrates away from the general will of the "body of the state" and induce them to conspire against the common good. Thus each member of the polity possesses "three essentially different wills: first, the will pertaining to the individual, which tends only to his particular advantage; secondly, the will common to the members of the government, which relates solely to the advantage of the ruling body"; and, finally, "the will of the people or the sovereign will." Unlike the "sovereign will," which is "general both as regards the state considered as a whole and as regards the government considered as part of the whole," the "collective will of the magistrates" is "general in respect of the government and particular in respect of the state, the government being a part of the state" (97). The collective will of the members of the government thereby constitutes a "corporate will" that has precisely the same structure as the "associations" defined as "partial associations [that] arise at the expense of the greater one" in such a way that "the will of each of these associations becomes general in relation to its members and particular in relation to the state" (66). The very essence of government therefore entails an ironclad law, described alternately in historical terms or as a biological law that leads toward degeneration: "in the government, each person is primarily himself, then a member of government, and then a citizen—an order of priorities which is the exact contrary of the one demanded by the social order" (97). It follows that "[j]ust as a particular will constantly acts against the general will, so too the government exerts itself continually against the sovereign. . . . This is an inherent and unavoidable defect which, as soon as the body politic is born, tends ceaselessly to its destruction, in the same way as old age and death eventually destroy the human body" (118). The downward tendency to "degenerate" (118) can be abated, but its effects cannot be totally eliminated, because the different types of will are affected by different forces. The force of will is in every body, whether individual or general, and the less general it is, the stronger it is. The need to take this unfortunate law into account is what leads Rousseau to condemn the idea of representation (Furet 1981a, 196).

The capacity to assume three different states, a capacity with which every person is endowed, constitutes the fundamental problem posed by the conclusion of tests of worth during which persons take stock of one another. In the civic polity, persons are more or less worthy depending on whether they are viewed as individuals or as citizen members of the sovereign, that is, depending on whether the will that drives them to act is particular or on the contrary directed toward the general interest. By the same token, if not to the same degree, as in the polity of inspiration, worth is presented in the civic polity first of all in the form of a quality of conscience, a genuineness of the inner being; this quality is objectified only weakly, and it can be feigned, because it is not readily available to the judgment of others through easily identifiable outward signs. Especially when one has to evaluate decisions involving the future that are thus subject to validity tests referring to a distant horizon, as is often the case in politics, how can one know whether those who claim to heed only the general will are not actually slaves of their passions, motivated by their particular desires rather than by virtue? Because persons have the possibility of concealing from others, and sometimes even from themselves, their true designs and the state—particular or general—in which they happen to be when they take action, their association may be nothing more than a deal made with dupes, a strategy by which the cunning secure the cooperation of the virtuous and the naive.

As a consequence, human relations are easily marred by suspicion. For before a person consents to what others ask of him, and especially before he consents to what governing bodies ask of upright citizens, he has to test not so much their acts, in their seeming factualness (for these can have a strategic thrust and be deliberately deceptive), but rather their intentions—in other words, precisely what they are hiding in the depths of consciousness or even in the dark corners of false consciousness. Under such conditions, the pursuit of truth has to rely on circumstantial evidence that is slight enough and involuntary enough to have escaped the strategists' notice. In contrast to the spontaneity and warmth that ought to reign in human relations, this watchful stance is needed to unmask the all-powerful selfish interests that lurk behind fine, altruistic discourse. Such vigilance is justified by the risks incurred by the state owing to the inclination of individuals to establish direct personal bonds in pursuit of partisan interests, rather than agreeing to establish them indirectly by participating in the body politic as a whole. Political action consequently demands not only virtue but also clairvoyance from those who carry it out. These persons must possess the cognitive ability, that is, more precisely, the critical capacity, needed to interpret the signs of selfishness and corruption and to unmask the personal appetites that are hidden under the appearance of virtue: "when in each man's heart the social bond is broken, when the crudest self-interest insolently adorns itself with the sacred name of the public good, then the general will falls silent: the motives of all are kept secret, their votes are no more the votes of citizens than if the state had never existed, and the decrees that are falsely passed, under the name of laws, have private interests as their only aim" (135).

The Social Contract had few readers during Rousseau's lifetime, but the French Revolution gave it a large audience. The "new principles" Rousseau articulated in that text make it possible to retranslate what Michael Walzer calls the "private intrigues with public effects" (1974, 28) that characterized court politics into the logic of conspiracy. But they also have the effect of extending to the entire set of persons encompassed by the political body the duplicity that constitutes the privilege and burden of Princes, treated sometimes as persons, sometimes as embodiments of the State. From this point on, as all persons are endowed with the capacity either for membership in sovereignty or for being only themselves, all may be required to justify, in public, the nature of their intentions and their acts: particular or general, selfish or altruistic.

This is also a way of saying that *The Social Contract* contains an anthropology and even a psychology as much as a politics. The two cannot be dissociated, and we probably have to attribute to the specialization inherent in the separation of university disciplines the division of labor that has tended to occur among Rousseauists between those who analyze his political works and those who study his personal writings. For in the personal texts, and especially in the *Confessions*, the problem of personal dependence occupies the same place it has in *The Social Contract*, although it is given a different treatment. As a response to his revelations of the personal suffering provoked by the impossibility of achieving authentically human relationships under the regime of personal dependence or that of the tyranny of opinion, Rousseau offers a solution constructed at the general level, that is, in the form of the political philosophy set forth in the *Contract*. Thus the conflicts among worths, and in particular the tensions inherent in the preeminence of domestic worth that are addressed in *The Social Contract* with the resources of political philosophy, are found in many passages in the *Confessions*, where they are developed in the language of feeling and emotion.

The difficulty arising from uncertainty over operative worths is most apparent in Rousseau's relation to "Worthies"; for example, in book 10, his relationship with the Maréchal and with Madame de Luxembourg (Berman 1970, 89–102) offers different variants of a typical sequence: humility, temerity, seduction, familiarity, abolition of distance, suspicion, unmasking, denunciation. Rousseau's convoluted compliments betray the complexity of an emotion that owes its ambivalence to the conflict of worths in which it is inscribed: "Ah, Marshal, before I knew you I used to hate the great, and I hate them still more now that you have shown me how easy it would be for them to make themselves adored" (*CF*, 488). The tension between the inspired worth of genius, the worth of fame to which the celebrated author may lay claim (although, being a genius, he is not unaware of its artificial character), and the worth bound up with rank is temporarily relaxed by the institution of an arrangement designed to bring the authenticity of inspired relations to the fore: communion in the love of beauty and the individualization of an unparalleled relationship (in the mode of a love affair) suspend disagreement about the relative worth of the famous writer and his noble, wealthy patron.

In the inspired relationship as it is described in the *Confessions*, each party rises above the attributes that belong to him or her in this world, casting them off into contingency. Two human beings then remain face to face, two people *in general*, in the sense defined above in which divine grace is directed to human beings detached from their earthly particularities, people coming to know one another in their most singular and most general aspects alike. Let us consider, for example, the Prince de Conti's visit to Montmorency: "I was the only person there who treated him as a man, and I have every reason to believe that he was truly grateful to me for it" (*CF*, 501). De Conti, who is a prince, pays tribute to Rousseau's talent—the writer having neither title nor fortune—and to his fame by paying him a visit in his "very small" apartment. Nevertheless, it is the prince who pays the visit, and Rousseau, as is his habit, introduces some play into the relations of equivalency. He honors the man who honors him with his presence by treating de Conti as though he had no claim to honor: he denies him his established honors as a way of honoring even more highly his natural worth. Then they test each other's skill at chess. Rousseau wins and, applying the same schema, he renders the prince the honors due him, addressing him by his title while retreating behind the outcome of a test to which they have both submitted and which is indifferent to their rank: "I honor your most Serene Highness too deeply not to beat you on all occasions at chess" (501). But, in the absence of a civic worth solidly rooted in state institutions, the goodwill of persons, their virtue, their mutual confidence, and their love for one another are not enough to take them beyond the relations of subjection inherent in forms of personal dependence, forms that invariably reappear and take over.

As Rousseau saw it, the civic polity existed in his day only in the form of a theoretical possibility, not as a concrete achievement, since the Republic of Letters, the ideal city founded on reason, is in reality nothing but a conspiracy of cunning minds. And outside the civic polity, dependence is unavoidable. It overwhelms all other forms of equivalence and measure, even if they emerge from an arrangement of justice that is indifferent to rank, such as a game of chess. A person who acts in particular as your benefactor is your enemy inasmuch as he is an enemy of the human race (Berman

1970, 96). With Rousseau, the sequence is virtually identical every time: through her marks of affection, one of the Worthies (a grande dame) encourages familiarity and even secrets. But effusiveness is met with politeness. One gives himself over while the other remains reserved; one abandons all caution while the other keeps up her guard. Injustice is presented initially in the form of a betrayal of one person's self-abandonment by the partner's self-restraint, for the latter keeps her distance while encouraging intimacy in a commerce that seemingly takes place between equals. Hierarchical dependence is thus doubled by an emotional, one-sided dependence:

> I have never been capable of moderation in my relationships, or of simply fulfilling the duties of society. It has always been all or nothing with me. Soon it was all; and finding myself made much of and spoilt by people of their importance, I overstepped the limits and conceived a friendship for them, of a kind only permissible between equals. I expressed it by complete familiarity of manners, while they continued to treat me with the courtesy and politeness to which I had grown accustomed. (483–84)

Under its troubled appearance of civic equality or inspired communion, which have yet to be completely disengaged from one another, lies the truth of a domestic relation. Relationships with the worthy are always those of servants to masters. To take just one more example, Rousseau's relationship with Madame de Vercellis is not genuine (for a detailed analysis, see Berman 1970, 102–4), because it rests on an injustice in communication which is one of the emotionally painful features of domestic subordination:

> I remember very well, however, that she showed some curiosity to know my story. She sometimes asked me questions, and was pleased when I showed her the letters I wrote to Mme de Warens or gave her an account of my feelings. But she certainly did not go the right way about winning my confidence, for she never confided in me. My heart loved to expand, provided there was another heart to listen. . . . In short, it is a bad way of reading another man's heart to conceal one's own. (84)

The achievement of a civic polity, whose theoretical possibility is demonstrated in the *Social Contract*, must offer persons a resource that allows them to bring to a halt the miserable tug of war between inspired worth, domestic worth, and the worth of fame, and it must provide them with solid ground on which they can overcome the uneasy uncertainty about worth and identity that is conveyed in so many pages of the *Confessions*. The civic polity must do for humanity taken as whole, as a body politic, what love never, or only rarely, allows persons to achieve in the order of individual relations.

The Industrial Polity

In civic worth, the relation of worth between the sovereign state of being and the particular state, between the general will and the splintering of the body politic into a multitude of particular wills, is present in each individual, since each one may be in either the particular or the general state. If Rousseau actually inaugurates the era of suspicion (or at least a secularized and politicized form of suspicion), the space of unmasking remains internal to the individual himself, the individual who may be authentic or inauthentic and who may disguise selfish motives in the discourse of the general interest. In the arrangement presented by Rousseau, the localization of the particular and the general within the selfsame individuals is what limits the scope of the organicist representation of the body politic. In market worth, the identification of external goods requires detachment in relation to others and to oneself if those objects are to serve as underpinnings for transactions. Sympathy toward others and the position of impartial spectator share equally in this tension between an intimate passion and a distance that is necessary for coordination.

For Saint-Simon, the space of unmasking is entirely detached from the individual: the task is no longer to explore hearts and souls but to penetrate reality and interrogate society. As Pierre Ansart shows, it is Saint-Simon who establishes the opposition between "the real and the not-real, the fundamental and the apparent . . . between a level of reality, of causal determinations, and a level of what is secondary or inessential" (1969, 2). This opposition makes possible the politics of unmasking that are based on "empirical observation and positive science," as these will be developed by Marx[13] and also, from a different perspective, by Durkheim.

Saint-Simon spells out the construction of an industrial polity through the intermediary of a permanent—though often implicit—critique of Rousseau; this takes the form of a questioning of "metaphysicians and jurists," who are sometimes called "intellectuals" and who are always contrasted with "industrialists and scholars" (1869, 1:189). In *Du système industriel*,[14] the author castigates "phrase-makers": the latter may well have been the first to expose the "vices of feudalism" and to form, "against the nobility and the clergy, a rampart in the shelter of which industrialists, along with scholars given to the study of the sciences of observation, were able to work in safety," but they themselves developed only a "half-science," a "bastardized and convoluted doctrine"; the "theory of the rights of man" is nothing but "an application of high metaphysics to high jurisprudence" (1:37, 62, 83, 2:92).

Authentic social science, the results of which do not depend "in any measure on our will, or our habits, or our beliefs," is thus contrasted with the half-sciences we know as metaphysics and law, as when Saint-Simon refers to the "passage from the conjectural to the positive, from the metaphysical to the physical" (1:6, 137). As Henri Gouhier (1970) reminds us, this opposition, later developed in the form of the law of the three estates in Auguste Comte's philosophy of history, had already been given systematic expression in Turgot's writings. In his *Plan du second discours sur le progrès de l'esprit humain*, he sketched out the evolution of the human mind from the state in which "everything that happened" had "its god" to the state in which events are explained by the "mechanical action of bodies," passing through the state preceding "real enlightenment about natural history" in which philosophers multiplied the "capacities to account for every effect" (13). However, Saint-Simon proposes an elaboration of the positive that benefits from work done in anatomy (by Vicq-d'Azir) and in physiology (by Cabanis and Bichat) to found a "social psychology" of "organized bodies," and to make up for the deficiencies of the eighteenth-century philosophers. In his "Introduction aux travaux scientifiques du XIXᵉ siècle," he expresses dismay that "Condillac and Condorcet [did not] study either anatomy or physiology. Their ignorance about these essential aspects of the physics of organized bodies was the cause of the critical errors that they both committed" (1965 [1808], 49). His first sociological project is justified in *Lettres d'un habitant de Genève à ses contemporains* in the following terms: "My friends, we are organized bodies; it was by considering our social relations as physiological phenomena that I conceived the project I am presenting to you" (45).

Some ten years later, in *De la physiologie sociale*, he proposes a description of society in terms of an "organized machine" whose parts are "organs" that fulfill different "functions." Organs and functions are opposed to a definition of society based on the "arbitrariness of individual wills," and they play a role in the constitution of a "true being whose existence is more or less robust or shaky depending on whether his organs carry out more or less regularly the functions assigned to them" (57). Like other living organisms, society can be treated for pathologies, and the new science of society is also therapeutic: "Political economy, legislation, public morality, and everything that constitutes the administration of the general interests of society are only a collection of *rules of hygiene*" (57). The guarantee of a "solid and durable constitution," understood as the healthy constitution of a living being, is found in "the natural progression of things" (*Syst.*, 1:68). The industrial polity is thus established in the objectivity of things that are formed naturally: "One does not create a system of social organization, one perceives the new linkage of ideas and interests that has been formed, and one points it out, that is all. A social system is a fact, or it is nothing" (*Org.*, 179–180).

This is the position that leads Durkheim to see Saint-Simon as the inventor of "social psychology" and thus as Comte's predecessor in the history of sociology. In "Sociology," first published in *La Science française* in 1915, Durkheim said that Saint-Simon was "the first to declare that human societies are surely realities in their own right, different from those found in the rest of nature but subject to the same determinism. Social organisms, therefore, ought to be the object of a science comparable to that which deals with individual organisms: and for this reason, he suggested that this science be called Social Physiology. . . . In one sense, all the fundamental ideas of Comtean psychology can be found in Saint-Simon; Comte took them from his master" (Durkheim 1960b, 377).

In *L'industrie* (1869 [1817], vols. 2–4, cited here as *Ind.*, 3 vols.), Saint-Simon identifies the origin of morality with that of society, and enjoins his readers to move on from heavenly to earthly morality (*Ind.*, 2:32, 37). Morality is conceived as a system of functional rules ensuring harmonious relations among two types of beings, individuals and society, "so that both will be as happy as possible" (30). Political laws are opposed to the real forces of society as form is opposed to substance, and "jurists and metaphysicians are apt to mistake form for substance, and words for things" (*Syst.*, 1:13). The question of property, for example, refers directly to the regime of production, and property ought to be "constituted in such a way that the possessor has an incentive to make it as productive as possible" (*Ind.*, 2:43). It is the "substance" that is concealed by "quibbling" over "the division of powers" and over "the form of government": "There is no doubt that the parliamentary form of government is highly preferable to all others; but it is only a *form*, and the constitution of property is the *substance*; thus it is this Constitution that really serves as the basis for the social edifice" (2:83). From here on there is no more need to "seek the goal toward which society ought to be directed"; jurists will have to get busy "quite simply making the laws that can best ensure the prosperity of agriculture, trade, and manufacturing" (*Syst.*, 1:145). As an extension of morality, politics manages the powers at work in society: "the government" is "society's chargé d'affaires," protecting "workers against the non-productive action of the idle" (*Ind.*, 2:36). "Affairs of state" have to be treated "in absolutely the same way as the private interest of an individual" and "a national association" has to be "viewed as an industrial enterprise whose aim is to procure for every member of society, in proportion to his stake, the greatest comfort and well-being possible. One can only admire the wisdom that the learned economists have brought to bear in this work" (2:153). "The business of government is idleness," the struggle against "parasites," "do-nothings," and "thieves," which means that it must be strictly limited to the management of work and production; "as soon as its action goes further, it becomes arbitrary, usurping, and thus tyrannical and inimical to industry" (*Ind.*, vol. 1; 1965 [1808], 72).

While for Rousseau the term "utility" meant conformity to the interests of the State and was thereby synonymous with virtue, without any special reference to work or to the production of material goods, in the industrial polity the term is associated with the satisfaction of needs, and on this basis it constitutes the higher common principle. Whereas Rousseau, in his *Discourse on the Sciences and Arts*, deplores the "preference given to pleasing talents rather than useful ones" (19) and blames a society in which "we have Physicists, Geometers, Chemists, Astronomers, Poets, Musicians, Painters; [but in which] we no longer have citizens" (19), Saint-Simon, in *Du système industriel*, proclaims that the "only true organs of common sense or common interest are industrialists," along with "physicians, chemists, and physiologists who are part of the same body" (*Syst.*, 1:63, 46). He rails against the fact that they are "reduced to a subordinate position by princes and other governments" (*Org.*, 1869, 24) and supplanted by "jurists and metaphysicians," "phrase-makers" more preoccupied with "principles than with facts" (*Syst.*, 1:35–37). It is not principles but "the force of things" that compels "farmers, traders, and manufacturers to band together in combining the general interest with the calculations pertaining to their particular interests" (63). These subjects, who are "superior in terms of acquired intelligence" and who have done "the best in administrative studies," cannot "organize themselves in their own interest" without serving "the interest of the majority," for, "in the present state of civilization, the primary political ability is administrative ability" (46–48).

The worth of people, in this polity as in others, corresponds to the generality of their state. The lowly man is "the least well-endowed with intelligence, a man whose ideas do not extend beyond domestic matters" (*Ind.*, vol. 1; 1965 [1808], 73). The worthy "work to discover and coordinate the general facts apt to serve as a basis for all combinations of agriculture, trade, and manufacturing" (*Syst.*, 1:46). "The work undertaken by industrialists has differing degrees of generality, and this basic disposition produces a sort of hierarchy among the various classes that make up the enormous mass of citizens who are active in production." Farmers and craftsmen are "bound together by the merchant class"; this latter has bankers as its "common agents," so that bankers have to be viewed as "the general agents of industry" (36–47).

The government, like any system for managing goods, can be the object of a calculation of costs, and "in the current state of enlightenment, what the nation needs is not to be governed, but to have the best possible market administered for it" (*Syst.*, 1:151). Saint-Simon also assesses the cost of the "three or four hundred thousand jurists, apprentice jurists, or servants of jurists, that there are in France, [who] are all men who produce nothing, and are consequently a burden to industry, which feeds them, houses them, clothes them for nothing" (*Ind.*, 2:115–16).

The fundamental law of the State is, in the industrial polity, the rule governing the budget, for "money is to the body politic what blood is to the human body. . . . Thus the law of finance is the general law; it is the law from which all others derive or ought to derive" (*Ind.*, 2:93). Among the "measures to be taken to end the revolution," Saint-Simon proposes that a council be created to vote on the budget, a "council of industrialists that will be given the name 'chamber of industry,' [a council] made up, first, of the four farmers who cultivate the most land; of the two merchants who do the most business; of the two manufacturers who employ the largest number of workers; and of the four bankers who have the most credit" (*Syst.*, 1:107). In *L'organisateur*, Saint-Simon proposes that a "Chamber of Invention" be convoked, with the following composition: "The first section will be made up of two hundred civil engineers; the second of fifty poets or other literary inventors; the third, of twenty-five painters, fifteen sculptors or architects, and ten musicians" (51). This chamber will present "a project for public works to be undertaken in order to increase France's wealth and to improve the lot of its inhabitants, in terms of usefulness and pleasure of all sorts; next, every year, it will give its opinion about the additions to be made to its original plan and about the improvements it thinks appropriate" (51). The industrialists "are the only ones capable of dividing national respect and rewards among the members of society in the appropriate way, so that justice will be done in every case according to merit" (*Syst.*, 1:133); for "France has become a great factory, and the French nation a great workshop. This general factory has to be managed in the same way as private factories" (3:91).

In attributing responsibilities to these chambers, Saint-Simon also specifically provides for attention to the expression of the higher common principle, thanks to the creation of museums and public festivals. Plots of land will be

> chosen from among the most picturesque sites [to hold] a museum of natural products, as well as industrial products from the nearby regions; they will also include residences for artists who want to live there, and a certain number of musicians will always be supported, for the purpose of inspiring the inhabitants of the *canton* with the passion whose circumstances will require development for the greater good of the nation. French soil in its entirety must become a superb English-style park, embellished by everything that the fine arts can add to the beauties of nature. (*Org.*, 52)

"Festivals of Hope" will be ceremonies celebrating the glory of the projects of planned investments: "orators will set forth before the people the work projects that Parliament has approved, and they will stimulate the citizens to work with passion, by making them feel how much better their lot will be after they have brought these projects to completion" (53).

The judges of industrial worth are the experts; politics is the "science of production" and must take a stand against the "dominant ideas" and "opin-ion" (in Saint-Simon, *Lettre à un Américain*: 1965 [1808], 78–79). The rep-resentative assembly of industrialists establishes the standards of worth in a system in which justice rests entirely on the distribution of rewards be-tween "producers" and "consumers." This jurisdiction stems from the "positive scientific capability" that is the prerogative of scholars. Saint-Simon, rising up against the thesis of an "innate political science" (that is, implicitly, against Rousseauist influence), observes that "when politics has been elevated to the level of the sciences of observation, something that will surely happen before long, the conditions of capacity will become clear and definite, and political culture will be exclusively entrusted to a special class of scholars that will "reduce chattering to silence" (*Syst.*, 1:17).

The sarcasm that Saint-Simon directed at belief in the innate character of political science and in the universality of the capacity to govern could be compared to the critique Sieyès addressed to "the raw democracy so named by analogy with the materials that nature offers everywhere to man but that man has everywhere devoted his industry to modifying." Sieyès in fact counters Saint-Simon with a political representation that is not unre-lated to a division of labor, given that "the distinctive feature of human be-ings in the social state is to express themselves reciprocally, as certain mathematical values express other values, by virtue of a sort of general plan that presides over collective life" (Bastid 1970 [1939], 369–70).

The order of political capacities outlines a hierarchy of states of worth defined by unequal degrees of social utility, a hierarchy that makes it pos-sible to contrast "nobles, clergy, jurors, and idle owners" with "manufac-turers, farmers, merchants, scholars," and "positive intellectuals" (*Syst.*, 1: 140–41, 190).

PART THREE

THE COMMON WORLDS

Five

JUDGMENT PUT TO THE TEST

Situated Judgment

AMONG THE ELEMENTS that produce justification, we began by isolating all those pertaining to evaluation of the persons involved, since the imperative to justify requires that each person be assigned a legitimate qualification. Along the way, we encountered the long-standing preoccupation of political philosophy with establishing equivalency classes and an order applicable to the members of a society. We examined a category of political constructions of legitimate orders that people use to assess one another in everyday acts. The fact that people may choose among a number of different ways of establishing equivalence raises questions (which we shall address directly in later chapters) about how these approaches are interrelated, and how people deal with such complexity. We have already suggested, however, that the order of each polity makes it possible to reduce complexity by reducing forms of generality characteristic of other polities to instances of particularity.

Our decision to focus first of all on the assessment of persons, and on the possibility of constituting an order of states among which persons may be distributed, corresponds to the tradition out of which we are working. Extending from political philosophy to the social sciences, this tradition bears traces of its break with earlier cosmologies that still included a physics and a world of ordered objects. Nevertheless, our decision has to some extent skewed our subject as we would like to constitute it now, by suggesting that a general order, a more or less secularized theological order, is imposed on everyone and governs people's actions, which thus turn out to be harmoniously coordinated. In part 3, we introduce a considerable modification in our trajectory. We shall focus on the ways in which judgment and justifications are tested, in trials that bring into play the objects that are involved with persons in the situations being judged.

Political philosophies remain at the level of principles; they tell us nothing about the conditions under which an actual agreement is reached. As we have already seen, the polity model is based on differentiation among states of worth, and it makes the legitimacy of these states manifest; it sheds no light on the ways in which states of worth are attributed to particular persons. The question of how states of worth are assessed is thus what will concern us here. After studying the constraints under which principles of justice are established, we propose to examine the conditions under which they are applied. How does one move from legitimate argumentation to the actions on which the social sciences focus, actions that are coordinated in actual practice? How can one account for the way the principles of justice are put into practice in particular circumstances? Making this shift entails a presupposition that the scope of the classic manuals of good conduct can be extended to include the implementation of aesthetic and technical principles along with those ordinarily qualified as moral. Is this move condemned to fail, as is suggested by a tradition of thought that sets up an opposition between justification—in the sense of formal argumentation detached from the constraints of action (an approach that rationalizes action a posteriori)—and the irreducibility of the circumstances of that action?

Emile Durkheim, for example, contrasts the "metaphysical and idealist abstraction" of economic theory with circumstances, reality, or nature, the sociological laws of which have to be established: "This man in general, this systematic egoist of which [economic theory] speaks is nothing but an abstraction. Real man, whom we know and who we are, is complex in a different way: for he belongs to a specific time and place" (1970 [1888], 85). Durkheim clearly uses "circumstances" to establish real laws and to denounce the abstract figures constructed by economics, in a move that we examined in chapter 1 and that is expressed in symmetrical terms in economic theory. The fact remains that the emergence of "practice" in the explanatory discourse of the social sciences reconfigures the place formerly occupied by "prudence," and it often only encourages social scientists to give up analysis in favor of concentrating on circumstances. In response to these objections, we shall try to dismantle the foregoing opposition and to develop a theory of agreement and disagreement that does not merely entail an encounter between arguments and principles; we shall attempt to present a theory that accounts for the confrontation with circumstances, with a specific reality, that is, a theory that accounts for the involvement of human beings and objects in a given action.

We shall thus set aside instances that teeter on the brink of chaos owing to the accumulation of disagreements, as well as those that produce an informal or private arrangement. The concession that is made in a private arrangement consists precisely in avoiding recourse to a principle of justice: people come to terms among themselves—that is, locally—to bring a disagreement over worth to an end without exhausting the issue, without really resolving the quarrel. Ruling out private arrangements, then, we shall concentrate instead on cases in which the quest for agreement leads the persons involved to rise above the contingencies while taking the circumstances into account, and leads them to make the relevance of the beings involved apparent in relation to a single general principle of equivalence. The question of what is just, the question of the justice or justness of the situation, can then be raised. It becomes possible to justify certain associations, while others can be deemed unjustifiable.

Let us picture, for example, a group of young people fooling around in a bar. They are throwing chunks of bread at one another; they are just having fun, and nothing that matters is involved in the circumstances. But now let us suppose that an old man speaks up and reminds them that bread is not a toy, and that, in this very city, during the war, people went hungry. The old man, who has kept quiet behind his newspaper up to this point, involves himself by intervening in a situation that can be judged in terms of whether or not it is equitable. He states what matters.

The move by means of which someone rises above the circumstances, by recognizing what matters and who or what will have to be involved in the action, is illustrated in Carl von Clausewitz's analysis of warfare. Starting from the tension between "absolute war" and "real war," between the philosophical principle of war and the chaos of the battlefield, a place of contingency and uncertainty, Clausewitz sets out to deal methodically with testing by fire, with *engagement*, which is the mode in which war is actually experienced (1984 [1832], 579). He seeks to show the internal logic behind the "art" of choosing one's objective in the heat of combat, "the faculty of using judgment to detect the most important and decisive elements in the vast array of facts and situations" (585). Developing a manual of battlefield behavior requires a thorough examination of the circumstances, and Clausewitz devotes much of his work to this undertaking. The principle of "victory or defeat" establishes, above and beyond the circumstances, an equivalence that allows for assessment and reduces "uncertainty about the proper scale to use" (586). Clausewitz's approach thus consists not in considering all possible circumstances in their contingent singularity, which would be an endless task, but in specifying the possible circumstances by involving them in a test of engagement that qualifies and integrates them. For instance, the relevance of a large rock is determined by its capacity to offer shelter or support, in the same way that Sartre's rock "appears [to him] in the light of a projected scaling" (1956, 488). However, unlike Clausewitz, Sartre refuses to draw upon any principle of justification that would make it possible to qualify beings. For him, the naturalness of a situation is entirely the product of a particular gaze; a different gaze would abolish it in favor of a different nature. Thus Sartre defines the situation through the relation between "my" project, which constitutes the rock as having to be climbed, and the way in which that "brute being" lends itself to climbing, whereas, for a different gaze and a different project, the rock would be subject to judgment solely in terms of whether it is beautiful or not.

The Polity Extended to a Common World

Recourse to reality has its place in an extension of the framework we have begun to develop. The *qualification* of persons according to worth cannot be taken for granted, since a state of worth cannot be attributed definitively on the basis of personal characteristics, by virtue of the requirement of common dignity (a3), which forbids the permanent attachment of a state to a person. The basic property of the polity model, which is to ensure that all members of the polity have an equal capacity to accede to all states, introduces an uncertainty that weighs upon the assessment of worths, thus making this assessment the point of contestation whenever a dispute occurs within a polity. The assignment of a specific state can always be called back into question, and bringing a polity into being depends on *tests of worth* that make it possible to attribute these states to beings.

The attribution of a state—which presupposes a general equivalence—to a particular person is an operation subjected to the paradox of encoding. A code or category is a form of equivalence that by definition transcends the particularities of a given being. How, then, can we relate forms to particularities, an act that the very operation of encoding presupposes? If we declare that we are encoding on the basis of one or more criteria, as formal presentations of classifications invite us to do, the question is still not resolved; rather, it shifts focus and bears upon the way the criteria themselves result from a previous encoding. Thus the proof of a person's worth cannot be based simply on some intrinsic property, for this would presuppose that a prior form of equivalence rooted in that property had already been established. The proof must be based on objects that are external to persons, objects that will serve in some sense as instruments or devices for determining worth. As with the establishment of proof in a legal context, what is telling is the coherence of an arrangement comprising beings that hold together, and a test requires that the things brought to bear must be relevant, must be qualified to serve as conclusive evidence. The reference to *qualified* things thus leads to an extension of the framework of coherence by which *polities* unfold in *common worlds*. In order for persons to reach agreement (and we have shown how agreement reaching is supported by qualification of persons in terms of states of worth), the quality of things must have been determined in a way that is consistent with the principles of worth invoked. The various metaphysics of worth now bring us to the point where we need to examine the conditions under which assemblages including both persons and things can be coherent. The question of agreement reaching thus leads from justice to adjustment.

The coherence on which judgment rests does not lie in language alone. Relevance is not simply a matter of stylistic figures, as a reductive grasp of rhetoric would have it. Thus two equally committed persons may confront one another with the following contradictory arguments: "This must be right because I am convinced of it," and "It seems to me that this is not proper." Neither an examination of the argumentation nor close scrutiny of its immediate context will allow us to understand oppositions in judgments as thoroughgoing as this one; hence we may be tempted to conclude that arbitrariness is at work here, that the conflicting viewpoints are wholly subjective. But in fact the convictions of each party are unshakable because each of the two utterances can find support for its proof in a different *world*: the first is based on the world of inspiration, in which conviction arises from the inner soul, while the second is grounded in the domestic world in which personal judgment takes second place to good manners.

If disputes are to be resolved, if uncertainty about states of worth is to be removed, and if these states are to be made demonstrable, the polity model has to be extended to beings that are not persons. Persons and things offer one another mutual support. When they hold together, they prove that agreements concluded among persons entail a type of justice that is in conformity with a type of justness or fitness characterizing harmony or "agreement" among things. With the help of *objects*, which we shall define by their belonging to a specific world, people can succeed in establishing states of worth. A test of worth cannot be reduced to a theoretical debate. It engages persons, in their bodily existence, in a world of things that serve as evidence, and in the absence of which the dispute does not have the material means for resolution by testing.

Principles held in common do not merely orient argumentation or action the way "value systems" do (in the sense, for example, in which Raymond Aron, discussing Max Weber, speaks of "value-reference" orientation [1998, 249]). More crucially, principles held in common are grounded in different common worlds. Something that belongs to and exists in one common world may be unknown in a different world. The world of inspiration, for example, is inhabited by demons and monsters, while the domestic world includes household pets, which go unrecognized in the civic world along with children and old people, and so on. Objects that constitute tools for making the worth of persons manifest in one world may not be taken into account at all in a different world.

The involvement of objects requires human beings to rise to the occasion, to objectify themselves by bringing objects into play and *valorizing* them, that is, endowing them with value. The use of valorized objects allows people to compare the singular situation in which they find themselves with other situations; recourse to the higher common principle can be achieved by means of tools. Objects substantiate worth, but at the same time they impose constraints on tests by calling for valorization. If someone evokes an object lacking valorization, someone else may well say: "He has it, but he doesn't know what to do with it." A test does not depend on the viewpoint of an individual, nor is it a ritual or a ceremony that could be properly called symbolic on the grounds that it depends on objects or relationships that are deviant or artificial. The mutual substantiation that these simultaneously present beings provide one another is what consolidates a given reality and provides proof. This accomplishment is especially evident at points where a single world unfolds in its greatest purity, because any beings on which reference to other worlds might rely have been shunted aside. Thus it is possible to set up self-evident situations whose plenitude depends on the fact that, in them, each being turns out to be in its proper place.

Objectivity presupposes that verifiable connections and acceptable forms of evidence have been defined in relation to a particular world and to the tools for establishing worth that are attached to it. Each of the various ways of determining worth corresponds to a way of constructing a reality test. Depending on the world under consideration, one can conduct a test by referring to the testimony of a worthy person whose judgment is beyond question, or by displaying the degree of credibility one has in the eyes of the greatest number, or by invoking the general will, or by paying the established price, or by relying on the competence of experts. The various forms of knowledge are adapted to the various procedures for evaluating worth. Whereas industrial worth is attested by assessment, domestic worth calls for reasoning by way of anecdotes in which a certain level of generality is always embodied, just as the person of the king is always concretely present in the king's body and has a more general existence beyond the bodily level at the same time (Turner 1967). To evaluate domestic worth, one does not refer to codes and criteria, as one would in the industrial world, but rather to the great feats of the worthy, to the lives of the famous. Moving from what is close at hand to what is farther away, one gradually assimilates the proximities that express personal relations and that are achieved in a domestic space made up of houses, properties, and neighborhoods. These forms of identification create borderless associations organized around a core, like the archetypal forms of characterization observed by cognitive psychologists (Rosch and Lloyd 1978).

Worth is the way in which one expresses, embodies, understands, or represents other people (according to modalities that depend on the world under consideration). Worth is thus associated with a capacity for expression in general terms. The relation between people's worth and their mastery of general forms is posited in each world, especially people's ability to formulate utterances that are said to be general, authentic, true, and so on. As Bossuet put it, "the great have great thoughts," that is, the worthy have worthy thoughts, and only the truly worthy manifest to the fullest this cognitive capacity for generalization. Transgressing this principle leads to behaviors deemed abnormal, as for example when a mere miller tries to discuss theology (Ginzburg 1980).

We should like to emphasize that, except as it relates to our interest in justification, the question of the existence of things in the universe is not our concern. We shall consider the ontological problem of the existence of beings and the modalities of their presence in the world only to the extent that these beings may be said to be *engaged* by the *justifiable acts* in which persons are implicated. It is from this standpoint that we shall envisage their coherence, in worlds that determine both natural beings and relations of natural engagement among those beings, worlds that are used for judgments of worth. These worlds cannot be described without reference to the reports people make about them. Still, the worlds are not impossible to pin down; they do not run together in the sort of cacophony produced when a variety of subjective viewpoints are brought to bear. Our aim is to bring to light the constraints that prevent such relativism when they are applied to the descriptions inscribed within the framework of a given world, and to relate these constraints to the ones that apply to the qualification of persons within the framework of a given polity.

Tests

The absence of an attachment of states of worth to persons is thus a favorable condition for what we shall call a *contention*, that is, a disagreement over the worths of persons, and thus over the equitability of the way worths have been distributed in the situation at hand. Challenges to this distribution take the form of tests that bear upon the factual nature of the elements that have been invoked to establish worths. A situation that holds together, a stable situation in which beings from the same world are arrayed in natural relations compatible with their states of worth, naturally demonstrates its own justness. The relative worth of the beings involved in such a situation has a self-evident character. Thus it would be preferable, if our language made the word available to us, to speak of "monstration" to bring out the active character of the situation that obtains, and to reserve the term "de-monstration" to signify the reaction that leads to debate and that presupposes the targeting of an interlocutor who has to be convinced. A contention will thus originate in a challenge to the view according to which the prevailing situation is well ordered, and in a demand for a readjustment of worths. For example, a situation is not harmonious if in that situation the way a qualified operator works is not adapted to the capacities of his machine. Such a situation calls for a readjustment of the arrangement.

Let us note that this contention over states of worth has to be distinguished from a more fundamental disagreement over the nature of the beings that matter, a *clash* between orders of worth, which we shall study later on. The fact that beings matter must not be confused with their state of worth. In a worth whose states are distinguished according to a finely graduated hierarchy, it is easy to see how someone can matter without being worthy. In a domestic situation, for instance, the least worthy matter just as the most worthy do (consider the case of valets and masters in domestic subordination: cf. Tocqueville 1988 [1835], 177–85), whereas neither a *public collectivity* (the civic world) nor a *technician* (the industrial world) has any status—neither matters—in the domestic context. But the worth of beings and the degree to which they matter still cannot be completely dissociated, and we shall see that the less worthy the beings, the less their engagement in a given situation is assured. The least worthy, remote from the common good, are less implicated than the most worthy in the nature of the situation; they can more readily detach themselves and slip into a different world. As we have seen, the degree of importance of what is sacrificed governs a being's installation in another world, where beings find themselves established all the more surely to the extent that they are more clearly justified by the sacrifice of self-satisfaction.

An initial challenge to a situation comes when disharmonies between the worths of the persons and objects involved are made manifest and translated into terms of *deficiency*. The scene of contention is then developed around the exposure of a lack of worth, and thus of some injustice or lack of justness in an array. This lack gives rise to discord that may take the form of a breakdown or a rejection in the industrial world, a quarrel in the domestic world, or a social conflict in the civic world. Objects may fail, and may not occupy the place that is incumbent upon them in the situation. People fail when they cannot rise to the occasion, when they do not attribute the appropriate degree of worth to objects and thus do not carry out the sacrifice presupposed by their own apparent state of worthiness: examples include the mother who can no longer face her children's demands and who breaks down in tears during dinner, the worker who gets out of synch, the professor who cannot figure out what to say in the middle of a class, and so on. In the second example, the deficiency, when it is attributed to a machine operator, casts doubt upon his worth—in this instance, on his industrial qualification, which is thereby modified—and he will have to be trained or replaced by a more competent operator.

But deficiency may also be imputed to the machine, which may turn out not to meet all the specifications set forth in the contract or instruction manual, and which thus needs to be improved or modified. In fact, in the course of a test, the observation of some disorder or inconsistency in the configuration of the beings involved will generally produce a challenge to the objects: not only can their worth be questioned, but also their status as objects, and indeed, they may lose this "objectivity" by collapsing into the noisy confusion of chaos. The test will thus include a second argumentative move that resembles a scientific controversy, except that it may take place in any of the worlds under consideration and it may have a quite different form in each one. The controversy at issue here has to do with distinguishing between facts that can legitimately be invoked in a proof, on the one hand, and contingent circumstances, which are irrelevant, on the other. In the example we have been considering, the controversy will focus on the contingencies that might have circumstantially disturbed the test and interfered with the efficiency of the operator (illness) or the machine (malfunction). When a controversy arises, it leads to a decision: either the beings who have been found deficient are diminished in worth by the observation of their deficiency and have to be excluded from the situation or else the observation that they are deficient is deemed inconclusive and they are given another chance to prove themselves.

A third move in the line of argument may involve a challenge to the claim that the contingencies invoked are purely accidental, and new objects may be drawn from the circumstances in an attempt to reduce the contingent character of the situation. This move leads to a test that absorbs and integrates the contingency. The disorder of the circumstances is overcome by a test that is purer than the defective situation. An accident becomes a deficiency. From one natural engagement to another, the distribution of beings among states of worth can be modified, but always in conformity with the same principle; traces of the other natures are reduced to the noise of the contingent circumstances.

It is important to note that no situation, however pure, can permanently eliminate the diversity of the contingencies whose static is maintained around the edges of what is in order. The persistence of this commotion brings uncertainty to bear on worths. The situation always threatens to get out of hand and to lead the parties involved to conduct another test, the way throwing the dice or drawing a card can start a game up again. In the absence of external noise, a final judgment would prevail, justifying a harmonious distribution of the states that no new element would call into question. Thus the noise of the world, although it can be temporarily silenced by a test, is what moves the world. Owing to this commotion, each of the worlds in which the polity model is realized, each particular world that, taken in itself, is characterized by completeness and self-sufficiency, bears traces of the possibility of other worlds. A universe reduced to a common world would be a universe of definite worths in which a test, always conclusive (and thus finally useless), could absorb the commotion and silence it. Such an Eden-like universe in which "nothing ever happens by chance" is maintained by a kind of sorcery that exhausts all the contingencies. Victims of paranoia seek to reconstitute such a universe against all odds, by multiplying and reshuffling associations without taking into account the particular worlds in which the associations are relevant. Their efforts bring to light, a contrario, the relation between contingencies and the plurality of common worlds. The breach in paradise that allows commotion to come rushing in is the temptation of the particular and the resultant fall that opens up the possibility of a universe containing a multiplicity of common worlds. In part 4, we shall show how the operation of denunciation, by relying on the deficient beings situated in close proximity to the contingent, leads to the valorization of a worth from a different world.

Our description of the extension of a polity to a world does not result, then, from a conventional choice in the order in which we expose the elements of our analytical framework. It corresponds rather to the movement of creation through which the repertory of objects belonging to a world is gradually extended as tests are conducted. This continuous creation is not simply an effect of the presence of an observer. Even in the inspired world, where objects are not very objective at all, in the ordinary sense of the term, creation goes on continuously, in synchrony with tests of grace that invite people to read the hand of God in the shape of a stone. Creation in the industrial world lies in the process of production, in the ordinary sense. Our approach is the inverse of the one taken by political philosophers who find the principle of the polity in nature. It differs, too, from the critical operation by means of which people can situate themselves in a different world and have their eyes opened, coming to see the world they left behind as artificial, the product of an illusion, a "naturalization." In contrast, our descriptive enterprise, conducted from within each world, requires our reader to suspend the critical outlook that results, as we shall see, from familiarity with several different worlds, and to plunge into each world in turn as one would do in a situation in which the sincerity of one's adherence to principles would be a condition of the justification of one's action.

A contention and the litigious process that expresses it thus lead to a test that is expected to bring the disagreement to a close by establishing a new just distribution of the persons and objects to which worth has been ascribed. Tests, whose outcome is always uncertain, are not the same thing as the demonstrations that are produced when worths are deployed in a situation that holds together. Scenes of the latter sort sound right and feel right; there is nothing to say about them. It is as though nothing has happened: agreement prevails among all parties. The completeness of a situation that holds together must thus not be confused with the tacit "taken-for-granted" approach that prevails in such circumstances. Indeed, a situation that holds together is prepared for judgment, whereas the circumstantial "taken-for-granted" approach is maintained, conversely, only so long as the question of justification is suspended. Foreign beings whose presence is disruptive are shunted aside, or simply deactivated, in order to forestall controversy, on the horizon of a test that no one has called for and that no one is contesting. This is a situation ripe for proof, which offers resources for treating maladjustments or injustices.

Every time a professor gives a class, for instance, she is demonstrating her knowledge. The demonstration may fail, and thus every class is, in this sense, a test. However, the purpose of the class is not to test the professor's knowledge, but to transmit it. In contrast, the lesson presented by a candidate for a teaching degree is the kind of class in which the arrangement is explicitly set up so as to test the future professor's knowledge and to assess his worth in relation to that of other candidates. The test is administered under very strict controls in order to ensure its validity—its "purity"—and so are the procedures for appealing its outcome. In a civic test, for instance an administrative formality or a university examination, market beings or external signs of wealth are deactivated. They are not appropriate to the situation, and if they call attention to themselves by their profusion, they threaten to upset the situation, as we shall see in part 4. Such situations—examinations in particular—call for a straightforward, sober presentation, for reasons of justice. Extraneous worths that would disturb the presentation—a candidate wearing overly expensive jewelry or very shabby clothes—are not supposed to be introduced. Circumstances such as these disrupt an arrangement that is designed to produce agreement on principles of justice without distinction as to persons, as St. Thomas Aquinas indicates (1981 [1265–73], 1456–59), in that such circumstances may tempt the examiner to assess the person being examined, and to compare himself to that person, according to worths that are foreign to the ceremonial arrangement.

Disturbed situations are often the ones that lead to uncertainties about worth and require recourse to a test in order to be resolved. The situation is then purified; that is, in order to settle the controversy, the parties involved draw exclusively upon the resources of a single world. The testimony of a faithful household servant makes it possible to unmask the usurper, a younger son who has taken the place of the legitimate heir, benefiting from the confusion caused by a shipwreck (domestic world); a rigorous analysis by experts makes it possible to test the efficiency of a procedure (industrial world) that had been adopted without experimentation owing solely to the esteem in which its inventor was held (world of fame); the meeting of a congress or an assembly puts an end to rumors that were circulating and to the threats of schism being raised by factions (civic world). In a true test, deception is unveiled: the pea under the mattress discloses the real princess. The masks fall; each participant finds his or her place. By the ordering that it presupposes, a peak moment distributes the beings in presence, and the true worth of each is tested. The happiness of the worthy converges with the common good, and in such moments the worthy are at their best; their worth is thereby confirmed.

When a contention calls for a test, the situation is set up so as to remove uncertainties and settle disagreements through an appeal to the higher common principle, in order to establish the relative worth of the people involved. These moments of truth presuppose situations that have been purged of any ambiguities that might allow alternative worths to emerge. The situation achieves purity only if measures have been taken and arrangements set up to establish it in a common world. The beings and objects that cohere in the situation are brought in, activated, and arrayed; each person involved is prepared to enter into the appropriate state. To single out the beings that matter and eliminate those that do not, the participants must rise above the particular circumstances and aim at a general principle that makes it possible to justify associations and reject beings that do not matter, shunting them aside into the order of contingency. This is what people do, for example, when they clarify a situation in order to ward off misunderstandings and forestall disagreement. The generality of the principle of association provides assurance that agreement can be reached. Participants in testing must be able to remain within a single world, and they must avoid distracting elements at all costs: they must pay no attention to anything that might introduce distortions. The risks of distraction are significantly reduced in a situation prepared for testing because the test framework itself presupposes limits in time and space.

Reporting on Situations

A comparison between a *test*, in the sense in which we have defined the term, and an athletic contest or a court trial may help clarify the way in which a higher common principle, if it is to be activated, must take the form of beings that include not only persons in their state of worthiness but also objects.

The sports world offers a reduced version of a developed polity, in a way. This world differs from a full-fledged polity only because certain limits circumscribe the practice of sports; it could become a polity only if the restrictions imposed on the persons and situations involved were lifted. This would bring us closer to the sort of "hygienic polity" that has been repeatedly sketched out but never successfully implemented. Such as it is, limited to a single sphere of activity and to certain persons, the world of sports nevertheless makes it possible to construct a value that may be seen as verifying the axioms of the polity model: *common humanity* (a1) (all the participants in an athletic context are equal, and people do not run races against dogs); the distinction of *ordered* (a4) *states* (a2) of worth potentially *accessible to all* (a3). This last hypothesis is not entirely self-evident, of course, in sports, where access does not seem to be unequivocally open to all if inherent physical differences are taken into account. Nevertheless, what results from a trial or test in a sport resembles a world ordered by a higher common principle from which all contingencies have been removed. The example of athletics makes it quite clear how situations are prepared for testing so as to make the tests conclusive. Once the circumstances—which are apt to be called "external" in order to indicate clearly that they do not stem from the principle of justness being applied (for example, a contest in which the wind is in one competitor's favor)—are set aside, ratification of the test results is ensured. If everything goes according to the rules, the circumstances are not even taken into account, either because their effect is viewed as negligible or because they have been integrated into the test itself. To create a new competitive sport is precisely to codify a test and to define the equipment to be used, the relevant objects, in such a way as to minimize the circumstances, absorbing them into the test or rendering them contingent.

As for the establishment of proof within the legal system, the range of relevant objects is much broader. However, the process of establishing the facts also illustrates the constraint that weighs on the form things must take in order to be qualified and presentable as evidence. While the comparison with a legal system may help clarify the transition, in a polity, from agreement about the worths of person to agreement about things and the way they are compared, and while the idea of justice may make the idea of justification easier to grasp, this comparison must not be allowed to limit the way our undertaking is understood. Taking a number of different higher common principles in turn as our starting points, we have identified forms of worth that are in fact quite remote from the judicial register (even though they may leave traces in that register by way of references to mitigating circumstances); these forms can be called economic, technological, or even aesthetic. Similarly, the need to reach agreement on things involved in testing draws us away from the legal context and may lead either toward technological objectivity or toward supernatural evidence. However, so long as we keep in mind the extended meanings we propose to give the terms "justice" and "judgment," we shall be able to put these comparisons to good use, especially when we examine the relations between the availability of the beings that may be involved in a just action and the form of those beings, which endows them with a capacity to constitute proof.

The comparison with proof in a court of law brings to light in particular the relation between the possibility of establishing facts involving persons and the recording of those facts in a coherent *report*. Like tests of judgment conducted in court, tests of worth are always put down in a report in which the beings involved are qualified and their relationships with one another are established. A just judgment thus shows the two-sided character of the objects and facts that together constitute proof: they are at once objective and capable of being reported in a developed argument. Things have a real impact on the judgment reached; they may be summoned up and manipulated during a test, and their actual involvement may be challenged during a reconstitution of the facts. However, the way the beings involved are arrayed is not defined apart from a report that records them, a transcript that sets down their presence and their relationships. It is impossible to imagine anything like a "pure situation" unrelated to any report. For instance, the objectivity of the proper functioning of a machine appears utterly remote from the imperative to justify, yet the machine does not operate "all by itself," even when there is no one to run it and no one to look at it, except to the extent that it functions according to a set of protocols for its use. Similarly, justification in the inspired polity presupposes a report, and in the description of this polity we have seen how an inspired transcription can be reported as a confession.

A Framework for Analyzing the Common Worlds

Tests are thus subjected to constraints that introduce into the objective order the sort of rules that govern the construction of a well-founded argument, requirements that we related earlier to the ordering of the common good. What we said above about transcripts implies that an array that holds together and that can constitute proof is subject to requirements resembling those of a grammar. To the extent that it is identified in reports, the natural order in a given world can be described via categories defining subjects (the *list of subjects*), objects (the *list of objects and arrangements*), qualifiers (*state of worthiness*), and relations designated by verbs (*natural relations* among beings). The qualification of these relations makes it possible to distinguish between circumstantial actions, which cannot bring accidentally juxtaposed beings into mutual engagement, and coherent actions based on a higher common principle. These categories allow us to constitute the following analytic framework, which we shall use in the next chapter to present the various worlds in which testing occurs.

Higher Common Principle. The principle of coordination that characterizes a polity is a convention for establishing equivalence among beings. This convention stabilizes and generalizes a form of association. It ensures that beings are *qualified*, qualification being the condition for assessing *objects* as well as *subjects* and for determining the way in which they matter, objectively, and have value beyond any contingencies. We can say that "*a*" is the equivalent of "*b*" in terms of some higher common principle: for instance, "in terms of fame, person *X* is more important—matters more—than person *Y*."

People tend to make the higher common principle explicit only as a last resort in the process of justification. Most often, they need only refer to the qualification of *states of worth*, or to the *subjects* and *objects* that are present. Moreover, the higher common principle cannot always be summed up in a single term.

State of Worthiness.   The way the various *states* of worth are defined depends chiefly on the way the state of worthiness is characterized. The state of deficiency is defined either negatively, as lacking the quality of worthiness, or, less directly, by an indication that the deficient are reduced to enjoying only their private happiness, in which case their petty expressions of self-satisfaction are condemned.

By virtue of the character of the order established among states of worth, and by virtue of the attachment of that order to a form of the common good, each order of worth corresponds to a scale going from the general to the particular (and not simply from higher to lower, as in physical measurements). Worthy beings are guarantors of the *higher common principle*. By their presence, they make available the yardstick by which importance is measured. By their high level of generality, they serve as reference points and contribute to the coordination of the actions of others. Thus the attempts of the deficient to belittle the worthy (by paying obsessive attention to their ignoble or petty sides) and to cast doubt on their superiority remain limited. The deficient are constrained by their concern that the principle from which they derive the share of worth from which they can benefit, however slight that share may be, might collapse and upset the very order of things.

The coherence between the qualities of worthy objects and those of worthy subjects is manifested in the fact that the qualifiers used in each case are often the same.

Human Dignity.   In the model of legitimate orders of worth that we have identified, people share in a common humanity that is expressed in a common capacity to rise to occasions in the service of the common good. Because this common dignity is rooted in nature, people tend to relate it to a "true" and "innocent" nature. The innocence in question can be seen in the way people give themselves over to the paradise of a natural situation, closing their eyes to the insinuation of dubious beings into that situation.

The specific features characterizing human dignity in each polity must be inscribed in human nature, and they must anchor the order of worth in a particular aptitude possessed by human beings. We shall thus be able to recognize, in each polity, a focus on some physical faculty (emotion, memory, habit, desire, and so forth) and its transformation into a capability that allows persons to reach agreement with others.

List of Subjects. For each world, it is possible to establish a *list of subjects*, most often qualified by their state of worth (*unworthy beings* or *worthy beings*). Thus, to take just one example, in medieval aristocracy the *juventus* are not characterized in terms of their age class but in terms of their inability to embody a lineage and to be invested with a domain, owing to celibacy, the absence of children, and so on (Duby 1964).

List of Objects and Arrangements. In each world, the *lists of objects and arrangements* are unequally developed. When *objects*, or their combination in more complicated *arrangements*, are arrayed with *subjects*, in situations that hold together, they may be said to help objectify the worth of the persons involved. All objects can be treated as the trappings or mechanisms of worth, whether they are rules, diplomas, codes, tools, buildings, machines, or take some other form. In the inspired world, it is hard to separate mechanisms from persons; people's own bodies are virtually the only equipment available to them. The distinction between the material and nonmaterial character of equipment, which often underlies the opposition between the symbolic and the nonsymbolic, is not a fundamental property here. Equipment with quite dissimilar physical characteristics may also serve to set up equivalencies that make it possible to establish calculable worths. We should add that the greater or lesser possibility of implementing mechanisms of worth—and this varies according to the world we are considering—correlates with the greater or lesser ease with which the worth of persons can be assessed.

Investment Formula. As we saw when the model was presented earlier, having an *investment formula* is a key condition of a polity's equilibrium, since by tying access to the state of worthiness to a sacrifice, it constitutes an *economy of worth* in which benefits turn out to be "balanced" by burdens (to borrow the term used in the *Social Contract*: Rousseau 1994 [1762], 59).

Worth procures benefits to the person who reaches the state of worthiness, but it also benefits the less worthy, who are thus the constituency of—both "expressed by" and "included in"—the worthy and who find in the worthy the possibility of increasing their own worth in keeping with their own dignity. But worth also presupposes the sacrifice of the private pleasures associated with a state of lesser worthiness.

Relation of Worth. The *relation of worth* specifies the relation of order among *states of worth* by spelling out the way in which the state of worthiness, because it contributes to the *common good*, encompasses the state of deficiency. Canonical presentations of the various polities all make clearly explicit the way in which the worthy express the deficient in terms that are not the same as those used to qualify worth (cf. Sièyes, cited in Bastid 1970).

Natural Relations among Beings. These relations, expressed by verbs in reports ("marvel," "honor," "promote," "elect," "buy," "operate"), must be in harmony with the worths of the *subjects* and *objects* that they unite according to relations of equivalence and order established by the polity (thus the fact that relations are harmonious does not imply that all beings are in the same state). Some natural relations entail worths of equal importance, while others indicate a hierarchical distribution.

Although these qualified relations presuppose an imperative to justify, on the part of human beings, the beings they bring together may consist of several objects. In the industrial world, for example, which is highly objective, objects are arrayed without the help of persons. Similarly, the market world is anchored in reality by the place it allots to goods; the inventory of these objects is of course constantly growing.

The sociological problematics of "the social construction of reality" presupposes, conversely, an emphasis on the opinion and beliefs of persons and a skeptical view of the objectivity of objects. This problematics is very unevenly adapted to the various worlds. It calls the industrial world into question by a shift into the world of fame that leads to rediscovering the symbolic and conventional character of signs in the most objective of beings. Sociology's oscillations between positivism and phenomenology thus have to do with its shifting from one world to another.

Harmonious Figures of the Natural Order. The relation of equivalence can be known only to the extent that it is revealed by a harmonious distribution of states of worth, that is, a distribution in conformity with the investment formula. Harmonious figures of the natural order are invoked as *realities* that conform to the principle of equity. In each world, it is possible to verify that the prevailing figure of the higher common principle "is reality" itself. Thus in the world of fame, one might ask: "Isn't an opinion also a *reality*?" and, in a market world, one might say: "[H]e has the facts, knows what people want, and figures out a way to give it to them" (McCormack 1984, 54).

Model Tests. A model test, or peak moment, comes about in a situation that holds together and is prepared for a test whose outcome is uncertain, a test that entails a pure and particularly consistent arrangement of beings from a single world.

Mode of Expression of Judgment.   The judgment that ratifies a test is expressed differently in each world. The mode of expression in which the judgment is expressed characterizes the form in which the higher common principle is manifested.

Form of Evidence.   The form in which evidence is presented is the modality of knowledge appropriate to the world under consideration.

State of Deficiency and Decline of the Polity.   The qualifications of the state of deficiency, which is characterized by self-satisfaction, are often less clear than those of the state of worthiness (when they are not the simple negation of the latter), either because identification ceases to be possible on the brink of *chaos*, when beings are on the point of being *denatured*, or else because a designation of deficiency reveals a worth of another nature, one that has been denounced and thus denigrated.

The Sense of the Common: The Moral Sense and the Sense of What Is Natural

The achievement of a justifiable agreement not only presupposes the possibility of devising a system of constraints that will govern the agreement-reaching process, but it also implies that persons are endowed with the abilities they need in order to accept and function within these constraints. Our project takes into account what people know about their own behavior and what they can invoke to justify it. In so doing, our undertaking respects a distinguishing characteristic of human beings, namely, that they are reasonable: they have judgment. In order to judge justly, one must be able to recognize the nature of a situation and adapt to it. In turn, in order to identify a situation, one must possess a certain competence, because the process of identification cannot be reduced to the outward projection of one's own intentionality. It does not depend on the pure subjectivity of a subject; subjects do not constitute the meaning of a scene by the gazes they bring to bear on it. How could people adopt the requisite stance and direct their attention appropriately, how could they even set their sights on order amid the chaotic multiplicity of possible associations, if they were not guided by principles of coherence, principles that are present not only in the persons themselves, in the form of mental schemas, but also in the arrangement of adjacent beings—objects, persons, preestablished arrangements, and so on? All these resources, masked in the course of circumstances by the ambient static, are *selected* in the process of justification to provide a basis for proof.

Knowing how to act naturally means knowing how to deal with the situation at hand. In order to face the imperative to justify, one must not shirk a situation that, like a task or a duty, calls for completion; one has to see it through to the end. Just as we assume that everyone is inherently capable of recognizing whether something is well founded or not, we shall assume that all persons are inherently endowed with the equipment they need to adapt to situations in each of the worlds we have identified. Since the principles of justice and the worlds in which they are realized are not attached to persons or groups but are instead embedded in situations, everyone encounters situations in daily life that arise from the various systems of justice, and in order to behave with naturalness, everyone has to be able to recognize these situations and adjust to them. People in whom this ability is lacking or impaired are deemed psychologically abnormal.

Just as every fully developed political philosophy characterizes human understanding or human psychology in a way that is consistent with its definition of the common good, the development of the polity model likewise goes hand in hand with a hypothesis about the mental instrumentation people can use to reach agreement about a polity. The same competence has to be present in all persons; this requirement of universality means that it will be useless to look to political philosophy for models. Here we shall simply propose a hypothetical description of the mental competence that is adapted to the minimal requirements of agreement reaching in a polity.

In the restricted context of the order characteristic of a polity, this competence—which we shall call a *moral sense*—implies the integration of the two basic constraints that underlie the polity: a requirement of common humanity, meaning that one must recognize the human beings with whom agreement is to be reached as sharing a common human identity, and a requirement of order, meaning that one must recognize a general principle of worth governing possible associations. In order to agree on what is just, then, human beings must be acquainted with a common good, and they must be metaphysicians. The ability to think in metaphysical terms is not required by reductionist theories, which are grounded in biology or economics, or by behaviorist theories, which hold either that human behavior is determined by external forces or that it results from mechanical responses to stimuli. Nor is this ability recognized by culturalism, which holds that persons are all programmed in the same way, so that they act in concert without any deliberate coordination; culturalism can thus maintain the postulate of nonconsciousness, whose importance in most sociological and anthropological traditions we have already noted. In our view, agreement cannot be reached simply through a kind of ongoing negotiation among beings who are unable to set aside their own points of view and adopt others, beings who are unable to establish generalizable equivalences—beings who function, in short, the way baboons do, in societies in which the order of worths is constantly breaking down and being repaired. This comparison has led Bruno Latour (1994) to suggest that the way ethnomethodology depicts human societies is perfectly illustrated by baboon societies.

However, one consequence of extending a polity into a world is that the competence required has to entail more than a moral sense. To judge justly, one also has to be able to recognize the nature of the situation and be able to bring into play the corresponding principle of justice. In order to function in a natural situation, in order to recognize objects and involve them in ways appropriate to their nature, human beings have to have a sense of what is natural. Thus they must be endowed with the ability to make coherent associations, so that they can identify beings detached from transitory circumstances and bring them into agreement. A coherent association presupposes a relation—one that can be described in explicit terms—to something more general, something that the associated objects have in common. A coherent association is distinguished in this way from a simple, ordinary association (one based for example on spatial or temporal contiguity). The fact remains that while people can be pressed to make their associations explicit, they are not necessarily obliged to do so, nor, a fortiori, are they obliged to base each of their associations on a principle, and we have to allow for the possibility of associations that are not well founded, for example, a statement such as "this is a very gentle landscape." Everyone has the right to make such a statement and go no further. Here, we shall not study the ability to make associations in its own right, but we shall try to clarify the way people discriminate in practice between justifiable and unjustifiable associations.

The ability to detach oneself from the immediate environment, to remove oneself from the confusion of what is present in order to attach the available beings to an order of importance constitutes the minimal ability human beings must have if they are to involve themselves in situations without getting lost in them. This ability has to be acquired, and it can be seriously impaired, as is suggested for example by J.-P. Barret's work in an institution for schizophrenic children. The children Barret observed seemed to have great difficulty rising above chaotic circumstances, whose compelling nature meant that every day was experienced as a series of incomparable and unpredictable instants.

People who are behaving naturally enter into an identifiable situation in a given world and adopt an attitude in keeping with the nature of the situation. Making oneself available to the situation means adapting one's gaze so as to stop noticing the presence of beings that do not matter, contingent beings without importance, and concentrating one's full attention on the beings that do matter. To adopt the attitude called for by the situation is to become a being belonging to the world from which the situation arises (when one adopts the attitude appropriate to a voting booth, for instance, one becomes a citizen). This is why there is something inhuman in the objectivity of the stance adopted by the worthiest beings. Conversely, it is because persons exist in all worlds that they have to be identified in the appropriate one (consider the example of a scientific colloquium where a researcher has given a talk before an audience that includes her father, and where the father participates in the discussion while showing that he identifies his interlocutor as a lecturer rather than as his daughter).

Lending oneself to a natural situation means doing everything in one's power to keep from being distracted by beings belonging to other worlds—and human beings are always distracting because they are protean, always in all worlds. The stance people take and the direction of their attention combine to obscure the beings lacking in importance that have to be deactivated and ignored, beings that may have to remain present without attracting attention (in testing, they can actually be set aside and kept out of sight). These contingent beings may be noticed, but they are perceived as inconsequential: one may notice spots on the classroom wall, but they have no bearing on the degree to which a situation is properly arranged, and they will not be included in any report. Natural situations present themselves in a similar way to everyone. This is what gives them a mandatory aspect: one cannot avoid the obligation of taking their nature into account, whether by accepting it, denouncing it, or trying to reach a compromise with another world. One's engagement makes it imperative to stay with the process to the end. But the situation still has to have been prepared: if a participant were to limit her involvement to a gaze, it is not clear how she could identify the situation and adopt the desired stance, how she could make herself available to the situation. A factory is not a factory just because people have viewed it as such. It is a factory because an array prepared in the industrial world requires a specific attitude on the part of observers: people have no choice but to see the factory as a factory and notice what is relevant in it.

Our analysis of testing suggests that learning to function in a common world—that is, learning which beings matter—may be a gradual process. People learn to behave naturally through the experience of testing. A test brings to light the principle of equivalence, set forth in its purest form, that orders each person according to his or her worth. For example, when we speak of "great moments" in sports, we are referring to peak moments in which no external circumstances intervene to disturb the contest and in which both sides excel. In such tests, the participants are fully caught up in the situation. Engrossed, defenseless, stripped of their critical faculties, they are in the right frame of mind to grasp the principle of worth and to acquire the ability to put it into practice. By the light of the principle deployed in all its purity, the worth of beings that matter is revealed as self-evident. In the world of fame, this is what happens when the media broadcast a scene showing a star getting an award. Similarly, an excited consumer who has just bought his first car exults in the plenitude of the market world; the same feeling will come back the next time he hears about a sale, a promotional event, or huge discounts in a department store. In short, this person will acquire the ability to involve himself in situations based on a market principle of justification by going to an automobile showroom or a supermarket, not by going to a library to read Adam Smith.

The Arts of Living in Different Worlds

We began by spelling out various forms of the common good on the basis of canonical texts from the political tradition; now we shall attempt to see how these forms take shape in situations. The initial result will be a record of the beings and arrangements that stem from the various worlds: putting this information together in more extensive inventories is the first step toward constructing instruments for systematic encoding. Such instruments are necessary for the analysis of reports and situations and for the identification of worths. We have been able to identify principles of the common good and its primary forms in the writings of political philosophers, because the authors we chose were seeking precisely to constitute a foundation for those principles. But where can one go to find worlds, since they derive their existence only from the coherent engagement of objects in acts? Where can one look if one wants to study the relationships between principles of action and their implementation?

To establish these primary data, we began with works designed to help people behave normally and to show them how to adopt an acceptable demeanor within specific situations. Intended to teach people to recognize situations and set them up correctly, these works are anchored in the tradition of manuals to which the rhetorical tradition gave the name *prudence*, or "practical wisdom"; examples include Baldassare Castiglione's *Book of the Courtier* and Baltasar Gracian's *The Courtiers Oracle; or, The Art of Prudence*, also translated as *The Art of Worldly Wisdom*.[1] While none of the authors of the practical manuals we shall draw upon here would claim to be producing a work of philosophy, our earlier examination of philosophical texts will help us situate these manuals within the tradition. At this point, it will be useful to recall some of the aspects of that tradition that shed light on our own undertaking.

The Aristotelian notion of phronesis-prudence goes beyond the Platonic concept of phronesis-contemplation; it goes back to the traditional idea of a second-rate calculating wisdom (Aubenque 1963, 25). Prudence is neither an art—because the category of action is not the same as that of production—nor a science (Aristotle, *Nicomachean Ethics*, 1140b [6.5.3]), because it "deliberates about the contingent and is thus the opposite of demonstrative science" (Jean Tricot, in the notes accompanying his translation of *Organon*, 1984, 285): "Nor is Prudence a knowledge of general principles only: it must also take account of particular facts, since it is concerned with action, and action deals with particular things" (*Nicomachean Ethics*, 1141b [6.7.7]). Aubenque points out that while Plato seems never to have doubted that "sufficiently transcendent knowledge could come to terms with the totality of particular cases, Aristotle despairs of ever deducing the particular from the general" (Aubenque 1963, 43). Practical wisdom addresses this hiatus and can thus be compared to equity as opposed to law, for "law is always a general statement (Aristotle, *Nicomachean Ethics*, 1137b [5.10.4]), the way the square a carpenter uses in his work differs from a geometer's square (1098a [1.7.19]), or the way "the leaden rule [is] used by Lesbian builders; just as that rule is not rigid but can be bent to the shape of the stone, so a special ordinance is made to fit the circumstances of the case (1137b [5.10.7]).

When Cicero describes the practical application of *prudentia* (the term he uses to translate Aristotle's *phronesis*), the ability to adjust to circumstances and the "calculation of duties," the examples he gives make it clear that these circumstances can be identified in a variety of registers:

> [I]n the performance of all these duties we shall have to consider what is most needful in each individual case and what each individual person can or cannot procure without our help. In this way we shall find that the claims of social relationship, in its various degrees, are not identical with the dictates of circumstances; for there are obligations that are due to one individual rather than to another: for example, one would sooner assist a neighbour in gathering his harvest than either a brother or a friend; but should it be a case in court, one would defend a kinsman and a friend rather than a neighbour. Such questions as these must, therefore, be taken into consideration in every act of moral duty . . . , in order to become good calculators of duty, able by adding and subtracting to strike a balance correctly and find out just how much is due to each individual. (Cicero, *De officiis*, 1.18.59)

Finally, we should note that Thomas Aquinas, although he relies on Aristotle's definition of practical wisdom, especially as it relates to contingent realities and to action as opposed to production (*Summa Theologica*, pt. II, qu. 47, 5th art.), takes a rather different position by anchoring prudence to a greater extent in the immutability of universal rules, and by placing higher consciousness, *synderesis*, in a governing position:

[6th article] *Reply Obj.* 3. The end concerns the moral virtues, not as though they appointed the end, but because they tend to the end which is appointed by natural reason. In this they are helped by prudence, which prepares the way for them, by disposing the means. Hence it follows that prudence is more excellent than the moral virtues, and moves them: yet *synderesis* moves prudence, just as the understanding of principles moves science. (Aquinas 1981 [1265–73], 1387; see also T.-H. Denan, app. II, in the French edition [1949])

To deal with the question of equity and the relation between the general and the particular within a single framework, one that could account for the confrontation between several different principles of justice, has been our aim from the outset. The development of this framework has allowed us to understand how a universe comprising several worlds can be reduced to a single world defined by the distinction between the general and the particular, a structure common to all the polities we describe. Equitable judgment seeks to appease the tensions inherent in the plurality of principles of agreement manifested in this universe, by making accommodations and by taking recourse to mitigating circumstances. The ability to deliberate, which is a mark of a prudent person (Aristotle, *Nicomachean Ethics*, 1140a [6.5.1], thus finds its modern expression in the imperative to justify, as it is manifested in a universe comprising several common worlds.

We thus proceed to study the implementation of the higher common principles in the various worlds, using action-oriented manuals as our source texts. Written for neophytes and intended for everyday instructional use, these manuals describe typical situations or model scenarios, and they constitute a valuable stock of utterances characteristic of each of the various worlds. They offer elegant solutions to the tensions underlying the stock situations they present, and they often adopt the lapidary form of precepts to set forth rules that serve as premises for the invention of ordinary situations, without having to develop the abstract and systematic formulations of political philosophies. These works providing instruction in "prudence" and "civility" thus offer compilations of practical advice about normal modes of behavior; they are well suited to our study because, unlike ordinary manuals that teach a skill or an art, these ascribe value to the behaviors they teach in terms of the common good. This aim characterizes such diverse texts as Ferdinand Lhote's precepts, guides to proper etiquette, manuals of good citizenship, and so on.

The analysis of such works might seem to lend support to an idea we do not share, the idea that each sphere of pertinence has its own separate space, an idea that might imply that people themselves are specialized. We chose to avoid this "easy way out" and to confront the question of relations among worlds as it arises for persons who do in fact shift from one world to another; thus we did not want to rely, for example, on a domestic manual dealing exclusively with the way one should conduct one's household affairs, and in which we would find a presentation of natural groupings but not the pressures and threats of controversy attached to the possible presence of beings from another world.

We therefore imposed two conditions on the choice of manuals we would study: first, each of the works had to correspond to one of the polities presented in the previous chapter, and had to depict this polity in the purest and most exemplary way possible; second, all six manuals had to be applicable to a common space. Rather than hypothesizing that value systems or cultures are tied to members of a single social group or a single institution, rather than presuming that values internalized in the form of ethical precepts or postures can be respected by a particular person in all circumstances of life, we hypothesized that a given person can refer to any and all measures of worth. We were convinced that if our hypothesis were not mistaken, then for a given type of universe or institution, and consequently for a given set of persons, it would be possible to find manuals corresponding to each of the polities we had identified. So we sought manuals of behavior dealing with a space in which diverse natural resources are always available, allowing for the possibility that persons may invoke any one of a number of higher common principles in support of a justification. If coherent engagement is to be maintained in such a setting, it is necessary to set aside any beings that would constitute a distraction in the situation by referring to other forms of justice and would thus produce a *clash* between orders of worth (we shall examine such clashes in part 4).

Business today offers a space of the sort we were after. What is problematic in businesses is that they encompass resources that are heterogeneous in terms of their mode of coherence and the underlying principle of justice on which that coherence is based. In the business context, situations that are juxtaposed in time or place are justified according to a variety of principles; thus business offers a good context for bringing to light the various ways in which the different worlds make objects available for use in justification. The business universe has given rise to a large number of works designed to teach people how to behave and what methods to follow in order to set up the most varied situations. Thus even though the manuals we chose have a common theater of operation (a business), and even though they address a common audience, they imply experiential engagements in different worlds, and they impart principles of correct behavior derived from different principles of justice.

These contemporary manuals or guides are intended for cadres. Each of the texts was chosen because it focuses on one of the worlds we had identified, and because it tells its readers how to set up the most natural situations that would be the least charged with underlying tensions: how to en-

courage people's creativity; how to cultivate appropriate domestic relations and make a good impression on one's boss, subordinates, colleagues,
visitors, or clients; how to promote the image of a business, a person, or a
product, and how to use the image to advantage in public relations; how to
set up situations in which the various persons in a firm are in civic relationships with one another (for example, how to elect or appoint delegates); how to set up situations defined exclusively in terms of a targeted
market share (commercial effectiveness); finally, how to set up situations
based entirely on workforce efficiency (productivity). These texts offer
practical advice about behavior rather than systems of political philosophy,
unlike the canonical texts from which we extracted the various polities
(and of which the authors of the manuals by and large show no awareness).

Nevertheless, it is important to emphasize that all the manuals we selected have some connection to the industrial world, if only through the
methodology they share. The salience, in businesses, of a world based on
utility tends to blur the distinctions among the various forms of generality,
given the mode of expression in which technology is formulated, and it
encourages the transmission of the various forms of practical wisdom (despite their considerable diversity), bringing them together in the various
worlds by means of pedagogical tools that are normally used, in the industrial world, to transmit technologies and that are expressed in the language
of skill: pedagogical techniques.

To take just one example, the premises that subtend worth in the inspired world and that are expressed in canonical texts by way of anecdotes
or enigmas, that is, in terms of singular, nonreproducible situations, often
take the form of reproducible arrangements in the manuals we analyze
here. This also means that the manuals used to depict the worlds corresponding to the various polities will often present impure forms, at least
with reference to the canonical models. It may even be the case, as we shall
show more clearly later on, that utterances that go right to the heart of a
polity seem to be tinged with irony or distance, that is, they may be formulated as criticisms rather than as precepts or rules, as if the author had
been unable to escape completely from the industrial world that is
brought to bear on his pedagogy. But we shall put this feature to good use
when, after an initial inventory of the various worlds at the end of this
chapter, we attempt to register the most frequently attested forms of *critiques* and of *compromises* between worlds.

Using only terms and formulations that appear in each of the manuals,
we seek to extract six representative samples of the worlds in which the
polities we identified previously are found, set forth, and realized in accor-
dance with their respective principles of worth. We reconstruct these samples following a single model, based on the categories presented earlier in
this chapter (*higher common principle, human dignity, state of worthiness*, and
so on). This approach makes it possible to compare worlds, to shift readily

from one to another by tracking a single category and reading the pictures, as it were, in a linear fashion.

Under each heading, the substance of the picture is sketched in matter-of-factly, without critical distance. If critical distance were to be introduced, it would have to be based on the suspicion that there is some truth hidden beneath surface appearances; it would entail a "depth" perspective such as is commonly practiced in the social sciences. But such a suspicion would be based, as the next chapter will show, on the very same figures of denunciation of one worth by another as the ones we propose to study in political position-taking, in economic affairs, or in the interactions characteristic of personal relations. Establishing critical distance from the worlds in question in this way makes it impossible to see their reality, even though this reality is well known not only to grammarians but to anyone who finds himself at some point involved in a situation that is in harmony with a given world, a situation that can be described without recourse to the notions of "game" or "role." Suspicion necessarily puts our exercise at risk, through the parasitic introduction of a foreign worth that serves as a lever to open up the critical gap. Thus reading each description of a world column by column invites the reader to abandon his critical sense; it facilitates an immersion that produces a sense of extreme self-evidence, of banality, in short, a sense of *naturalness* in the world in question, precisely the naturalness required of every person involved in a *situation that holds together*, the naturalness we have taken as the object of our study. And like every person engaged in a situation, the reader can only rid himself of local adherence, of full commitment to one particular world, by turning to a different one, by skipping from one description to another.

The samples we present thus show how the various worlds and the polities to which they refer may take shape today, in situations realized within a single space (that of a business firm) and among a single set of persons (the firm's employees). In addition, our samples will serve as a tool for readers: by referring to these imagistic reductions, readers will have a practical way to position themselves quickly within one of the worlds or to recognize the presence of one of the worlds in the entanglements of a complex situation. As work based on other corpuses has shown, especially a set of observations and interviews with employees of a bank who were asked about the right way to behave and make judgments in granting credit (Wissler 1987), the choice of source texts is not of great significance for the resulting inventory. All works designed to govern the management of situations defined with reference to a common polity contain roughly the same terms and refer to the same objects.

The Inspired World. To represent the *inspired world*, we chose a work by Bernard Demory, *La créativité en pratique* (Creativity in practice; Paris: Chotard et associés, 1974). This text, a manual intended for business use, was written by a creativity counselor. At first glance, Demory's book might seem the least appropriate of all the works we selected to identify the pertinent arrangements and beings in the various worlds. Indeed, since the inspired polity relies very little on instruments or tools (because it presupposes the establishment of a direct relation between persons and the higher common principle), a text in the form of a manual can only betray it. Creativity counselors have to teach something that cannot really be taught, and they have to ensure that everyone has access to inspired states, even though—according to the descriptions offered by the canonical texts on the inspired polity—such states cannot be achieved on demand. Thus the creativity manual used here, like all works of its kind, has to sustain an unstable position. Situating itself within the inspired world, it makes a sharp distinction between creative situations and situations constructed according to the operative principles of other worlds, mainly by denouncing those principles (as we see, for example, whenever creativity is contrasted with the standardized rote learning to which an industrial worth can be attributed). But the creativity manual must also exit from the polity and even denounce its canonical expressions in order to open up the possibility *that creativity can be learned*, by means of methodical exercises of an industrial nature that justify the manual's existence and, more generally, the *profession* of the person who wrote it. This means that compromises with the industrial world, which can be found in all the manuals relating to other worlds that we analyze here, are particularly pronounced in the case of inspired worth.

The Domestic World.   To represent the *domestic world*, we use a work by Pierre Camusat, *Savoir-vivre et promotion* (Human relations and promotion; Paris: Editions d'Organisation, 1970). As the introduction makes clear, this text was written explicitly to convey the art of harmonious personal relations to employees with no formal training who have been promoted within a company. Camusat's manual is thus particularly useful for analyzing the way a domestic world can take shape in the workplace. In fact, a large number of elements that actually belong to the industrial world (including those that management science classifies under "human resources") are found here retranslated into the domestic world.

Camusat's text deals primarily with businesses and work relations. But one section focuses on families and family relations; the author accounts for this by stressing the connection between professional success and family life: "[S]ome readers may find it surprising that, alongside professional and public life, private life is also included in this Handbook. Private life is nobody else's business, they will argue. It is certainly not my intention to intrude on anyone's personal life, but rather to deal with family issues which are of crucial importance to success in businesss" (49).

The World of Fame.   A work by Christian Schneider, *Principes et techniques des relations publiques* (Principles and techniques of public relations; Paris: Delmas, 1970), introduces the *world of fame*. This text deals with the art of public relations, an art that is not entirely limited to the world of fame. As the term "relation" indicates, public relations always lie on the borderline of the domestic world; Schneider makes this clear in describing the relationship between press agents and reporters. Still, the goal of public relations is to build a measure of worth based on fame.

Public relations can also tilt toward the market world. Schneider asserts more than once that the goal of public relations is to enhance a reputation, not to sell a product, and several of his examples are designed to show that one can engage in public relations in order to increase the prestige of something that is not for sale (a city, a politician, and so on). But in a number of cases, and especially whenever enhancing the reputation of a product is at issue, he presents sales as both an indicator and a goal of increased fame. This tension appears in the distinction, clearly marked in several places in the book, between public relations and advertising or marketing. Advertising and marketing focus on persons as consumers; their effectiveness is ratified by a purchase. Public relations efforts focus on persons as sources of opinion about a product, whether favorable or unfavorable. It is in this sense that people constitute a public and establish fame (public opinion). When a company engages in public relations, some compromise between the world of fame and the market world is necessarily implied.

Finally, public relations involve an industrial relation to the world of fame, for the same type of compromise is produced in surveys. This can be seen, for example, in the opposition stressed in Schneider's manual between public relations campaigns and rumors: a public relations effort is required to control the rumors that arise and proliferate spontaneously when information is lacking. Public relations activities use the same sorts of instruments as the industrial world. Their productivity can be measured, they may be subject to a criterion of utility, and so forth.

The Civic World.   To analyze the way in which situations in the *civic world* are set up in businesses, and to begin to identify the arrangements and beings whose presence becomes apparent to persons in civic situations, we use two complementary labor union manuals published by the Confédération française de travailleurs (CFDT) and distributed by Montholon Services: (*a*) CFDT, 1983, *Pour élire ou désigner les délégués* (Electing and appointing delegates); (*b*) CFDT, 1981, *La section syndicale* (Union chapters).

Governed by labor laws, the organization of personnel in businesses and more specifically in labor unions in France is directly inspired by instruments established after the French Revolution and developed throughout the nineteenth century in efforts to implement a higher common civic principle. As we saw in the formulation excerpted from Rousseau's *Social Contract*, this principle does not lend itself to heavy instrumentation, and indeed neither delegation nor representation is exempt from criticism. Thus the objects and arrangements described in the CFDT manuals often borrow their forms and trappings from other models, especially from the industrial world.

The first brochure, on the election or appointment of delegates, is the purer of the two. Indeed, it is clear that elections as described in this manual correspond precisely to the tests that characterize the civic world. They may be held within the workplace (implying a compromise with the industrial world), but the instruments and language used unmistakably belong to the civic world. The civic scenarios and postures and the numerous references to statutes and laws in this text are associated with explicit or implicit denunciations of business situations that turn out to be ordered according to another world, especially when they are governed by market logic or, as in the present case, when they are based on connections belonging to the domestic order. Thus the reader is often reminded that the possibility of establishing situations within a company in which civic procedures are implemented requires a detour by way of the general interest and recourse to a disembodied sovereignty. Such detours imply breaking with another form of professional tie, one that is realized, conversely, by bonds of the domestic type founded on personal dependence—in other words, from a civic viewpoint, arbitrary and unjust bonds.

The Market World.   To represent the *market world*, we have had to turn to a foreign work, Mark H. McCormack's *What They Don't Teach You at Harvard Business School* (Toronto: Bantam, 1984), for we could not find a contemporary French text that presented the art of succeeding in business in the form of a how-to manual. In France, works dealing with trade or sales present few purely market assemblages; the industrial world as expressed in sales techniques, merchandising methods, planning, calculations, graphs, and so forth is too pervasive. This lack brings out the fact that even though market principles use the tools of a scholarly discipline, and even though the market world is frequently involved in ordinary situations in which people display their wealth, market worth has considerably less political impact in France than in the United States. We should add that McCormack himself clearly indicates the incommensurability between market worth and industrial worth in his many denunciations of the latter. Indeed, commenting on his choice of title, he remarks: "This 'product,' for instance—this book—if it were titled *Principles in Practical Management*, would certainly appeal to a different audience and probably, at least in terms of potential, a much smaller one" (114).

While we chose this particular text (there are many others like it in the

American context) because it existed in translation and was thus available to a French public, it nevertheless met our requirements quite well. It offers a compendium of practical advice on the art of business drawn from the author's personal experience (the French version has a subtitle that can be translated as "Notes from a street-smart executive"), and it focuses on market goods that are particularly detached from the arrangements of industrial production. When the issue is how to profit commercially from the name of a celebrity (for example, a sports figure) or of a well-known institution (the Nobel Foundation, the Vatican), the impact of technical constraints in the manufacturing process is reduced, whereas such constraints weigh much more heavily on marketing precepts applying to traditional manufactured goods. The most highly developed compromises in McCormack's work thus come into close proximity with the world of fame.

The small world of sports, which the author knows well, has its own measures of worth, its tests, and its rules, and it can serve as a reduced model of a polity, as we have already seen. The image of a champion ("I have long been fascinated, both professionally and psychologically, by what makes a champion," 255) makes it possible to shift from the value system of athletics to measures of worth in the world of fame or in the market world: "Had it not been for Arnold [Palmer]'s previous 'up-market' affiliations, he would not have been so perfect" (124). The analogy between the market world and the world of sports is reinforced by the fact that the higher common principle of the market polity, competition, includes personal rivalries that can be compared in some respects to competition between athletes. McCormack explicitly marks the difference between the two worlds, however, emphasizing the fact that in the market polity, the insuperable primacy granted to champions does not exist: "[T]here is a major difference between competing in business and competing in sports. In both cases the idea is to win, to beat everyone else. But in business there is no end to the game. There are no insurmountable leads. The competition always has time to catch up" (205).

The Industrial World.   As our data base for the *industrial world*, we use Maurice Pierrot's *Productivité et conditions de travail: Un guide diagnostic pour entrer dans l'action* (Productivity and working conditions: A diagnostic guide to action; Paris: Entreprise moderne d'édition, 1980). Its title indicates at the outset that this manual is intended to go beyond the framework of the *industrial world*, unlike the innumerable technical papers describing the mechanisms and routines of normal business operations. Pierrot's goal is to harmonize the imperative of productivity—an imperative that perfectly expresses the higher common principle in the industrial world—with a call for improved working conditions, a call that, like all precepts proposing to take the social aspects of a business into account, implies a compromise with the civic world, one that gives priority to the human dignity of the workforce. Thus in Pierrot's text we can find not only the basic trappings of industrial worth (a necessarily incomplete set, given the highly developed objective structures that proliferate in the industrial world), but also a variety of compromises with the civic world; we shall investigate these compromises in chapter 6.

We have addressed each of the six works in the same way. We set ourselves the goal of isolating, extracting, and combining in a readily accessible form the main elements that would be needed either to reconstitute the initial text as faithfully as possible, if by some accident the original version were destroyed or lost, or else to produce new statements that could be seamlessly incorporated into the original text. To this end, we developed a preliminary inventory in which we brought together the beings that are specific to the world under consideration; each entry is accompanied by at least one example. We then processed this inventory using the analytical framework presented earlier in this chapter, a framework that extends the elementary categories of the common good and thereby accounts for the natural order, for the relevant arrays and the potential reports about them. The list of beings (subjects, objects, relations, and so forth) extracted from the inventory is indicated at the head of each category in the grid, followed by a text put together in such a way as to encompass the largest possible number of natural beings. This text, intended to strip the readers of their critical distance and bring them fully into the world in question, into the very process of its fabrication, cannot help but create an impression of self-evidence and redundancy closely resembling the impression one gets during peak moments of adherence to a natural situation. A certain reality is laid bare, a world without depth is disclosed, a world lacking an "elsewhere" and consequently lacking any place from which "what is" could be denounced.

Thus we have *composed*—to borrow from the vocabulary of music—a sample of each world by picking out the objects that are in harmony. As we shall see in the next chapter, the confrontation between incompatible harmonies or agreements is what makes it possible to unmask the artificiality of opposing worlds, somewhat in the way Berg uses "the C-major triad," according to Adorno, in passages that otherwise have no tonality, "as often as money is mentioned," "triadic harmonies" comparable "to turns of phrase in a language and especially to money in economics" serve to denounce the "banality" and the artificial nature of market relations: "The little C-major 'coin' is *denounced* as counterfeit" (1973, 58 n. 18, emphasis added). Everything that makes it possible to construct the worth of a polity can thus be used to deconstruct worths established with reference to other higher common principles, so that the same devices serve alternately for topical composition and critical unveiling.

Six

THE SIX WORLDS

The Inspired World

THE INSPIRED WORLD, in which beings must be prepared to welcome changes of state, is weakly equipped and not very well stabilized. All the things that support and outfit equivalence in the other worlds, such as measures, rules, money, hierarchy, and laws, are missing here. Given its weak level of accouterment, this world tolerates the existence of internal tests that are minimally objectifiable, if at all. This practice shelters inspired worth from the opinions of others—worth in this world is indifferent to signs of contempt—but it also accounts for the fragility of this form of worth. The inspired world has to confront the paradox of a worth that eludes measure and a form of equivalence that privileges particularity.

In this world, persons may be more or less worthy inasmuch as they are all capable of experiencing the outpouring of inspiration and thus of acceding to perfection and happiness.

In an inspired world, the state of worthiness has the attributes of *inspiration*[1] itself, in the form of *illumination*, a gratuitous benefit that is at once external and internal, felt in the *experience* of an inner movement that takes over and *transforms*: the state of worthiness is *spontaneous*—both sincere and involuntary—because it is an inner state that beings receive from outside themselves. It is manifested by *feelings* and *passions*, and it is *experienced* as *devouring, terrifying, enriching, exciting, exalting, fascinating, disturbing*, and so on. What is worthy is what cannot be controlled or—even more importantly—what cannot be measured, especially in its industrial forms. Worth is often qualified negatively in such a way as to emphasize what is lacking, what would be needed in order to grasp, evaluate, and stabilize a situation. Inspired persons are not afraid to define themselves by using terms that would

The outpouring of inspiration (HIGHER COMMON PRINCIPLE) Inspiration.

Inexpressible and ethereal (STATE OF WORTHINESS) Bizarre, Unusual, Marvelous, Unspeakable, Disturbing, Exciting, Spontaneous, Emotional.

devalue them according to a different logic, as for example when one qualifies oneself as *irrational*. In the inspired state of worthiness, beings are not subject to industrial measures, reason, determination, or the *certainties* of *technology*; they deviate from the ordinary and "take on *bizarre* airs*." They are exempt from domestic arrangements as well; they abandon common sense in favor of *extravagance* and they "make the familiar *strange*." They know how to recognize and welcome what is *mysterious*, *imaginative*, *original*, *unspeakable*, *unnamable*, *ethereal*, or *invisible*, and they are at ease in *informal* situations.

The anxiety of creation (DIGNITY). Love, Passion, Create.

The passion that moves them instills in them at the same time a *desire to create*—a desire *awakened* by inspiration—along with *anxiety* or *doubt*, *love* for the object pursued, and suffering.

Visionaries (SUBJECTS) Spirit, Shade, Monster, Fairy, I, Child, Woman, Madman, Artist.

The worthiest persons in terms of inspiration are often despised by the world at large; they may be poor, dependent, and useless. But their deficient state actually enhances their access to knowledge of the world's truly harmonious figures (*heaven, the imaginary, the unconscious*, and so on). This holds true for *children*, who are "curious, *inventive*, *passionate*," for *women*, the *simple-minded*, and *madmen*, and also for *poets*, *artists* (who are of the same "nature as *women*"), *monsters*, "*frightening*, *imaginary creatures*," and other *freaks of nature*. In this world, in which beings are appreciated for their *uniqueness* and in which the being with the highest degree of generality is the most *original*, the worthy are at once unique and universal. One shifts without transition from the singularity of the *I* to the generality of *man*. Thus *artists*, who often embody inspired worth today, are worthy because they include the others in the singularity of a proper name: *Baudelaire, Cocteau, Einstein, Galileo, Mozart, Shakespeare*, and the like. According to this logic, there are beings even worthier than artists, beings who inhabit *magical* worlds (*shades, fairies, magi*), but when these are evoked in the work we are drawing on here it is always in a desecratory mode.[2]

The waking dream (OBJECTS) Mind, Body, Dream, Unconscious, Drug.

Poverty leads to worth through a stripping away that leaves the body bare. Indeed, in the inspired world, the objects and arrangements that equip worth are not detached from persons. They stem equally from a *mind* and a *body* (a *gift* may be manifested either in gestures or in words) that are prepared to receive inspiration—in other words, that are cut off from what connects them to arrangements of other natures and placed in a state of availability. To *surpass oneself*, one must *plunge down* into the place where worth can be manifested—that is, into *oneself*—"take a sort of *mental voyage*," "a trip without *drugs*, as it were"—in order to *awaken* one's "*dormant faculties*" by means of *dreams* and *fantasies;* one must "know how to use *sleep*," give oneself over to *daydreaming*, "not always think about being useful, efficient, logical, rational." The same results can be achieved with the help of "devices borrowed from *religions of the Far East*, from *zen*, and from *psychoanalytical approaches.*"

Access to inspired worth thus calls for sacrificing forms of stabilization and the contrivances that ensure the identity of persons in other worlds. One must "*break out* of habits and routine," "accept *risks*," "reject habits, norms, sacrosanct principles," and *call* everything *into question* while shaking oneself loose from the "inertia of knowledge." The terms that designate the operation of avoiding alternate worlds (which are denounced as illusory) take on particular relief here: to prepare oneself for worthiness is to "*shed* one's rational mental outlook," "*give up*" everything in order to *devote oneself* to one's vocation, *shed one's skin, get rid of* one's old self. However, what provides access to worthiness—a state whose advent is never predictable—is not renunciation per se, but a "sequence of *singular chance occurrences*": "No *painter*, no *musician*, no *writer*, no *scientific researcher* can claim to succeed every time. . . . He knows, on the contrary, that he will have to experience *failures, run in place* for long periods, start over again and again before succeeding." The "*unforeseen accidents* of creation" ("with all its—happily—*uncontrolled* and *mysterious* aspects"), its *detours*, call for *humility*, which allows one to "transcend the prideful assurance of the expert."

Escape from habits (INVESTMENT) Calling into question, Risk, Detour.

Worthy persons in the inspired world understand other beings, encompass them and bring them to fulfillment, not by representing what they all have in common (as spokespersons do in the civic world, for example), but rather by asserting their own uniqueness. It is through what they have that is most *original* and most *peculiar to them*, that is, through their own *genius*, that they give themselves to others and serve the common good. They

The universal value of uniqueness (RELATION OF WORTH) Genius, Independent.

thus have the duty of shaking off the yoke, of separating themselves from the herd, of seeking *individual liberation*, not in order to pursue a selfish goal but in order to achieve human dignity while reestablishing authentic relations among human beings.

The alchemy of unexpected encounters (RELATIONSHIPS) Create, Discover, Quest, Imagine, Dream, Explode (cause to).

In the inspired world, natural relationships are relationships of creation. Each being creates and allows itself to be created by others. One must thus adopt a state of *openness*, a *welcoming attitude* in order to allow "the mysterious *alchemy* of *creation*, the *alchemy* of things and the *alchemy* of *words*," an alchemy that *composes* an ever-new and shifting world: "we are speaking in vague terms of unheard-of riches, of significations that are infinite in their variety and by that very token highly imprecise." The inspired person is inclined to put himself in a *questing state*, to "enter into *affective relationships*, the only ones that generate *warmth*, *originality*, and *creativity* among individuals"; he is inclined to *dream*, to "*imagine*," that is, to "*conceive* what does not exist," to *create* (*art, cinema, literature, painting, theater*), to seek *encounters*, to "raise *questions*," to produce *word plays and witticisms* that lead "into other universes" and thus to achieve *transmutations*.

The reality of the imaginary (FIGURES) Imaginary, Unconscious.

Indeed, only in universes detached from reality—from "demoralizing reality," or what purports to be such in other worlds, and especially in the industrial world—can true worths be manifested: thus it is necessary to "explode what is called reality." The way to escape from reality is to "let *imagination* run *wild*," "turn individuals into explorers of the *imaginary* so they can succeed in "descending into the *unconscious*," for "all *creation draws upon the unconscious*."

Vagabondage of the mind (TEST) Adventure, Quest, Mental Voyage, Pathfinding, Lived Experience.

A true *adventure* is an *inner adventure*, and a true *voyage* is a *voyage* of the *mind*, a *pathfinding*, a *quest*. This mode of translation is opposed to everything that, in other worlds, and once again especially in the industrial world, grasps movement in the accomplishment of a determination, in a *trajectory* that is predictable and thus "boring." The *path* toward inspiration is "an ill-defined path, full of *detours*, made up of *encounters* and changes of direction," a *path through the underbrush*, a *path of invention* on which one can *wander* "beyond the marked borders," open to *adventure* "with its *exhilarating promises*." To follow this route is to "find one's *own paths*." It leads to the *experience* of *par-*

ticular states "in which the barriers are down," bodily states and *mind-fests* that are moments of plenitude and inspiration.

In such peak moments—in the *creation* of a *masterpiece*, for example—inspiration manifests itself *spontaneously*, *suddenly*, in a disorderly fashion, gripping the creator and obliging him to "*surpass himself.*" Its way of *appearing* is to deposit a *breath* that animates, that draws "imagination out of its stupor" and prods it to *take off*. It is in the nature of inspiration to *pour out*, to *spring up*, to manifest itself through a "*flash* of *genius*," a "*spark*" that will provoke the appearance of an idea, an *illumination* or *unusual intuition* that *disturbs*, bringing in its wake a "confused *bubbling up*," a "*strange whirlwind.*" In this state, one grasps the world by way of *impressions* and *feelings*, through an *aura* of happiness, *vertigo*, *fear* and *trembling*.

The stroke of genius (JUDGMENT) Illumination, Intuition, Spring Up, Appear, Chance, Bubbling Up, Revolution, Vertigo, Surpass (Oneself), Masterpiece, Planet, Aura.

For the real world is not directly accessible to the senses. It allows itself to be known by means of *signs* that unveil its existence and suggest what it may be, but without making itself present. These *signs*, conveyed through *words* or *images*, take the form of coincidence, *analogy*, or *metaphor*. All coincidences are relevant because "relationships, often tenuous or purely intellectual ones" exist "among all the elements of our universe." The manifestation of the probable accordingly calls for an arrangement in which correspondences can be unfolded and transfers of meaning can be freely operated in such a way as to give rise to *unusual ideas*. One must adopt a "different *language*," that of "*images, phantasms, symbols, myths, legends,*" shot through with *associations*, open to the *fantastic*, to *dreams*, and "nourished by the prodigious accumulation of *images, memories*, and *myths* that has built up without our conscious awareness." Evidence takes the form of an affective state, a *feeling* that is spontaneous, involuntary, and fleeting; its validity demands neither approval from others (as it would in the world of fame) nor the construction of a routine that stabilizes relationships among objects (as it would in the industrial world).

The certainty of intuition (EVIDENCE) Phantasm, Symbols, Signs, Analogy, Images, Myths.

Retreat outside dreams leads to a fall. Beings in the state of unworthiness are defined with reference to the world of fame, in that they seek respect and attach "importance" to "social position" and to "external signs of success." They are also qualified by properties that ex-

The temptation to come down to earth (THE FALL) Paralyzed, Habit, External Signs, Reproductive.

press both the determination and the reproduction of sameness (as opposed to *originality*) and also the fixity and stability of that which, lacking impetus or held in restraint, cannot grow: they are *frozen* in the repetition of (industrial) *routines* or (domestic) *habits*, and *locked into* the reproduction of what is already known. *Knowledge* acquired through *education*—the routines of schooling or the habits of family life—thus constitutes an obstacle to what leads toward worth: *amazement* or *enthusiasm*. The polity comes undone when the *temptation to come down to earth* wins out over the impulse to *take flight*.

The Domestic World

The domestic world does not unfold inside the circle of family relationships alone, especially given the restricted notion of family, detached from any reference to the political order, that is accepted in our society today. When this world unfolds, the search for what is just stresses personal relationships. The worth that, in the domestic world, is a function of the position one occupies in chains of personal dependence can only be grasped in a relational sense: *worthier than . . .* , *less worthy than . . .* For the same reasons, the exercise of worth is subject here to constraints of place and time linked to the need to present oneself in person in the presence of others, in order to manifest one's own importance. This need underlies the interest taken in everything having to do with the body, its clothing and its presentation. Arrangements of a domestic nature are weakly equipped with instruments for acting from a distance; such instruments are particularly well developed, in contrast, in the civic world, which lays emphasis on the objectivity of rules detached from persons and on mechanisms of representation. In the domestic world, objects are not apprehended according to their own worth, as is the case in the industrial world, but essentially according to how much they contribute to establishing hierarchical relations among people (we find examples in objects used in the context of social encounters) and also, necessarily, according to the degree to which they facilitate the inscription of the worth and thus the identification of persons during en-

counters. In the domestic world, where beings are immediately qualified according to their worth, in such a way
that their manifestation necessarily entails a determination of their position in a hierarchy, the inscription of
signs of worth in the form of titles, heraldry, clothing,
marks on the body, and so on, is sought in order to limit
the uncertainty of situations involving personal encounters and to reduce the costs of identification. But the importance that the processes of inscription take on tends to
attach worth to persons. The case of irrevocable titles
and especially hereditary titles is exemplary: such titles
render critiques powerless, because in most instances they
cannot reach their intended goal, namely, the institution
of a new test. Tests thus often take the form of confirma-
tions; this is apparent in the archaic expressions of the
domestic world offered by fairy tales, which are saturated
with anecdotes in which a worthy person, disguised as
someone of lesser worth, is subjected to a test that reveals
his own inherent worthiness (for example, "The Princess
and the Pea").

It is through reference to *generation, tradition,* and *hierarchy* that order can be established among beings of a
domestic nature. These three terms themselves are in a
relation of equivalence, because the bond of personal
dependence that connects a less worthy person with a
superior—always constructed in the image of the *father,*
whose state of worth is highest because he is the incarnation of the *tradition*—can be conceived in more than one
way: since the worthiest person is found at the point of
origin, the bond can be read as a link either in the chain
of generations or in a hierarchical chain.

In domestic worth, beings in a state of worthiness
achieve superiority in each of the three components: as
part of a *hierarchy,* they are worthy owing to the relation
that connects them to worthier beings by whom they are
appreciated and *valued,* beings who have attached them to
their persons. It is in this way that they are *distinguished*;
the quality of distinction does not presuppose here, as it
does in the world of fame, a competition of all against all
in a marketplace of esteem, but rather the exclusive *judgment* of a *superior* or *leader* and the elective choice that
makes someone *stand out from the ranks.* Beings are also
worthy because they are rooted in *tradition,* that is, they

*Engenderment
according to tradition
(HIGHER COMMON
PRINCIPLE)
Generation,
Hierarchy, Tradition.*

*Hierarchical
superiority (STATE OF
WORTHINESS)
Benevolent, Well
brought up, Wise,
Distinguished,
Discreet, Reserved,
Trustworthy, Honest,
Faithful.*

are *proper* (as opposed, for example, to *legal* in the civic world, or to *exact* in industrial arrangements). They exist in *continuity* (a property of the unworthy in the inspired world), and they possess all the qualities that manifest *permanence*, such as *firmness*, loyalty, *punctuality* ("*punctuality* is the politeness of kings"). These virtues are manifested in behavior that varies depending, on the one hand, on whether the relationship with *intimates* or with *outsiders* is emphasized and, on the other hand, whether the relationship with *superiors* or with *inferiors* is emphasized. *Attentive* to *intimates* (for example, a *spouse*), to whom one owes *thoughtfulness, attention, and propriety*, the worthy person is *cordial* with *visitors*: "The reputation of households is often made by *visitors;* thus one always benefits from being very *cordial* toward them, whether they are important or not." When they *face* superiors, beings worthy of esteem are *deferential*, which "does not however imply *obsequiousness, opportunism,* or *flattery*." In this context, they are *honest*, presenting "their viewpoint . . . with *frankness*" but without offering "systematic opposition," and they maintain relations of *trust*. This attitude "will tend to create a climate of *understanding*" based on *discretion* and *reserve*: "the best way to appear *well brought up*." Nevertheless, less worthy persons "avoid *familiarity* with their *hierarchical superior*, even if they *know him personally*, especially in front of *third parties*, and they are equally *reserved* if the superior is a *relative*." Inspiring *trust* in *others*, superiors are *informed* and *wise*. In the domestic world, where worth presupposes personal loyalty to a worthy being and membership in the closed universe of a household, objects are all the more *private* in character (letters, for example) to the extent that they are associated with the more worthy beings, and *discretion* consists in "refusing to listen to *gossip* and especially in refusing to pass it along." In relation to the less worthy beings for whom he is responsible, the superior has the duty to share with them, according to their *rank*, the qualities that constitute his own worth. If the superior is *benevolent* and *helpful* with everyone, "everybody will be grateful to him." True worth in fact presupposes simplicity (acting "in all *simplicity*"), *delicacy* (of *feelings*), and *thoughtfulness*: "Nothing is more despicable than the person who, *moving up to a higher station*, behaves disagreeably with his *subordinates* on the pretext that he is now the *boss*. This is where *upbringing* shows its full value. . . . Thus it is absolutely useless to be *distant, bossy, humiliating*. Quite the contrary. Even if niceness can sometimes look like *weakness*, it always ends up being recognized as a form of *upbringing* and is accordingly all the more appreciated." Still, "*delicacy* does not exclude *firmness*." Upbringing, which produces "the *well-brought-up* person" in whom *reserve* is combined with *poise*, is in the end precisely what associates the worthy state with *generation*, a relation that is established here (as is often the case when an utterance reveals what lies at the heart of the natural order) in the mode of what we shall designate further on by the term "desecration": "Those who hold or who believe they hold the secrets of a good *upbringing* claim that it takes at least three *generations* to produce a *well-brought-up* man."

The worthy act *naturally* because they are moved by *habits*. This arrangement, locked into the body, ensures the stability of behavior without requiring obedience to instruction, as industrial *routines* do. Thus it is "necessary" to give "children" good *habits* from the start, for *habits* adopted early are never constraints and they quickly become *natural* behavior. "Only *habit* gives *poise*," because it makes *good manners natural* ("*natural courtesy*"). These attitudes are also *natural* when they are based on *good sense* ("*principles* based on good *sense*") or on *predispositions* ("get a favorable *predisposition* right away"), as they often turn out to be naturally in *harmony* with the way the world is evolving. The term "*natural*" ("*drive nature out the window and it comes right back in the door*") also designates, finally, the *character* that is revealed in one's behavior toward *other people* and "reflected" in one's *personal presentation* and *bearing*. In this world, *bearing* is inherent in persons because it manifests *character*, which is *habit* made human ("*personal bearing* reflects the individual").

The poise of habit (DIGNITY) Good Sense, Habits, Naturalness, Character.

In a domestic world, beings are immediately qualified by their relationships with others. When beings belong to the same *household*, the relationship is one of order. Here, the terms used to designate specific beings express their importance and define them as more or less worthy, in the sense of *more worthy than* . . . or *less worthy than*. . . . The terms thus refer to the beings that encom-

Superiors and inferiors (SUBJECTS) More worthy beings: Father, King, Ancestors, Parents, Family, Grownups, Leader, Boss. Less worthy beings: I, Unmarried Person, Foreigner, Woman, Child, Pet. Others: Visitor, Surroundings (members of), Neighbors, Third party.

pass them or to those that they themselves encompass, that is, those (superiors) from whom they derive their origin or those (inferiors) to whom they themselves have given rise. When the principle of subordination is engenderment and when the relation to origins is established by means of reproduction, the more worthy beings precede and the less worthy follow in the generational chain: thus *forebears* and *ancestors—grandfather and grandmother, father-in-law and mother-in-law, uncles and aunts, parents*—are more worthy; *children*, or *girls*, are less worthy. But the principle of engenderment is not limited to procreation, and within a given *household* the more worthy beings are the primary causes of the less worthy ones, apart from blood ties: thus the *husband* (more worthy) makes a woman his *wife* (less worthy) by *marriage*; the *master* or the *mistress* of the *household* contains, and is, the beings included therein: *unmarried persons, children, servants* (designated here as *domestic workers* by comparison with the industrial world), household pets ("*spoiled cats and dogs*"). In a domestic world, in which beings can be qualified according to an extensive range of different states of worthiness, the *less worthy* are always present and designated as such because they are the very substance with which the worth of the *more worthy* that include them is constructed. Thus persons who possess dignity in subordination, however unworthy they may be, are only truly deficient when they find themselves detached from the units that included them, either by distancing (*foreigner, outsider*) or owing to their own *selfishness*: "As a general rule, it is always best to replace noisy *asides* and the imperative '*I*' with *conversations of general interest* led by the *father*, for *mealtimes* are actually the only moments that find the *family all together*." The *father* is principle of cohesion in the *family*, the one who establishes the link to an origin; like the *boss*, or, earlier, the *king*, the *father* is the one who lifts beings up by means of the dependence in which he holds them and who thus gives them access to all the worth they are capable of achieving according to the level they occupy. Since beings are always defined by a relation of subordination, and since all relations of subordination are equivalent to the relation of *child* to *father, grownups*, the *elderly*, and *important persons* are homologous. Similarly, less worthy beings are equivalent, and no particular feature of childhood distinguishes small *children* from the other subordinate beings (*unmarried persons*, *servants*, and so on) for whom the more worthy beings are responsible. Finally, when beings are not directly qualified by belonging to a hierarchical unit (*household*, guild, and so on), the relation that defines them does not specify their worth, which depends on that of a person with whom they have a *relationship*: a *friend*, a *confidant*, an *intimate*, a *guest*, an *acquaintance*, and so on, may be more or less worthy according to the worth of the other term, and association with a worthy person, which raises one's status, is opposed to *undesirable associations*, which lower it.

In the domestic world, objects are primarily determined by the way they support and maintain hierarchical relationships among persons. Thus "small *gifts* nourish *friendship*" and foster bonding because they call for something in return: "*Thanks* are owed for everything received: *flowers*, *gifts*, candy, books, and so on," and—"a sacrosanct principle—every *letter* requires a *reply*." "*New Year's greetings*" create "a *family tie* and *habits of courtesy* that characterize *well-brought-up children*." The same thing holds true, in life's peak moments, for *congratulations*, *condolences*, *good wishes*, and also *recommendations*, which provide opportunities to exchange marks of *trust* from person to person: "When we entrust a *letter* to someone so that he or she will transmit it on our behalf to another person (a *letter of introduction* or *recommendation*, etc.), the letter must be presented unsealed. This proves that we *trust* the messenger. But *etiquette* requires that the latter seal the letter himself in the presence of the sender." Similarly, the "*rules of etiquette*," like the *rules of correct behavior* or *good manners*, which are the trappings of worth in the domestic world, link and separate by opening and closing *doors*: "The *good manners* cherished by our ancestors used to open many *doors*." Conversely, "a *failure* to observe the *rules of good behavior* can close *doors*, and the slightest *blunder* may have consequences at the level of the *situation* (a term that here designates a professional state precisely in that it depends on the position occupied in chains of personal dependence and on the *favor* of *superiors*). The objects that circulate, *flowers* or *gifts*, right down to the "smallest *courtesy* toward oth-

The rules of etiquette (OBJECTS) Good manners, Proper behavior, Rank, Title, Dwelling, Introduction, Signature, Announcements, Gifts, Flowers.

ers," indicate, by their direction, the relative worth of the persons among whom they are exchanged. Thus, in *introductions*, "one always introduces the other person to the one to whom the greatest *respect* is owed," so that, "in practice, the least important person is named first." Similarly, *polite formulas* vary depending on whether they are addressed "to *subordinates*," "to more or less everyone to whom one has no particular obligation," "to acquaintances with whom one is on *equal footing*, to persons with whom one is in a relation of *equality* with a nuance of *respect*, to a *hierarchical superior*, to a client, to an *older person*, to an *important person*, to a *lady*, to *acquaintances* with whom one's relation is *friendly*, or to *intimates*," that is, in function of the respective position of the persons involved according to hierarchy, sex, age, or degree of *intimacy*. A *handshake* is also an instrument of worth, a tool devised from the body itself; depending on the order of gesture, a handshake may raise or lower a person's standing: "It is up to him (the *leader*), not you, to *offer his hand* first." Objects and arrangements are thus the means by which beings recognize one another's worth, just as they know their own; this is the way they know and deploy the relative worth of the persons involved and also the way they make themselves known. The ordering of *ranks* and *stations* ("*rise above one's station*") makes it possible to find one's place in *hierarchies* and to allocate *deference* and *respect* in such a way as to "be *correct* in all circumstances": "In *principle*, if there is a *hierarchy*, there are *ranks* and, normally, there are reasons for which the *leader* is superior to you . . . ; consequently, he is owed a certain *deference*." Arrangements indicate the identity of persons and *announce* them: "It is preferable to arrive early and to *announce oneself*." *Visiting cards* ("on white card stock in the *classic* shape and design"), *letterheads* on which "one's *title* is included," *signatures*, which put an end to anonymity ("the rather disagreeable *anonymous* aspect of illegible *signatures*"), *handwritten letters*, which identify because they bear the mark of a unique handwriting (as opposed to typewritten letters, of an industrial nature, which are not suitable for "personal correspondence"), the *announcements* by means of which one "*informs* of the *birth* of a *child*," are all "*ways of introducing oneself* . . . that make it unnecessary for the interlocutor to ask who you are."

Such a question is *displeasing*, because it includes a reproach to the interlocutor for failing to inform of something that should be known. These identifying arrangements reveal persons by linking them to a *household*, a
family, a *milieu*, a *society* (in the sense of "*a respectable social
group*"). Indeed, "personal *introductions* reflect an individual's temperament and *character*" in the same way that
one's place of "*residence*" (in the literal sense of *dwelling* as
the materialization in accouterments of the worth of a
household and a *family*) "is in the image of its occupants."

In the domestic world, the more worthy beings have
duties ("even more than *rights*") with respect to those in
their *entourage*, and especially with respect to those
whom they include and for whom they are consequently
responsible. These *duties* call for "the rejection of all *selfishness*": "discomfort is produced in *social life* when one approaches it only in terms of oneself and not in terms of
others." One's *duties* include, for example, the *pleasant demeanor* and *obliging manner* that "make human relations
smoother," in the *consideration* for others that "makes *life
in society* more agreeable," or in the *helpful*, *disinterested*
behavior characteristic of persons who do not *take advantage* of the *weak*. Carrying out these *duties* is what makes
"life in common" *pleasant*, what "makes life *enjoyable*,"
what allows *individual relations* to be *harmonious*.

*The rejection of
selfishness
(INVESTMENT)
Consideration, Duty
(and Debt), Harmony.*

In the domestic world, in fact, the more worthy include the less worthy as if they had created them. The
former have precedence over the latter in the order of
generations, and by the same token also in *hierarchies*.
This primacy is a source of *authority*. Thus "the middle
generation has an all the more thankless role in that it
must both demonstrate *authority* over *children* and *respect*
and *consideration* toward *grandparents*." The more worthy
constitute the very being of the less worthy: *hierarchical
superiors* supply the worth of *inferiors* and define their
identity. *Leaders* are thus the *honor* of *subordinates*. Conversely, the less worthy, who share by way of personal dependence in the worth of those to whom they are *subordinated*, are part of the more worthy who include them and
who bear *responsibility* for them. The two groups are not
separate from one another, but rather *of the same flesh*.
This mode of understanding beings is expressed in *pride*,
respect, and *shame*. The less worthy are *proud* of the more

*Respect and
responsibility
(RELATION OF WORTH)
Authority,
Subordination,
Respectability, Honor,
Shame.*

worthy who complete them, and *subordinates* have *respect* for *superiors* who have *consideration* for them: "A *subordinate* is always very sensitive to the *consideration* and *trust* he is shown. He will do everything possible to justify them, and this climate of *trust* makes relations more *pleasant*." Similarly, the more worthy are *proud* of the less worthy who are parts of themselves: "Never let a *child* leave the house without checking quickly to make sure that everything is in order and that one can be *proud* of him." Each understands the others in terms of the *respectability* conferred on him by the *degree* of *subordination* in which he finds himself. Thus, for example, one must never "do an end run around a *subordinate* by giving an order to staff working under that person." But those who are really *respectable* know, on the other hand, how to *earn respect*. Thus parents whose children treat them disrespectfully are at fault: "They have *brought up* their *children badly*, since they have not managed to *make their children treat them with respect*." Inferiors indeed have the ability to lower the standing of their *superiors*, whom they implicate by their own actions. They can do this by tainting their superiors' honor; this presupposes a compromise with the world of public opinion: "What can be said of the *wife* who, through her own fault, compromises her *husband's* honor or reputation?" But inferiors can also *squander* their *inheritance* (which involves a market worth), as in the case of "a *child* . . . who quickly *fritters away* the fruits of his *father's* labor." And it is this aptitude for winning *respect* that creates real *superiority*: "There is only one *superiority*, and it is not the superiority conferred by *good manners* and their application to utilitarian and social climbing or quite simply conventional goals, but the *superiority* of the 'gentleman' that gives meaning to life, in the rejection of all *selfishness* and in *respect* for *others*. Thus it is not a matter of appearing 'as one is supposed to appear,' but of being a man of worth who adds to these deeper qualities the indefinable quality that allows him to live better and to communicate better with those around him." So "true *superiority* is inherently self-evident. Moreover, it is real only when it goes entirely unchallenged."

The company of well-brought-up

Access to superiority comes by way of a good upbringing. In a domestic world, in which beings have to ensure

the *permanence* and the *continuity* of a *tradition*, relations
concern *upbringing* first and foremost. Indeed, "your own
upbringing will be judged by that of your *children*." It is
through *upbringing* that *naturalness* is transmitted. To
have good bearing and to behave *correctly* and *naturally*,
one must have been *well brought up*: "*drive nature out the
window and it comes right back in the door*. . . . One must do
everything one can to make sure that *naturalness* results
from a *good upbringing*." A well-ordered world is thus first
of all a world in which the children have been *well
brought up*, and are trained in *good manners*. It is the *parents'* duty to *inculcate proper etiquette* and *behavior* in their
children in a *continuous*, lasting, and thoroughgoing way,
so that the children in turn will become *well-brought-up*
adults: "To be *well brought up* is to know how to conduct
oneself *correctly* in all circumstances. To be *well brought up*
is to know how to behave *with poise*, without *shocking*, *ir-
ritating*, or *annoying others*. Indeed, *good bearing* is above
all a *habit*." And this *training* in *habit*, a "second nature"
that creates the *natural* faculty of *poise* (as opposed to the
deliberateness and awkward artificiality of effort), is
formed through *imitation* and *example*: "the climate in
which *children* are immersed from their earliest years . . .
will have a decisive influence" because "*children* like to
imitate." "Playing at being *grownups*" is one of children's
"favorite pastimes." A child will thus "carefully *reproduce*
everything that he sees or hears around him." In a domestic world, a *child*, who has no distinguishing features
as such, is thus only a small *grownup* who—since every *hierarchy* leads back to the *father*, or to another worthy who
has equivalent status—is not sharply distinguished from
the other less worthy beings in the *home (unmarried persons, pets, servants*, and so on), or from *inferiors* more generally, for the state of *subordination* in which the latter
find themselves always confers something of the status of
children. *Training* is thus "first and foremost a *family* affair," because it is within the *family* that the child ac-
quires the *bent* that results from a *permanent and ongoing*
pressure that creates his *character*. In this world, relationships among beings are *personal*. One *receives* and one *is
received*. These relationships can only unfold in contiguity or in the presence of *others*, and each individual is
known *in person*. Thus, for example, discourse that can be

people
(RELATIONSHIPS)
Reproduce, Give birth,
Train, Invite, Give,
Receive, Return,
Recommend, Thank,
Respect.

produced in the world of public opinion or in the civic world in front of an audience or at a meeting can only be addressed in the domestic world to an identified being whom one knows or to whom one has been *introduced*: "First of all, a basic *principle:* one does not speak to people one does not know." For *opinion* (in the sense of "having a good *opinion* of someone"—which is distinct, owing to its personal character, from opinion in the sense of reputation or from public opinion in the civic sense—is formed through *individual contact*. And judgments, too, are formed through *regular contact* with a person whose *introduction* makes a good or a bad *impression* depending on whether the person is or is not capable of being "*good company*." Thus the art of composing a harmonious world is first of all, here, the art of bringing people together, of *gathering* them together at key moments such as *mealtimes*, and of harmonizing them according to their state of worth—in other words, the art of knowing whom to *include* and whom to *exclude*: "Either one *respects* the *rules* and is *included*, or one cheats and is *excluded*." Made up of chains of personal dependencies (*households, milieus*, and so on), the world is ordered by the opposition between inside and *outside*, spaces between which passageways are opened or closed: dealing with insiders, one *welcomes*, one *calls for collaboration*, and, acting with "*respect* for the laws of *hospitality*," one *invites*. Dealing with *other people*, one *confides* (which is "always inappropriate"), one *lends*, one *returns* ("a loan is worth something in exchange"), one *makes recommendations*, one gives *gifts*, which entail *obligations*: "To give an expensive *gift* is a delicate matter. Either it *embarrasses* the recipient, if he knows that the giver's means are modest, or else it creates an *obligation* or a commitment on the recipient's part." In the same way, one offers *thanks*, one *returns invitations*, one *respects*: "one has to *respect* those with whom one lives" and treat them with *consideration*. One also has to *go by way of* persons in order to move up the hierarchical chain, or *pay visits* to carry out a *succession* in the *correct* way: "In the work context, the *predecessor* often presents his *successor* himself. This *undertaking* is at the same time a *farewell* visit."

The soul of the home (FIGURES)   Given the primordial importance granted to *hierarchy*, the natural harmony of the world that is expressed by social *conventions*, *customs*, or *principles* shows up in particular in figures that present an ordered series of beings in their various states of worth. This is the case with the *succession of generations* ("*children* are the reflection of their *parents*"), with *society*, in the sense in which we speak of *life in society* (for example, "the *pleasure* of the little *society* constituted by the workplace"), or with the *milieu* ("to be *accepted* in a certain *milieu*"). But the arrangements associated with *family* and governed by the formula of the *household* are the ones that lend themselves best to the manifestation of *harmony*. Thus professional life cannot be separated from *family* life: "There is so much interdependence between professional life and *family* life that problems arising in the workplace have their repercussions at *home* and vice versa." A business enterprise can be compared to a *house* (a "house of commerce") which has a "spirit," the way a *home* has a "soul": "Don't forget that for practical purposes the *spirit* of a company or a service depends on the *leader*, and that as a result it is he who will make it *pleasant* or not to work under his orders." Conversely, the degradation of the *family*, corrupted by the introduction within it of forms ("associations") that belong to the civic world ("these associations of *outsiders* from the same *family* that are being prepared for us") is the very epitome of failure in the domestic space. "If you are tempted to speak ill of [your company], remember the Chinese proverb: 'If you don't sing the praises of your *house*, it will fall down on your head.'"

It is also within the family that most model tests occur. These generally take the form of social situations such as *receptions* "held in the context of *celebrations*, *birthdays* and *anniversaries*, *baptisms*, *first communions*, *Christmas*, and *New Year's*, or on such occasions as *weddings*, *childbirth*, the receipt of an *award* or a *nomination*." Such celebrations may be marked by a new distribution of states of worth, for that distribution is often modified by an event that has something to do with *generation* or other major milestones: *birth*, *marriage*, *death*. They inevitably provide an opportunity to bring together, through *conversation*, more worthy and less worthy persons whose relations of worth can thus be confirmed: "In a *conversation* involving several persons, never address just one of them. Doing so makes it seem as though you are trying to ignore the others."

Household, Family, Milieu, Principles, Customs, Conventions.

Family ceremonies (TEST) Celebration, Birth, Death, Marriage, Social events, Conversation, Distinction, Nomination.

Knowing how to bestow trust (JUDGMENT) Appreciate, Congratulate, Compliment, Criticize, Report.

The higher common principle is manifested in demonstrations on the part of a *superior* who, acting in person in face-to-face contact, *bestows his trust, appreciates, respects, congratulates, judges,* betrays *contempt,* delivers *criticism,* makes critical *observations,* or *administers a dressing down.* In a hierarchical order, judgment belongs to the most worthy person, who must thus not be kept in the dark about anything so that she can issue an informed ruling: "Don't let [the leader] *remain unaware* of the problems about which she should normally be informed. . . . Ask for a meeting with her while respecting the ground rules (company policies, *hierarchical* order)."

The exemplary anecdote (EVIDENCE) Example (give as an), Prejudice.

The forms of evidence that support judgment belong to the category of *examples,* cases, especially anecdotes in which exemplary behavior on the part of *appreciated* persons is identified and offered as a model. The order of the world can be grasped in its full generality through the unfolding of uniqueness. In the domestic world, the forms in which nature is inventoried are collections of narratives, curious and instructive stories, allegories, and also collections of personal objects and relics, objects worth keeping because they have been used by a worthy being. Thus in this world the forms of the general are identical to the forms of the particular in the industrial or civic worlds.

Lack of inhibition (THE FALL) Impolite, Blunders, Loudmouth, Gossip, Troublemaker, Indiscreet, Disorderly, Vulgar, Envious, Flatterer, Traitor.

Instability and precariousness characterize the most deficient beings. In the unworthy state, beings do not stay in place. Their *character* incites them to act with *ostentation,* by *attracting attention,* by *speaking in a loud voice,* that is, louder than their worth would warrant, by acting in such a way as to *be noticed,* by showing themselves to be *uninhibited, impolite, familiar, excessive:* "Girls and women will avoid *excessive* makeup, *flashy* jewelry, and *glaring* colors." Since they do not live according to their rank, the unworthy do not stay in place. They are rootless. As a result, the slightest incident can intervene to distract them. They have "the detestable habit" of *contradicting* and *answering back,* and they are always causing *problems:* the *leader* "will always be grateful to you for making his job easier and not complicating it by inopportune demands, conflicts with your colleagues or your *subordinates, problems* of any sort." Not knowing who they are ("Who do you think you are?"), the deficient beings of the domestic world cannot give themselves over to what they do; always apt to be distracted, like the children whom they resemble in all respects, they disturb the ordered arrangement of situations in which they are involved: *muddled,* they *"let themselves go."* They are *overly casual, disorderly, awkward,* and *talkative.* They make *errors of judgment, awkward mistakes,* and *inappropriate remarks,* behavior that turns people *against them* and makes them *despicable* in the eyes of the more worthy. The same tendency not to stay in their place inclines them to *envy,* which leads them to be *gossipmongers*: "Who would have no reservations about hiring someone who talks too much without being aware of it, or someone who spreads *malicious rumors?*" In a domestic world, *trust* is immediately oriented in the direction of the *hierarchy:* "Don't trust *familiarity* and *confidences.* Be aware that the person in whom you have confided may be your *subordinate* or your *superior* tomorrow. You will then bitterly regret your lack of inhibition." The tendency of the *unworthy* toward "*indiscretions* that foster *malicious gossip*" derives, like *envy,* from the relations the unworthy maintain with those upon whom they have to depend, and by that token with what qualifies the state of worth with which they themselves are imbued: the superior beings are constantly present in their minds, as a source of ongoing concern, because they are necessarily the source of lowered or increased status, the very principle of dignity and indignity. It is indeed via the more worthy that persons find themselves diminished, since, better placed in the chain that binds them to their origins, they intervene by rendering superfluous the beings that they include and of which they are the accomplishment. But they are also, and for the same reasons, the unique source from which dignity and worth may be drawn, since it is only in contact with them that participation in what constitutes superiority can be achieved. *Indiscretion,* a passionate attraction to what is hidden, is thus always directed, in a domestic world, from the less worthy toward the more worthy. With tireless attention it targets the unworthy behaviors of the worthy (for example, the *bad company* they may keep). This fascination is mingled on the one hand with the satisfaction of catching the worthy off guard, of positioning oneself closer to them by diminishing them, and on the other hand with the disappointment of seeing true worth by the same token become more remote, for true worth no longer resides authentically in those who turn out to be its natural heirs, and is no longer accessible through the mediation of dependence. But *malicious gossip*, transmitted in person-to-person *chitchat*, from mouth to mouth (*gossipmongering*), only diminishes the unworthy who lend themselves to it and who, by circulating *rumors*, which the worthy refuse to do, *betray* their superiors: "If you are not in *agreement* with your *superior* and if he maintains his position, do not criticize him *outside* [i.e., to others]. . . . This would be to *betray* his *trust*." *Betrayal* is an extreme case of deficiency, because it disaggregates and takes apart: it finishes the job of setting apart and detaching the person who, by making his independence known on the *outside*, undermines the unity of the *house* and thus makes it vulnerable. The person who commits an act of betrayal is thereby *excluding* himself and reducing himself to a nonentity.

The World of Fame

Unlike the domestic world, but similar in this respect to the market world, the world of public opinion places little value on memory. Unlike the market world, it does not even recognize the form of memory of past tests that is constituted by the durability of money beyond the moment of the test during which it was transferred. *Celebrities* can be *forgotten* from one day to the next. This is the feature Andy Warhol was alluding to in his famous announcement that a world is coming in which "everyone will have fifteen minutes of fame." In the world of fame, there are few things that can consolidate and stabilize the relation between worth, which comes exclusively from the opinion of others, and the bearer of worth, an entity (person or thing) that is not qualified by properties inscribed in its being in a lasting way. This nonessentialist and purely relational character of the worth of fame may be precisely what has encouraged its adoption as a universal standard of measure by the schools of thought within the social sciences that like to highlight the structural and relativist properties of the social world. But the same feature also makes this form of worth fragile and easy to criticize. It is noteworthy that this form of worth was sketched out in texts that sought to criticize it well before it was established as a positive doctrine, and even today it still seems to be ill-equipped to resist the many attacks that continue to be made on it.

In the world of fame, people may impose an order on beings and reach agreement in a just world by taking only the *opinion* of others into account. It is *opinion* that establishes equivalence, and the worth of each being depends on the *opinion* of others: to a large extent, the reactions "of *public opinion* determine *success*." Persons are relevant inasmuch as they form a *public* whose "*opinion* prevails," a *public* "that creates *public opinion*" and thereby constitutes the only "true" *reality*: "Isn't an *opinion* also a *reality*?"

The reality of public opinion (HIGHER COMMON PRINCIPLE) Others (the), Public (the, at large).

Fame establishes worth. In the world of public opinion, worthy beings are the ones that *distinguish themselves*, are *visible*, *famous*, *recognized*: their visibility depends on their more or less *attention-getting*, *persuasive*, *informative* character. Let us note that, in this world, the qualifiers of worth are applied without distinction to persons and to other beings, even though, as in the other worlds, only persons can reach the highest state.

Fame (STATE OF WORTHINESS) Reputed, Recognized, Visible, Success (to have), Distinguish (oneself), Persuasive, Attention getting.

People are all capable of reaching that state because they share the property of being moved by *self-love*. Self-love is what creates their dignity as human beings. They have a common *desire to be recognized*, a common craving for *respect*. Thus, for example, it is "for reasons of *self-love*" that "the staff . . . likes to be made aware of the *role* it plays." In the same way, "questioned by someone from outside his own company . . . , the participant wants to be able to explain what his own *role* is, and to be *respected* everywhere, since part of the *reputation* of the company for which he works *reflects back* on him."

The desire to be recognized (DIGNITY) Self-love, Respect (desire for).

Since worth derives solely from opinion, the other qualities, and in particular one's profession, are not taken into account in the operation of establishing equivalences that makes it possible to identify *personalities* or *stars*. A *surgeon* and an *explorer* may be equivalent when they are considered from the standpoint of fame: "When a *cosmonaut*, a *famous surgeon* who has done successful heart transplants, or a *celebrated explorer* is featured at a company event, this is certain to *attract* the *attention* of

Stars and their fans (SUBJECTS) Personality (a famous), Opinion leader, Spokesperson, Relay, Journalist, Public relations agent.

the *public*." However, arrangements of worth may include persons who are neither *big names* nor their *fans* but who serve as judges responsible for focusing attention on the worth established by fame. This is the case, for example, with *opinion leaders* "whose *opinion* prevails and who determine *public opinion*," *journalists* who judge whether or not *public opinion* is "*receptive*" or not, *public relations agents, hostesses, spokespersons*, and *press agents*.

Names in the media (OBJECTS) Brand, Message, Sender, Receiver, Campaign, Public relations, Press, Interview, Bulletin, Medium, Brochure, Mailing, Badge, Audiovisual, Atmosphere, Setting.

Access to fame, which is potentially possible from one day to the next for any being, however lacking in resources it may be, can also be supported by an arrangement of objects. To make oneself known, it is a good idea to have a *name*, or, for products, a *brand name*, inscribed on a *medium* such as a *label* or a *badge*. *Communicating an opinion* to the largest possible number of persons allows fame to spread by contagion; this is accomplished within an arrangement that includes a "*sender*, a *receiver*, and a *medium*, an *intermediary* charged with *conveying* the message to its *intended audience*." Rooted in the world of fame (and not in the industrial or market world), a business enterprise can be thus defined as a *sender* addressing a *receiver*: "The *sender*, that is, the company, and the *receiver*, that is, the public." An effective arrangement, a good *campaign* that makes it possible to *plant* an *image*, thus presupposes "a *medium* that is perfectly adapted to a specific *message* and capable of putting this *message* in the best light." The tools that help establish the worth of fame include *brochures, flyers, booklets, magazines, newsletters, books, public relations offices, audiovisual productions, press releases*, and *interviews*. It is essential to "have the [company] leaders *interviewed* if they are *well known*; it is obvious that via a statement made or a position taken by Mr. X, *a big name*, the company of which Mr. X is president will be *in the limelight*." As instruments for the worth of fame, objects that represent compromises with the industrial and civic worlds may be used, for example, *public opinion surveys*; by means of an industrial apparatus, these supply a "yardstick for *opinion*" or for the *penetration* of a *message*, that is, "the fraction expressed in terms of the percentage of a population *reached* by a given *medium*." However, in the logic of public opinion, this yardstick is sought not merely for its own sake, but also for the way it helps spread the message: "The increasingly frequent recourse to *public opinion surveys* allows us to state the following fact: the publication of results indicating that a majority of persons has a given *opinion* reinforces the *opinion* of these persons, underwriting it, as it were, and *influencing* the *opinion* of others." The regular publication of surveys thus contributes to ensuring the transparency of the state of worthiness of famous beings who cannot *hide* the fluctuations of their *standing*.

Having no *secrets* is the price paid, more generally, for reaching the state of worthiness in this world. To be *known*, one must agree to *reveal* everything, keep nothing back, *hide* nothing from one's public. "*The public* has a real allergy to *secrets*." *Stars* thus give up not only their private lives but also individual or personal attitudes, which are denigrated in this world as extravagances or whims that might displease the *public at large*. Similarly, one must abstain from any "esotericism" (a mode of expression that has high value in the inspired world), for this mode is treated as a manifestation of ostracism with respect to the *majority*. "If a *message*, some bit of *information*, is too esoteric, only the most sophisticated sector of the *public at large* will be reached, while the rest, that is, the *vast majority*, will fail to perceive—let alone understand and remember—anything at all. As a result, every act aimed at *public opinion* has to be carried out in relation to the least sophisticated sector, which implies that the same *information* must also be delivered to the most sophisticated sector."

Giving up secrets
(INVESTMENT) Reveal.

In the world of public opinion, the relation of worth is a relation of *identification*. The most worthy include the others because the latter *identify* with the former, as the *fan* identifies with the *star*. But persons may also *identify* with objects that have been *successful*, and through these objects with the *celebrities* who have adopted and displayed them. Thus "every satisfied driver identifies with his car and 'defends' it against judgments formulated by others." To include others is *to be recognized* by *others*, *to attract their attention*, *to convince them*, to obtain *respect* from them, *to earn* or *win* their *support*. A being of great fame creates a public, constitutes it as such, just as much as that being is created by its public. The person that succeeds in *breaking through*, in capturing the attention of the public, includes and *imparts reality* to the being of

Being recognized
and identifying
(RELATION OF WORTH)
Identification,
Strength.

those who, owing to the *recognition* that they grant that person, ensure his *celebrity*. Such a person "takes on the potential *strength* of each of his *audiences*" and manifests that *strength* by concentrating it in himself. The term *strength*, although it is ambiguous, is used in the manual we are referring to here, as it is in Hobbes's canonical texts, especially in the evocation of the way in which a famous person encompasses his *public* and increases in stature in proportion to its *support*.

Persuasion
(RELATIONSHIPS)
Influence, Convince,
Sensitize, Attract,
Seduce, Hook,
Penetrate, Capture,
Launch, Emit,
Circulate (cause to),
Propagate, Promote,
Orient, Amplify, Talk
about, Cite.

The relation of inclusion among the worthy through their fame and their audience is expressed in terms of *influence*. To establish a relation of *influence*, one has to *hook, attract, alert, gain a following (fans)* or a *reputation, persuade, reach, sensitize, mobilize, interest, inform, seduce.* Subjected to such *influences, opinion* creates *fashion;* it *circulates* the way a *rumor* does in a *communications* network, and thus *imparts value* to the beings of that nature whose *fame spreads* mutually from one to another: "If for example a company succeeds in inviting *big names . . . , stars,* the *reputation* of those *big names* will carry over to the company itself." *Being acquainted with* something is equivalent to *having heard of* it: "By virtue of *hearing of* [someone or something] in any number of ways, the *public* has the impression, even if it is not involved in a consumer relationship, that it *knows* [that person or thing]. *Talking about* something, *mentioning* it, *dropping* a *name,* and *publishing* a *book* are all ways of "*getting* a *message across,*" of *releasing, spreading* a piece of *information.* In this world in which everything that has value is immediately *known* and *visible,* persons are constantly making *comparisons.* Thus, for example, "the *press,* in all its forms, allows employees of a company to *compare* their company, their own working conditions and salaries, to other companies in the same sector, or even in other sectors." These crisscrossed comparisons weave a *network.* Persons who are *receptive, receivers* of the message, in turn become *senders.* Public relations offices are used to stimulate the process by creating "a *network* of free *press agents.*" In fact, those who have *heard about* something become its *echoes, retransmit* it, guaranteeing its *repercussions;* they *convey information,* they *maintain* the *image,* by *multiplying* and *amplifying* the *message* as a "center of resonance." Thus "it is extremely useful to *sensitize* members of the teaching profession, because of the power of *amplification* . . . that they represent." Similarly, "a good *public relations* policy may make it possible, for example, owing to good contacts with the *press*, to *amplify* 'good *information.*'" "A *public*" thus plays "a dual role: *spectator* and *actor.* The public is a *spectator* when it receives certain *information* that may prompt a reaction of *endorsement, opposition,* or *indifference.* But then the public becomes an *actor,* for in most cases it will *talk about* that *information* to other *publics* to which it can *communicate* its *opinion.*" One can intervene in this *communications* network, *manipulate* it in order to *plant* an *image, launch* or promote a product: "*information emanating* from the *press, personalities, opinion leaders*" "*appears in the public eye*" and, by *orienting* and *manipulating* the *image transmitted* to the public, it *positions* the product.

The natural order distributes the range of *images* by *positioning* them in relation to their *publics*, which are *divided up* into *targets* or *audiences.*

In the world of fame, the peak moments are those during which these images become salient, for example during a *presentation* that places them in the spotlight *under the gaze* of *others.* Beings achieve worth only if the presentation is made *visible*, in a transparent space in which it can be *looked at* and *compared. Presentation* "*in the* public *eye*," intended to give *visibility* to a being, for example by means of an "*open house*," is the object of a staging that makes it possible to *manipulate* the *ambiance*, the *climate*, the *atmosphere*, and the *setting*, which, during a demonstration, "must not simply be designed to dress up a room or an assembly line, but must contribute to creating an *atmosphere* in relation to the *message* that the company wants to *transmit*." In a desecratory formulation, the author of the manual speaks of *provoking*, of "creating an *event* out of nothing." The *presentation* may take the form of a *press conference*, "during which some *important information* is *transmitted* to *journalists*," or it may take the form of an *inauguration* or *launching* "that *brings together big names*, carefully chosen and *important audiences*, and *journalists*," and which makes it possible, while producing "as great a sensation as possible, . . . to *alert* visitors and incite them to come in." "A *demonstration* serves as a *medium*, from the *vehicle* to the *message*, obvious or im-

*The public image
(FIGURES) Audience,
Target, Positioning.*

*Presentation of the
event (TEST)
Demonstration, Press
Conference,
Inauguration,
Open house
(demonstration).*

plied, which makes it possible to achieve the desired goal. Consequently, the *message* may *take on* the form of a true *message*, it may *communicate* some *information*, or it may be only an *ambiance*, a *climate* that is created and that acts almost unconsciously on the *audience present*."

The judgment of public opinion (JUDGMENT) Rumor, Unconfirmed Report, Fashion, Standing, Sensation, Repercussion, Proper proportions (reduce to), Measure (the audience).

The *brand name* makes it possible to crystallize a *trend* in public opinion, through a *brand image*. Turning the press into an instrument ensures the objectification of this demonstration by its *repercussions*, the *sensation* that is produced: "The *press* is generally quick to *echo* the *rumors* and *unconfirmed reports* it picks up." In the world of public opinion, judgment is in fact manifested by the convergence of *opinions* that produce a *rumor*, an *unconfirmed report*. The demonstration is patent when this convergence is *visible* owing to the affluence of the *world* and can thus *amplify itself* on its own like a *fashion*: "It is well known that the *world attracts* the *world* and that the circus atmosphere (in the good sense) is always a safe bet." The absence of judgment, in this world, consists in deluding oneself about one's own worth. Only a demonstration of the judgment of public opinion makes it possible to reduce the tension between the worth one attributes to oneself (ideal) and the worth that is attributed to one by others (real): "Before undertaking any action at all on a *brand image*, it is important to know the *real image* (or the absence of a real image); to define with precision the *ideal image* that it would be desirable to *promote*." To reduce a *rumor* or an *unconfirmed report* to its *proper proportions*, one must resort to the "*reactions* of *public opinion*." The judgment may be supported, as we have already seen, by survey techniques that allow the establishment of a measure, a *standing* that helps reassure the *celebrities* of the undeniable *worth* that they are afforded by the recognition granted them.

The evidence of success (EVIDENCE) Known.

Indeed, in the world of public opinion, what is known is what is already obvious, and, conversely, what is either unknown to the majority (*esoteric*) or indistinguishable and lacking in relief is debatable.

Indifference and banality (THE FALL) Unknown, Hidden, Indifference (encounter), Banal,

To be unworthy, in the logic of public opinion, is to be *banal* (not to have been "debanalized"), "not to have any *image* at all, which in general signifies a complete *ignorance* of the product," or else to have an *image* that is *fuzzy, degraded, faded, lost*; to be *forgotten* or *hidden*, to en-

counter *indifference* or *opposition*, in short, to *disappear*":
"Certain companies struggle . . . not to *lose* it [their *im-age*], not to *disappear.*" "All one has to do is *keep a close eye* on the *press* for a month to *be persuaded* of this: *events* that mobilize *public opinion* in a country for several days run-ning are completely *forgotten* from one day to the next because they have *disappeared* from the *newspapers*. Now, if a *journalist* does not return to the subject, it is because he judges that *public opinion* is no longer *receptive*, 'that it has already had enough,' and that other *information* is more important."

Forgotten, Fuzzy image, Deteriorated, Faded, Lost.

The Civic World

The distinctive feature of the civic world is that it at-taches primordial importance to beings that are not per-sons. In this world, the ones who accede to higher states of worth are not human persons but rather the collective persons that they constitute by meeting together. Insofar as human beings belong to or represent collectives, their worth can be taken into consideration. But the very exis-tence of such collective beings, which have no bodies of their own, can easily be challenged: "Only individuals truly exist." Thus the things and arrangements included in the civic world are destined above all to stabilize and equip the collective persons, to *objectify* them in such a way as to give them body, permanence, and presence.

A relation of equivalence can be established among beings insofar as they *all* belong to a *collective* that in-cludes and transcends them. *Collective* beings themselves are included within other, larger *collectives*, embedded in sets of which the most inclusive is humanity itself. Per-sons are all subject to the same justice because everyone possesses a conscience that is fashioned in the image of the *collective* conscience and because everyone is capable, by listening to the voice of this conscience, of subordi-nating his or her own will to the *general will*. This act of becoming aware gives persons "the *will* to organize themselves," that is, to surmount the singularities that *di-vide* them in order to bring about the *union of all*. Thus a "*collective workers' organization*" is "open to *all* workers, whatever their political or philosophical opinions, na-

The preeminence of collectives (HIGHER COMMON PRINCIPLE) Collective, All, Will (general).

tionality, age, or sex." People's actions are relevant when, as participants in a *social movement*, they take part in a *collective action* that gives meaning and justification to their own individual behavior: this "action . . . is not a simple accumulation of *positions* or *individual initiatives* but *collective action.*"

Rule governed and representative (STATE OF WORTHINESS). Unitary, Legal, Rule governed, Official, Representative, Authorized, Confirmed, Free.

In the civic world, the worthy beings are the *masses* and the *collectives* that assemble and organize them. Their worthiness is qualified first by their dimensions: *confederate* ("*confederate congress*"), *national* or *international*, and by the fact that they belong to *public* space as opposed to the "private" world: one speaks of "*public* agencies." Moreover, persons or collectives gain in worth when they work toward union, when they strive to "*unify*" people, to "*break down* their *isolation*," to concentrate "the *collective* power of salaried employees *grouped* around *common objectives*," and when they manage to *express*, in a "*unitary concept*," the "problems *common* to *all.*" This activity is *liberating* because it frees people from the oppression of selfish interests. The "labor movement," which ensures "the *unity* of workers," can thus be qualified by its "liberating mission." A being can also be qualified as worthy if it is *recognized* as *representative*, a term that, in the civic world, designates the way in which other beings are included and the relation of worth among beings. To be a representative gives *authority* within an *organization*, and confers the *capacity* to exercise a *power*. The representative is *qualified* to "accomplish the *mission*" that is its *vocation*, its *calling*. Thus "only labor unions . . . are *qualified* to negotiate with management." The representatives are duly *mandated*. The law, for example, confers a "*legal* character on the *representatives* of the personnel." *Legality* defines a form of worth that is particularly appreciated in this world. It belongs to texts when they are *regulatory* or *legislative*, to *representatives* when they are *official*, to *members* when they are confirmed as such, to *delegates* when they are *valid*: "the *validity* of the *delegate's nomination*" must be "subordinated to the preexisting *constitution* of the *chapter.*" It is similarly necessary to verify the legality of *candidates*, who, in order to be *eligible*, must be *free*, that is, detached from the bonds of personal dependence that constitute the worth of people in the civic world: "To be *eligible*, one must . . . not be a near relative or the spouse

of the employer." This detachment is what guarantees
the candidates' *independence* and "*freedom* of speech": one
must "respect . . . the *independence* of *judgment* that is
necessary in such circumstances"; and a "lack of *independence* with respect to management suffices in itself for a
labor union to be declared non*representative.*" *Freedom* is
the condition of *dignity*, because it respects the aspiration
of citizens to *unity*.

Beings may escape from chaos—in this world, that
means from *division*—and thus attain worth because they
are naturally *political*. They harbor in themselves an *aspiration* that inclines them toward what is *common*, toward
what *unites* them and incites them to *break down their isolation*. This is what confers on them the quality of citizens invested with *civil rights*: "The salaried employees of
the company are *presumed* to enjoy their *civil rights.*"

The aspiration to civil rights (DIGNITY) Civil rights, Political aspirations, Participation.

The common aspiration to unity defines the dignity of
persons. In the civic world, beings are persons when they
are capable of having rights and obligations, that is, when
they have been *created* or *authorized* by an *act* in which the
will of all is expressed. The worth of persons depends on
the state they are in: as particular persons, they are unworthy because they are reduced to being merely *themselves*, "isolated *individuals*," slaves of their own particular
interests and condemned to powerlessness; they become
worthy when they accede to the general state and make
themselves the *expression* of a *general will* and the embodiment of a *general interest*. Thus the local *chapter* is a *collective* person because it *assembles* several *individuals* in a
form that has been recognized and *constituted* in a *legal*
process that confers *rights* upon it: "A *chapter* may not be
instituted . . . on the *basis* of a single person." Its worth
depends on its *capacity* to bring its *members* to the general
state by *mobilizing* them around a *common interest*: "The
chapter has to seize the moment when the workers *become
aware* of their exploitation and of the need to fight, in order to *transform* them into *members*, into *militants*." It can
then fulfill its *vocation*, which is to "*take charge* of the
workers' entire set of *interests*." In this state, where they
are worthy because they have achieved *solidarity, individuals* are *members, militants, representatives, elected officers,
collectors, treasurers, secretaries, delegates*. But the *chapter*,
like the other collective persons of the civic world (*offices*,

Collective persons and their representatives (SUBJECTS) Public collectivities, Party, Federation, Chapter, Office, Committee, Elected official, Representative, Delegate, Secretary, Member.

committees, federations, confederations, parties, commissions), and like the moral beings that *represent* the *collective interest* (*elected officials, representatives, delegates*) can lose its worth if, backsliding into the particular in the wake of a *deviation*, it ceases to "function *democratically*": the union *chapter* is not exempt from *deviations*, and it is appropriate to "control the *delegates*," to remain *vigilant*. If these "fundamental *principles*" are forgotten, the collective being breaks down and is *diluted*, becoming no more than a sum of individuals moved by their individual interests: "When *interventions* (in *meetings*) are numerous, and *contradictory*, the final decision can only remain with the *delegate* or *delegates*. That is why the union *chapter* has to play its full role under the circumstances, by proposing *initiatives*. . . . Indeed, it is inconceivable that it should refuse these *responsibilities*, that it should be *diluted*, and disappear at the high points of its action."

Legal forms (OBJECTS) Rights, Legislation, Decree, Order, Measure, Courts, Formality, Procedure, Transcript, Infringement, Capacity (electoral), Code, Criterion, District, Slate (of candidates), Program, Policy, Statement, Poster, Brochure, Ballot, Tract, Slogan, Seat, Headquarters, Local office, Acronym, Card.

To resist the tendency that attracts them toward the particular, moral beings in the civic world have to be stabilized by means of equipment. The collective will from which they derive—and the more general it is, the more worthy it is—must be provided with its own instruments in order to express itself. To make itself heard, it requires "*seats* to be *filled*," *polling places, voting booths, ballots,*" "*measures* allowing an *electoral campaign* to take place normally"—*slates of candidates*, for example. Next, in order to sustain their existence, collective persons must assert their *presence* and acquire *headquarters*, endowing themselves with a material existence that renders them *concrete*; they must manifest themselves in objects. The claim that a collective person endowed with a "*civil status*" has its own *personality*, is indeed a person, is a reasonable one in the civic world. Yet this fact is challenged from the standpoint of the other worlds, which deny the reality of collective persons and accredit only the diversity of the individual persons of which they are composed. In order to make "concrete . . . the *presence* and the *active* role" of collective persons, *material* means are used that allow their *presence* to be brought out in a form accessible to the senses. Thus the local branch needs to have "*offices* in large corporations." Having *headquarters* indeed constitutes one of the main devices a collective person can use to objectify its existence (see Boltanski

1987, 144). In order to make itself visible, the *chapter*, like any other collective person, must have at its disposal the *"equipment* needed to produce a *tract, a typewriter* and a *copy machine*," and it must acquire "useful and indispensable *tools* in order to *express* and defend the workers' *interests*," such as "highly visible" *posters*, informative *signboards, newsletters*, and *brochures*. Thus the brochure we are using here as our reference states in its introduction that it "has to be a *basic* tool for the *militants* who *participate* in the life of a *chapter*." If their material existence is to appear in a striking fashion, collective persons must also be circumscribed in space by *boundaries*, which assign them a *sector* or *district* (*"electoral district"*). Furthermore, their *vocation* has to be specified by a *definition* that spells out the organization's goals and thereby endows it with legal existence ("the *law* itself gives no *definition* of . . ."). This definition provides *criteria*, for example *"criteria* of *representation*," and *codes* making it possible to *identify* the various collective persons and to distribute among them the *individuals* whose *identity* may be defined in turn by their membership in collectives. It confers on them a *right of presence* and a *right to vote, prerogatives* that are attested by *cards, contributions*, and *receipts*: "The *receipt* for *contributions* on which the *collector* records the sums received." To maintain their standing, collective persons must also be associated with symbols and emblems, with identifying *acronyms*: "The *acronym* . . . must always be clearly apparent." Possessing neither a body nor sense organs, the will of a collective person, if it is to be clearly expressed, must be summed up in ready-made formulas allowing for repetition by multiple voices without alterations or *deviations*, such as *slogans* (which "are to be used often"), *resolutions* ("the *resolution* on democratic procedures adopted by the 28th Congress"), *objectives* ("salaried employees *banding together* around *common objectives*"), *positions* ("publicize the union's *positions*"), *programs* ("the *program* developed by the National Resistance Council"), *policies* ("base our practice on a set of *common policies*"), or *lines* (*"party lines"*). The will of these collective persons is less subject to caution when it is asserted in *official* forms such as *orders* (a "group *created* by an *order*"), *decrees* (*"decree* of application"), *rulings* ("the basic text of the ruling dated February 22, 1945"), *disposi-*

tions ("dispositions peculiar to certain professions"), *judgments* ("*judgments* handed down by *courts*"), and also *proclamations* ("the *proclamation* of the *elected officials*"), *proposals* ("the *proposed text*" of a law), and *protocols* ("the *protocol of understanding*"). Even exceptions, which lack worth in this world because they are singular by nature, can be acknowledged when they are codified under the legal form of *infringement* ("*infringements* of the conditions of *seniority*"). When actions are undertaken in *legal* forms, they give rise to *procedures* such as the production of *transcripts* ("the *transcript* of the *election*"), *measures* ("the establishment of *measures*"), or *formalities*. Thus the *notification* to the company of the *election* of a *delegate* in a *registered letter* with *return receipt requested* is an "important *formality*," because "the date of receipt of this letter marks, in principle, the starting date of the delegate's protected status."

The renunciation of the particular (INVESTMENT) Solidarity, Transcending (divisions), Renunciation (of immediate interest), Struggle (for a cause).

In the civic world, one attains worth by sacrificing particular and immediate interests, by transcending *oneself*, by refusing to place "*individual interests* ahead of *collective interests*." Thus militants *renounce* "forms of *action* in which only the *immediate* and sometimes *personal interests* of the workers are taken into account." The rejection of the particular makes it possible to *transcend the divisions* that *separate*, in order to act *collectively*. This is the condition of *solidarity*. But people's attachment to their own particular interests, their selfishness and their *individualism*, are such strong tendencies that the creation and maintenance of collectives requires a tireless *struggle*: "A *chapter* cannot be created from one day to the next. The building of this instrument demands constant *struggle*: *struggle* against the bosses, who are hostile toward its existence, and at times *struggle* against oneself." Collective persons are in fact confronted with a particular difficulty. In order to exist, they must *express themselves* ("the right for the union *organization* to *act* and *express itself* directly") in *declarations*, yet they cannot *take the floor* except by borrowing the voice of a representative or of a *responsible official* who tends, as a *private individual*, to *monopolize* the *interventions* that belong to *all*. It is thus necessary to "*control the elected officials*." One may seek to prevent the *dissolution* of collective persons by *codifying* them, by *subjecting* them to a *legal obligation*, by *consecrating* them with reference to a *legal framework*. A *delegate* may, for example, be *author-ized*, "*invested* with specific functions" that are *codified* in *texts* (such as *collective conventions*), that define his *status*, acts relating to his *competence* and the *incompatibilities that* concern him: "The *mandate* of *delegate* is *incompatible* with the *mandate* of administrator." When the *obligation* is not respected, *subjection* to a *legal framework* ultimately au-thorizes the collective person to "take any needed *steps*," to take appropriate *recourse* ("*appeal* to the judge"), or to *exclude* the offender, which precipitates him back into a state of unworthiness.

Civic worth depends first and foremost on *membership*. The person who *becomes a member* gains in stature be-cause he breaks out of his *isolation*. "Broad-based *mem-bership* on the part of the workers" is what constitutes their worth. But it is the mechanism of *representation* that expresses the relation of worth in this world in a specific way. The *power* of *representation* granted to a person who benefits from a *mandate* is what authorizes him to encompass others, to speak in their name, to be their *spokesperson*. *Representatives* and *delegates* are more worthy because their *mission* is to *translate* and express the *aspira-tions* of the *masses*. They have the *capacity* to *represent* the others' *interests*, that is, to transform the interests of each into a *collective interest*: "The feeling of dissatisfaction is spontaneous—the sense that something is wrong. The job then is to find out what is wrong, what has to be changed, and turn that into a demand." In the civic world, finally, in order to be legitimate, the relation of worth must be exercised within *legal forms* that define and limit *representation* according to the domain (political parties, unions, and so on), and according to time (the length of the *mandate*). The *legitimate representative* must *report back* to the base, that is, to the people whose *associa-tion* constitutes the collective.

Relation of delegation
(RELATION OF WORTH)
Membership,
Representation,
Delegation, Expression
(of aspirations).

The principal mode of relation in this world is the *as-sociation* that makes it possible to turn a multitude of *indi-viduals* into a single person. To create a *collective*, it is nec-essary to *assemble, regroup*, reunite, *unify*. The *capacity for collective action* is manifested by *recruiting, extending, im-planting*, or *spurring initiatives*: "It may be a matter of an *initiative* on the part of some workers who, although *in the minority*, contemplate *initiating an action*." But this

Gathering for collective
action (RELATIONSHIPS)
Unify, Mobilize,
Assemble, Exclude,
Join, Support,
Appeal, Debate
(democratically),
Speak out

(take the floor),
Inform, Codify,
Legalize, Authorize,
Refer (to a court).

world, always inclined to lapse into the *particular*, requires conscious and *active mobilization* if it is to hold together. Persons must be continually on the alert to avoid *splintering* and to preserve a collective character. *Representatives* must be "in close *liaison* with the workers"; *members* must "remain *in constant contact* with the *organizations* . . . and with their *policies*." They must "*come to terms* and *organize themselves*," launch *appeals*, debate democratically, pursue *discussions*, *publicize* their *policies*, inform, and, in order to be *heard, multiply explanations* as much as possible."

The democratic
republic (FIGURES)
Republic, State,
Democracy, Base,
Electorate, Institutions
(representative),
Parliament.

The civic world, which can develop only in the context of a State, finds its most perfected form in *republics* and in *democracies*, which ensure the *representation* of citizens united in *electoral bodies (electorate, electoral college, representative institutions, parliamentary democracy)*. Thanks to such institutions, the *general will* can emanate from the *base*: "In the framework of these activities, union members know the pulse of the workers. They know what . . . *aspirations* come to light in the workplace. If the *chapter* has a tendency toward apathy, they can

Demonstration for a
just cause (TEST)
Assembly, Congress,
Council, Meeting,
Session, Movement,
Presence (manifest the
presence of), Dispute,
Recourse, Justice
(demand).

arouse it, spur *debates*, and so on. The *members* are truly at the *base* of the *union chapter*." Democracy is the most appropriate political form for the manifestation of the general will that constitutes the model test for the civic world. The peak moments in this world are thus moments of *unity, meeting*, and *membership* ("call a *meeting* of the *membership*") in which the reality of the collective person is confirmed by the physical presence of its members: *demonstrations*, movements, *assemblies*, councils, *sessions, congresses*. These gatherings are particularly favorable to the development of collective worth when they aim at *demanding justice* by taking *recourse* to the *law* to settle a *dispute* or, better yet, when they provide the opportunity for a *reconsideration* that appeals to the judgment of all against institutions and against *judges* accused of *monopolizing* the *law* and bending it in favor of the particular interests of certain parties.

The verdict of the vote
(JUDGMENT) Voting,
Election, Consultation,
Mobilization, Cause
(support a) Awareness
(achieving).

Judgment is the expression of the general will that may be manifested in the inner self of each person through the *achievement of awareness* ("it is within the company that workers begin to *become aware* that they have *common interests*"); this may be manifested by a *collective reflection* or in the form of a *mobilization* around a *cause*, or it may use democratic instruments: *voting, elections,* the *designation* of *representatives.*

The form taken by evidence is the *law* in which the expression of the general will is inscribed. Its reality is clear when it is embodied in texts that can be invoked and in *legal rules* that can be applied: "The new *delegates . . .* will find useful information here on the *legal rules* that are applicable in such circumstances."

The legal text (EVIDENCE) Law (the), Rules (legal), Statutes.

The polity comes apart when it yields to the *particular*. Whatever *dilutes, splinters,* or *restrains* is unworthy: "What would the *chapter* be if it were limited to a *restricted* number of *members*?" Thus the domestic bonds of *corporatism* are constantly denounced because they *divide* workers: "*corporatist* demands that only contribute to *dividing* the workers still further into different *categories.*" To put an end to this divided state, it is necessary to "break down the trade structure that has splintered the working class." Beings, when they are not strongly held together by bonds of *solidarity,* go astray and allow themselves to be led into *deviations*. They dissolve into subgroups, or, worse, into self-serving *individualism*: "*Democracy* cannot be improvised in this world shaped by *individualism.*" People left to *themselves,* prey to their own appetite for *personal power, monopolize speech* and, "practiced in *influencing assemblies,*" "make decisions along lines that have very little to do with the *interests* of *all* the others." *In the minority,* they form a *tight inner circle*: "There is a great risk that a hierarchy will be constituted among the *militants* and that a *tight inner circle* will be created, one that cannot really use the existing possibilities." They are finally *isolated* and *cut off* from the *base,* and this absence of grounding in the general will gives them an *arbitrary* character contrary to the rule (*irregularity*) that leads them toward *a fall* and *annulment* (qualities that characterize the greatest deficiency imaginable in the civic world): "salaried workers who have been *removed* from their union functions"; "*irregularities* that may lead to the *annulment* of the *elections.*"

Division (THE FALL) Divided, Minority (in the), Particular, Isolated, Cut off (from the electoral base), Individualism (self-serving), Deviation, Subgroup, Irregular, Arbitrary, Annulled, Removed.

The Market World

The market world must not be confused with a sphere of economic relations. We have tried to show, on the contrary, that economic actions are based on at least two main forms of coordination, one by the marketplace, the other by an industrial order, and that each has its own way of setting up a reality test. This analytic distinction, supported by empirical observations based on situations that lead to carrying out one or another of these tests, sheds light on certain problems encountered in economic theory that have to do with the confrontation between these two orders. Such problems surface in particular when time is introduced as a factor in market relations, which are atemporal by nature. The comparative picture of the *market* and *industrial* worlds lays the groundwork for the analysis—to be carried out in chapter 7—of the critical relations between the advantages associated with coordination by market goods and the advantages associated with the implementation of efficient technologies. The gap between these two worlds cannot be filled by the formal addition of a new (temporal) dimension, and thus it cannot be interpreted as the distance separating a static equilibrium from a dynamic equilibrium. From Thomas Aquinas (who supplemented existing critiques of the practice of lending money at interest with the observation that time, a public good, cannot be sold) to Keynes (who noted the contradiction inherent in financial assets, which are caught between an evaluation dependent on fluctuations in profits and a judgment as to the solidity of investments), the interest rate never ceases to appear as an ambivalent object bearing the critical tension between these two worlds, despite attempts to turn it into a price like any other.

Taking a symmetrical approach to the two worlds allows us to avoid another reduction of their relations, one that would consist in relating the market world to subjective desires expressed in consumer demands while relating the industrial world to objective constraints inscribed in the functions of production. Despite its impressive arsenal of technological objects, the industrial world of efficiency is no less political than the others, and tests in it are just as dependent on a common judgment. As for the market world, it is not animated exclusively by business relations between buyers and sellers. This world is also peopled with omnipresent objects; the economist can overlook their role in the coordination of actions only when he treats them as endowed with a nature independent of the interventions of others. In this he displays the attitude of a person acting normally in the market world; in order to reach agreement on a transaction, such a person has to rely on the objectivity of the item and on its independence with respect to the various persons implicated in the transaction.

It suffices, however, to play each of these worlds against the other—to put my uncle André's knob-handled cane on the market—to allow all that distinguishes a market object from objects to which value is attached in other worlds to rise to the surface, through the disturbance that follows. By bringing to light the quality of objects of a market nature and their role in coordination, we are preparing to deal with the complex situations in which ambiguous objects disturb this coordination: something scribbled by Picasso on the corner of a table, a dented tank that does not meet industrial contemporary standards, a used car, and so on.

By distinguishing a market order, we are making ourselves vulnerable to critics who stress the lack of realism in the construction of a competitive market equilibrium. Our intent is not to seek to rehabilitate such an equilibrium on a new basis as a model of society, but to show that the order actually serves, among other things, to coordinate local transactions that seek to reach a certain form of generality. Doing so by no means ensures the achievement of a general equilibrium in conformity with the theory. In the first place, the complex societies that we are studying cannot be confined within any one of the worlds that we have identified. Moreover, within the market world itself, tests lead to the readjustment of states of worth only gradually, and not by recourse to the centralized arrangement of criers postulated by Léon Walras as necessary for establishing perfect market equilibrium at a given moment (1954 [1874], 84). As for the theoretical critiques that reveal, under the appearances of market relations, the role played *in fact* by trust, by beliefs, and so on, they converge at more than one point with the ordinary critiques that we shall seek to identify systematically in chapter 8.

Yet another difficulty poses an obstacle to the exploration of the market world. Even if one agrees to distinguish the objects that sustain it, one may have reservations about the prospect of dealing with the market according to the same model as constructions of the common good such as those referring to the general will. Can we accept this challenge and go against firmly established distinctions between the individual and the collective, between selfishness and altruism, or between the play of free choice and the weight of social norms? Can we recognize in an individual who has no homeland and no future (Nietzsche 2001, sec. 23, pp. 48–49) a being qualified to participate in a form of the common good? In this paragraph, we are pursuing the demonstration we undertook in our analysis of the market polity, by indicating how the market world can be related to the same model of worth, and what specifications are established in it for relevant beings and relationships.

Competition (HIGHER COMMON PRINCIPLE) Rivalry, Competitors.

In the market world, actions are motivated by the *desires* of individuals, which drive them to *possess* the same objects, *rare goods* whose ownership is inalienable. The characterization of this world by the dignity of persons, all equally motivated by desires, and by the adequacy of the objects that equip it already encompasses the principle of coordination, *competition*, which can be made explicit in the justifications to which tests give rise.

Viewed from the outside, the constitutive convention of competition plays the same role as the conventions that serve as higher common principles in the other worlds. The construction of the market is neither more nor less a metaphysics than the construction of the orders that refer to trust and tradition or to the general will. Each of them supposes at least two levels, that of particular persons who are on the verge of escaping from the convention and that of persons of worth who are participating in the common good.

Desirable (STATE OF WORTHINESS) Value (of), Salable, Millionaire, Winner.

The *competition* between beings placed in a state of *rivalry* governs their conflicts through an evaluation of market worth, the *price*, which expresses the importance of converging desires. Worthy objects are *salable* goods that have a *strong position* in a market. Worthy persons are rich, *millionaires*, and they *live the high life*. Their wealth allows them to *own* what others *want*, valuable objects, *luxury items*, *upscale* products. Their wealth is proportion-

ate to their own *value*, which they know how to *sell*, and
which is expressed by their *success*, designated in particular
by the vocabulary of competition: *getting ahead*, challenging oneself, *taking the edge*, being a *winner*, a *top dog*.

The deployment of market worth is inscribed in a
space that has neither limits nor distance, in which the
circulation of goods and persons is *free*. Businessmen and
women *think big*, oversee *world markets*, and do *international deals* throughout the world.

Market worth does not participate in a construction of
time. The state of worthiness includes no memory of the
past, no plan for the future. In business, one *gets ahead* by
leaping to the top, just as one unexpectedly goes bankrupt. Instability does not imply a defect, as it does in the
industrial world. Luck may go the wrong way, but one
can take advantage of *insecurity*. *Fate* can usually be made
to turn out in one's *favor*, transformed into *good luck*, if
people *exploit* the situation *opportunistically* and *take advantage of opportunities* that arise.

The state of unworthiness is one in which persons *fail*,
stagnate, and *lose out*, and in which goods are *rejected*,
spurned, *hated*, instead of *desired*.

*Unwanted (STATE OF
UNWORTHINESS)
Hated.*

Lacking any means of buying or selling, poor persons
come close to escaping the convention of the common
good and to being deprived of the dignity of human beings in this world.

The human nature that flourishes in the market world
is characterized by a desire as innocent as any dignity.
"Go for Profit. Samuel Johnson once said: 'There are few
ways in which a man can be more innocently employed
than in getting money'" (McCormack 1984, 202). This
capacity is inherent in everyone: "Most people, I believe,
are born salesmen" (89). It precedes consciousness itself:
"[T]he art of selling is the *conscious* practice of a lot of
things we already know *unconsciously*—and have probably
spent the better part of our lives doing" (89).

*Interest (DIGNITY)
Love (of things),
Desire, Selfishness.*

It is by expressing their dignity that persons come clos-
est to truth. Interest is thus their *real motivation*, the property of their *self* that makes them be *themselves* by *wanting*
to obtain *satisfaction*. One *succeeds* through the strength of
this *desire*, because one *loves*. *Real* life is what people *want
to acquire*.

In the manual we are using, the author recounts a scene

in which the participants are playing with the limits of humanity and having fun by attributing to nonhuman beings this dignity of desire, this capacity to *love* or to *hate*. At an annual sales convention, the president of a dog food company summed up the situation this way: " 'Over the past few days,' he began, 'we've heard from all our division heads and of their wonderful plans for the coming year. Now, as we draw to a close, I have only one question. If we have the best advertising, the best marketing, the best sales force, how come we sell less goddamn dog food than anyone else in the business?' Absolute silence filled the convention hall. Finally, after what seemed like forever, a small voice answered from the back of the room: 'Because the dogs *hate* it' " (117).

Since dignity designates a capacity to participate in a common good, the fact that it takes the form of a selfish desire in the market world is almost paradoxical. By recognizing dignity in persons occupied with satisfying their self-centered desires, utilitarian philosophy has contributed to establishing the modern image of the individual detached from the chains of belonging and liberated from the weight of hierarchies. However, the success of the figure of the individual has been largely dependent on proof that individuals can find a place in an order in which their actions are coordinated with those of others. Political philosophies have demonstrated the benefits of competition only by establishing this possibility of coordination, which makes it possible, today, to refer to a market polity.

Only if one loses sight of the convention that creates bonds between people as *individuals*—a convention that operates via their desire for the same objects—and if one forgets the way in which this convention of competition governs its own *free* play, do the terms "individual" or "freedom" become susceptible to the semantic slippages that lead to the presentation of the market world as the sole guarantor of people's autonomy and freedom.

Competitors
(SUBJECTS)
Businessman,
Salesman, Client,
Buyer, Independent
(worker).

The market world is thus populated with *individuals* seeking to satisfy desires; they are in turn *clients* and *competitors*, *buyers*, and *sellers*, entering into relations with one another as *businessmen*.

The fact that the deployment of objects is required for market coordination becomes obvious, in contrast, when the identity of market objects is lacking. An object of a market nature is a thing toward which competing desires for possession converge: it is a *desirable, salable, marketable* thing. Market objects do not have the same quality as objects in the industrial world, which are valued for their efficiency, their functional character. Unlike the standardization of industrial products, on which the effectiveness of those products depends, the identification that is common to market objects inscribes them as inalienable property, objects that are common to diverse desires.

Let us note that of all the social sciences, economics is the one that grants the most space to objects, although the status of these objects is not made clear in economic theory. Industrial tools remain largely external, developing as technology advances, even as they contribute actively to the production of merchandise. Market goods are so natural that their role is rarely addressed, apart from considerations about public or collective goods. Recent theoretical developments regarding the quality of goods do touch on the crucial hypothesis of a common identification of objects, but the problems raised are reduced to a matter of asymmetrical information. The value of the item is determined in a market test, and problems dealt with as instances of cheating on real quality are raised by the implicit reference to a different form of value, often industrial in nature (Eymard-Duvernay 1989b, p. 127). Similarly, the implications of a theoretical slippage from a market of goods to a market of contracts are not clearly distinguished, since the role of the hypothesis of the objectivity of a medium for the expression of competing desires is not taken into account.

The common identification of objects of a market nature is closely linked to the requirements of aggrandizement in a market world, to the investment formula that ensures access to the common good by means of a sacrifice. The selfishness of subjects in the market world has to go hand in hand, if any order is to result from their competition, with clear-sightedness as to the limits of selves; this is the other side of the picture, where the common identification of external goods is concerned. This requirement, often forgotten in methodological or political approaches to individualism, is the one that de-

Wealth (OBJECTS) Luxury (item).

Opportunism (INVESTMENT) Liberty, Opening, Attention to others, Sympathy, Detachment, Distance (emotional), Perspective (getting some).

fines the *individual* as a social being, socialized by desires that converge toward external goods.

In the market world, people are thus *detached* from one another (and in particular from any domestic bond), *liberated* in such a way that they lend themselves willingly to every opportunity to engage in a *transaction*. In short, subjects are as *available* as goods on the *market*. Here, too, the adoption of this approach to the market world makes it possible to dispel ambiguities about freedom and liberalism. Rather than to consider, as the saying goes, that each person's freedom ends where another person's begins, thus suggesting a topographic approach to the question, it might be preferable to recognize that the freedom of free-market liberalism has meaning only insofar as it is an expression of choice for external goods, and that this externality is acquired only if one starts out with a detachment that presupposes seeing others the way one sees oneself.

Perspective, emotional distance between the situation and oneself, *control* with respect to one's own emotions (emotions that, as we have seen, express the state of worth in the inspired world) are the weight that this worth brings to bear. The *opportunism* that characterizes the worthy—those who know how to *make the most* of everything, in the market world—thus goes hand in hand, unparadoxically, with a certain *attention to others* that presupposes "the ability to listen, really to hear what someone is saying" (McCormack 1984, 8) (inasmuch as others are detached individuals themselves, and not inasmuch as they form an opinion from which one has to protect oneself, like "the others" in the world of fame). This attention does not serve to temper selfishness; it is consubstantial with selfishness in the market order.

Just as the work by Adam Smith from which we extracted the canonical presentation of market worth invites us to associate a theory of the wealth of nations foregrounding the principle of competition, on the one hand, with a theory of moral sentiments based on the position of impartial spectator and sympathy, on the other, the manual we are using here makes visible the relation between the satisfactory progress of *business* and a state of persons characterized by *detachment* with regard to themselves (a *distance* that recalls the "equal distances with respect to great and small objects" at which Smith positioned the spectator) and by *attention to others* (*sympathy*, in Smith). The author of the manual brings to light the complementarity between the value of the monetary instrument of the market and the value of feelings toward others, by attributing them respectively to his mother and his father, in the dedications in which he pays his parents tribute: "To my mother, Grace Wolfe McCormack, who instilled in me, always with a twinkle in her eye, an awareness that money was indeed worth being concerned about"; "[t]o my father, Ned Hume McCormack who, more than anyone I have known, demonstrated to me the importance of being highly sensitive to people's feelings no matter how difficult the circumstances" (vii).

Possess (RELATION OF WORTH)

Even if the market world is not reduced to a collection of atoms deprived of connections with one another, market relations propagated in networks can easily be contrasted with hierarchical relations embedded one within another. And yet the market order also espouses the order of the general and the particular that implies such embedding. Market worth is not so very different from the worths that serve as examples for the notion of hierarchy, the domestic order of authority, or the industrial order of competence. Since market objects encompass the desires of others, their possession implies a hierarchical relation in the ordinary sense of the term. The state of worthiness encompasses the state of unworthiness in a relation of *possession*. The *price* of an object is the proof of the attachment of others to the good that one is holding. Since not all persons can satisfy their appetites equally by acceding to the same rare goods, the wealthiest incorporate the others by *possessing* the *desire* of those who are less wealthy and who remain deprived of goods. *Millionaires* are defined by their possession of things everyone wants.

When they are engaged, the beings of the market world are *doing business*. *Business* consists of at least two *individuals* plus an object whose *purchase* and *sale* they *negotiate*. The object, a *good* or a *service*, helps to fashion a link between people by *attracting*, by *interesting*. The *transaction* presupposes that people have enough *perspective* and that the object is *detached* enough to allow the *play of competition* with others. Local transactions thus

Interest (to) (RELATIONS) Buy, Get (for oneself), Sell, Business (do business with), Negotiate, Benefit (from), Market, Pay, Compete.

exceed settlements and become a market that takes into account the entire set of the others' desires through the prices that will be *negotiated* and *paid*. This *distance* has to produce indifference with regard to all the qualities that are foreign to those of buyer or seller in the persons with whom one is *dealing*, qualities that would express worths in other worlds ("I've come . . . to see the relative insignificance of outward glitter, be it celebrity, position, or appearances" [14]).

The assemblages are coherent when the market beings are of the same worth, when the *product* is well *positioned* in relation to the buyer and the seller. This operation takes into account the *reality* of the *buyer's* desire for the object. At the end of this harmonious process of composition, the persons doing business find their worth naturally in relation to the object negotiated. Being in a *business deal* that holds together requires persons who meet, often *face to face*, to *negotiate head to head*, far from the influence of others; they must *take one another's measure* accurately and "never underestimate [the] competition" (205).

Market (FIGURES)

The harmony of the natural order stems from the way in which *goods* acquire their *price* in a *market* that determines the distribution of states of worth. The test is the moment, uncertain in its outcome, when a *deal* is *done, settled, in the bag*. The end of the test is expressed by the signing of a *contract*. The test is also an opportunity to extract new objects from chaos, to discover new things that might *interest* a client and give rise to a transaction—an opportunity to extend the market world.

Deal (TEST) Done deal, In the bag, All wrapped up.

The common identification of goods and the generality of the worth known as *price* associates the face-to-face aspect of a business deal with other transactions taking place elsewhere, with other individuals; these can thus be equated. Price, which sanctions the test by modifying the distribution of worths, takes into account the negotiation between the two subjects involved. But this takes place on the horizon of a general price, a requirement expressed in the fact that the price has to be *reasonable* and must correspond to the *real* value.

Price (JUDGMENT) Value (justified, reasonable, real).

Money (EVIDENCE) Benefit, Result, Payback.

The generality of the price is ensured by a monetary standard. *Money* is the measure of all things, and thus constitutes the form of evidence. The *profit*, the *benefit*, the *payback*, the *result* of the transaction is thus expressed in *cash*, a *commission*, a *fee*, or an *honorarium*. This place assigned to money in market world tests does not allow us to settle any debates over monetary theory, of course, but it suggests that money, in its function of reserve value attached to a projection onto the future, is an ambiguous entity that opens up a passageway to other worlds.

The inhuman limit of the market world is marked in a long tradition criticizing the vanity of the possession of riches and advocating an attitude of wise detachment toward material wealth. In distinguishing between goods and a person's other qualities, Seneca—unlike Hume or Smith—denied that the former expressed the latter in any way and that they might serve to justify any sort of worth whatsoever: "I own my riches, yours own you. . . . I shall not look up to myself on account of these things, which, even though they belong to me, are nevertheless no part of me" ("De Vita Beata," 157 [22.5], 165 [25.1]). Just as domestic authority, taken to an extreme, can lead to a servitude that inscribes the servant himself within the master's domain as part of the patrimony, wealth can lead, in a confusion between persons and things, to the direct possession of another person rather than of the goods that that person may desire. Among the Scottish philosophers, it is the construction of a sphere of interested relations that makes the existence of disinterested relations possible (for example, friendship) (Silver 1989).

Enslavement to money
(THE FALL)

The Industrial World

The *industrial* world is the one in which technological objects and scientific methods have their place. The terminology adopted must thus not lead to the assumption that this world is fully inscribed within the limits of industry. Conversely, the workings of an industrial enterprise cannot be understood on the basis of resources stemming from this world alone, even if the aim of efficient production based on functional investments finds its justification in the industrial order.

If, as we shall see, a canonical judgment as to the quality of a scientific phenomenon allows us to illustrate the reality test of the industrial world, the fact remains that the development and diffusion of a discovery cannot be justified simply by the test examined here; these phenomena exceed the framework of the industrial world by a wide margin. Works on the history or the sociology of science and technology bring out the heterogeneity of the resources and actions involved in the processes of innovation, and they are even joined today, on this point, by economic approaches to technological change. Certain actions are inscribed in an *industrial* test where the intent is to establish scientific proof. Others are implicated in the peak moment when a singular phenomenon emerges, an innovation announcing a break with tradition according to an *inspired* justification. Still others rely on the worth of *fame*, a worth that implies a concentration of credit in terms of public opinion based on distinctive signs and marks; others depend on the venerability of *domestic* bonds guaranteeing a solid reputation or on the establishment of *market* value in an immediate response to clients' desires.

Just as the recognition of the market order is obscured by a misunderstanding of the conventions that accompany the affirmation of an individual, the understanding of the industrial order is blocked by a treatment of technological objects that locks them into an instrumental relation to nature and fails to examine the conventions supporting agreement about the scientific phenomenon in question. The observation of the conditions under which industrial objects are put to work shows that they lend themselves to the same type of test as the one already identified in the other universes. Testing these beings and establishing their objectivity presupposes a detour through a collective form, a higher common principle that governs the way they are judged. By highlighting this industrial test, we are distancing ourselves both from an approach in which science and technology are openings onto an external world, and from a radical relativism that construes facts as arbitrary beliefs attached to communities.

Efficiency (HIGHER COMMON PRINCIPLE) Performance, Future. The ordering of the industrial world is based on the *efficiency* of beings, their *performance*, their *productivity*, and their *capacity* to ensure *normal operations* and to respond usefully to *needs*.

This *functionality* is expressed in an *organization*, and it implies both a synchronic articulation with other beings and a temporal articulation. Efficiency is in fact inscribed in a regular bond between cause and effect. The proper *functioning* of beings extends the present into a *future*, opening up the possibility of prediction. The industrial form of coordination thus supports an equivalence between present situations and situations *to come*, and constitutes a temporality. *Tomorrow* is what counts: the *"machines of tomorrow,"* the *"worker of tomorrow,"* "the *organization of tomorrow."*

The quality of worthy beings, beings that are functional, *operational*, or (when humans are involved) *professional*, thus expresses their capacity to *integrate themselves* into the *machinery*, the *cogwheels* of an organization, along with their *predictability*, their *reliability*, and it guarantees *realistic projects* in the future.

Efficient (STATE OF WORTHINESS) Functional, Reliable, Operational.

People are in a state of unworthiness when they produce nothing useful, when they are *unproductive*, when they fail to do much *work*, owing to *absenteeism* or *turnover*, or because they are *inactive, unemployed, handicapped*, or— when they turn out work of poor quality—because they are *inefficient*, unmotivated, *unqualified, unsuited* to the job. Things are unworthy when they are *subjective*. Beings are also unworthy when, instead of being open to the *future*, they cling to the mold of the past, by failing to *evolve*, by remaining *static*, rigid, *ill-adapted*.

Inefficient (STATE OF UNWORTHINESS) Unproductive, Not optimal, Inactive, Unsuited, Breakdown (in a state of), Unreliable.

Waste (especially waste of "human *capabilities*" resulting from "*unqualified* work that . . . does not correspond to the *real capabilities*"), *spoilage, rejects, pollution, deterioration*, these are all *negative* signs of worth; they manifest *weak control*, the poor *functioning* of a *disturbed system* ("the *quality* of the *raw material* is *uneven* and *disrupts production*"), and they originate in *random events, incidents*, and *risks*.

The questioning of the industrial order is expressed in a non*optimal* situation, as when one *"observes* that the *programming* of *production* is not *optimizing* the *costs."* This contentious situation is a *malfunctioning*, a *problem*, a *breakdown*, an *accident*: "The reduction of rejects, accidents, and nonproductive time often makes it possible to reduce physical costs and wastes of human energy" at the same time.

The dignity of persons, the aspect of human nature on which the industrial order is based, lies in the human po-

Work (DIGNITY) Energy.

tential for *activity*. This capacity is expressed in *work* that is the implementation of the energy of *men of action*. "To invest in human *capabilities* and *energies* is to use the best *means* for economic *efficiency*." Consequently, the failure to *use* the available human *potential* is a serious breach of human dignity.

Professionals (SUBJECTS) Expert, Specialist, Person in charge, Operator.

In the industrial world, people have a *professional quali-fication* (the term *professional* is used, moreover, as a sub-stantive to designate them) related to their capability and their activity. This scale of qualification underlies a hier-archy of states of worth, a hierarchy marked by compe-tencies and responsibilities (*management, leaders, decision makers, supervisors, technicians, operators*, and so on).

In work relations and systems of remuneration, the formal qualities that express industrial worth are opposed both to a market evaluation that would result immedi-ately from a service provided and to a domestic judgment that would evaluate a person's authority.

Means (OBJECTS) Tool, Resource, Method, Task, Space, Environment, Axis, Direction, Dimension, Criterion, Definition, List, Graph, Chart, Calendar, Plan, Goal, Quantity, Variable, Series, Average, Probability, Standard, Factor, Cause.

The objects in the industrial world are instruments, *means, mobilized* for an action that is presented as a *task* of production. This instrumental construction of action, im-plying a spatial and temporal detour by way of objects that serve as relays, is thus envisaged here as a specific feature of the industrial world and not as a property that would be of a higher order of generality characterizing the actions of human beings endowed with reason.

Production activities are not organized in the same world as the actions of a market nature analyzed earlier, contrary to what is implied by the reduction of the pro-ductive function brought about in the economic theory of general equilibrium. Production is carried out in a de-ployment of objects of an industrial nature that is ex-tended from tools to procedures. The manufacturing of *products* brings into play *raw materials* plus *energy, ma-chines*, and *methods*: "A whole *panoply* of *tools, organiza-tions, methods* and *methodologies* must be available so that at every moment the best available *equipment* can be used and then set aside as soon as it is no longer *appropriate*."

The human body is the primary tool that works through *effort*, and objects of an industrial nature are merely instruments that extend the efficiency of the body's work. The economic theory of capital converges with the sociology of science and technology when it uses military metaphors to describe "enlisting . . . potent forces as our allies in the task of production." "Every 'detour' denotes the conscription of an auxiliary power that is more potent or more clever than the human hand" (Böhm-Bawerk 1959, 2:13, 14). The coherent assembly of these objects sustains a causality inscribed within a temporality: once the arrangement is in place, only a modest gesture is required to unleash a series of significant effects (2:13, 14).

Objects of an industrial nature contribute to shaping a *space* in which effects are transported by means of mechanisms. Space is organized in such a way that distant zones, or zones unrelated to the action, according to a domestic topography, are treated as an *environment* as soon as functional links have been established. The various actions are integrated into a single *homogeneous* plan which is *governed* by *axes, guidelines, dimensions, degrees,* and *levels.* Objects are related to one another within this space with the help of *lists* and *inventories* dealt with by *lot.* Measurable space can be projected on a piece of paper where part of the test is played out, thanks to the construction of *grids, states, graphs, charts, flow charts, frameworks, accounts, indicators.* The spatial articulation of objects presupposes a capacity to *define* that is equipped with a *measuring instrument.* The *measuring instruments* used are actually machines that are incorporated into the workspace. They *standardize* by using *definitions* and *investigations* to produce objects in due form whose functions can be grasped by *criteria* or *characteristics.* Even human bodies can be caught up in these measures and inscribed in the ergonomics of the *task* to be carried out: "*Ergonomics* can help us *determine* the physical *cost* of a *workstation* and *express* it in kilocalories per day. . . . The *stations* have been *modified* (height, position, seats) as a *function* of the *average measurements* of *segments* of the *personnel.*"

Function is a notion that must be understood in a spatial articulation and a temporal liaison, as mechanical devices illustrate. The temporal equivalence instituted by industrial worth is particularly visible in objects apprehended according to their aptitude for managing the future, such as flow charts, *plans,* and *budgets:* "By *making adjustments* to the *planning calendar,* we are *integrating* the *project* into the *plan,* the *working* and *investment budgets.*"

The tools for measuring time take advantage of the regularity with which industrial objects function and endow the industrial world with a representation of time that is not unlike the topography of this world, in which one can be transported without friction, can move ahead or make a retrospective return to the past. *Calendars* and *timetables* make it possible to establish *states of periodic advancement*, to trace *stages, phases, deadlines*. This shaping of time models in return the reference points for action constituted by *goals* and *missions*.

The analysis of the objects of the industrial world makes it possible to understand the possibility of *calculations*, by reversing the perspective adopted when one reduces calculations to the exercise of a mental faculty belonging to beings endowed with reason. The instruments for defining and measuring constitute the situation of action as a *problem* leading to the formulation of *hypotheses* and calling for a *solution*. The articulation of *elements* or *segments* obtained by the *decomposition* of the *complexity* of the *universe* can be accomplished by mathematical operations, since the calculations are based on *quantified variables*: "The *inventory* of *problems* and their alternative *solutions* is subjected to the *method* of economic *evaluation* that makes it possible to *quantify* the various *hypotheses* for improvement."

Progress
(INVESTMENT)
Investment, Dynamic.

Progress is the investment formula in the industrial world. It is associated with the operation of investment (in the classical sense of the term) that weighs the "price of *efforts*," "heavy in time and in money," and the "*middle-term profitability*" that they *ensure*: "The *investments* will open the way to new *development*." Industrial worth requires this *dynamic* in order to avoid obsolescence, the "*future obsolescence* of the existing *organization*." The temporal orientation is constructed on the basis of the future (as is seen in investment decisions or in arguments for optimization by "*backward induction*"), unlike the temporal orientation that prevails in the domestic order, an orientation generated by the past.

Let us note that the calculation of the profitability of an investment, as soon as it takes an interest rate into account, integrates the constraints of a financial market that is not inscribed in the industrial order.

Control (RELATION OF
WORTH)

It is in a relation of *control* that the state of worthiness encompasses the state of unworthiness. The word *respon-*

sibility may be ambiguous here, because it also serves to designate the relation of domestic worth. However, the industrial responsibility of the worthy person does not imply that he has power over a less worthy person who owes him respect in return. The control one exercises depends only on the possibility of predicting less complex actions by integrating them into a larger overall plan. A more worthy person is in relation with a less worthy person primarily through the *"responsibility* he assumes" for *production*, by the *control* he has over the *future*: "To *determine* the *future* accurately in order to *control* it is an *indispensable task* of *factory management*."

Natural relations are those required by the regular *functioning* of beings of an industrial nature. They are thus dependent on the qualities of the objects already identified.

In the first place, they *put to work production factors* organized in *structures* or systems made up of *adjusted mechanisms, adapted machinery,* and *interactions.* The functional connections are established in the mode of the *necessary,* the *required.* These *inexorable, indispensable* requirements take the form of *constraints* that *condition* action and must therefore be *taken into account;* one must *take responsibility* for them. Persons themselves are *integrated as a function of* the more or less *complex competencies* they exercise: "Each *hierarchical level takes upon* itself what cannot be *delegated* to a *lower level;* in exchange, it has access to *efficient tools* for *control.*"

The functional relations of the industrial world share in a temporal *stability* that is favorable to *forecasting*: "The *production unit* appears on the whole as a rather well-*stabilized* universe that is very well *controlled.*" The organization of the beings installed in an industrial arrangement goes hand in hand with an *organization* of its functioning, with *stabilization* procedures that, in production, work primarily through stocking operations.

The *implantation* of an industrial arrangement presupposes *adjustments* in the environment, *adaptations, redefinitions*: "The *overall program* is *adapted* to each particular *terrain* and all its *phases* are *redefined as a function* of the *characteristics* proper to this *terrain,* while the overall *framework* is maintained." *Industrial* action requires a *correct* vision of this space in which the problem is inscribed, so as to

Function
(RELATIONSHIPS) Put
to work, Machinery
(liaison of), Function
(to be a function of),
Cogwheels, Interact,
Need (to),
Condition(to),
Necessary (relation),
Integrate, Organize,
Control, Stabilize,
Order, Anticipate,
Implant, Adapt,
Detect, Analyze,
Account (take into),
Determine, Light
(bring to), Measure,
Formalize,
Standardize,
Optimize, Solve,
Process.

detect, discover, identify, bring to light, measure, analyze, and *decompose* the relevant elements. Similarly, the results of the action taken are apprehended through their *traces* on this space. From space to *class*, the code breaks a path. The operations of *standardization* and *formalization* make it possible to see the world through data *expressed* in numbers, *quantified,* ready to be *processed,* combined, *added up.*

The description of the constitutive elements of the time and space proper to the industrial world makes it quite clear that the operation of *optimization* is possible only in an environment of beings of an industrial nature. Rational optimization is not situated in continuity with the immediate satisfaction of a desire, in the extension of a market coordination. In fact, the temporal extension of the criterion of optimization in economic theory, which passes through an optimization of expectation of the anticipated utility, confronts difficulties that result from the introduction of irreversibilities inherent in the investment decision (Favereau 1989b).

*Organization
(FIGURES) System.*

The harmony of the industrial order is expressed in the *organization* of a *system,* a *structure* in which each being has its function, in short, a "technically predictable universe": "No blatant contingent *malfunctions* are visible; all the *cogwheels* of the *organization* work *together* without a hitch." However, the equilibrium is not static (which would lead to a rapidly *outdated* state) but dynamic; the equilibrium is one of *growth, expansion.*

*Trial (TEST)
Launching, Setting up,
Putting to work,
Achievement.*

The testing of this organization presupposes *verifying* that things function as predicted, that the solution to the problem is *realistic.* Once the *decision* is made, the arrangement *set up,* the project *launched,* the mechanism *started,* its proper operation can be judged by an evaluation of its *performance* on the basis of the *effects produced.* It remains to be seen whether the arrangement *functions correctly,* whether everything is *in working order,* whether "it's going well." This functioning may lead to a reordering of the *hierarchy* of *functions*: "The *qualification* of the *tasks evolves* in the opposite direction from the *hierarchy* of the original *functions.* The preparation is gradually *disqualified* owing to *automatization.*"

*Effective (JUDGMENT)
Correct, In working
order, Functioning.*

The test is also an opportunity to reveal new objects. The measuring devices mentioned earlier contribute to the process of revelation by achieving spatial and temporal equivalencies, by carrying out operations *in series*. They make it possible to establish laws on the basis of *frequencies*, and to reduce the role of *chance* by exhibiting *probable* relations on the basis of *averages*. Proof is grounded in a temporal regularity, the methodic repetition of measurement. New *causes*, new *factors* capable of *giving rise to effects*, are thus identifiable during tests.

Measure (EVIDENCE)

In the industrial world, the distinctive dignity of humanity is threatened by the treatment of people as things. The worth of the objects and arrangements created can be confused with this dignity to the point of blurring the boundary of humanity. Deprived of tests, protected from the risk of contingencies that can call the order of competencies into question and allow new objects to emerge, industrial worth can become frozen in the monumental order that is regularly depicted in critiques of technology.

Instrumental action (THE FALL) Treating people as things.

PART FOUR

CRITIQUES

Seven

WORLDS IN CONFLICT,

JUDGMENTS IN QUESTION

Unveiling

BY FOLLOWING the deployment of objects in a coherent world that we have considered, from a viewpoint stressing the formal constructions of political philosophy, only as a polity, we have seen how judgments could converge in tests and could thus engage with reality. But in the tests that we have examined up to now, only beings belonging to a single world were involved. What happens when persons and things from different worlds present themselves together in a test? And, more generally, how are relations among different worlds established? The search for a satisfactory response to these questions leads us to leave natural agreement behind in order to contemplate new figures. We shall first examine figures of critique that arise in situations of discord, and then, in part 5, the particular form of return to agreement that we shall call compromise.

The problems raised by relations among worlds cannot be dismissed by associating the various worlds and the worths they manifest with different persons, cultures, or milieus, the way classical sociology treats relations among values and groups. To attach persons to worlds would mean pinning them down in a single form of worth, and this would run counter to the principles of justice on which the polity model is based. One of the chief guiding threads of our undertaking consists, to the contrary, in the observation that human beings, unlike objects, can manifest themselves in different worlds. We are investigating the possibility that people can reach justifiable agreements despite the availability of multiple principles of agreement, and can do so without acknowledging a relativism of values, or attributing ownership of the principles in question to persons or groups of persons, as a way of sidestepping difficulties. Indeed, the latter approach leaves the question of agreement without a response. If the various persons involved corresponded to different groups, these persons would be indifferent to one another (as in Rousseau's version of the state of nature) and thus would not form a polity; they would never succeed in agreeing on the higher common principle from which the situation arises, and every test would quickly turn into a dispute leading to an impasse.

Thus we have to give up the idea of associating worlds with groups; we can attach worlds only to the arrangements of objects that qualify the various situations in which persons are acting when they attribute value to these objects. However, in a differentiated society, each person regularly has to confront situations stemming from distinct worlds, has to recognize such situations and prove capable of adjusting to them. Every differentiated society may be qualified as "complex," in the sense that its members have to possess the competence needed to identify the nature of a situation and to navigate situations arising from different worlds. Since the principles of justice invoked are not immediately compatible, their presence in a single space leads to tensions that have to be resolved if the action is to take its normal course. The most inspired artist cannot let the inspiration of the moment determine his course of action in every situation; in order not to be perceived as mentally ill, he has to stand in line at the post office like any other customer. Similarly, actors whose professional universe is deeply embedded in an industrial world, with its workshops, offices, and construction sites, are nevertheless not stuck fast once and for all in the world of industry. Even at work, they have to be able to shift into situations in which objects and worths from a different world are deployed—perhaps from the world of inspiration, to take an example that appears particularly incompatible with the industrial order. Certain manifestations of working-class resistance that seem at odds with demands consistent with a properly industrial worth and are expressed in physical exploits or physical violence (Sabel 1982; Luedtke 1986) constitute ways of increasing one's worth that stem from inspiration, on the same basis as exercises of self-mortification in classical asceticism.

Our analytic framework is distinct in this respect from paradigms based on the hypothesis of an internal guidance system that works by means of a program inscribed in persons in advance. Whatever the origin of the program and the mode of its inscription may be, its function is to maintain the subject's identity while guaranteeing a more or less automatic repetition of behaviors that remain in harmony with one another no matter what situation is confronted. Our own framework seeks, on the contrary, to preserve uncertainty about people's actions, an uncertainty that has to have a place, it seems to us, in a model purporting to account for human behaviors. Although the room to maneuver is strictly limited by the way the situation is arranged, a model incorporating several worlds gives actors the possibility of avoiding a test, of challenging a test's validity by taking recourse to an external principle, or even of reversing the situation by introducing a test that is valid in a different world. The model thus includes the possibility of a critique for which determinist constructions fail to account.

To undertake an analysis of competence in a society that includes a plurality of principles of agreement, we shall start with situations featuring beings that are relevant in different worlds. Among these composite situations, we shall begin by examining disputes unlike the disagreements evoked in the preceding chapter, in that persons who reject the outcome of a test are not content to invoke the effect of unfavorable circumstances in order to demand that the test be annulled or repeated. To support their demands, they call attention to the presence, in the situation that was unfavorable to them, of beings that do not belong to the world in which the test has to be set up in order to be valid. They thus seek to attribute value to beings of a different nature whose intervention introduces worths that are foreign to the test, thus rendering the test invalid. This operation of *unveiling* extends the possibilities of disagreement, which are limited in a one-world model by the impossibility of producing arguments that arise from principles other than those governing the situation at hand.

To carry out this operation of unveiling, beings that do not belong to the nature that is present have to be removed from the circumstances surrounding the test. When the validity of the test goes unchallenged, these beings are submerged in contingency. They are there, but weakly illuminated, without being subject to precise identification, irrelevant unnamed *items* whose presence is purely circumstantial; thus they have no effect on the order of worths among the beings in presence. The family photograph on the boss's desk is not relevant in the scene in which he is confronting an employee he is about to fire. The photo may remain in contingency; it need not intervene in the negotiation that is under way in an attempt to determine, for example, whether or not the employee is guilty of professional misconduct. But the photo can also be imbued with value in a way that brings a different world to the surface, along with a principle of domestic justice that might attenuate the rigor of the verdict if it were taken into account. "Ah, you have children? So do I!" This appeal to equity would be more incongruous, harder to get away with, if there were no objects at hand that could serve as operators. The unveiling thus consists in drawing on contingent items in the circumstances and wresting them away from contingency ("it's no accident that . . ."), while making it clear that they are indeed involved in the test. Such items then count, inasmuch as they are of a different nature and bring to light a different world: the situation turns out to be denatured by them.

Persons may remove themselves from the grip of a situation and call the validity of a test into question because, since they have the potential of belonging to any of the possible worlds, they have the ability to be *distracted*. If they were attached to a single world, like things, they would not be in a position to reidentify contingent items and wrest them away from the surrounding chaos. These foreign beings may be more or less *distracting*, moreover, and the more they disturb the present situation through their commotion, the easier it is to get a grip on them and involve them in the test.

Even if no object of a different nature is at hand, a test can still be derailed by persons who do what is necessary to transform their own state and manifest themselves according to the requirements of an external world. A mayor wearing the insignia of his office (a civic person), an entrepreneur talking business with promoters (an industrial person), and the eldest son of a family that is respected and well established in the region who is having lunch with friends or relatives (a domestic person) share the same body and have identifying markers that make it possible to connect the three persons. A participant may distance herself from the civil ceremony presided over by the mayor and unveil the latter's election as fraudulent, "arranged by his friends" to serve "private interests," while attributing value to the presence of a dignitary in the garb of a judge. But this clairvoyance presupposes that the person doing the denouncing has herself changed state: if she were there simply in her civic mode (as a member of the city council, for example), she would not pick up the signs of connivance the mayor is addressing to local dignitaries. In order to grasp the relevance of these signs and attribute value to them, the denouncer has to detach herself from the civic test in which she is participating and position herself in the domestic world, for example, inasmuch as she is subordinated to the mayor's person by ties of personal dependence, and because, owing to her situation, she has picked up certain anecdotes arising from the private domain (anecdotes therefore defined from the standpoint of the civic world as petty, trivial, and misplaced, or as illegal and scandalous). Thus it is by relying on her own body, imbued with value in a different nature and in conformity with an absent world, that she can remove herself, without the help of anyone or anything else, from the test that is under way in order to consider and judge it from the outside.

We shall now turn to some illustrative cases in which knowledge of other worlds makes it possible to extend disagreement to the test itself. We shall first analyze cases in which reference to other worlds seeks not to challenge the test's relevance or the principle on which the test is based but, on the contrary, to reinforce its validity by purifying the conditions of its realization, which are the only aspects called into question.

Next, we shall present more extreme situations in which the presence of beings of a different nature is exploited in order to challenge the very principle of the test, and to try to overturn the situation by replacing the test that is under way by a test relevant in a different world. Only in the latter case is the operation of unveiling fully accomplished. This figure al-

lows us to associate two movements. The first consists in highlighting beings of another nature whose hidden presence has debased the test, and
thus in dismantling the common good by denouncing it as a private good
(unveiling in the sense of unmasking false appearances). This first movement is followed by a second, which consists in attributing value to the
common good of a different polity (unveiling in the sense of recognizing
true worth). This reversal is signaled by the use of connective phrasing
that links the unveiling of a reality to the revelation of a principle of determination that had hitherto remained hidden: "in fact," "in reality," "to tell
the truth," "what is called," "what is labeled" ("what is known as reality"),
"is only," "subtends," "is subtended by," "in the guise of," and so on.

Causes of Discord and the Transport of Worths

Since they can be acquainted with more than one world, persons may
challenge the validity of the tests to which they are subjected, and they are
not limited to questioning the distribution of worths. Knowledge of other
worlds makes it possible to challenge the validity of a test by showing that
it is affected by the presence of beings of a different nature, or by the lack
of objects belonging to the world from which it stems. If the test carried
out is to be valid, then, a new, purified situation has to be set up, one from
which foreign beings have been removed so that the test can be conducted
without impediments. Purification requires the involvement of beings better identified in the world from which the test stems, beings that are consequently more worthy, as is the case for example when, during a civic test,
someone appeals to a judge. Let us consider two travelers arguing over a
seat in a train that each says he has reserved. The situation is well equipped:
there are numbered seats, tickets, posted rules. In order to avoid coming
to blows, to avoid giving up on justice in favor of force, the persons involved make a further commitment to the civic nature of the situation by
calling on the conductor and presenting their tickets, reservations, cards
indicating a privileged status, and so on.

A challenge to the validity of a test always relies on the unveiling of a
disharmony between the state in which the persons engaged in the test
find themselves and the nature of the objects that they must accredit. This
challenge takes two forms. Someone may show that the test is unfair because the objects needed for its completion are lacking. The test is considered valid in principle, but it has not been properly carried out: in this
case, we shall say that it is a mere simulacrum, and we shall speak of inval-
idation owing to the lack of an object. In another case, someone may show
that a test is unfair because it takes into account objects belonging to a different nature. Here again, the test is considered valid in principle, but its

realization must be more closely controlled so as to remove the foreign beings that are disturbing it. In this latter instance, two new possibilities arise. First, someone may criticize the way the worth of persons is evaluated by showing that this evaluation takes into account their capacity to accredit objects that are foreign to the world from which the test stems, either because the persons involved have brought these objects with them or because they have picked them up from among the circumstances (accusation of a *transport of worth*). A person whose worth has been unjustly overvalued will be said to have benefited from a "privilege." Conversely, someone may demonstrate that the deficiency of a person in a different world has followed her into the test in spite of herself, and has affected her performance. This person will be said not to have met the test under satisfactory conditions of justice because she suffers from a "handicap" (accusation of a *transport of deficiency*).

Let us examine the first figure of accusation more closely. The validity of the test is challenged because objects that ought to be accredited in order to test worths are faulty or lacking. Since the world from which the test stems is not fully exhibited in the situation, the persons involved have not really had the means to make their case in that world, have been unable to show their true capabilities. The rigged test diminishes these persons with respect to others who have been subjected to a test carried out under satisfactory conditions. Consequently, it is unjust to hold them responsible for their defects, and the test, if it is to be conclusive, must be repeated under valid conditions, that is, in the presence of adequate objects. This is the argument put forward when someone judges, for example, that a high rate of abstention must not be attributed to an absence of democratic spirit among the citizenry but to an insufficient unfolding of the civic world, as a result of which the democratic expression of popular sovereignty is impeded (for example, when access to polling places is blocked or entails a physical risk, when the anonymity of the voting booth is not respected, and so on). Or someone might show that the poor results achieved by managers and engineers in a third world country cannot be attributed to an inability to act in a rational way—an inability of which they have been accused—but have to do with the fact that these persons had been placed in situations of industrial testing where, for want of suitable objects (owing to material of poor quality, absence of information, and so on), the possibility of engaging fully with the industrial world was not really available to them.

Let us now attempt to account for accusations of the second type. To do this we need to specify more fully than we have done so far the capacities attributed to persons in a multiworld model. We must recall that people may be in any and all of the worlds in turn, and also that from the vantage point of one world they may be familiar with others (a position that offers

the possibility of an unveiling). The second property is not a direct consequence of the first; one can imagine a universe in which persons would be
plunged by turns into situations arising from different worlds without any
means of coming to know several worlds at once and, as a result, without
being aware of the plurality (this is the case with hysterics). But a universe
of this type does not correspond to the ordinary experience of normal
people; what is more, it would offer nothing for description to latch onto.
When the validity of a test is challenged, persons are accused of being engaged in that test without having disengaged themselves from a test of a
different nature. The test is not a fair one because the persons involved
have not all been engaged in it in the appropriate state: some of them remain imbued with an acquired worth of a different nature. It follows that
the distribution of worths among persons does not correspond to the importance of the sacrifice they have accepted. They will then be accused of
benefiting from a special privilege. The unveiling aims to reveal the presence of this foreign world not in order to challenge the relevance of the
test but to show its irregularities, and to ask that the situation be clarified
in order to ensure that the test will be repeated under satisfactory conditions of validity. To describe this figure of accusation, we shall speak of *preoccupation*: the persons are accused of being concerned with objects from
another world instead of being engaged with what they are doing in the
current world. Still preoccupied with matters involving other worths, they
are not in the state that is appropriate to the test: they import the beings
that preoccupy them, and these can be picked up by other persons who
share the same preoccupations. Preoccupation is thus the most general expression of the transport of one world into another. The transport of worth
and the transport of deficiency are denounced as unfair because they are
based on the possibility of attaching worth to persons as if it were consubstantial with them.

Let us note that the figure of preoccupation is always polemical. It is
based on an interpretation of the state of persons, an interpretation that
may be contested. During a dispute, a person who is deemed to be preoccupied may reject this accusation by denying that it has any basis: to be
sure, the student who turns up for the examination is wealthy, but he has
not made a display of his wealth and the examiner has not taken it into
account in any way. The student's knowledge alone has been evaluated.
To be upheld, the accusation has to stem from the presence of objects of a
market nature, signs of wealth (items that have no importance in the logic
of an academic test) and the accusation has to show that these objects
have been put into play by the student in an effort to gain appreciation.
The accusation must also show that the examiner did not remain blind to
this transport of worth (otherwise it would not have affected her judgment), and that she allowed herself to be distracted by the signs of wealth

to which she was attentive, thus suggesting that she was no less preoccupied than the candidate by the presence of objects that enhance a person's worth in a market world. If she had been doing her job properly in the academic test, she would have remained blind to the candidate's expensive clothing (market worth) and elegant manners (domestic worth); she would have set them aside during the test as superficial ornaments of no importance. She would have assessed the student's value fairly, that is, by taking into account only the student's qualities in the industrial world, his work, his reliability, his competence, and so on. The possibility of challenging the validity of the test thus results in making the justification more demanding: it favors an explicit account of the sacrifice accepted that, without the prodding of the critique, might be tacitly presupposed. The critique thus contributes to the knowledge that the worthy have of their own worth, a worth that they have to justify in order to face accusations intended to disqualify tests in which they have distinguished themselves.

But one may also contest the verdict of a test by showing not the advantages that the transport of worth confers on the worthy (privileges) but the disadvantages from which the deficient suffer. In this case, it is established that the test is not pure, in that it is affected by the deficiency of those lacking worth in another world, and that this *transport of deficiency* results in diminishing them in the current world (handicap). This is the figure at work when someone invokes mitigating circumstances and declares that a judgment that takes the handicap into account is equitable: a worker is late to work, but the penalty imposed on her is suspended when it is learned that she is the single parent of a sick child. Her hierarchical superior will be said to have been equitable, or to have proved his "humanity," when he took the mitigating circumstances into account. However, in the course of the dispute, this evaluation may obviously be challenged in turn, and the leniency of the equitable boss may be qualified as "inappropriate indulgence," "weakness," "cowardice," or "favoritism"; in other words, it may be denounced in turn as the unfair manifestation (unfair because it affects the outcome of the test) of a particular interest on the part of the boss in the worker, who must bring into play the presence of objects of a domestic nature, such as her status as relative or neighbor, in order to pass the test. In the transport of deficiency, the things from a different nature that constitute obstacles to the accrediting of objects from the current world are treated as burdens weighing people down. Equitable judgment takes this weight of things into account in the evaluation of the sacrifice accepted. There will thus be an effort to neutralize the effects of the burden by a compensatory move that takes the handicap into account. To correct the injustice and give the less favored person "another chance," someone will propose to lighten the weight of things by a corrective arrangement (redistribution, compensatory education, and so on). In this case, as in the case of the transport of worth, the dispute may be suspended and agreement restored by the setting up of a test that is purer and thus can be viewed as more just. Strictness toward the worthy and indulgence toward the deficient thus shatter the scale of worth and leave intact only the smallest possible distance between the worthy and the deficient. The convergence of judgments on this minimal gap, treated as natural, has to do with equity.

Clashes and Denunciations

In the cases we have examined up to now, the disputes had to do with whether or not the test was pure and consequently whether or not it needed to be clarified; the world exhibited in the situation was not called into question. However, this world is itself subject to challenge. The impossibility of reaching agreement on how to set up a valid test leads to a confrontation between two worlds, and thus to the possibility of clarifying the test in one of these worlds or the other. Given that reestablishing agreement depends on carrying out a new test recognized as valid, anything that stands in the way of repeating the test (for example, when the test's verdict turns out to be attached to a person) or anything that impedes purification of the test keeps the dispute alive. The party that deems itself disadvantaged can make a legitimate challenge if it can show that redress of the injustice by means of a new test cannot take place. The dispute then moves on to a new stage in which the very reality of the common good underlying the legitimacy of the test is contested. The disagreement then has to do not only with the test's outcome and the distribution of states of worth but also with the principle that is to govern the way the test is carried out and with the world in which the test has to be set up if it is to be conclusive.

In the *clash* between worlds that arises here, the dispute no longer has the relation between the importance of the sacrifice and the distribution of worths as its sole object. The challenge to the relation between the sacrifice accepted by a person and the state of worth to which that person accedes (the worthy do not deserve the place they occupy because they have benefited from a privilege and have not actually carried out the sacrifice that they are invoking to justify their rank) is accompanied by a reconsideration of the common good denounced as mere self-satisfaction in opposition to other principles of justification: the worthy are not producing the common good but their own happiness; their wealth is not the condition of the well-being of all—it serves only their own well-being; the work they accomplish is not useful to the common good, but is rather at the service of their vanity or their personal ambition, and so forth. In clashes, the discord thus has to do not simply with the worth of the beings present, but with the very identification of the beings that matter and those that do not; it has to do, then, with the true nature of the situation, with *reality* and the common good to which reference may be made to reach agreement. The goal is no longer to repeat the test in a purer and more equitable fashion by eliminating privileges and neutralizing handicaps, but to demystify the test as such, in order to place things on their true ground and to institute a different test that will be valid in a different world.

This development of a dispute into a clash over the very nature of the common good may come about if persons involved take recourse to operations intended to challenge a test's purity. Indeed, we have seen that in order to challenge the validity of a test and show that it is affected by the presence of beings foreign to its true nature, it is necessary to reveal the presence of these beings, contingent items whose importance is exposed so as to be denounced, entities brought to light and identified so they can be set aside. But as soon as one of the parties present has identified them by associating them with a different form of the common good, these items can no longer be left out. They must then either be included in the current world, where they are deficient, while being qualified by means of the terms used to designate the most deficient beings, or else their worth has to be taken into account, whereupon the situation finds itself reversed.

This operation of reversal consists in showing that false worth conceals deficiency; it corresponds to the first stage of unveiling, which we shall call a *critique*. Critiques are articulated by operators such as "in fact," "in reality," "are only," and so on. A clash, in which several incompatible principles of justice may enter into competition, thus includes the possibility of several tests. The parties involved disagree about the world in which the test must be carried out if it is to be legitimate. The clash is thereby a necessarily unstable moment in a dispute. At a supermarket cash register, if a customer were to claim a right of free access to all goods, the same for everyone, he would be denouncing the market test as an act of theft on the part of the supermarket; if a customer waiting in line at the post office were to claim the right to go straight to the window because he is wealthy, he would be denouncing the validity of the principle of justice on which public service relies. In order to disentangle the clashing elements, it is necessary to go back to a single test, either by reversing the situation to make it shift into another nature, which is the aim of the critique (the so-called public is only the juxtaposition of self-interested clients, or, conversely, the so-called client is in fact a citizen with the right to a public service open to all) or else by setting aside the items on which the unveiling depended in order to seat the test once again in its world of origin. The unveiling may also serve to set aside disturbing objects of a foreign nature and to restore the conditions of a test on which judgments can converge.

The more or less explicit character of the critique depends on the level of the dispute. As long as the dispute remains limited, denunciations may be carried out without being completely clarified with reference to a principle. For instance, tactics of disengagement such as irony, hyperbole, or understatement, which, through an exaggerated inversion, increase, or reduction of the worths at stake tend to discredit the principle of evaluation at work in the situation and open up the possibility of reference to alternative worths. The same thing holds true for "displays of humility" (grotesque compromises between inspiration and opinion, which are referred to only in critical terms, as when one speaks of "ostentatious humility") or self-denigration. These figures are first attempts at critiques. Self-deprecation, "putting oneself down," consists in lumbering oneself with attributes that, with reference to other ways of establishing worth, qualify what is deficient; this amounts to critiquing worths that one is claiming to lack, in other words, essentially, here, fame and wealth.[1] In fact, in a natural situation, no one can boast of being deficient. No one, without losing his dignity, can flaunt defects that diminish him in the world he currently occupies. Glorifying oneself on the basis of a lack thus necessarily presupposes an external point of reference. When this "inversion of the gaze positing values" (Nietzsche 1971, [1887] 234) remains implicit, we find ourselves in the presence of what Nietzsche denounced under the heading of *ressentiment*. But the mere fact of not lending oneself to the situation, not yielding to it naturally, considering it from the outside, refusing to go along with the others and engage in it even while remaining in it as an outsider, is a critique in action (a category to which inspired gestures belong), one that, while unveiling the artificiality of the situation, stirs up trouble in it and creates awkwardness. For example, a reception on the occasion of someone's departure, a party attended by colleagues, requires that the participants change their state in order to leave industrial worths behind and take on domestic worths, a change that is sometimes difficult to bring off if it is set up in the workplace; some participants refuse to drink, joke around, or dance, and instead withdraw into a corner to talk shop or to look on the entire scene with the absent air of inspired idiots.

The Monstrosity of Composite Setups

Since critiques rely on the presence of beings from a different world, the possibility of taking recourse to that other world depends on the way the situation has been set up. Particularly pertinent here are the *awkward situations* with composite setups that make available to persons certain things stemming from different worlds that are capable of being engaged in a test. The ambiguity of composite setups arouses feelings of awkwardness and anxiety in participants when they are involved in a test. They have to select objects from among the disparate resources offered by the situation and prevent the situation from coming apart. But the coexistence of objects of different natures makes several groupings equally possible and creates uncertainty about the nature of the test under way, and especially about the state in which the persons involved find themselves. Each of the participants presents a murky aspect: they all have something disquieting about them, and their engagement in several natures may be denounced at any moment. Let us take, for example, an official commission charged with judging proposals, only a small number of which will be retained. The arrangement includes civic elements (the scene takes place in a government office) and measuring instruments of an industrial nature (the feasibility and usefulness of the work under consideration) and also of a market nature (the cost of the project). But worths of fame (are the persons present well known?) and inspiration (are they gifted, imaginative?) come up constantly during the meetings of this commission; its members know each other personally, are on a first-name basis, and chat about all sorts of things, all of which pulls the situation in the direction of a domestic test.

To bring to light the incongruous groupings formed of beings from several worlds, we can either observe them directly or extract them from reports made by people about awkward situations in which they have been ill at ease. The awkward situations, collected in the form of typical anecdotes that make them easily accessible, lend themselves to retelling. Their import and the interest they arouse derive not only from the feelings with which they are associated but also from their ability to deal, in a stylized way, with tensions between worlds that may be associated in different versions of an anecdote by different persons, whose experience is thus made available for sharing. But one can also attempt to reconstitute such scenes artificially by combining persons, objects, and relations deriving from different worlds. Even more than striking anecdotes drawn from daily life, these artificial constructions have the power to evoke and reveal the ordinary sense of fairness. Thus, for example, the simple permutation among forms of relationships and objects stemming from two different worlds suffices to engender monstrous hybrids: to offer (domestic) a political tract (civic) as a gift to an employee; to allocate (civic) bouquets (domestic) to one's grandparents. The permutation introduces a discordance among worths: by saying that the militant "offers" tracts as if these were personal objects, we remove him from his role, which is to represent the general interest; by saying that a child "allocates" bouquets as if these were impersonal objects, we lose sight of the respect a child owes to his grandparents. To construct such chimera, as biologists call synthetic beings created in the laboratory, we shall use the inventories established to describe each world. We shall thus be able to reconstitute reports of composite scenes and measure to what extent these disconcerting utterances distance us from the obvious plenitude encountered in the tableaus that led us into the heart of each of these worlds.

Let us take as examples the following situations (it should be intuitively obvious that there is something incongruous or awkward about each one):

- at home, to get his children's attention, a father presents a glowing picture of his ability to direct a project at work;
- at a meeting, a chapter secretary suddenly appears on the podium, takes the floor and speaks passionately; he lets his imagination run wild, makes bizarre wordplays, and finally confesses that he is unsure of his own thinking;
- in a workshop, a machine operator offers a gift to the expert who has come to measure the production capacities of the machine for which the operator is responsible, and asks the expert to write a recommendation for his son, a well-mannered computer technician who is unemployed.

These three scenarios, composed by putting together elements extracted from the descriptions of the various worlds, all offer pictures of awkward situations that are troubling for the actors, who cannot be at ease in them. The first combines elements borrowed from the domestic world (a father and his children), from the world of fame (attract attention, present a glowing picture), and finally from the industrial world (ability to direct a project). What makes these situations awkward? Attracting attention and shoring up one's personal image are not among the sorts of relations that a father is supposed to have with his children. Attracting attention is a behavior that qualifies the least worthy beings in the domestic world: impolite children attract attention. Moreover, a father does not talk about his work and his professional qualifications at home, with his family, in terms stemming so directly from the industrial world, with the goal of enhancing his own worth in his family members' eyes (this would suggest that he must be very impoverished in domestic worth if he is seeking to improve his standing by such an incongruous transfer of worths). The ambiguous test is not adapted to any of the worlds to which the beings present in the scene belong.

The second scenario, no less awkward but closer to those presented in novels, brings together elements belonging to the civic world (secretary, office, chapter, podium, meeting, taking the floor) and from the inspired world (appearance, passion, imaginary, word plays, unusual, expressing self-doubt). The representative of the collective person is exposing in public what is most singular about himself. This conduct, which would be qualified as indecent in the domestic world, is actually scandalous in the civic world. As is often the case when the composite setup includes numerous elements of an inspired nature, this scene evokes what might be called "temporary insanity."

In the third scenario, elements from the domestic world (offering a gift, soliciting a recommendation, son, well mannered) are inserted into an industrial situation (operator, workshop, expert, production capacity, machine, computer technician, unemployment). As for responsibility, it may be relevant in either of the two worlds.

These scenes all open up the prospect of several different tests, and in each of them one can imagine various outcomes aiming at clarification in a single world. The children in the first story may seek to get their father's attention in their turn by speaking louder than he does and boasting that they know some stars from the music world (clarification in the world of fame), or, on the contrary, embarrassed by his indecent attitude, they may respectfully display their disapproval and dismay by keeping silent (domestic clarification). The strange chapter secretary may be led away from the podium, relieved of his functions, and expelled from his organization as a result of his peculiar and irregular behavior; the meeting would then return to its regular agenda (civic clarification). But the secretary may also win the support of the assembly in a broad movement of spontaneous enthusiasm that leads everyone else to share his or her personal experience in public (inspired clarification). Finally, the expert may turn down the gift and focus solely on the capacities of the machine (industrial clarification). But he may also set aside the task of measuring and, attuned to his friend's concerns, give his full attention to the problems of the son, with whose excellent upbringing he is familiar; the scene then ends up in a café or at home (domestic clarification).

Setting Up Situations That Hold Together

One may seek to prevent the appearance of clashes by *setting up* situations that *hold together*; the scene prepared in view of a test has to be able to be coherent in a single world. To ensure that the situations develop properly, one cannot count entirely on persons, since they have the possibility of changing nature and of belonging to different worlds. One must therefore establish an arrangement of natural objects that makes it possible to stabilize persons by attaching them to the world involved in the situation. This preparatory work aiming to control the circumstances by setting aside beings that are capable of intervening to disrupt the situation is particularly clear in situations that are explicitly oriented toward judgment: examinations, trials, auditions, and so forth. But it also appears, to varying degrees, in all the commitments whose consequences are viewed as particularly important and whose legitimacy has to be spotless.

However, even in the best-prepared situations, foreign beings may not all be set aside; the proper development of the situation thus always requires active intervention on the part of persons so that they themselves will remain in the appropriate state of mind. Indeed, the test's coherence also depends on the mental dispositions that the resources of the situation have activated in the participants. They need these dispositions in order to identify correctly beings that may belong to any of several different worlds (for example, "reputation," which, in its various senses, may enter into domestic configurations or stem from the world of fame) and shift them into the one that is most appropriate to the situation. One way of absorbing beings stemming from a different world that cannot be set aside and on which an unveiling might rely consists in bringing them back into the world adjusted to the situation, at the price of a translation that identifies them as deficient: teachers who stage a demonstration on the day outside evaluators are visiting their school are simply written off as lazy and incompetent. The setup of a situation in a world is thus often accompanied by a critique of beings who might well be worthy in a different world. Thus, for example, in the works used in the previous chapter to depict the various worlds, manuals that set out not only to teach readers how to behave in each of these worlds but also how to support each particular world and defend it against the outside, critiques have the function of establishing equivalences between the worthy of other worlds and the deficient of the world to which value is being attributed: the being bubbling up with ideas in the inspired world is boiling over in the domestic world.[2]

Even the purest situations are never completely protected against denunciation, however. They often retain a lingering clutter of foreign objects, a clatter of irrelevant noises that can be put to use as a way of detaching the situation from the present. For want of objects belonging to a different nature, one can always detach oneself from the present by dint of one's own strength: human beings belonging to any of the worlds can denature a situation without relying on external objects if they involve themselves in the situation as beings stemming from a different world. In the absence of external resources, these denunciations embodied in persons are often carried out through a shift into a state stemming from inspired nature. The more peculiar the denunciation is—the more the procedure adopted is foreign to the nature of the test under way—the more salient it is: for example, someone may interrupt the work of a commission in order to put forward farfetched ideas for getting the nation out of a crisis, or someone may write to the president of the Republic to complain about a neighbor who has embezzled funds. But these denunciations are also particularly dangerous for those who carry them out, since these persons, forced to commit themselves fully without any possibility of turning back, risk being considered insane and going down to defeat even as the situation called into question by their acts is falling apart. For want of objects on which to rely, the being who seeks to reverse the situation all by himself has to collect in his person the nature into which he wants the test to shift, and by his very act has to make the higher common principle present. He throws himself *body and soul* into an enterprise entailing a physical risk that helps establish its authenticity, as we have seen in the case of martyrs. The worth of reference is then confused with the worth of the person who presents himself as the measure of all things; this "madness of worths" may constitute the ultimate way of unsettling a situation that holds together.

For example, at a concert given in Paris by a conductor from a country where the rights of man are not respected, a spectator leaps onto the stage and interrupts the performance to demand the liberation of a political prisoner. He throws himself in person, in his status as a citizen defending a collective cause, into an operation of clarification ("in fact") that aims to reveal what really matters—the prisoner's suffering—and to thrust the music being performed into contingency: this concert does not belong to the realm of artistic judgment; the spectators are "in fact" covering up a political propaganda maneuver in the guise of an artistic manifestation. The denunciation aims to make the public aware of the "real" meaning of its participation in the spectacle and seeks to *reverse* this meaning, that is, to transform an audience that exists in the world of fame (it has been attracted to this place by the reputation of the conductor and the orchestra) into a public opinion stemming from the civic world and capable of manifesting itself, on this basis, in the form of a collective expressing solidarity. But the person who undertakes to bring about this reversal on his own, relying only on his own speech, voice, body, and personal conviction as his resources, has no protection against the failure of his enterprise, which may be disqualified as incongruous or abnormal. Things may turn out differently if the situation includes beings that can readily lend themselves to a civic nature: the presence of official personalities in the audience, for example, or a reference in the program to the celebration of an anniversary or a cultural agreement. The act of clarification accomplished by someone acting alone presupposes a commitment of the whole person, with conviction and passion for truth. In that sense, such a person always has an inspired aspect. There is no hope for him if he is not immediately supported by others who have come for the same purpose and—even more importantly—by an instrumentation that is invasive enough to produce a change of state in the dumbstruck audience: spectators (world of fame) who turn out to be militants (civic world) who unfurl banners repeat the same slogans from the balcony, and so on. The possibility of managing to distract the persons present and overturn the situation in order to subject it to a requirement of collective solidarity also depends on the state in which the persons find themselves. This possibility is increased to the extent that the persons involved remain under the influence of—preoccupied by—an earlier situation stemming from a different nature from which they are unable to detach themselves. Preoccupied persons who are not fully attuned to the current situation and who retain a hope of reinstituting another nature are easy to distract, if the situation can be denatured so that it shifts in the direction of their preoccupations.[3] In the case of the concert, the disruptive elements can overturn the situation most easily if the persons present are not all caught up in the pleasure of the music, if they are not fully attentive to what they are doing and remain preoccupied by the presence in themselves of a state corresponding to a different commitment; this might come about, for example, if the concert were taking place during a time of political unrest and the street outside were occupied by demonstrators.

The Humanity of an Equitable Judgment

The possibility of breaking free from the grip of a situation may lead to an equitable judgment denouncing the intervention of worths foreign to the nature of the test, but it may also lead to inequity, by way of a transport of worths. A judgment is deemed equitable when it takes into account the existence of worlds external to the nature of the test. Only a judgment bearing upon persons can be qualified as equitable. "Human" judgments inspired by *prudence* (practical wisdom) are opposed to "inhuman" verdicts deriving from the strict application of a rule of justice. The former take into account properties that, in the polity model, characterize human persons—that is, the fact that, in advance of a test, all persons are equally capable of being in any state of worth and of participating in any world. It is by bringing this possibility into play that persons manifest their dignity. As an example, let us consider the case of deficient persons who, when a test is unfailingly unfavorable to them (here we approach a model in which states of worth would be attached to persons), can escape despair by challenging the relevance of the test through denunciation and can get out of the situation by creating a distraction, making an ironic remark, or stirring up a commotion that mocks the worthy and relativizes their importance. However, this possibility cannot be taken for granted. Even if their engagement is more uncertain than that of the worthy, the deficient cannot extirpate themselves without cost from the privileged moments in which they benefit from belonging to the polity and from the share of common happiness that it bestows on them. Moreover, when they are engaged in a natural situation, they cannot step back and calculate their interests, taking into account their present deficiency and the advantages that might accrue to them if the situation were reversed. In fact, there is no higher vantage point above any of the worlds, no external position from which the plurality of justices could be considered from a distance, as a range of equally possible choices.

The ability to free oneself from the grip of a situation is no less necessary to the worthy. In order to make themselves human, they too must show that they are capable of openness, must shed the rigid coating that weighs them down and binds them to the tests in which their worth is manifested. Worthy persons must attend to what they are doing without letting themselves be distracted by the circumstances. They must pursue what they have to accomplish (a task or a speech, for instance), and they are the last to hear the noise rising outside, the last to look up at the window and worry about the external clamor. Someone who is in mourning and who nevertheless gives himself over fully to the task at hand, unpreoccupied and untroubled, will be described as someone manifesting self-control, but that attribute may also be viewed as having an inhuman aspect. Like a mechanism that starts up again on its own, the person is reactivated, immediately at ease in the world that is appropriate to the situation. Thus, on the one hand, a constantly repeated critique results in a vain flight into alternative worlds; on the other hand, an excessive identification with the series of objects in the world at hand results in a petrified attachment to a specific worth.

Free Will: Knowing How to Close and Open One's Eyes

In order to complete the model of competence that we are sketching here and to construct what, in a multiworld model, can be described as *prudence*, we need to take into account the faculty of detaching oneself from a situation and getting out of a test. It is by taking plurality into account that prudence distinguishes itself from the forms of justice that figure in the political philosophies on which we based our initial analysis of the various principles of equivalence. In fact, in a single world in which, in the absence of external reference points, people would be one with the thing in which they found themselves engaged, with no possibility of detaching themselves, prudence would be useless. On "the islands of the blessed, as the fables relate," says Augustine, citing Cicero, "we would have no need . . . of prudence. . . . We should be blessed merely by learning and knowing nature, and for this reason alone is the life of the gods also to be praised" (Augustine 1963, 428–29 [14.9.12]). A multiworld justice thus presupposes free will on the part of persons who are capable in turn of *closing their eyes* (in order to attend fully to what they are doing in the situations in which they are involved, to resist distractions and engage themselves in the tests that the situations have in store for them) and of *opening their eyes* (in order to challenge the validity of a test and, by breaking free from the grip of the situation, to distinguish beings deriving from other worlds).

Persons incapable of immersing themselves in the fullness of situations cannot stay in place or engage themselves. Unimportant items become salient for them, and the objects that the test is intended to emphasize do not stand out. These persons cannot disregard what is inessential. They are vigilant, always on the alert, and they do not know how to be present without denouncing what surrounds them. They are prevented from realizing themselves by identifying themselves with the privileged moments in which each of the worlds, exhibiting its own form of worth, offers itself to be experienced by those who know how to immerse themselves in the scene and set aside all other preoccupations in order to be fully present to what they are doing. This state of vigilance is manifested especially when persons are attached to a world in which they are at ease and which tends to reemerge to disturb the situation, whatever it may be. These "characters" who are deemed "too consistent," for whom nothing ever happens by chance, take no notice of the circumstances and unveil, in every situation, the hidden result of the same underlying causes. Their preoccupation with a single nature absorbs them and makes them conform to the image of human beings that theories of personality often present.

However, the capacity to know what matters while testing the authenticity of pure situations is not all there is to knowledge. In order to challenge the validity of a test and to denounce its injustice, persons must also be able to extricate themselves from the grip of a situation in order to gain knowledge by means of a critical judgment, that is, by opening their eyes to look at other worlds and at the beings that ensure their presence. By letting the scales fall from their eyes, an act that brings to light something to which they had paid no attention before, prudent persons can establish themselves as judges of what really matters and can say in what the reality of things consists. By using their ability to open and close their eyes, persons actualize their free will. This knowledge is tested in the peak moments in which each of the worlds exhibits itself in a particularly pure form, as can happen in a dizzying fashion in ceremonies, for example, or when someone cannot resist falling outside the plenitude of the moment into a lapsus, a blunder, or a fit of irrepressible laughter.

But the ability to open and close one's eyes, to let oneself be caught up in the nature of the situation or to avoid doing so, is not manifested in critiques alone. It is also at work whenever persons have to complete the passage between situations arising from different worlds; in a complex society that includes multiple arrangements, this capacity is thus indispensable to the normal conduct of daily life. The passage from one natural state to another cannot be conceived as a mere mechanical effect of the situation. It is not entirely determined by the situation, and it demands on the part of the persons involved an effort to eliminate the traces, in mind and body, in memories, thoughts, and feelings, of what has been experienced in a previous situation. Thus in order to excuse someone who has not succeeded in navigating this passage, for example in the aftermath of a difficult test, one says that that person has not gotten back to normal, is not himself, is still upset, needs time to get hold of himself, and so on. The art of managing a passage between two situations is manifested, for example, in anticipatory behaviors that go from sensitivity to the premonitory signs of a modification in resources, through the anticipation of predictable maneuvers on the part of others, to maneuvers intended to prepare a change in the mood of the persons present by introducing new resources. Thus one may activate the resources of the domestic world during a meeting set up in a civic world by going to shake the president's hand, by renewing personal connections with other participants through signs of recognition, smiles, nods, and so on. Carried out injudiciously, such marks of friendly relations may also be interpreted as symptoms of peculiarity or even mental illness by the other people present, who then refuse to play along with these maneuvers and to respond in kind. The work required by the passage from one world to another is especially apparent when test situations in different worlds come up in close succession, so that the persons who retain the aftereffects of the previous situation in the new test have to assume their relation to different realities and their sequential adhesion to truths whose incompatible character cannot be ignored. Consistency in the way one behaves in different worlds, which does not impose itself with the same urgency when the situations are sharply detached, has to be managed by the person involved. This person may be led to denounce or relativize her own earlier behaviors, which she then describes in the register of artifice and theater, joking or playacting ("I had to play along"), playing a role for the benefit of others, in contrast to the authenticity of the present moment. Past behaviors, in which one had nevertheless been engaged without reservation but which have become foreign to oneself with the shift into a different world, are held at a distance in the register of *cynicism*. We see this, for example, when it becomes necessary to shift from a civic situation to a domestic one, where the tension is retranslated in terms of an opposition between the artifice of the "official" and the reality of the "unofficial," or, in Pascalian terms, between "established worth" and "true worth." These reversals of reality are particularly awkward when several participants have to shift simultaneously between situations in different worlds: while the passage is taking place, each one remains uncertain about the state of nature in which the others find themselves. This is the case, for example, when supervisors have to go as a group straight from a management meeting in which they participate in the name of the company to a union meeting in which they participate as exploited workers. The behaviors, ritualized in the extreme, that can be observed in these delicate moments are destined to produce a change of state that, to be carried out simultaneously by all, requires a coordination that is particularly difficult to ensure (as one sees in meetings that have trouble getting off the ground because some of the participants are not fully attending to what they are doing, are instead joking around and continuing to linger in the previous situation). It suffices for a single member to be elsewhere, for him to show by expressive behaviors that he is exempting himself from the grip of the situation, to make the situation fall apart.

Taking several worlds into account makes it possible to specify the constraint of justification. The persons involved would not be subject to it if they were not confronted with a critique. The possibility of exiting from the present situation and denouncing it by relying on an external principle and consequently on the plurality of worlds thus constitutes the condition of a justified action. But for the same reasons the constraint of justification may weigh unevenly on the actions of the persons involved depending on the degree to which access to the different worlds is open to all. In a universe in which slaves were held in a state that abolished or restricted in the extreme the possibility that they could produce critiques, and in which they were consigned through violence to a world in which they became objects, the masters could view themselves as gods and assert their will without having to justify it. But once they destroyed the polity by shifting the boundaries of humanity and by introducing a radical discontinuity between the dominated and the dominators, they would abolish the framework in which their superiority was asserted, and would lose the sense of their own worth.[4] The construction of a universe subjected to a constraint of justification, that is, of a universe in which the rationality of behaviors can also be put to the test by a critique, thus presupposes an array of different worlds in which the objects accessible to all permit the attribution of worth, and by the same token it presupposes practical control of the forms of justice that have been established in principle.

Eight

THE CRITICAL MATRIX

Critiques from the Inspired World[1]

Addressed to the Domestic World.   In the inspired world, persons have no hold over the powers that may come to them and raise them up to worth—or may leave them in the lurch and cause them to fall. But to a limited extent they can lend themselves to or resist the action of these powers. Worth in this world thus has a precondition: one must prepare oneself resolutely to welcome these powers if they appear. To act accordingly, one must live with uncertainty (since one's own resolve has no influence over the action of the powers that are indispensable to worth and is not a source of worth in itself), and one must sacrifice everything that might constitute an obstacle to inspiration, anything that might keep it from being recognized and embraced. This is why critiques issuing from the inspired world are addressed first and foremost to the aspects of other worlds that situate persons within the continuity of time. What is stable and *fixed* is devalued: for example, *sacrosanct principles*[d] or *norms*[u], which are *shackles* that inhibit *creativity*.[i] Constraints of this sort bring to bear on people's actions the weight of engagements made by others in the past (for example, *traditions*[d]), commitments for the future made by persons themselves (for example, *promises*[d]), or, in the industrial world, *forecasts*[u] and *plans*[u] that entail obligations. Such constraints limit a person's availability, which must be continual if inspiration is to be recognized and welcomed at the very moment, the unpredictable moment, when it strikes. In the same way, one can criticize everything that shores up states of worth in other worlds, such as *hierarchies*[d], *titles*[d-c-u], domestic *habits*[d], or industrial *routines*[u]. By inciting to constancy, these instruments diminish the capacity of persons to allow themselves to be overcome by inspiration as it *pours forth*[i]: "For [the creative person], the notions of *hierarchical* situation[d], established order,

The shackles of habit

respect due to rank[d] or *social position*[d-m], are dead letters."
Similarly, forms of address, marks of respect, *polite*[d] *formulas*, all the "verbal precautions" of the domestic world, are criticized as ponderous and artificial formalities that contrast with "informal" exchanges and authentically human relationships: "Behind all the social façades[f], [the creator] sees only the man[i]." The positive valuation of unstable emotional states associated with outpourings of inspiration correlates with critiques of control, moderation, and the establishment of worths. *Habits*[d] and *rules inherited*[d] from an *academic culture*[d-u] are opposed to *originality*[i], genuine—that is, inspired—thought, and the *enthusiasm*[i] that accompanies creation. *Academic culture*[d-u] is criticized as *traditional*. *Knowledge* that is relevant in the industrial world is constantly denigrated in the inspired world for its stability and its objectivity. Worthy figures in the industrial world—*experts*[u], *authorities, VIPs*—are "dangerous characters" here: "With all the weight conferred on them by their *titles*, they dictate directions and condemn those who take *roundabout paths*[i]. . . . And *casting doubt*[i] on their discourse is out of the question: they shore it up with so many *references*[d], so much *data*[u], so many *numbers*[u]."

Give everything up   The inspired requirement of "giving everything up" to follow *one's own path*[i], *giving oneself* over entirely, also leads to critiquing the weight of personal bonds and domestic worths. To reach *independence*, to shed the "old skins" that drag them down, creators have to be able to *call into question*[i] the *masters*[d] whose existence the inspired world nevertheless recognizes, in a domestic compromise. The requirement of *giving everything up* also includes a critique of the industrial world, when the *roundabout paths*[i] of inspiration are contrasted with *trajectories*[u], predictable and calculable paths.

Addressed to the World of Fame.   A person who recognizes the mystery of inspiration is *humble*[i]. Self-love, the quest for *respect*, vainglory, and "*external signs*[f] of success" are constantly criticized in keeping with the classic model of the inspired polity. Granting importance to *opinion*[d-o] *The vanity of* (used here in the sense of a compromise between the domestic world and the world of fame) leads to discord and *appearances* *personal rivalries*[d-o] that silence the *imagination*[i]. Among

Theodoret's lives of the saints, a particularly good example of such a critique appears in the person of St. Marcian. Not content to hide the miracles he was given to accomplish, as other Church Fathers did, he even refused to help someone seeking aid in order to avoid the "thoughts of vanity" that might come to him under the circumstances. The miracle that nevertheless occurred thus took place without his knowledge and against his will (Arnauld d'Andilly 1736 [1647–53], 2:369–72). As we saw in the moralists' portraits of courtiers, inspired critiques of worldly worths thus posit the existence of an authentic reality on the basis of which the *theater of the world* can be unveiled: inasmuch as relations with others are part of a *worldly*[f] *exchange*[d] in the world of fame, this world is only a *stage*[f] on which inauthentic persons play *roles*[f]. In the social sciences, this critique corresponds to the movement that leads social psychology—a scientific mode of knowledge in harmony with the nature of fame—to *go beyond*[i] *measuring*[u] *influences*[f] and take a critical look at the world, unveiling the *comedy* that *actors put on for themselves*; in order to reveal the underlying reality, social psychology must thus seek principles of interpretation deriving from the civic world, such as *collectives*[c] or *social structures*[c-u].

The inauthenticity of the theater of the world

Addressed to the Civic World.   In the context of a revolution, civic worth can enter into a compromise with inspiration. It is criticized, from the standpoint of the inspired world, when it is envisaged in its most institutionalized forms, heavily instrumented and detached from persons; in this respect, critiques of civic worth intersect with the industrial world. Thus we encounter challenges to "the frigid *legalistic-economic* relations[c-u] that confine and stifle us"; their coldness contrasts with "the *warmth* of *affective* relations[i], so long forgotten."

The inhuman state

Addressed to the Market World.   Subjection to *money*[m] (venality) is among the forms of bondage from which one must free oneself to be in the right state to receive inspiration: like *respect*, which expresses the opinion or esteem of others, money is said to be "of little importance." Subjection to money may be criticized either because it presupposes enslavement to desires oriented toward the satisfaction of personal pleasures or because it implies

Interested parties

submission to other parties during the process of making a deal. The world of inspiration can unfold only if the market world, with all its unworthy beings, can be set aside. Compromises implicating these two worlds will thus be denounced, whether they involve acts performed in a religious context, in the art market, or in a creative endeavor where an idea is commercialized and turned into a "concept" or an "innovation." Creativity itself "is not a *commercial* product," and "*merchants*[m] of *creativity*[i] will stop at nothing to seduce [naive persons]." *Stopping at nothing* is an expression used here to stigmatize the dealings of an opportunistic businessman who is seeking a compromise with inspired worth.

The rigidity of routines

Addressed to the Industrial World. The incongruity of stable forms in the inspired world, forms criticized above in the context of domestic *habits*[d], is even more clearly expressed where industrial *routines*[u] are at issue. *Habits*[d] are distinguished from *routines*[u] by the instruments used for their repetition. In the case of *habits*, the body itself does the reiterating—unlike the inspired body, which is stirred by emotion, the domestic body is activated by the memory of previous gestures. In contrast, the repetition of *routines* depends on permanent, impersonal extensions of the human body. The resultant stability protects against disturbances that might lead to the inappropriate resurgence of a habit or the uncontrolled irruption of inspired manifestations. Safety precautions, for example, often take the form of routines implying the utterance of explicit "instructions," as when an airline pilot orders flight attendants to lock the doors before takeoff instead of relying on their habits. However, critiques issuing from the inspired world often target both *habits*[d] and *routines*[u], for both practices stifle inspired outpourings owing to their inscription in time. Thus well-established methods and ways of doing things are accused of inhibiting creative spontaneity, and schools are criticized for their *traditional routines*: "Education . . . has done all it could to stifle in us the *madwoman in the attic*[i] [*la folle du logis*] whom Pascal evoked[i]"; "*teachers*[d] look at *creative*[i] students . . . as troublemakers."

The oppression of the reasonable

In addition to condemning temporal stability, inspired critiques also target oppression by a hierarchy of *authority*[d] or *competence*[u] that inhibits inspired worth. Critiques of this sort may lead to a radical hierarchical reversal, in which the *authority*[d] of the *elders*[d] is abolished by the *naive* gaze cast upon it by newcomers or the young.

Critiques of the *functional* objects characteristic of the industrial world give us a picture of inspiration rising up larger than life against the constricted measures used to assess industrial productivity: "I still hope to have made it clear [to the reader] that *creativity*[i] is more than a *sophisticated*[u] *tool* for developing new products and increasing a company's *profitability*[u]." Such critiques are rooted in the "profound antinomy between *reason* and *logic*[u] and all that belongs to the realm of *dreams*[i] and *imagination*[i], to all that remains *unspoken*[i], and to the "fascinating world of the *irrational*." Critiques of *technologies*[u] or *methods*[u] arouse suspicion about the facts on which the sciences rely; this attitude is conveyed in the slogan suggesting that people ought to "explode what is commonly called reality."

Critiques from the Domestic World

Addressed to the Inspired World.   Domestic bonds are opposed to inspiration, for with its unstable character and its inhospitability to graduated states of worth, inspiration disrupts configurations set up according to hierarchies and customs; indeed, it plunges them into *disorder*. The manual on which we based our analysis of the domestic world does not refer explicitly to inspiration. But a large number of the properties it attributes to unworthy beings are, conversely, attributes of worth in the inspired world. Inspiration is thus most often criticized in the domestic register by way of defects, qualities designated in a derogatory fashion that correspond to forms of inspired worth. This is the case, for example, with *effusiveness*, a negative term applied to behaviors in which the inspired world recognizes the expression of something that contributes to the dignity of persons, such as *emotions*[i] or *feelings*[i]. The same thing holds true for many other attributes characterized negatively in the domestic world, for example in references to behaviors manifesting instability as opposed to stability, spontaneity as opposed to control, unpredictability as opposed to predictability. Any

Lack of self-restraint

behavior that betrays a lack of self-restraint—or, as Norbert Elias said about court society, a lack of "restraint of the affects" (1983, 110–16)—is criticized; for example, the action of *bursting in* (to *burst into* an office or a meeting "out of the blue"), *calling out* to people, *talking to the company at large*, spilling one's soul by "telling one's life story," passing judgment on the basis of one's own convictions and boasting about one's own "frankness," or, in the case of *children*, "climbing into someone's lap," "tugging on someone's clothes," "rummaging in a woman's handbag," "calling everyone by their first names," "interrupting someone who is speaking," or *contradicting*. At issue, here again, is an absence of control—especially over one's emotions and one's body—that is associated with the spontaneous character of inspired states. This failing is targeted by critiques of any sort of *sloppy* and *unrestrained* behaviors that betray a *lack of self-control* or a lack of *composure*.

The good manners of the sycophant

Addressed to the World of Fame.   Knowing how to behave has to be valued for itself; such knowledge should not be put to a *self-interested*ᶠ use in order to gain approval or win favor. Similarly, *true superiority* is contrasted with the *appearances*ᶠ of worldly *pretensions*ᶠ, and with *social climbing*. The domestic world, which privileges *discretion* (in keeping with the saying "children should be seen but not heard"), also takes exception to behaviors intended to impress an audience.

Not making a spectacle of oneself

Still, given the ambiguity of the opposition between "public" and "private," in domestic configurations it is sometimes hard to distinguish between critiques aimed at the world of fame and those directed toward the civic world. Thus the domestic precept according to which "differences should not be aired in public" may be addressed either to the civic world or to the world of fame without any mark of distinction between these two different ways of breaking down the domestic distinction between inside and outside, between space divided into separate territories, "domains" or *houses*ᵈ (*"houses of commerce"*) on the one hand and a homogeneous expanse on the other. In the first instance, the designation *public*ᶜ includes a reference to the State (as when one settles a difference defined as "familial," "private," or "internal" by calling on the judicial system and proceeding to a trial during which the disagreement is made public). In the second instance, the term *public*^c refers rather to spectators, and what is criticized is *attracting attention* ("all you have to do is avoid *attracting attention*"), for attracting attention signals a lack of self-restraint—or *making a spectacle of oneself* (as when a husband and wife quarrel in public and make a spectacle of their disagreement); this latter case suggests even more clearly the theatrical analogy that is a frequent figure of speech in denunciations of fame. In a space divided into *homes*, domains, and territories, a space organized by the opposition between inside and outside, the person who *makes a spectacle of himself* risks harming *his loved ones* by betraying *secrets*^d. The practical wisdom or *prudence* of *important persons* incites them to *be cautious*^d. In contrast, less worthy persons (*women, children, subordinates*), who are less *responsible*, are inclined to *attract notice*, to *talk too loudly, ostentatiously*, in order to *attract attention*^f, without *being suspicious of their neighbors*^d, which leads them to *betray secrets* (especially during *working dinners*^{d-u}). *Discretion* and *reserve*^d, attributes of domestic worth that contrast with the show-off tendencies of the *social climber*^{f-d}, are themselves criticized, from the vantage point of the world of fame, as marks of a *lack of ambition*. They characterize *self-effacing* persons who are destined to *remain unknown*.

The discretion of trustworthy persons

Addressed to the Civic World. The domestic world, which recognizes only the worth of personal attachments, takes exception to *anonymity*, but this critique is sometimes addressed to the "they" of the world of fame, sometimes to the "collective" of the civic world. These two forms of impersonality are confused, for example, in references to the *anonymity* of public places: "One of the hypocrisies of our time . . . lies in the way people exempt themselves from all restraints under cover of *anonymity* . . . at the wheel of his car, he is no longer *Mr. So-and-So*^d but Mr. Nobody^{f-c}. . . . We have the impression that everybody says to himself unconsciously: 'Here I am *known*^d, so I am going to *behave well*^d. There, nobody knows me, so I can do anything I want.'" The same ambiguity makes it possible to move easily from a critique of media-based instruments of fame to the critique of legal relations that are civic in nature; in the fol-

The irresponsibility of Mr. Nobody

lowing example, the critique of *television*, a standard[u], impersonal[f], public[c], technological[u] object belonging to the media[f] that is contrasted with the *personal responsibility* of the *father*[d], leads to a denunciation of the transformation of *family*[d] ties into *associative*[c] ties that are civic in nature: "*Television*[f] runs counter to the *spirit*[d] of the *family*. The central focus is no longer the *father* with his *authority*, his *experience*, and his desire to *educate*, but a *piece of furniture* that produces *pictures*[u] (the same ones for everybody, moreover) and that lacks *warmth* and *soul*[d]. The '*Associations of strangers*[c] from the same *family*[d]' that are being prepared for our future are not very appealing."

Addressed to the Market World. The arrangements and beings of the market world go virtually unmentioned in the manual we used to analyze the domestic world. This is all the more remarkable in that the work in question is a guide intended for companies. When references to the market world do appear, they are not purely critical: things being what they are, money is a necessity; people can't get along without it. But this drift toward a compromise with the market world is contradicted by a critique of an extension of the market that corrupts domestic relations and worths. The author thus makes a point of recalling the limits of market relations. *Money*[m] must be subordinated to *merit*[d], in a world in which *not everything can be bought*: "[Children][d] need pocket money[d-u], but they should nevertheless not get used to coming by it too easily[m]. If they have to *deserve*[d] or *earn*[d-u] it, they will have a better understanding of the value and difficulty of getting it for themselves. . . . Still, they must not be given the idea that *everything can be bought*[m]." Money is damaging to personal relationships, as well. Money is not to be discussed in the family. It is generally inappropriate[d] to sell[m] family property (*houses, jewels, pets*[d], and so on): by nature, such items should circulate through inheritance or as gifts, because they are *attached* to the domestic realm (Mauss 1990 [1923], 74).

Not everything can be bought

Domestic property, inscribed in a chain of ownership rooted in the past, contrasts with market goods, which are completely alienable. This opposition generates a large number of critiques denouncing the distortion of relations of trust when they are perverted by interest, and the troubles that interest introduces into family ties, bonds of friendship, or a *good environment*[d].

In his chrematistics, Aristotle clearly distinguishes between two ways of acquiring things. The natural "art of acquisition" is manifested by the appropriation of goods in the context of the "household art," so as to ensure the subsistence of the domestic unit by way of "supplies," for nature provides animals it has engendered with "enough sustenance to suffice." Conversely, the art of business "is not natural," and it threatens the polity with disorder (*Politics* 1256b, 6–10). Property acquired in the first manner cannot be extended indefinitely, and it is inscribed within the boundaries of the domain or "household," unlike goods acquired by appropriation in a market context; the quest for the latter is spurred by unlimited desire (1256b, 30–38; 1258a, 1). If Aristotle criticizes interest-bearing loans as "contrary to nature," it is because they presuppose treating relations between money—"invented . . . for the purpose of exchange" (1258b, 4–5)—and interest as if they were comparable to relations between parents and the beings that they have engendered in their own image (the word *toxos* means at once "child," "small," and "usury"). Bentham makes fun of this position by noting that, despite his considerable efforts, Aristotle did not succeed in discovering any mechanism in a coin for generating other coins.

Even today, certain moneylending arrangements continue to support this tension between domestic and market property; this is the case, for example, when a request for a small business loan is submitted to a regional bank, whose "credit committee" includes both officers of the bank and elected representatives from among its clientele (Wissler 1989b). The roots of the tension become clearly apparent if we look at the way a decision to grant credit is justified in the two different worlds. In the domestic context, justification is oriented toward the maintenance of an inherited local business underwritten by relatives or friends. In the market context, in contrast, justification is oriented toward profit, and it offers flexible credit opportunities at the moment of purchase that authorize an expansion of spending beyond the borrower's budgetary limits.

Addressed to the Industrial World. In the domestic world, worthy subjects and worthy objects *generate* benefits. Critiques that contest the scope of industrial arrangements rely on the opposition between the process of *generation* in which *trust* is rooted in *functional efficiency*. A domestic being "gives according to what he is given," in proportion to the *domain*[d] that contains it. Objects of a domestic nature are goods belonging to the patrimony; these include "supplies" destined to benefit the beings that will be engendered in the future. In *Politics*, Aristotle cites the example of milk (1256b, 13–15) and declares that "it is the work of nature to supply nourishment for her offspring, since every creature has for nourishment the residue of the substance from which it springs" (1258a, 36–38). Thus in the patrimonial model for managing nature, nature itself is bequeathed as an inheritance from the past that has to be protected against opportunistic dealings of a market orientation (Godard 1989).

The poor quality of standardized products

The application of productivist techniques aiming to control this engendering in a *production function*[u] will inevitably disturb the domestic engendering that underwrites quality (Darré 1986). "Producing volume" or "producing profits" (Dodier 1989, 291) are activities that prevent domestic relations from guaranteeing the quality of the beings that depend on resources of a domestic nature.

The lack of professionalism of workers with diplomas

In the manual we used, we do not find any critiques focusing on the incompetence of people with *diplomas* as opposed to the competence of people with *experience*, those who have learned on the job; professionals are praised only via the figure of the *good worker*. But earlier research (Boltanski 1987) showed the virulence of such critiques in companies in which value is attributed to resources of a domestic nature, anchored in *habits*[d].

The measure of professional competence that relies on formalized criteria and standardized procedures—among which diplomas rank high—is of little weight with regard to the authority that will be manifested in a trade. The forms of judgment differ in the same way, as we see both in moments of recruitment (Delamourd 1988) and in moments of evaluation: "If all job candidates had an inkling of the degree to which they are judged, from the very first encounter, by the way they present themselves, they would pay more attention to appearances."

The technician who is prisoner of his formal methods, the expert whose eye is riveted to charts, the manager obsessed with written instructions, all these are called into question for their very way of being, which denatures domestic worth. Data recorded in the forms that constitute proofs of an industrial nature through an accumulation of statistics are not suited to supporting a domestic judgment based on an experience stockpiled in *examples* or *cases*. Numbers without importance are contrasted with testimony validated by recollections of exemplary cases, even when, in the inverse critique, the lack of reliability of domestic data would be denounced in order to show that "figures speak for themselves" (Wissler 1989a, 100). This tension is often reduced to the application of a rule; the gulf that separates it from the circumstances is filled by links viewed as ad hoc by ethnomethodologists, whereas it actually results from the confrontation between two different modes of generalization (Dodier 1989, 298, 304). The radical difference between ways of collecting, recording, and storing information, depending on whether the objective is a domestic judgment or an industrial judgment, corresponds to the dualism present in the history of probabilities, between probability according to authority and probability according to frequency (Hacking 1975). This makes it possible to clarify the debates that have been going on in the social sciences from the time of Le Play and Cheysson over the respective merits of the so-called qualitative and quantitative methods of monography and statistics (Desrosières 1986, 1989).

Ill-adapted formalism

Critiques from the World of Fame

Addressed to the Inspired World.   The worth of fame, which depends on the opinion of others, is incompatible with inspired worth, whose confirmation depends on the certainty of an intimate conviction. In the world of inspiration, the temptation of fame is one of the chief causes of a fall. Conversely, in the world of fame, inspiration is criticized as madness, because it is assimilated, as we saw in Hobbes, to a personal opinion that is blind to the opinions of others. Thus in the manual designed to transmit the art of *public relations* that we used to analyze

False depth

the world of fame, we find a critique of *esotericism*[i] insofar as this tendency ignores the tastes of the *public*[f] and fails to direct its *messages* to the *largest possible audience*[f]: "If your *message*[f], the *information*[f] you are trying to convey, is too *esoteric*[i], you will reach only the most sophisticated sector of the *public at large*[f]; the rest—*the vast majority*[f]—won't even notice it, let alone *understand* and remember anything about it." Inspiration is also criticized in the warnings designed to reveal the limitations of what one can expect from *public relations*[f] *experts*[u] (the label "expert" presupposes a compromise with the industrial world), by recalling the primacy of opinion (the higher common principle), a *reality* to be reckoned with: "You must not imagine . . . that a *specialist*[u] in *public relations*[f] is a *magician*[i] capable of '*getting across*[f]' any *message* you like and getting the *public* to accept it." The expert can succeed only to the extent that the *message*[f] and its vehicle[u] are *deduced by the public*[f], and not the other way around." The critique of inspiration—a worth that dispenses with acquiescence by others—provides an opportunity to reassert the economic principle underlying the world of fame, where the renunciation of secrets, of singularity, of solitude, of private life, a renunciation often attributed to *stars* and *celebrities*, is the sacrifice to which the worthy must agree in order to be recognized by others. This is what distinguishes a *message* in the world of fame, where people speak of "delivering a message," from the inspired *message* (a prophetic announcement, for example) whose expression conforms to an inner necessity that is not exhausted by its delivery to an addressee. Sacrificing the privacy of one's thoughts, the singularity of one's speech or writing, the particularity of one's *message*, is the price paid for *success*: "A star's private life has to be public" (Morin 1972, 55). A *star* does not belong to herself: she has to give herself to others so they can *identify*[f] with her. Media revelations of the hidden underside of *stars'* lives (*rumors*[f], gossip, the sorts of tales that no longer simply circulate from person to person but are *echoed*[f] in the media by *journalists*[f]) are exciting because they project familiar personal objects (cigarette lighters, articles of clothing, homes, pets) that belong to the domestic context into the world of fame. They open doors into the *intimate space*[d] of *famous* people[f] who become *known*, through

Stars deprived of private life

their image in the media, the way one would know them if one *socialized*[d] with them in person. But the opposite effect is no less troubling: a *star* who appears in person in a domestic context (as a fellow shopper, for example, or as a neighbor) brings two mutually exclusive worlds into coincidence in a single situation. Inasmuch as he derives from the world of fame, he is recognized as a *celebrity*[f]. But while in terms of fame he is inaccessible and untouchable (characteristics that contribute to his image, just as the inaccessibility of works of art exhibited behind the glass windows of a museum contribute to their aura [Benjamin 1969, 229–30), his presence in a familiar context makes him accessible, even though it does not subject him to the natural order of the domestic world into which it transports the worth of his fame; he seems both remote and within reach at the same time.

This disturbance takes a paroxysmal and systematic form in delusions of grandeur, which confuse the different ways of "knowing" that characterize different worlds. Thus Jacques Lacan's patient Aimée does not distinguish between her *responsibilities* toward her son[d] and the *responsibilities* of heads of state facing the risk of war whom she reads about in the *newspapers*[f], and she sends *personal* letters[d] or *love poems*[i] to famous people with whose lives she is familiar thanks to the *press*[f], writing as if she knew them personally[d]: for example, she addresses the Prince of Wales as if she were a servant writing to her master (1980 [1932], 153–245). She also seems to think that because she "knows" them she is necessarily known to them; she transports the reciprocity of domestic relations into the world of fame.

Addressed to the Domestic World.   Critiques of *reputation* in the sense appropriate to the domestic world are necessary to accredit *celebrity* in the sense appropriate to the world of fame. It is precisely because these two arrangements share certain properties, in part, that they must be sharply distinguished. Thus utterances proffered in face-to-face exchanges[d] (*rumors, congratulations, confidential disclosures, observations, reproaches, examples,* or *anecdotes*[d]) are differentiated from *information*[f], which, in the world of fame, *spreads*[f] into public *opinion*[f], and is *broadcast*[f] not to a particular recipient but to the *public*[f] as a

Giving up the habit of secrecy

whole, to *the largest possible audience*. The transparency of the information circulated via a *public relations* campaign contrasts with the opacity of personal relations, which are criticized, as they are from the vantage point of the civic world as well, under the heading of *paternalism*: "The goal you are trying to achieve in greeting the public is completely free of *paternalism* (a notion totally foreign to *public relations*[f])." Domestic secrecy, the practice of *hiding things*, is criticized by the same logic as inspired esotericism. It will be said, for example, that "a staff member who is not kept *informed*[f] is always under the impression that what is *hidden*[d] from him has to do with him personally, and that he is a victim." In the same spirit, one finds critiques in the world of fame that focus on whatever is transmitted "via the *hierarchy*[d]," "from the top down." When a message follows the chain of dependencies, it loses the impersonal character that certifies the *reality* of the *information*[f] transmitted: "People are afraid of *demagogy*, and they are suspicious of any *information*[f] that comes from the *top*[d]."

Addressed to the Market World. In spite of a highly instrumented compromise with market worth (see *Brand name*, below), the latter is criticized because of the risks of compromise to which *publicity*[m] exposes the formation of opinion. For example, in *public relations*[f], "arguments that are essentially advertisements, or that focus too much on *selling*[m]," are to be avoided, and during a public relations presentation, one must be careful not to "give one's guests the impression that they are being subjected to an *advertising* campaign[m]." The author of our manual clarifies the nature of testing in the world of fame by contrasting "the goal of advertising and promotion, [which is] essentially to *sell*[m] something," with the aim of public relations, which "is to *inform*[f]" consumers, to *attract their attention*[f]. When it is denatured by the addition of beings of a market nature, a test in the world of fame "cannot fool the *press*[f] for long, for journalists will immediately—and perhaps for a long time to come—reject all *information*[f] put forth by the company." *Public relations* are also clearly distinguished from *marketing*: "In *marketing*[m], the key is to adapt the *product to the market*[m], that is, to the *consumer's*[m] conscious or unconscious *desires*

Self-interested publicity

and needs. In *public relations*ᶠ, the key is to establish a network of good *relationships*ᶠ."

Addressed to the Industrial World. In the public relations manual we examined, which dates from the 1970s, critiques of technicians or experts cut off from the mass of information seekers are not as highly developed as they are today. The theme of the scientist who is a prisoner in his ivory tower has been reinforced in recent years by the development of arrangements providing instrumentation for the worth of fame (print media, audiovisual and electronic media) that make it possible to objectify the assessment of public opinion. Thus it may no longer be enough simply to publish the results of scientific research; they may need to be subjected to a test in the world of fame, for example, a press conference. Recognizing the legitimacy of a scientific test that relies in part on the world of fame goes hand in hand with a denunciation of experts who are so isolated and esoteric that they are unable to guarantee on their own that their work will find an echo in public opinion.

The esotericism of the expert

Critiques from the Civic World

Addressed to the Inspired World. In the civic world, inspiration is criticized as *impulsivity*ⁱ/ᶜ ("an irresponsible and *impulsive* approach") and as *individualism*: "The appearance of this *subscribers' newsletter*ᶜ must be the result of a *sudden inspiration*ⁱ on the part of a militant or a handful of members." *Impulsivity* leads to *improvisation*; "*union action*ᶜ," however, "is not compatible with *improvising*ⁱ/ᶜ." *Individualism* is typical of *avant-gardes* that are in a *minority*ᶜ and *cut off from the base*ᶜ. It is a trap for those who seek to "play at being an enlightened *avant-garde*." Similarly, *ferment*ⁱ, an attribute of worth ("bubbling up") in the inspired world that is the object of a civic compromise when it is associated with revolution, is criticized as a barrier to the *unity* (*coordination*) of collective persons: "A general *ferment*ⁱ does not suffice. What is required is a steady flow of information, *collective* reflection*ᶜ, coordination*ᶜ."

The impulsivity and ferment of the enlightened avant-gardes

Addressed to the Domestic World. In the civic world, references to domestic relations are most often critical.

Overcome paternalism

This should not be surprising, since the civic bond is defined precisely as one that liberates from relations of personal dependence. Domestic bonds in business contexts are criticized because they help "isolate union militants" and "cut them off from the employees." They are characterized as "petty" and "underhanded." This is the case with appeals to *"company spirit*[d]," which is a "sneaky" way of "hindering" the action of *delegates*. But the same thing holds true for other manifestations of *paternalism*[d/c], as we see in the following example, a scene of *reproach*[d] (which constitutes a mode of expressing judgment in the domestic world): in order to intimidate one or more delegates, "a *paternalist* sermon is sometimes delivered in the director's office. . . . 'You think your *parents*[d] would be happy if they knew this? And here I've hired you to *please them*[d].'" *Paternalism* is often criticized when there is a clash about whether a conflict is *collective* or *personal* in nature. This is an important issue because "collective conflicts" fall under the authority of unions and can be addressed by instruments of a civic nature, whereas "conflicts among persons" have to be settled "amicably" in the register of the domestic world. The importance of the way the issue is qualified, as "personal" or "collective," escapes no one, and the nature of the conflict constitutes one of the fundamental stakes for which the persons involved compete; depending on the positions they occupy in the conflict, these persons may try to accredit its *collective* character or, on the contrary, may seek to bring it back into the universe of personal relations. In the first case, it will often be said that "the true dimension" of an issue "has been revealed," and in the second, that the matter has been "reduced to its proper proportions." Conversely, in the first instance, someone may retort that that "generalization" is "excessive" and that what is at stake is a "special case," "a mountain made out of a molehill," while in the second instance, on the contrary, it may be argued that it is "misleading" to "personalize" the conflict, which actually has an "exemplary" character and "a general import" that people are trying to "stifle." In an argument of this sort, bonds of a domestic nature are treated as singular bonds incapable of acceding to generality. In our day, indeed, beings of the domestic world are viewed as singular entities from the vantage point of the civic world, in keeping with the current forms of the State, for these forms are no longer of a domestic nature (as they were in France under the Old Regime). Thus in work relations, union representatives often accuse management of "personalizing" conflicts in order to dissimulate their collective dimension, with the goal of *demobilizing*, that is, *separating* those who are naturally drawn toward *unity* by the goal of the common good. On other occasions, in contrast, people may seek to present themselves simply as individuals with no particular ties to others—in order to defend themselves against an accusation of conspiracy or collusion, for example. In cases like these, management may seek to *restore authentic human relations*[c/d] by criticizing antagonisms blown out of proportion and denouncing the *abuses*[d] of the union movement, which artificially creates *discord* in the workplace. Within unions themselves, *hierarchical* relations of a domestic nature are also criticized, because they imperil the cohesiveness of collective persons: "Right from the start, it is important to avoid any gaps among the *militants*[c] in terms of the level of *information*[c] and *consciousness* on the part of each member. Otherwise, there is a great risk that a *hierarchy*[d] will develop among the *militants* and that a *limited core group*[d/c] will be created, one that will not be able to exploit existing opportunities." Similarly, domestic *authority*[d], denounced as *authoritianism*[d/c], is rejected because it subordinates *everyone's* destiny to the decisions of a single person: "For instance, we cannot advocate a *democratic*[c] society for tomorrow and develop authoritarian relations[d] today."

Free oneself from authoritarianism

The tension between the civic world and the domestic world is particularly evident in connection with election proceedings, because these generally presuppose complete independence on the part of persons who have to be disengaged from subjection to *others*[d] and sheltered from *influences*[f]. In order to create the *collective* being of an *electoral body* one must "respect . . . the *independence of judgment*[c] that is necessary in such circumstances" and comply with legal principles that guarantee the impartiality of the elected officials: "In order to be *eligible*[c] one must . . . not be a *close relative*[d] or *spouse* of the *employer*[c-u]"; "lack of *independence* from *management*[c-u] suffices in and of itself to make a *union*[c-u] *nonrepresentative*[c]," and so on.

Prevent corruption

It is this principle that *management* ignores when its representatives participate in "repression ... by trying to add the *director*[u], his family[d], and his *housekeeper*[d-u] to *candidate lists*[c]." Here it is a matter of applying to companies a more general rule that is valid in municipal and other elections as well, a rule intended to detach the civic bond from the domestic bond and, secondarily, from the market bond. Thus according to the Electoral Code in France, "in communes of more than 500 inhabitants, parents and children, or brothers and sisters, cannot be members of the municipal council at the same time." Similarly, the law spelling out incompatibilities specifies that owners of businesses supplying municipal services, along with salaried employees of the commune who might have relations of personal dependence or market relations with a sitting judge, are not eligible to serve on

Combat the old boy network

the municipal council. *Knowing one another*, as persons, already implies involvement in a personal coalition that is a source of *deviations*. We see this in the case of the "search for candidates" discussed in the brochure we used to depict the civic world: "The solution that involves '*taking the same people* and starting over' is often the lazy way out. It is 'too easy' to claim that there are no new *candidates* who are willing to *run*[c]. It is also sometimes more 'comfortable' to find oneself with *the same little team*[d] of *delegates*[c] who *know one another*[d] and are *used*[d] to working together. These tendencies must be resisted. The *entire*[c] *chapter*[c] has to be notified of the search for *candidates*[c], either during *general meetings*[c], through the *members' newsletter*[c], or both." The tension between the principles that guarantee the purity of *mass beings* rooted in a *cause* and singular relationships woven from person to person is particularly strong in unions, political parties, or other organizations that associate arrangements of a civic nature (*vote, mandate, representation*) with local structures and with modes of recruitment and cohesiveness that rely to a large extent on ties of proximity (working in the same shop, living in the same neighborhood, sharing domestic bonds, and so on). Thus for example most of the incidents that attracted media attention to the French Communist Party in the 1970s and 1980s included the revelation of ties of personal dependencies (cliques) that have secretly brought together, in a common sectarian interest, militants who had been assumed to be entirely devoted to the common cause. But similarly mixed situations (for example, ceremonies surrounding the renewal of Party cards), suspended between respect for legal forms and the most familiar casualness, can be depicted by insiders as *trusting, fraternal, and welcoming*[d], and by those *excluded*[d-c] as conspiracies against the common good.

The same remarks apply more broadly to denunciations of scandals. These always consist in the unveiling of a domestic bond beneath a civic relation: the denouncer brings to light the existence of a secret association based on personal relations—familial, friendly, emotional, or sexual—among persons who ought to be united only by *commitment* to a *cause* and respect for the *law*[c]. An *affair* becomes scandalous when the bonds that unite persons are revealed in public, when a family's "dirty linen" is "hung out" on "the town square." *Scandals* develop in the tension between the domestic world and the civic world (*"forme affaire"*; see Boltanski 1990b). In the French context, scandals are connected with the separation brought about under the Revolution between the domestic polity and the State, now two incompatible worlds: on the one hand, we have "small" incidents involving people, their "intimate secrets," the details of their intrigues, and on the other hand we have "History writ large," History with a capital *H*, the "political" or "economic" history of the Nation. This separation confers a scandalous character on the unveiling of private bonds among persons who should be connected only by the public good, and it confers a murky, soiled, indecent character on the use of civic arrangements to deal with domestic conflicts that could be settled amicably, it is said, without making a big issue out of them—without turning each one into "a federal case," an affair of State. In such murky situations, the act of making public revelations and the act of keeping secrets are criticized by turns. Whereas the civic world unfolds in a homogeneous and transparent space, the domestic world, where space is centered on *homes*, is organized through the opposition between inside and outside, and *betrayal* consists precisely in making *public* on the outside what is supposed to be known only on the inside.

Denounce scandals

The civic critique of domestic discretion as a "conspiracy of silence" that reserves family secrets for insiders has as its counterpart the domestic critique of public testimony as a betrayal that weakens and dishonors the "clan" in front of *outsiders*. Denunciation of a scandal consists in showing the true nature of the relations among people who present themselves as public persons dedicated to the common good but who are in fact serving private interests. Under the appearances of a civic configuration (for example, a municipal council or a court of law), the real domestic ties that unite persons are unveiled. To achieve this, the denouncer must rely on resources that are not present in a civic situation, such as ties of kinship or friendship, ties that are discovered with astonishment, discreet signs of connivance that have to be interpreted, evidence of string pulling, and so on. Such resources make it possible to recompose the situation in a different world, and the object of scandal is the tension between the apparent arrangement and the underlying world; beneath civic appearances, the situation dissimulates another reality, which is domestic in nature. But this reality is condemnable and must be denounced in turn if the situation is to be reestablished in its full purity: the trial is a simulacrum because the defendant maintains personal ties with members of the jury, who came to an agreement among themselves beforehand at the hotel (Claverie 1984), or because the judge maintains private relations with the defendant and was seen eating with him at a restaurant. The shared meal deepens the scandal because it introduces a reference to bodily appetites, and there are no more particular interests than those that, destined as they are to ensure that one's own body experiences pleasure, by their very construction cannot be shared.

Bodily appetites are especially incompatible with civic worth, which ignores them as either hungry or sexual beings depending on the *collective* character of persons. A judge has no body. That is why the denunciation of a scandal revels in inflammatory language (Angenot 1983), one of the characteristic features of which is the way it associates loftiness with baseness, pomposity with obscenity; it expresses virtuous indignation in scatological and pornographic terms. Such stylistic discordances are at the service of denunciations, for these must reveal in broad daylight the particular interest hidden beneath declarations of general interest, and they are never as conclusive as when they can contrast the search for pleasure with a righteous respect for rules, and contrast attachments to the body—which subordinate the social bond to the pleasure that each person draws individually from his dealings with others—with group solidarity.

Local ties, which engage persons in face-to-face relations, tug them toward the domestic world and are for this reason always suspected of opposing the opacity of a *milieu*[d] and the favoritism of a particular attachment to the transparency and egalitarianism of civic relations. The locality, an agglomeration *rooted* in a *region*[d] invested with unique features, customs, *habits*, and so on, is thus opposed to *local premises* in the civic world (the *local seat* of a political party or a union, the *local headquarters* of an *association*, the *local offices* of a government agency), which owe nothing to the particularities of the environment. *Local premises* of a civic nature ensure the presence of the collective person (the State, the Party, the Union, and so on) in a point of space, conceived as a homogeneous expanse. This presence is manifested by such markers as emblems, insignia, *badges*, acronyms, or *posters*[c], which are identical everywhere and which negate distance (for example, a poster denouncing apartheid in South Africa in the local headquarters of a political party in a suburb of Paris). The *local premises*, which owe nothing to the singularities of the persons who occupy them, on a temporary basis and for the length of their *mandate*, can also be criticized from the vantage point of the domestic world as *anonymous*[c/d] and without *warmth*.

Rise above parochial bickering

The tension between the worths attached to having roots in a locality (the "local worthies") and the worth of the nation is inscribed in constitutional forms that provide instrumentation for the civic world: we know, for example, that in France a deputy is not the "natural trustee" of a body, nor does she represent the interests of the inhabitants of a locality or a *region*[d] corresponding to the *district* in which she was *elected*[c] and to which she would be linked by a compelling mandate. She embodies the "general will" as a whole, the general interest of the nation (Furet 1981a, 180–81). Considered from the standpoint of the civic world, the locality is thus the place of the particular and the idiomatic, the place of a particular way of speaking ("the regional accent") or a patois that is characterized by a relation of "proximity to" or "distance from" the "national language" (de Certeau, Julia, and Revel 1975, 53–60); it is also the site of the *prejudices*[d] that public schools are charged with eradicating (Bourdieu 1991).

Public schools, in the many projects debated under the Revolution whose aim was to "put citizens as a whole" "in unison with the enlightenment of a deliberating nation" (Julia 1981, 195), are "indivisibly the instrument whereby prejudice was to be extirpated and the home of the learning of liberty" (Furet and Ozouf 1982, 98), freedom being understood as detachment from familial or local bonds of personal dependence. In the domestic world, a child has no distinguishing features and is only a small-scale potential adult, more or less worthy according to the position he occupies—on the same basis as adults—in the political body, which is itself conceived in the image of the family. In the civic world, a child is a hybrid being, still dependent on a line of descendency and a home; in order to become a citizen, he has to detach himself from *inherited*[d] memberships and fortunes, by acquiring knowledge that will raise him to "the status of a man," a rank in which he will have few equals (Rousseau 1974 [1762], 158–59). Rousseau's Emile owes to the practice of an artisanal trade his ability to retain his independence with respect to others and his quality of citizen under any and all circumstances.

This type of critique, which appeals to the opposition between local and national, private and public, can also be associated with the *affairs* that lead persons attached by family ties to question those ties, taking recourse to civic beings in order to transform a domestic arrangement. This is the case for example with divorce, in which the civic instrumentation may go beyond classic legal proceedings and invoke causes that make universal claims, such as custody rights for divorced fathers (Chateauraynaud 1986, 201–40). Finally, particular allegiances to specific trades are denounced in the same way, because they *divide*[c] workers, as petty bickering divides citizens. Such particularisms are identified with *corporatism*[d], which, by evoking the institutions of the Old

Transcend corporatist divisions

Regime and, more recently, the institutions of Fascist states, brings out a *traditional*[d] character in harmony with domestic arrangements and with *paternalism*. Civic critiques are addressed for example to "the *narrow corporatism*[d]" of those who practice "trade unionism" in the limited sense, "the structure of trades that have *chopped up*[c] the working class into autonomous segments" and the "*corporatist*[d] *demands*[c] that only help further *divide*[c] workers of different categories."

Addressed to the World of Fame. *Public opinion* has different meanings in the civic world and in the world of fame. In the civic world, the opinions of independent individuals express the general will that is attached to the collective as such through the process of voting; this contrasts with public opinion in the world of fame, where opinion is constituted by the converging adherences of persons who are subjected to the influence of others. Critiques of opinion polls and especially their publication during an election campaign point up this ambiguity: because they simply tally personal opinions, which depend on particular interests, polls disrupt collective suffrage. In a civic context, a reference to summation often constitutes a critique of the world of fame, by the same logic: "Union action . . . is not a simple *summation* of positions or *individual*[f] initiatives but rather a *collective*[c] action." Likewise, the critique—a virtually desecratory one in a civic context—of political propaganda and of maneuvers intended to encourage the adherence of others ("certain very politicized types are experienced in *winning over*[f] assemblies[c]") allows objects of a civic nature to be clearly distinguished from arrangements that serve fame.

Ban polls during an electoral campaign

Addressed to the Market World. In the manual we used to present the civic order, the market world is recognized only to be criticized. This refusal to come to terms (which may depend here, at least in part, on the fact that we chose to use a labor union document) is not so surprising if we recall the difficulties that have been encountered by efforts to bring about a compromise, in French society, between the civic form of coordination, supported by the general will, and the market form. As an example of the expression of an irreducible opposition

The selfishness of owners

between the public good and private interests, we can turn to the pre-Revolutionary debates over the relations between the right of residency and the possession of goods, and especially Condorcet's position on the subject (Baker 1975, 253). In his 1788 *Essai sur la constitution et les fonctions des assemblées provinciales*, Condorcet agrees with Turgot on the division between "fractional citizens" and "full citizens" "who have enough revenues from real property to ensure their subsistence" (1986 [1788], 284), but departs from Turgot's position to "refute the opinion of those who would have liked to give a number of voices proportional to the value of the property" (288).

The civic critique of market worth, which has been the object of a great deal of study, can be expressed today in the lapidary form of *slogans*^c, as in stock references to *capitalism*, or in the conventional opposition between *owners*^m (characterized by *selfishness*) and *workers*^{c-u}.

Market individualism   Civic opposition to the market world may also be expressed by a critique of self-serving *individualism*: "Democracy cannot be improvised in this world shaped by individualism." It may also figure in statements pointing to the *deviations* to which collective persons may succumb when particular interests win out over the quest for the common good, as we see with regard to union dues: "It is not a matter of '*insurance*' but a way of *participating*^c in a *collective engagement*^c. . . . [T]he union is not a kind of insurance or security, it is rather an aggressive *collective*^c."

The definition of public services is built around critical opposition to a definition of market service. The compromises presupposed by the nationalization of companies such as those supplying electricity are subject to a powerful tension between a reference to *citizens*^c who have equal rights to benefit from the services provided and a reference to *clients*^m, as we see in controversies over the costs of connection to the grid (Akrich 1989, 184).

Avoid   ***Addressed to the Industrial World.*** Arrangements that
bureaucratization   stabilize the compromise between the civic world and the industrial world are also subject to critiques, especially in the canonical form (which is not present in the works analyzed) of critiques of *technocracy*^{u-c}. These critiques in turn open up passageways toward compromises with the inspired world, as we see in connection with *training*. The

operation by which *training*ᵘ (referring to the acquisition of a skill or competence) is detached from the industrial world and highlighted in the civic world elicits a critique of "knowledge cut off from life" and of "experts bringing information." Thus this civic critique shares some features with the inspired critique of school routines: "Training ᶜ⁻ᵘ by a union *militant*ᶜ has little to do with the usual practice in *schools*ᵘ of making people swallow information that is deliberately cut off from life and that is addressed to individuals for their individual advancement. On the contrary, union training . . . is meaningful only if it is conceived as *collective*ᶜ *enrichment* ⁱ."

Critiques that aim at compromises between the civic and industrial worlds take the standard form of warnings against the risks of *bureaucratization*: "The *structuring*ᵘ of the *chapter*ᶜ is indispensable. A rapid description such as the one we have just provided might leave the impression that a risk of *bureaucratization*ᶜ⁻ᵘ/ᶜ exists. We do not deny this. It is only to the degree that the *chapter* functions *collectively*ᶜ . . . that this pyramid of *responsibilities* will take on its true meaning, that of ensuring a *democratic*ᶜ operation."

Critiques from the Market World

Addressed to the Inspired World. Although motivated by desires that resemble passions, actions coordinated by the market rely on external goods and require the maintenance of a certain distance between the parties involved. Like the other worths, market worth thus governs a tension between a state of particularity and a state favorable to coordination. The investment formula operative in this world balances the wealth associated with access to the market against the sacrifices required by detachment with respect to oneself and attention to others (Adam Smith's "impartial spectator" and "sympathy"). *Emotional distance*ᵐ and *self-control*ᵐ are necessary conditions for seizing *opportunities*ᵐ and *making deals*ᵐ, without letting oneself be blinded by one's "impulses" and acting "on the spur of the moment," an expression that stigmatizes the behavior of a businessman who gives himself over to a sudden inspiration. The need for self-control in business dealings rules

Self-control in
business dealings

out effusive expressions that would stem from an inspired *authenticity*[i]. Getting carried away by one's own gestures may make the body a convincing object in the world of inspired worth, but it is a hindrance in market transactions, in which it is advisable to ward off emotional crises by remaining coolheaded, managing one's emotions by compartmentalizing them: "In the end, compartmentalizing is mostly a conscious process of putting some emotional distance between yourself and the situation" (McCormack 1984, 49).

The achievement of the distance required for a market bond leads to a critique, similar to one issuing from the domestic world (*Lack of self-restraint*), of any eccentric and thus *disturbing*[i] manifestation either in people's dress or in their emotional expressions: "Dress as though you mean business. . . . People who show up for business meetings wearing loafers with no socks, their shirts half unbuttoned, and gold chains visibly exposed can evoke disturbing generalities about their entire personalities" (32–33).

Addressed to the Domestic World. The market world, because it is not firmly seated in a particular space and lacks the support of a precise time frame, gives rise to critiques of the elements of the domestic world in which these two notions are anchored. Specificities, personal attachments, and local ties are particularities from which one must free oneself in order to gain access to an anonymous, borderless market. Traditions, prejudices, and routines are only shackles that prevent the development of opportunistic market relations.

Free oneself from
personal relationships

The *distance*[m] and *detachment*[m] achieved in relations among beings of the market world presuppose both control of emotions (and thus a critique of inspired worth) and *freedom*[m] from personal dependencies and from *influences*[d] (critiques addressed to the domestic order): "away from the *influences of others*[d], we concluded *negotiations*[m] for a rights agreement that has been in effect ever since" (McCormack 1984, 53); "I don't think there is any way I can overemphasize the importance of *confidentiality* in *business*" (44). Relations with influential persons, like the relations of trust maintained by confidences, which are quite naturally at home in the domestic world, cast troublesome shadows over free market contracts. In a business, appropriate practices such as staff rotation must be instituted to lessen the threat of personal or local attachments, for these are sources of prejudices that hinder adjustment to market conditions.

This critique, applied repeatedly in our manual to everyday situations, echoes earlier challenges to a traditional political order that could rely on the foundations of a market order. For example, Ludwig von Mises identified bureaucracy with an order that "consists in intrigues at the 'courts' of those in power. There was a good deal of flattery, adulation, servility, and cringing at the courts of all despotic rulers" (1944, 105). Critiques such as these perpetuate a shift—a critical one for the understanding of the legacy of liberal philosophy (in Locke's sense)—between the notion of freedom or autonomy and the requirements of free exchange. The critique is also reflected in the social sciences, in debates in which anthropologists and economists confront one another over the nature of relations of exchange and over the limits of the market in traditional societies (Mauss 1990 [1923]). The value that an object may have as a gift derives entirely from the bonds that attach it to the person of the giver. Conversely, when an object appears as the object of a transaction, an object of exchange in the marketplace, its fundamental property is its independence of the personality of the seller and the buyer. Personal bonds are thus criticized as impediments to an individual's free access to the market. In this light, the critical figure that invites people to *free themselves from personal relations* may recall the inspired critique of domestic bonds (*Give everything up*), as well as the civic critique of these bonds (*Conquer paternalism*; see also, in Rousseau's writings, the conditions that have to be met in order for the general will to be expressed: the settling of "small differences"). Personal bonds of trust, reduced in a civic world to a conspiracy against the general interest, are criticized here as understandings that hamper competition.

A client's attention to the singular (domestic) properties of merchandise and the mode of investigation that this attention entails are incompatible with the market nature of goods detached from persons. Thus an "intensive" search for the singular bonds between a secondhand article and its former owners can be contrasted with a comparative appreciation (*"survey form"*) of the price in an official market (Geertz 1978).

In a similar spirit, the domestic quality of persons that is expressed in age or seniority is insignificant in the market world, where value does not depend on age or length of service: "I have no psychological hang-ups about the people who work for me making a lot of money at a very young age" (McCormack 1984, 193).

Break local attachments

Lacking limits in time or space, the market world contrasts sharply with the domestic world, whose topography is oriented around privileged domains. Local attachments, implantation in regional territories, all forms of provincialism are only shackles hindering the global extension of the marketplace: "I also felt the regionality of most team sports athletes would severely restrict their *marketability*[m]. Golfers, on the other hand, were almost as *salable*[m] in Tokyo or in Kalamazoo as they were in their *home towns*" (McCormack 1984, 164).

The territorial privileges of corporations are unfailingly criticized from the market perspective, which presupposes a constant expansion of the space in which transactions can occur (Kaplan 1984). In economic literature, elements such as the "barriers" delimiting domains, which stem from a domestic order, are criticized as impediments to the free circulation of merchandise, "barriers to entry" or "barriers to mobility."

Even authors who seek to show the place of relations that are not in keeping with the market world, especially in "labor markets," use this pejorative vocabulary. Thus the free play of the market is blocked by *"non-competing industrial groups"* (Cairnes 1874, 68), confined within limits imposed by the personnel department (Reynolds 1951, 42), "Balkanized" (Kerr 1954), or caught up in the local fabric of "internal markets" and their customs (Doeringer and Piore 1985).

Defy prejudices

Critiques of the disorder caused by the presence of domestic beings in the market world also bring out differences in the way the two worths relate to time. The market world has no use for the durability valued in the domestic world. "Preconceived ideas" and "popular wisdom," which draw their worth from tradition, are obstacles to the deployment of a market world that insists on *defying prejudices*. The shackles from which one must free oneself include cumbersome routines that are incompatible with market opportunism as well as with inspired spontaneity (see *The shackles of habit*). Similarly, the consumer loyalty sustained by branding arrangements can be criticized because it leads the consumer to miss opportunities and pay too much "for the brand name" (Eymard-Duvernay 1989b, 126).

Addressed to the World of Fame. The market world differs fundamentally from the world of fame, owing to the existence of external goods that serve to govern competition among appetites and to determine the measure of worths. When sought-after goods are no longer available, competing *desires*[m] for appropriation degenerate into the gregarious *adherence*[f] of persons who identify themselves with the same sign, like fans of a celebrity, or people who follow fashion rather than their own desires. Once they are blended together in this movement of identification, people behave in the same way, or as critiques of the world of fame put it, they imitate one another.

From the critical vantage point of the market world, *snobbery* is thus the attitude of someone in quest of goods who works out a compromise with the world of fame by imitating persons who have worth in terms of fame or by identifying with a fad or fashion and conforming to it with servility. A "snobbish" client may turn up his nose at *goods*[m] that are not sufficiently *distinctive*[f]. As we are told by sociological studies that unveil the mechanisms for accumulating credit stemming from the world of fame, goods are merely distinctive signs; when this becomes the case, the expanded use of the term "market" no longer includes the form of coordination that relies on competition to acquire rare goods.

When the market can no longer be invoked as the higher common principle, because goods can no longer be identified in a stable fashion, the shift toward the world of fame is manifested by a pathological fluctuation of prices that reveals *the damaging effects of speculation*. Thus in the speculative maneuverings of public opinion that help create artificial price variations by acting on individual expectations, the mediation of the product, which creates the reality of the exchange and which is the

The damaging effects of speculation

condition that allows the constraint of scarcity to work, disappears to the benefit of what can then be treated as the desire of others (Aglietta and Orléan 1982), in an extension of René Girard's analyses: Girard unveils a rivalry that does not result from an accidental convergence of desires but from two essentially "mimetic" desires converging "on one and the same object" (1977, 154).

The low value of celebrity

In the face of compromises with the worth of fame (*Brand name*), the author of our manual critiques appearances and *celebrity*[f], which are of *low value*[m] in the market order ("I've come . . . to see the relative insignificance of outward glitter, be it celebrity, position, or appearances" [McCormack 1984, 14]).

Blockage via collective action

Addressed to the Civic World. Action, in the market world, is a private matter. The term "private," inscribed in opposition to "public" space, nevertheless fails to illuminate the relation to others that is woven through the intermediary of the goods desired and that makes the market order as "collective" as the others, provided that the term "collective" is defined more broadly than it is in the civic world.

Deals are worked out *face to face*[m], and *group*[c] configurations are criticized: "Sell one to one. I hate sales presentations made to a large group of people and will avoid these situations whenever I can. To me, a large group is more than one" (136). Even for activities that slide toward the industrial world and conclude with a "decision" to embark on a *project*[u], all collective procedures are criticized: "While meetings are essential to the decision-making process, they are not the best forum for decision making, and if more than four or five people are in attendance, decision making is probably next to impossible" (224).

The cost of justice

When the only available form of justice is of the market order, legal activity no longer has any special status: it is reduced to a deal like any other, a more or less good one. The intervention of justice in market relations is criticized as soon as it diverts the participants from the direct face-to-face signing of a contract.

Even though he himself has had legal training, the author of our manual criticizes legal interventions in market relations: "Fights between law firms on behalf of clients are often mere vehicles for firms to charge time and earn money. I feel that if you can put the two parties in most legal disputes in a room by themselves—even two years into the legal dispute—the matter will get resolved, certainly more cheaply, and probably a lot more equitably" (207). The Japanese, preeminently worthy subjects from the viewpoint of our manual since they do business throughout the world, are cited as models because "there are . . . very few law firms in Japan" (208).

The gap between the legal construction of a contract and the establishment of a market bond is often attenuated in the composite arrangements in which property rights come to the aid of the market order, but it appears clearly in the following excerpt, in which the author challenges the juridical aspects of a transaction. He even calls the validity of a legal commitment into question, from the standpoint of the realism or opportunism that can push for settlement at any point without getting locked into a straitjacket of obligations: "As a lawyer, it's easy for me to treat a commitment as a commitment and a deal as a deal. But I've often found that by recognizing extenuating circumstances and letting someone off the hook I have accomplished much more for myself and my company in the long run" (40).

Addressed to the Industrial World. By virtue of the temporal engagement implied by its investment in technological objects, the industrial world is subject to criticism from the market standpoint for its rigidities. In addition, the anonymous and formal expression of worth that is natural in the industrial world is called into question because it leaves no place for the interaction of subjective desires: industrial capacities (of machines and experts alike) are only impediments to deal making.

The critique of *the rigidity of tools and methods* is addressed to *structures*[u] ("don't let structures run the operation" [McCormack 1984, 179], *flow charts*[u] ("companies never function according to their organizational charts" [75]), *systems*[u] ("systems . . . ride roughshod over everything, especially common sense" [175], and *organizations*[u] ("Income First/Organization[u] Later" [250]). All these objects disturb the market world and threaten to make the market subject forget his dignity, that is, his interest in getting rich: "The bigger the company, the

The rigidity of tools and methods

easier it is to get off on tangents and forget why you are in business in the first place, which is to make a profit" (202).

Owing to their temporal orientation and their propensity to map out the future, *plans*[u] are shunned and their "lack of realism" runs counter to market opportunism, which encourages people to leap at every chance to make a fortune: "Prospectuses Versus Real Life. I would be quite happy if I never saw another prospectus" (250).

The critique of the restraining effect of bureaucratic rules and especially of planning is particularly explicit among so-called free-market economists such as Ludwig von Mises and Friedrich von Hayek. Von Mises stresses that profits are tied to the underlying instability of the market order and that in a stationary world profits and losses would cancel each other out: "the total sum that a manufacturer must spend for the factors of production required would be equal to the price he gets for the product" (1944, 27–28). Von Mises and Hayek both refer to Saint-Simon, moreover, when they seek to challenge the systematic constructions of worth that they are critiquing (102; Hayek 1952, 105). Denouncing authors who advocate a society that ought to function just like a factory, Hayek cites Saint-Simon: "All men will work; they will regard themselves as laborers attached to one workshop whose efforts will be directed to guide human intelligence according to my divine foresight" (121). Hayek challenges "the characteristic mental attitude of the engineer (16), and, indeed, the first efforts of the founders of the Saint-Simon school were aimed at France's École Polytechnique, where propaganda was highly effective. As Prosper Enfantin wrote, "the École Polytechnique must be the channel through which our ideas spread into society. . . . We learned the positivist language there, along with the methods of research and demonstration that must drive political science today" (Charlety 1931, 45). Hayek stresses the incompatibility between a principle of action that he attributes to this mentality and that he recognizes behind the machinations of the "engineers and planners" (94–98), and the principle that governs commercial activity: "the merchant will constantly come into conflict with the ideals of the engineer, with whose plans he interferes and whose dislike he thereby contracts" (98).

The figure of the technocrat who wields tools and rigid methods looms large in critiques issuing from the market world. As the title of our market world manual indicates (*What They Don't Teach You at Harvard Business School*), and as a publicity blurb for the French edition insisted ("How to Sell—That's What They Don't Teach You at Harvard"), this work is first and foremost a critique of a false industrial worth in the name of the true market worth: "The real problems of selling^m have little to do with aptitude^u.... [T]o presume that *management^u skills^u* obviate the need for *sales^m* skills is a dangerous form of self-deception" (McCormack 1984, 90).

The bad deals of the technocrat

Industrial skill is often criticized via the academic training that produces it. Thus training is often associated with "intelligence," an illegitimate value accommodated in the industrial compromise that allows it to be *measured^u* in the form of IQ: "There is the old tale of two friends who met on the street after not seeing each other for twenty-five years. One, who had graduated at the top of his class, was now working as an assistant branch manager of the local bank. The other, who had never overwhelmed anyone with his intellect, owned his own company and was now a millionaire several times over" (McCormack 1984, xv). "[T]o assume, as I once did, that advanced degrees or high IQ scores automatically equal 'business smarts' has often proved an expensive error in judgment" (xv).

Critiques from the Industrial World

Addressed to the Inspired World.   Industrial worth, the support for coordination oriented toward the future, is disturbed by the eminently uncertain quality of beings from the inspired world. They are criticized for *the wastefulness of improvisation*, attributable to the unpredictability of "muddled" activity, as illustrated in particular by the erratic behavior of "visionaries." The intrusion of unforeseen events that is implied by the inspired gesture of an inventor is risky for the functioning of the industrial order and is subject to criticism for the breakdowns it causes.

The wastefulness of improvisation

Addressed to the Domestic World.   In relation to the industrial order of *efficiency^u* and *progress^u*, *what is old is out-*

What is old is outdated

dated, and what is *traditional* is *old-fashioned*[u], even "medieval." Older people[d], worthy subjects in the domestic polity, are put in their place, that is, they are qualified in terms of industrial worth by the *degree*[u] of their *activity*[u]: "As the average age rises, the company has to anticipate the development of a population of 'handicapped' personnel." Just like persons, things that have a past will be criticized as *ill adapted*, for example a "dilapidated" industrial building that is no longer "functional."

The inefficiency of particularisms

The difference in nature between domestic space and industrial space is highlighted in critiques that spell out the breakdowns resulting from domestic attachments. This critique focuses on the trouble caused by personal relations in the exercise of a task that presupposes an effort to distance oneself: "Do not mix your private life with your professional life. . . . [I]t is preferable not to make friends in the office." The domestic bonds inscribed in a familial capitalism unfailingly create critical tensions when they are judged from the viewpoint of industrial management of a company. The board of directors is an arrangement that is easily disturbed by a confrontation between domestic and industrial qualifications, as when "daddy" is also a "dear president" and a family quarrel is introduced into the heart of the firm (Chateauraynaud 1989b).

Customs, informal practices, domestic territories, reserved spaces, and local privileges are generally contested in the name of industrial efficiency. The methodical exploitation of beings that are poorly adjusted to a production function—natural resources, for instance—requires "investment in forms" (Thévenot 1984) intended to undo particularisms. Thus a systematic exploitation of shellfish may entail the deployment of an industrial arrangement stretching from fishing records to aerial surveillance by helicopter, so as to make the activity measurable (Callon and Law 1989, 20).

Compromises with domestic worth, developed around the construction of a "trade" or an "art," are thus criticized. The arrangements that sustain them are denounced as monstrous groupings and condemned as ignominious by expressions such as "guesswork" or "hunches," which point to practices inappropriately elevated to the rank of method.

Industrial and domestic worths, although they are both distributed according to very extensive hierarchical scales, are not based on the same principle of order, and the *incompetence of an unworthy leader*, a "boss by divine right," stigmatizes the domestic hierarchy in the name of the industrial order.

The incompetence of an unworthy leader

Addressed to the Civic World. The work used as a source of critiques issuing from the industrial world is too oriented toward compromises with the civic world (see below) to give free rein to possible critiques of civic worth. A common expression of this type of critique consists in underlining the *inefficiency of administrative procedures*. A more complex but no less common figure (see below) challenges legal compromises between industrial and civic worths in the name of market flexibility or even of domestic authority. Thus the owners of a small business may prevent a Labor Department inspector from entering company premises by gathering together in person in full force. The inspector has to call on the police for help. She can reestablish her own worth only by reconfiguring a civic arrangement and by transporting adequate civic beings into the situation.

The inefficiency of administrative procedures

Critiques may bear instead on legal compromises between industrial and civic natures, contesting "acquired privileges" ("these habits have characteristics of acquired privileges") or emphasizing the costs of a labor policy ("a company that practiced a costly labor policy not financed by increased productivity would go bankrupt and would be unable to ensure the welfare of its employees").

The costs of a labor policy

Addressed to the Market World. A challenge to the ambiguity of a policy can be expressed in critiques of the conspicuous consumption of "luxury" articles, which are *expensive*[m] but not very useful, as they do not satisfy real *needs*[u].

Useless luxury products

The ambiguity of a product, which can serve in a compromise between the industrial world and the market world, is at the heart of the scholarly controversies in economic literature that have to do with the formation of value and its respective expressions on the basis of desires or labor costs.

Unjustified prices

The tensions between industrial worth and market

worth are often manifested during market tests when it is time to *make a deal*ᵐ and agree on a *fair price*ᵐ. Market contentions that are expressed before a sale in the course of preliminary *negotiations*ᵐ often degenerate into clashes when the price is challenged in the name of a different worth—that is, when reference is made to the low degree of usefulness or *efficiency*ᵘ of a market being with respect to its *price*ᵐ, whether a person or a thing is at stake: "The president of a major apparel firm once told me that he wasn't going to pay an athlete more money than he was making himself. By this criterion, the seven-figure guarantee that we were asking for probably did seem outrageous" (McCormack 1984, 116).

The author reports another interesting case, an even more complex one because it also brings into play the world of fame and the inspired world. It involves a well-known anecdote about a woman who accosted Picasso in a restaurant. She "asked him to scribble something on a napkin, and said she would be happy to pay whatever he felt it was worth. Picasso complied and then said: 'That will be $10,000.' 'But you did that in thirty seconds,' the astonished woman replied. 'No,' Picasso said. 'It has taken me forty years to do that'" (McCormack 1984, 169). The situation is complex from the start: it includes a famous being, the worldwide celebrity Picasso; an inspired gesture, the scribble that bears traces of genius and is not quite the same thing as the autograph of a star, which is only his name; a market being, the sum of money that the woman proposes. After the master has done his drawing, the client criticizes the exorbitant price he is asking, relying on arguments of an industrial nature and stressing the small amount of work required, that is, demonstrating the low degree of industrial worth of the item produced in this way. Picasso remains caught up in the situation that is now purified according to this world and that takes the shape of an industrial contention over the amount of work incorporated into the product; he justifies the price by the preparation time (his training period, as it were) required for the production of the item. Another possible outcome, on the basis of this heterogeneous arrangement, would have consisted in purifying the situation in the inspired world (which would have required a new critique on the part of the artist) and highlighting the spontaneous, immediate, absolutely singular and priceless character of the creative genius.

The tension with market worth is expressed in the industrial world by a highlighting of the unpredictability, the *random* character, of market beings. The worths associated with these two worlds are opposed in terms of their stability, as in the case of "an urgent demand by a 'powerful' client . . . that has to be met at all costs." The market pressure exercised by the client shakes up industrial arrangements that presuppose planning and programming, and leads to deficiencies in industrial quality (Chateauraynaud 1989a, 267). In the industrial organization advocated by Henry Ford, the stress on *standardization*[u] and *utility*[u] leads to denunciations of the incapacity to invest and the volatility of the market ("presenting a new model every year—that's the notion women submit to for their clothes and their hairdos" [Eymard-Duvernay 1989a, 128]).

The whims of the market

This tension is at the heart of economic theory. When economic theory is based on an evaluation in terms of price and market coordination, it is ill adapted to account for a temporal orientation of the decisions and the irreversibilities resulting from investment, despite the extension of the notion of utility to include the expected utility (Favereau 1989b).

PART FIVE

ASSUAGING CRITICAL TENSIONS

Nine

COMPROMISING FOR THE COMMON GOOD

Beyond Testing to Compromising

COMPOSITE ARRANGEMENTS THAT INCLUDE persons and things capable of being identified in different worlds are not fatally undone by disputes. Relations involving such arrangements do not always arouse the sense of strangeness that is produced by the examples we have used to analyze critical operations. For instance, let us consider references to "workers' rights": this familiar expression associates an object from the civic world (rights) with beings from the industrial world (workers). This grouping is inherent in the union movement, and more broadly in all arrangements with which the term "labor" can be associated (labor movement, labor law, labor disputes); the phrase seems acceptable, does not strike us as foreign to the search for a common good. We shall refer to terms of this sort as *compromise* formulas.

In a compromise, people agree to come to terms, that is, to suspend a clash—a dispute involving more than one world—without settling it through recourse to a test in just one of the worlds. The situation remains composite, but a clash is averted. Beings that matter in different worlds are maintained in presence, but their identification does not provoke a dispute. In order to identify a compromise situation, then, it is not enough to note the presence of disparate objects. One must also verify that their importance has been established and that they are not treated by the participants merely as contingent *items* noted by a single observer. For instance, the existence of a personal bond between the manager of a local branch of a regional bank and someone who has come in to ask for a loan (Wissler 1989b) is a resource that is potentially available for use in a compromise. But a compromise can be reached only if familiarity between these business partners is brought into relief (through the use of first names, perhaps, or a recollection of common memories, or a reference to close relatives). More precisely, a compromise is possible here only if domestic arguments are equated with arguments that are relevant in the market world: a faithful friend is a solvent client. Such an equivalence is treated as self-evident; it is not made explicit. In a compromise, the participants do not attempt to clarify the principle of their agreement; they are favorably disposed toward the notion of a common good without actively seeking one. This objective is achieved by seeking the general interest, that is, not only the interest of the parties involved but also the interest of others not directly affected by the agreement. While the imperative of justification is not satisfied in this compromise situation, it is nevertheless not completely lost from sight, as it would be in a private arrangement—an understanding reached by mutual agreement—or in a situation where the participants yield to relativization (we shall look more closely at the figures of private arrangement and relativization later on). A compromise suggests the possibility of a principle that can take judgments based on objects stemming from different worlds and make them compatible. It aims at a common good that transcends the two different forms of worth in presence by including both of them: promoting "techniques of creativity," for example, entails a reference to an unspecified principle according to which industrial routines and inspired outpourings serve one and the same common good.

The Fragility of Compromises

The principle targeted by compromises remains fragile as long as it cannot be related to a form of common good that is constitutive of a polity. The establishment of a compromise does not allow persons to be ordered according to a relevant worth. For example, in the case of a civic-industrial compromise, it remains difficult to imagine, label, and justify a way of testing persons that would target their worth as citizens and their worth as workers simultaneously. Although compromise situations keep the general interest in view, they remain composite; a compromise will often be described as not entirely defensible in logical terms, even though it may be preferable to any other solution. The beings gathered together in a compromise situation continue to belong to their world of origin. It is thus always possible to reactivate the clash by relaunching the controversy over the nature of the objects that need to be taken into account in order to conduct a conclusive test. By relying on one of the worlds in presence, a participant may accentuate the troubling and distracting character of the beings that derive from other worlds and undertake to purify the test by denouncing the compromise as dishonorable.

One way of solidifying a compromise is to place objects composed of elements stemming from different worlds at the service of the common good and endow them with their own identity in such a way that their form will no longer be recognizable if one of the disparate elements of which they are formed is removed. Transformed in this way, the compromise is more resistant to critiques, because it now relies on indivisible objects. Thus, in the composite situation evoked above involving a "competitive public service," the compromise between the higher common principles of the civic world (public service) and the market world (competition) can be reinforced. References to compromise beings and compromise objects indicate ways in which the opposition between these two principles may be surmounted: the identity of a "user" encompasses the contradiction between a "citizen" and a "client"; when the instrument known as a "suggestion box" is made available to users, it absorbs the tension between a "list of grievances" and a "list of demands." As objects like these are multiplied and stabilized, the outline of a new world takes shape. An arrangement such as France's Economic and Social Council[1] associates an industrial preoccupation with a civic form in view of a common good; when such an arrangement is worked out, it anchors the compromise in the world of things. People may then turn to this state compromise, which is associated with a political regime and legitimized by its inscription in public law, for support when they seek to propose or defend other compromises of the same type. In the discourse of a company president, for example, a civic-industrial compromise ("we're all in this together: increased productivity is good for us all") will go over better than a domestic-industrial compromise ("we're all one big family with a tradition of increasing productivity") or an inspired-industrial compromise ("I had a dream: you got the spirit, and our productivity increased").

The multiplication of composite objects that corroborate one another and their identification with a common form thus help *work out* and stabilize a compromise. When a compromise is *worked out*, the beings it associates become hard to pry apart. In the phrase "workers' rights," the difficulty of dissociating the elements pertaining to civic worth from those pertaining to industrial worth becomes evident during debates over the "rights of foreign workers," when someone is trying to break down the compromise that is often implemented in this connection (as good workers, foreigners are useful to the national collectivity) in order to treat the professional identity of these workers without reference to citizenship. The operation is especially awkward when situations proliferate in which the arrangement has been constructed in numerous situations so as to ensure a maximum degree of association between these two types of worths (elections of employee representatives in various circumstances, for example). In the case of a particularly well-worked-out compromise, a test will sometimes resemble a contention in a single world, in the sense that without challenging the validity of the compromise and thus without raising the issue of its coherence, someone will accuse certain persons of not behaving a way that maintains cohesion among the beings involved in the compromise, of not being "up to" the level of the compromise and thus of helping to dismantle it.

A compromise can be worked out more easily when it can be made to accommodate beings or qualities that are *ambiguous* in the sense that they may derive, depending on the way they are understood, from more than one world. This is the case, for example, with "authority" and "responsibility": each of these terms may qualify the relation between a father and his children in the domestic world or the relation between a supervisor and his subordinates in the industrial world. "Consideration" is another example: in the domestic world, this term qualifies the trust granted one person by another ("appreciative of the consideration and trust that he is granted"), while in the industrial world the term takes on the meaning it has for Rousseau when he denounces the quest for consideration as an act of submission to the world's whims. Similarly, one can build bridges in a civic world in several ways: toward the domestic world, through the intermediary of "principles," by shifting from "fundamental principles" (civic) to "having principles" (domestic); toward the world of fame, via "the public," public opinion, campaigns, and demonstrations; and finally, toward the inspired world, when reference is made to a supervisor's "becoming aware" and to the conviction that "calls back into question" ("the ability to keep questioning one's own positions," "demands addressed to the company in connection with a more general questioning," and so on). The industrial world may enter into a compromise with the domestic world by way of quality and with the market world by way of products, technological objects, or coveted goods. Figures of the common good also lend themselves to compromises: thus one can refer to "society" and maintain an ambiguous reference to polite society (domestic), civic society as a political body, or society as studied by the social sciences (with its regularities and its laws, the latter has a strong industrial component).

In the absence of an ambiguous object, one can open the way to compromise by criticizing what is most worthy in the world from which one is extending one's hand toward a foreign nature. By this act of *desecration* (often signaled by quotation marks to suggest a distancing on the part of the writer), one escapes engagement in the plenitude of a closed world and indicates openness to an association between incompatible principles. In the works on which we have drawn to depict the various worlds—and we should recall that these are all guides intended for people in business—the figure of desecration is used in particular in support of compromises with the industrial world, which are often difficult to work out. Thus the guide we used for the domestic world, one written for the self-education of managers, makes desecratory remarks about domestic worths when it is advocating compromises with competence and efficiency, qualities on which its self-taught readers' advancement will depend. The author denounces social niceties (the term "good manners" must not be applied to social chitchat in "polite society" but rather "to daily relations with the population in general"), the archaic character of protocol, conventions ("reject conventions"), and even generation or birth, in order to anchor a compromise between (industrial) competence and the qualities of the "well-brought-up" person (domestic) without referring to family background. In the same way, from the standpoint of the world of fame, one can privilege an industrial compromise by denouncing rumors ("where the company image is concerned, you must be careful not to spread rumors") and a civic compromise by condemning slogans ("slogans must be prohibited"); from the standpoint of the market world, one can promote a compromise with the domestic world by denouncing money and self-interested behaviors (managers who keep "accounts of services owed and provided"), in opposition to the authenticity of affective relations. But it is probably in the manual used to present the inspired world—which, owing to its lack of equipment, stability, and measurements, is particularly resistant to industrial compromises—that the figure of desecration is found most frequently, with the denunciation of magi ("an image like this . . .—the poet is a magus who communicates directly with the heavens—gives an entirely distorted view of creators"), charlatans ("let's face it, creativity has its visionaries and its charlatans"), miracles ("a fair number of companies are always looking for miracle cures"), halos ("so it was inevitable that creativity, as a 'science' of discovery, would deck itself out in a halo right away to impress the masses"), genius (one must not "look at creativity . . . as a perfect weapon that can be introduced into a group and by some mysterious process instantly turn its members into geniuses"), and inspiration itself ("creators, that is, privileged individuals who have received a gift at birth and who are visited by inspiration on demand"), as opposed to a systematic transmission of creativity through teaching.

The identification of compromise objects presupposes a search for specific formulations and designations that establish references to the worlds of origin in a single utterance. A large part of the process of working out a compromise thus consists in reaching consensus as to the adequate term, finding a formulation acceptable to all—one that "sounds right." If the compromise is later denounced, this effort to get beyond the tension between opposing terms by searching for an acceptable designation will be presented as an attempt to disguise the truth in order to make it palatable: critics will charge that the neologism is "in fact" only a euphemism, and the objects associated in a compromise must be given back the names they had in their world of origin so that their true meaning will emerge. What someone calls a "domestic employee" (a formulation that presupposes a compromise with the industrial world and that opens the way to a civic compromise, as when one speaks of the "rights of domestic employees") is nothing but a maid (a being of little worth in the domestic world). To denounce the first term as a euphemism for the second is to unveil the persistence of the domestic condition and the maintenance of personal dependence, under the pretense of a deceptive label implying that a maid is a salaried worker "like any other."

An Example of a Complex Figure:
Denunciation Supported by Compromise

When a compromise is worked out, it can serve in turn as the basis for a critique. We are then confronted with a more complex figure, for more than two worlds are in play, and the critique is established with reference to a formula that arises from a composition involving two different natures. But in such a case the critique can never be completely clarified, because it is impossible to return to a higher common principle.

For example, the theme of "misunderstood genius" (which appears in the work we used to analyze the inspired world) looks at first glance like a critique issuing from the world of inspiration and addressed to the world of fame: a genius, a worthy inspired being, is unjustly treated as an unworthy being in the world of fame (where he is miserable because he is unrecognized). But this critique is inconsistent: if fame is of no value in the inspired world and if one of the qualities of an authentic genius is precisely his indifference to "vainglory," then he can only congratulate himself on the obscurity that surrounds him. To make a place for this formula in our analytical framework, we have to take it as an example of a more complex figure in which the critique is based on an already-worked-out compromise between inspiration and fame. This compromise identifies inspiration and fame within a single common good. The two worths are indeed treated as equivalent, since one can just as well denounce the fact that geniuses are not well known as the fact that well-known persons are not geniuses (the theme of "unwarranted fame"). However, the indeterminacy of the common good makes it impossible to get very far in pursuing the controversy: if she tries too hard to unmask charlatans whose fame is unwarranted and to denounce via the media, in the court of public opinion, the success that mediocre creators achieve with the public at large, the unrecognized genius who is caught reluctantly in the spotlight risks being accused in turn of seeking glory or of being bitter because she has not found it; in either case, the authenticity of her passion is discredited and she is diminished in the inspired world.

This example can be associated with the "paradox of the pamphleteer," evoked by Jean Starobinski in connection with Rousseau:

> A man who becomes a writer to denounce the social fraud places himself in a paradoxical situation. By choosing to become an author and, even more, to begin his career by winning an academic prize, Rousseau entered the social circuit of opinion, success, and fashion. From the first, he was therefore subject to suspicion of duplicity, contaminated by the very disease he was attacking. . . . The only possible redemption was to make a public statement of his separation: withdrawal became necessary, and a permanent disengagement

would serve as Rousseau's justification. . . . Even his excuse, so long as it remains public, is yet another link to public opinion and does not eradicate his mistake. (1988, 36–37)

Thus when he refuses to make Emile an author, Rousseau forestalls the anticipated objection, "You are an author yourself," in a remarkably pure statement of the pamphleteer's paradox: "Yes, for my sins; and my ill deeds, which I think I have fully expiated, are no reason why others should be like me. I do not write to excuse my faults, but to prevent my readers from copying them" (Rousseau 1974 [1762], 160). This formula often comes back, moreover, in "pamphleteering speech," with its "paradoxical mandate to try to make a case for the obvious" by publicly denouncing the "imposture" of opinion in the name of an "inner truth" that one must attempt to share with everyone (Angenot 1983, 85–92).

Composing Compromises and Forming Polities

Working out compromises helps to identify resources that can be mobilized in order to extend the polity model to new principles. The indeterminacy of the common good sought by a compromise becomes more and more problematic when, with the proliferation of composite objects, the outline of a new world takes shape and the tests in which these objects are engaged simultaneously increase in number. The fragility of such compromises, the ease with which they can be denounced, leads to frequent repetitions of tests that have not been judged conclusive enough to bring the controversy to an end. The clashes to which these tests give rise are particularly favorable to the work of explicitation that may lead to the establishment of new principles of equivalence and to the clarification of the common good that is being sought. During this process of generalization, qualities that are ranked according to particular aims are gradually extended in scope so as to qualify beings whose common property will be highlighted.

For example, in the polemics that accompanied the development of court society, with its proliferating tests and the resultant new clashes (in particular, between the worth of the nobility and the king's favor), the worth of fame is envisaged for itself. The work of specification sometimes takes the form of a denunciation (as when seventeenth-century French moralists denounce "vain" glory, or when Pascal distinguishes between established worth and natural worth); it can also take the form of an elucidation that seeks to describe reality without subjecting it to a value judgment and that thereby opens the way to a legitimization of what is already in place. This process is illustrated in the work by Hobbes (1997 [1651]) that we used to give an initial picture of the polity of fame. Challenging the validity of the test leads to formulating the principle that justifies it. Thus when La Bruyère writes that "there are some persons who, if they did know their inferiors and themselves, would be ashamed to be above them"[2] (1929 [1688], 227), he is sketching out an inversion of worths without bringing foreign beings into the domestic world. In most of the maxims in the essay he devotes to "the great," he observes a state of decadence: the great do not measure up to their own greatness. But in order to account for the reversal ("in what respect should the great be ashamed of taking precedence?"), qualities without relevance in this world have to be brought in and credited with a general value, which opens up the possibility of ranking persons in terms of other worths—for example, utility, a principle of industrial worth whose compatibility with the constraints of another polity must then be established.[3] Similarly, at the end of the eighteenth century, the defection of artisans who were breaking away from the system of bondage to masters and establishing themselves freely in the Faubourg St.-Antoine (a zone beyond the gates of Paris and thus outside the control of the trade corporations), and more generally the debates over the corporations that accompanied Turgot's reforms (Kaplan 1976), helped to determine new forms of justification, either in market terms or in terms of skills, and these new forms in turn entered into compromises with the civic worth of the collective when the establishment of procedures designed to allow the expression of the general will through voting led to political debates over the definition of citizenship.

Political philosophy systematically shapes such debates, which it subjects to criteria of internal coherence and compatibility with conventions accepted in other contexts. These constraints must be satisfied in order for a principle of justice to be endowed with a universal validity that guarantees its legitimate character. The philosophic undertaking thus constitutes a fundamental moment in the process of generalization that achieves universalization of values by devoting to the common good qualities that had been previously attached to particular aims. The process ensures the reproduction of the polity model in new forms of worth, without necessarily requiring a complete theoretical mastery of the structure of the model: the qualities revealed by the highlighting of new compromise objects are subjected to the control of logic and are systematically confronted with the requirements of justice, which derive from common sense. The rigor of this work of shaping helps explain how ordinary persons can have the necessary competence to recognize the validity of an argument intuitively, even though they may not be able to generate new principles of justification—principles that would belong in any event to the realm of utopias, in the absence of a world in which they could be deployed.

Developing a State Compromise:
Toward a Civic-Industrial Polity

To illustrate the foregoing analyses, we shall take the example of Durkheim's moral philosophy, one that is familiar to historians of the social sciences. We shall look closely at the way this "moral science"—which in fact constitutes a political philosophy—promotes the establishment of compromises and at the same time puts new worths in place, clarifying the common good that supports legitimate associations. To identify the compromises toward which Durkheim's work has led, we must first situate his moral philosophy in relation to the already established principles that circumscribe his universe of reference: the civic principle with which the notion of the collective is associated, the industrial principle that establishes the compartmentalization of labor and the orientation toward science, and the domestic principle that is present above all in his references to traditional corporations. The compromise between collective altruism and industrial efficiency shunts aside the market principle whose capacity to sustain a just and harmonious polity is challenged and whose utilitarianism and selfishness are tirelessly denounced.

Like political economics, Durkheim's moral science recognizes the principle of utility and the division of labor that underlie the industrial polity whose model we constructed by relying on the work of Saint-Simon. But unlike political economics, Durkheim's work detaches these two requirements from the market principle and associates them with a third, the requirement of *collective* justice based on solidarity. In order to bring about this change in alliances, Durkheim no longer settles for a simple functional division of labor; he confers a social character on the division of labor, stressing the unit within which this division takes place and thus emphasizing the necessary solidarity among workers specialized in different areas ("the *division of labor in society*"). Durkheim relies on the Rousseauist construction that had to be denounced as utopian in order to build industrial worth.

The construction of collective worth and the critique of values anchored in political economics are inextricably linked. Taking a polemical position in order to defend himself from the charge of falling back on "metaphysics," Durkheim insists most particularly on the reality of "society," the "collective being" as a totality, a "real being" that cannot be reduced to a "collection of individuals." He sometimes identifies this body as a "nation" or "State," thus emphasizing a connection with the thematics of political philosophy and the shift from the political body to the social body. The "social being" is not to be confused with any "one individual" or with "the majority of citizens"; rather, it is to be identified with "the nation in its entirety." Political economy, being based on "egoism" and "self-interest" as opposed to the disinterested sentiments of social morality, cannot claim to establish a polity: it is "radically separated from morality, if indeed any ethical ideal is left for humanity once all social bonds are dissolved."[4] "Interest," in the sense in which Durkheim uses the term here, is attached to the singularity of desiring persons. Consequently, it cannot serve as a principle of equivalence; this is consistent with the author's intention to demonstrate the impossibility of building a just and harmonious polity on market exchange.

The market polity can therefore be apprehended only negatively. For example, relations of competition are treated as purely contingent chance encounters, because, stemming from the domain of the individual, they escape the obligation of rules.[5] The extension of market relations creates a world without rules, without morality, and without justice, a world in which the polity falls apart. Thus in the preface to the second edition of *The Division of Labor in Society* (Durkheim 1997 [1893]), the term *"anomie"* designates the loss of the common good and the fall into a state of chaos, "disorders," arbitrariness, and discord, in which "success" wins out over "morality," force trumps justice, and the "law of the strongest" is characterized as a "physical law" as opposed to a "social rule."[6]

A first step toward the foundation of the worth of compromise that is Durkheim's goal consists in substituting the collective interest for the interest of individuals. It is through an analysis of socialism, via Saint-Simon's work in particular (Durkheim 1958 [1928]), that Durkheim undertakes to connect industrial worth with the good of all. Unlike "communism," which is "prompted by moral and timeless reasons," socialism "is bound to a socially concrete setting" and is driven by "considerations of an economic sort" (39–40).[7] For "socialists" as for "economists," "social relations will be essentially relationships of interest" (194). But while economists maintain "that there is nothing basic which is truly collective, that society is only a sum of individuals juxtaposed, and that social interests are the sum of individual interests," the former, and among them Saint-Simon above all, consider that "since economic factors are the substance of common life, they must be organized socially" (196).

But the subordination of industry to the common good that Saint-Simon sought is insufficient and utopian, because it does not take into account the violence of human appetites.[8] Indeed, in Durkheim's anthropology, no doubt inspired partly by Schopenhauer (Chamboredon 1984), which would account for its similarities to Freud's political philosophy (Nisbet 1966, 82–83), human beings are driven by unquenchable desires (Besnard 1973) which, unlike animal appetites, are not naturally limited by instinct: "there is nothing within an individual which constrains such appetites" (Durkheim 1958, 199). Thus if they are not to become "insatiable," they must be "contained by some force external to him" (199). This force is that of collective representations and, in the present case, of the moral representations that emanate from society, from the social being, from the group, as supraindividual instances of practical reason. Only collectives, sites where morality is generated, have the necessary authority to restrain individual appetites whose unbridled expression would return society to a state of disintegration and conflict close to the state of nature;[9] only collectives have the authority to impose on each person the "sacrifice" that is needed so that "private utility" can be subordinated to "common utility." For Durkheim this sacrifice constitutes, as it does for the other political philosophies we have used to present the polity model, the very basis for agreement among men in a society.[10]

Durkheim's construction of a collective worth detached from individuals and superior to them, the only worth capable of subjecting them to a constraint of solidarity, can be treated as a reelaboration of civic worth, whose model we established by turning to Rousseau's work; by this reelaboration, Durkheim is seeking to open up a path to an industrial compromise. In his course on Rousseau (1960a), he identifies what can serve to establish the reality and the worth of a collective being (Halbwachs does the same thing later in his edition of *The Social Contract* [1976]). Elsewhere, Durkheim criticizes Rousseau's lack of interest in economic activity, denouncing the purely moral and thus utopian character of Rousseau's "communism"; in another context, following Saint-Simon, he criticizes the "individualism" and "voluntarism" that underlie the very idea of a contract.[11] To be sure, he sets up a contrast between "the vitalist and substantialist conception of life and society" with which he identifies Rousseau's work and an "organic" conception, a "whole made up of distinct parts, which work together precisely because they are distinct" (1960a, 112); this leaves room for an opening toward a compromise polity, partly inspired by Saint-Simon, in which collective solidarity is based on the division of labor and on the complementarity of social utilities. Durkheim nevertheless places equal stress, in Rousseau, on all the texts in which the "body politic" is described as a "collective" being that is "superior to individuals," a "moral entity" sui generis, not reducible to the sum of its parts, and his commentary on these texts is quite laudatory (81–85). This is the case, for example, with the pages of the "Geneva Manuscript" in which Rousseau compares societies to "chemical compounds" with "properties which they owe to none of the components that make them up" (82).[12] "This remarkable passage," Durkheim writes, "proves that Rousseau was keenly aware of the specificity of the social order. He conceived it clearly as an order of facts generically different from purely individual facts. . . . In his view, society is nothing if not a single definite body distinct from its parts . . . a live, organized body, similar to that of man" (83). As Steven Lukes remarks (1973, 282–88), Durkheim retranslates the language of the "general will" into that of the "collective consciousness," for example when he speaks of the "collective will" (Durkheim 1960a, 107), or when he speaks of the "socialist principle" in Rousseau, the "base of his organic conception of society" (85) and of a supraindividual origin of morality: "Thus the moral order transcends the individual; it does not exist in physical or material nature" (103). Contrary to what can be understood when the reference to Rousseau serves to criticize individualism and by this detour to denounce market worth, the interpretation is drawn toward an industrial compromise. Durkheim is attempting to work out a passage from the "political body" that comes from a contract toward "society" as an "objective" being. Independent of individual wills, subordinated to an internal law, this being has its own regularities and can be subjected to measurement on the same basis as natural bodies. Durkheim then identifies those of Rousseau's analyses that seem to him to attribute to the social milieu "the invariability and necessity characteristic of the natural order" (95), to found "written law[s]" on "manners" and "diffuse custom" (122), and to confer on them "a force which by its impersonality would be identical, *mutatis mutandis*, with the forces of nature" (94). Similarly, to stress the transcendence of the social being, Durkheim appropriates Rousseau's opposition between "aggregation" and "association," between a "sum" and a "composition." In a text cited above, he writes that society is "something other than the arithmetic sum of its citizens" (1993 [1877], 65).

Finally, the way Rousseau conceives of the tension between the particular and the general within each person sheds light on Durkheim's conception of the relation between individual beings and the social being. If the construction of a just polity requires "sacrificing the individual to the social," this necessary sacrifice, "like Abraham's, is not made without stress, hesitation and compromise," as Georges Davy writes in his introduction to the lectures published in English as *Professional Ethics and Civic Morals* (Durkheim 1992 [1950], lv). Thus Durkheim is not unaware that he has to be able to account for individual acts. Although real beings are collectives, one still cannot forget that these collectives include "individuals": if "society is a real being," the fact remains that this being "does not exist outside of the individuals who compose it" (1993 [1887], 64). The place from which collective representations emanate, the society or the group, is also, in Durkheim, a normative agency. This is in keeping with the Rousseauist ethic that seats virtue in the obedience to the general will, which gives rise to law. But the movement that consists in detaching practical reason from the understanding proper to each individual so as to locate its origin in an agency external to persons, a movement already under way in Rousseau, is pursued here to its logical end.[13] Man for Durkheim is no less divided than man for Rousseau. For Durkheim, the tension between a particular interest and the general will, in each person's heart of hearts, takes the form of a tension between the individual's selfish desires, which are given free rein in market exchanges, and the altruistic tendencies that come from his belonging to a collective. In Rousseauist anthropology, particular interests always tend to win out, in each person, over submission to the general will, because the first depend directly on the natural appetites, while the second, lacking instrumentation, stems from pure will and virtue. Durkheim, in contrast, sees society as endowed with the stability and the objectivity that qualify things, and he seeks to understand how social nature can make itself master of human nature by imposing on individuals a respect for supraindividual rules. He consequently focuses on examining the conditions under which social constraints are implemented. For the authority of the collective body to be realized, each individual has to feel it in himself, and more specifically in his or her own body. Solidarity, to be effective, thus presupposes a double movement: the displacement of the rules on which judgment depends from persons onto the collective has to be followed by an inverse movement through which collective moral representations return to be inscribed in the heart of each person. If society is to offer resistance to the destructive anarchy of desire, the externalization of practical reason has to go hand in hand with a movement of reinternalization. Individual persons, even taken separately in an isolated state, may be in conformity with morality because they have internalized the collective representations. In the collective polity, this double movement of externalizing and internalizing is what ensures the coordination of individual actions and orients them toward solidarity.[14]

But this movement is not automatic. If the authority of the collective is to make itself felt and if the reinternalization is to be accomplished, the distance between the collective agency and individual persons must not be too great. The collectivity has to ensure its presence in the form of "institutions" that can provide instruments for establishing relations with others. This is a modification of the Rousseauist schema, for the latter is devoid of instrumentation; its coherence presupposes an inspired component, and intermediary bodies can only be envisaged in the form of "intrigues" opposing the resistance of the particular to the expression of the general will. Durkheim's modification makes it possible to connect civic worth with the division of labor: between the national collective and individual persons, there is room for groups, conceived as totalities in themselves that take on the contours of various professional states.[15] These groups are indispensable. They maintain the cohesion of the social body, which would come apart without them, would degenerate into a juxtaposition of self-centered individuals. Durkheim thus opposes the reality of a society that includes intermediary bodies to the abstraction of the Rousseauist republic where nothing is interposed between the individual and the state, where there is nothing that can exercise a restraining influence on the anarchy of market relations.[16]

The reference to "corporations,"[17] which is based on an analysis of Roman and medieval guilds, introduces a domestic component into the civic-industrial compromise that is the source of what might be called a collective polity:

> A common cult, shared banquets and festivities, a cemetery in common—are not all these features, when considered together, those distinctive of Roman domestic organization? Thus it has been said that the Roman corporation was "a great family." ... A commonality of interests replaced ties of blood. ... A professional grouping would not to this extent recall to mind the family grouping unless there was something akin about them. Indeed in one sense the corporation was heir to the family. ... Exercising a function that had first been domestic, but that could no longer remain so, it replaced the family. (Durkheim 1997 [1893], xl, xlv–xlvi)

The passage by way of the domestic polity is necessary to associate the regulatory agencies with the persons engaged in productive activities and to make up for the lessening of the constraints exercised by "domestic groupings" and "local groupings." With this shift, the functions of moralization and repression that these groups exercised in the play of relations of personal dependence are transferred to economic activities. For Durkheim, however, it is not a matter of counterbalancing decreased family dependencies by increased constraints of a professional order. Indeed, Durkheim strives to pry the principle of the family institution away from consanguinity in order to emphasize its character as a political bond, so that in his case it is by no means an exaggeration to speak of recourse to the higher common principle of a domestic polity.[18]

But corporations can no longer be purely domestic institutions. To enter into the compromise of the collective polity, they have to come to terms with industrial and civic worths. In the third of the lectures devoted to "professional ethics" (1992 [1950], 28–41), Durkheim goes into considerable detail about practical problems, and spells out the changes that would have to be made in the old corporatist institution to adapt it to industry and the modern State: delocalization (substituting a "comprehensive and national, unified" organization for a "local structure, an affair of the community" (37–38); the creation of independent electoral colleges for employers and employees, "at all events when their respective interests were obviously in conflict" (49–50); the attachment of corporations to the State (39), which could pass on to them the establishment of the legislative function in relation to the economy, which has to be "classified according to the industry," as well as management of retirement and emergency funds and the resolution of "labour disputes" by "special tribunals" (40).

The recourse to corporations as instruments for the relations between individuals and collectives thus constitutes one of the solutions proposed in the nineteenth century to resolve the problem of the "representation of professional interests" (Parrot 1974). It is indeed in these terms that the question of the relations between civic, industrial, and domestic worths has arisen historically; it has been made particularly vexatious by the development of industry and especially, in France, by the dissociation—after the passage in 1791 of the Le Chapelier law prohibiting workers' associations (a law used later to prohibit strikes and unions) and the French Revolution's dismantling of the trade corporations—between one's professional condition and one's political citizenship, the latter being conceived in the Jacobin spirit as the state attained by individuals divested "of all concrete distinctions" when they confirm their membership in the nation by voting (Furet 1981a, 174–75). This question has had a large number of other responses, such as workers' associations, which led to the union movement. Their formation between 1830 and 1848 was initially the fruit of an effort to reach a compromise between domestic worth and civic worth through which workers, as William Sewell shows, "combined their corporatist notions of trade solidarity with revolutionary notions of popular sovereignty" (1980, 14). It is also the aim of constructions intended to harmonize the tension between social utility, measured by competencies and participation in the exercise of national sovereignty, as we see from the history of the debates whose object was to establish the distinction, sketched out by Sieyès, between "active citizens" and "passive citizens" and to connect professional capacity with electoral capacity, in a compromise between industrial worth and civic worth that would set aside domestic worth (with for example the distinction between "superiority" and "privilege," "superiority of functions and not of persons") (Rosanvallon 1985, 95–132).

This means that one must not do what many commentators have done in order to extract Durkheim's construction from a hasty, summarial ideological critique; one must not detach it from other attempts to restore corporations, attempts that have been most fully developed in the political philosophies that have inspired certain legitimist tendencies and also social Catholicism in its traditionalist and anti–free market tendencies. These attempts led to a renewal of corporatist thinking in the 1930s and to the creation of corporatist institutions under the Vichy regime, in an effort to compromise with industrial worth. The abandonment of this first "third way" (between "collectivism" and "liberalism") favored the development and instrumentation (for example via a centralized planning system)[19] of a civic-industrial compromise. This second "third way" was based on a critique of "collectivism" and "traditionalism" (in the form of "Malthusianism," "paternalism," and so on), and it sought to connect industrial efficiency and social justice (systems of social protection, redistribution of industrial profits, and so on) in view of a single common good. It presupposes the establishment of new forms of representation, in the State, of the professional condition of persons (collective conventions, professional classifications negotiated with unions, and so on) that tend to modify the qualities associated with citizenship (Boltanski 1987, 66–154 and 170–78). But however instrumented this compromise may be, the fact remains that in the absence of a new polity in which the worths that find themselves associated would be surpassed, a person's profession, considered to be a fundamental attribute in a great number of situations, remains a passageway between worths and an object of tension. Its appreciation often gives rise to clashes, because it can call upon principles of equivalence that are hard to reconcile. As evidence, we may look back at the examples collected in the preceding chapter, where a significant number of critiques focus on professional status: for instance, the inspired critique of the false worth of experts, the industrial critique of traditional apprenticeship, and the civic critique of the familial transmission of professional positions.

Ten

FIGURES OF COMPROMISE

Compromises Involving the Inspired World

With the Domestic World. Inspiration, which coincides with its concept only as pure experience, cannot be inscribed in a polity and become the basis for a universal principle of justice without being transmitted and thereby compromised. We have already encountered this paradox in the arguments Augustine uses to justify writing and publishing a confession which is of no use in relation to God, since God already knows its full contents, and which can be excused in relation to humankind only if it is associated with a project of edification. Because the experience of the soul's movements under the influence of grace and the bodily states that these movements arouse are inherently ineffable, except in a metaphoric form that invites a mystical approach, the transmission of such experience requires a compromise, one often involving the domestic world. The initiatory relation of master to disciple is a case in point. Physical proximity, prolonged contact, a complete yielding of self, a sharing of emotions and affects, the monotony of chant, recitation, or psalmody, repetitions that lead to the formation of incorporated habits—all these factors facilitate the transmission and internalization of a type of knowledge that is very difficult to convey through writing alone, or even more simply through speech. In this sort of apprenticeship, which is almost always associated with the study of sermons or written texts, knowledge transmitted orally or in writing is constantly tested and reappropriated in another way: in practical relations with the master, with other people, other species, or supernatural powers. In this mode of acquisition of knowledge, faith precedes comprehension, is its precondition and is at the same time reinforced by it, in a continuous, circular fashion. The experience of apprenticeship thus merges with an

The initiatory relation of master to disciple

experience of ever-deepening understanding, an ongoing reorganization of one's relation to the world, the world being construed as a text whose meanings are inexhaustible.

This compromise is not fully developed in the work we analyzed, which was intended for use in businesses and thus necessarily included a major industrial component. However, its author repeatedly emphasizes the betrayal that inheres when knowledge is translated in the form of a standard message and transmitted in a uniform way; as we have seen, inspired denunciations of the knowledge of an *expert*[u] or a *mandarin*[u] point in the same direction. Our author suggests instead that a person who possesses knowledge, who has experienced in himself what he is called to transmit, is led to become a *master*[i-d,] to adopt a position of personal and corporal *authority*[d], in order to pass his own experience along to another person; he takes that person as a disciple on whom he will imprint himself through his own conviction, his commitment, his example, and also through his gestures and the sound of his voice. The master *arouses*[i] the disciple. "As one intern put it," says our author, "I am trying to be an *awakener*." But compromises with other worlds necessarily accompany the transmission of inspiration as it passes from person to person, not according to some inherent impulse but through the capacity of inspiration to espouse the will and actions of human beings. The compromises take different forms depending on whether the situation is pedagogical, as in the case just evoked in which a person *adopted*[d] as a disciple is reborn into a new *life*[i] (domestic compromise), or political, as when in a prophetic outburst someone issues an *appeal*[i] to the *people* in order to *mobilize*[c] them (civic compromise), or media-related, as when someone offers an inspired[i] act as a *spectacle*[f] by addressing a *crowd* in order to *seduce* it and win its *support*. This last possibility introduces a compromise between inspiration and fame; another example of the same type can be found in certain forms of *identification*[f] that give rise to spectacular[f] emotional[i] manifestations.

The hysteria of fans

With the World of Fame. Let us recall that in the world of fame, *identification* defines the relation of worth among beings. This mechanism is highlighted in Hobbes's

Leviathan, the founding text of this polity; here, the most worthy beings are "Actors" who encompass the least worthy by "Personating" them through signs, playing their role, giving them an "outward appearance," "representing" their "words" and their "actions" on a "Stage," by "bearing" their "persons" and "Acting" in their names (1997 [1651], 88–89). Thus, in the polity of fame, the least worthy *identify* with the most worthy, the *unknown* with those who are *in the public eye*, those who are *obscure* with those who *shine*, *stars* or *celebrities*; the former submit to the *influence* of the latter and *imitate* those with whom they *identify*. Writings on the *star system* and *media society*, which were especially abundant in the 1960s, describe these processes of *identification*—often in a critical mode—either in formulations that draw them toward the market world, when signs of fame are attached to products ("the star who appears in advertisements invites us to identify partially with her" [Morin 1972, 124]), or else in expressions that appeal to the resources of the inspired world: "The *cult* of the stars *reveals* its *deepest meaning* at certain moments of collective hysteria" (87).

As we saw in our reading of Hobbes (Hobbes 1997 [1651], 140–41), inspiration is a source of madness in a world based on fame. The two worths come together in a delirious crowd, where persons lose the individuality that they need in the world of fame in order to give or receive credit. They become one with the actor who personifies them; they identify with him and are penetrated by his presence as if by an external force. The "idolatrous mass of fans" yields to this state of inspired confusion with a *star* (Morin 1972, 65). When a *political[f] leader[c]* is taken as the model for identification, a civic denunciation typically ensues; in this case, identification is usually no longer couched in the canonical expressions of the worth of fame but depicted, much more clearly than in the case of *stars[f]*, in critical terms: suggestible "crowds under the influence" of a leader (Le Bon 1977 [1895], 37).

In the guide to public relations that we used, identification with a *political leader* is thus presented in a desecratory form, through remarks about the "mental age" of the "group" ("when a group is assembled, the greater the number of participants, the lower the mental age") and in a denunciation of *propaganda*. Propaganda constitutes an illegitimate form from which public relations efforts in business enterprises have to be distinguished if they are to be involved in a valid compromise. The illegitimacy of propaganda does not have to do with the association of fame and civic spirit—which can give rise, as we shall see later on, to the formation of acceptable compromises—but with the presence of an overly pronounced industrial component; when this component is used to deceive the critical capacities of persons, and ultimately to degrade their humanity ("brainwashing"), it contradicts the principles of common humanity and common dignity.

Man in revolt

With the Civic World. The requirement of *calling back into question*, which is common to the inspired and civic worlds, favors passages and compromises between these two worlds. Depending upon the configuration in which it appears, *calling back into question* may consist in a purely inspired manifestation that is necessary in order to attain *detachment*[i], or it may lean toward the civic world, if it is motivated by the goal of the *public*[c] *good*[i]. In this case, one speaks of "a more general *calling into question.*" When it is involved in an inspired-civic compromise, calling into question takes the form of a *revolt* that is initially *spontaneous*[i], but, unlike anarchic rebellions, it is then channeled into an *organized*[u] revolutionary *movement*[c], that is, a movement in which the construction of a civic bond is instrumented by means of "effective[u] methods of mobilization[c]," and in which political contestation can look to a *scientific*[u] theory of *political*[c] history for support. It is difficult for revolutionary action to reject compromises with inspiration, because its own legitimacy ultimately rests on the *actual experience* of *workers* and on their *heightened consciousness.* It is to the extent that leaders are close to "workers" in a company who are "beginning to *become aware*" of their "*common interests*" and can "draw lessons from the *actual experience* of militants . . ." that these leaders can craft the *union* of *all.* A movement that is disconnected from the experience of workers runs the risk of succumbing to *bureaucracy.* But "heightened consciousness" constitutes a revolutionary force only if it is incorporated into the program of a collective apparatus. It remains tacit, latent, an individual malaise, unless it is taken in hand by spokespersons capable of *arousing*[i] it, expressing it, and mobilizing it for constructive action: "In the context of their own activities, union members know the workers' pulse. They know what desires, what *dreams* come to light in the workplace. If the chapter has a tendency to fall asleep, they can *wake it up*, provoke *debates*, etc. The membership is really the *base* of a union *chapter*." Indeed, a *heightened consciousness* does not suffice to build and stabilize collective persons. To solidify the collective and give it a single will, the *workers' dreams* have to be *translated*. This act of translation is necessary in order to transform *revolt*, an *individual* manifestation that can be criticized as *individualistic*, into a *demand*, that is, into a civic expression of a collective interest: "The *chapter* must be attentive to hundreds of everyday phenomena, hundreds of questions that the workers ask themselves, sometimes *unconsciously*[i], if it wants to transform a *revolt*[i] into *demands*[c] and show that there are ways out, that resignation is not a solution." The recognition of a worth proper to *actual experience* makes it possible, as is often the case with compromises involving the world of inspiration, to play on the opposition between what is closed and what is *open*, between what stems from *organization* (a point of passage toward the industrial world) and what stems from *imagination*) ("the essential is also a matter of *imagination* . . . in the union context"), between what is stable and what is unstable, between what is congealed and what is *alive*: "The practice of unionism is *alive*; it is constantly evolving thanks to what we can learn from the *experience* . . . that our members accumulate in the course of their everyday actions."

Exchanges between the inspired world and the civic world are favored, moreover, by the uncertainties that weigh upon expressions of the general will, at least in the canonical version of the civic polity—inspired by Rousseau—that has prevailed in France. As we know, the definition of sovereignty elaborated under the French Revolution was traversed by an acute tension between "'pure' democracy," which rejects delegation of power, and a model of "representative democracy" that depends on suffrage or competence (Furet 1981a, 176–77; Rosanvallon 1985, 95–104). In the work we used to analyze the civic world, this tension between popular sovereignty and an apparatus for representing the national will in

The gesture of protest

a state comes up in the treatment of *"justice."* References to "justice" appear most often in a desecratory form that is signaled in particular by a systematic use of quotation marks whenever the term is used to qualify judicial institutions. This practice is designed to disqualify the state's judicial apparatus and the decisions made by its judges, indicating that these do not conform to true justice, whose legitimacy is based not on an institution but on the sovereign people. Manifestations of indignation or anger in the face of injustice and especially in the face of the unjust character of judicial decisions may be constituted as spontaneous expressions of the people's immanent sense of justice. This opposition between justice and injustice may also espouse the more general distinction between procedural law, treated as a technology that lends itself to instrumental (litigious) use, and justice treated as an extension of the moral sense.

The tension inherent in the civic polity between popular sovereignty and the apparatus of a state often finds an outlet in compromises with the inspired world. The same path is often taken by people who claim— sometimes explicitly invoking the Declaration of the Rights of Man and the Citizen while ignoring the constitution that followed—the right to carry directly to the sovereign people the causes they care most about and in which they are often interested parties inasmuch as they are victims. The expression of their cause and the unveiling of the injustices they are fighting are often accompanied by a denunciation of the judicial system and of the judges who have dealt with their case: the latter are accused of betraying the duties of their office to the benefit of the powerful.

In the absence of legitimate political resources that would make it possible to build a bridge between persons as citizens and the people as sovereign (for example, the right to petition or the right to direct expression in front of an assembly of representatives of the people), these defenders of a just cause can reach the sovereign people only via the *media*[f]. The only way they can take the injustices for which they are demanding reparation to the tribunal of the people is to contact *newspapers*[f] or radio or television stations. The media offer the sole channel of access they can use to gain access to *public opinion*. Now, this entity can tilt into different interpretations, depending on whether it is on the side of the civic world or on the side of the world of fame. The construction of an inspired-civic compromise almost inevitably leads people to make concessions to the world of fame as well. But it is hard to make this form of inspired-civic compromise hold together: for evidence, we can look at the way denunciatory protests of this sort are often discredited in the world's eyes, and in particular in the eyes of the journalists to whom they are addressed, by features that signal their strangeness. When a written text is involved (a lampoon, an open letter, a letter to a newspaper), it typically bears distinctive stylistic or graphic signs (taunts, insults, underlining, and other devices to mark emphasis) that are associated with forms of proof in the inspired world. They manifest the force of conviction of the writer's inner self, the vigor of the indignation, the authenticity of the revolt, made patent by the emotion with which the denouncer is carried away almost in spite of himself, and by the risks run, which guarantee the noninstrumental and disinterested character of the undertaking. But this way of leaning on the inspired world in order to ground the legitimacy of a public protest is a two-edged sword. For it is precisely the simultaneous appearance in a single context of beings stemming from different natures—principally (though not exclusively) from the inspired world and the civic world—that is interpreted by others as a sign of abnormality or even madness (Boltanski 1990a).

But the inspired *challenge* to civic worths is not limited to written protests. It can also be expressed through *gestures* of protest. The term *gesture* is often used to designate a sacrifice that is relevant in the inspired world but carried out to meet goals that are worthy in the civic world. Thus the term *gesture* may designate the act of someone who quit her job, refused to accept a prize, returned a medal, and so on, and who publicized the act. The renunciation of civic distinctions is not, in this case, a manifestation of inspired worth, for inspired worth as such disdains worldly honors. If such were the case, the act of publicizing the gesture would be incongruous. The sacrifice takes on its full meaning, on the contrary, in an inspired-civic compromise intended to support the unveiling of impurities that jeopardize civic proofs. For example, one may give back a medal in order to denounce the influence peddling that lay behind the awarding of the medals in the first place. The person who enacts a gesture of protest captures the attention of others by doing something out of the ordinary that requires interpretation. Such *spectacular*[f] *gestures*[i], which put the instruments of fame at the service of *collective causes*[c], thus presuppose the presence of others without being explicitly addressed to them. Indeed, in its natural purity, the inspired *gesture* is a solitary one, and as such it has no direct effect on others. In order to constitute an effective instrument of mobilization, the gesture must be visible and striking. But it is then in danger of shifting completely away from the inspired world into the world of fame, and this would deprive it of its demonstrative value. Here, then, is the paradox: a *gesture* can mobilize opinion only if it is known to others, and yet no one must be able to accuse it of having been carried out for the purpose of influencing others. If it can be so accused, it can be denounced as "interested" and "instrumental"; it may be described, for example, as a "calculated gesture" on the part of someone who seeks to *make a spectacle of himself*[f], *make himself interesting, make a good impression,* or *get people to like him.* The prospect of physical sacrifice constitutes one of the privileged ways of preserving the inspired dimension of the civic *gesture* by raising the cost of critiques seeking to unveil it as inauthentic, strategic, simulating, interested, or spectacular. This is apparent in cases of self-mutilation intended to protest prison conditions, for example, and in hunger strikes. A hunger strike accomplished by a *particular*[i] person but for a *common cause*[c] is a compromise object that engages intimate compassion for a body suffering from hunger, on the inspired side, and the public responsibility of judges, on the civic side.

But although this form of protest requires a high degree of engagement on the part of its practitioners, it can also be accused of insincerity or simulation, because the sacrifice can be made in a gradual way that ratchets up the threat to others. It is only when the *gesture* consists in making the sacrifice of one's own life that the accusation of inauthenticity can no longer be accepted. This sacrifice, which presupposes the possession of no goods other than one's own body, is for that very reason one of the ways through which unknown persons lacking authority or wealth can accede to a form of worth: " 'If it had not been for these thing,' declared Bartolomeo Vanzetti the day after his condemnation, 'I might have lived out my life talking at street corners to scorning men. I might have die, unmarked, unknown, a failure. Now we are not a failure. This is our career and our triumph. Never in our full life could we hope to do such work for tolerance, for joostice, for man's onderstanding of man as now we do by accident. Our words—our lives—our pains—nothing! The taking of our lives—lives of a good shoemaker and a poor fish-peddler—all! That last moment belongs to us—that agony is our triumph.' From a statement made by Vanzetti after receiving sentence, April 9, 1927" (Sacco and Vanzetti 1928, v).

The capacity to *create*, which is an attribute of *genius*[i] in the realm of inspiration, can enter into a compromise with the civic world when it is granted to a *group*[c]. The exaltation of the spirit of an entire people, that is, of its capacity as a collective to engender literary, artistic, and political forms in keeping with its own genius, constitutes one of the canonical expressions of this compromise. The compromise is expressed in a less ambitious fashion in the guide to creativity that served as our reference work, where we are told that "a group can learn to create on the same basis as an individual genius." This compromise, worked out through a connection with the industrial world (*learn*), is directly linked with the author's profession: he is a "creativity counselor" who works with groups brought together for a series of sessions. *Group creation*[i-c] can occur in a broader context, however, as we see from a reference to the events of May 1968 in France, when a collective *ferment* ("bubbling up") "made many people aware of the power of the imagination." The author also refers in this connection to the "warmth" of the no-holds-barred *meetings* that brought forth bursts of inspiration in opposition to the hierarchical rigidity of "society at an impasse."

Collective genius

With the Market World. In the market world as in the inspired world, actions are not coordinated in terms of temporal continuity; indeed, such continuity is discredited, because it blocks the impulses of *desire*[m] or *creation*[i].

The creative market

The instability of the two worths, market and inspired, can help to reconcile singular instances of *uncertainty*[i], moments marked by insecurity and worry, with *opportunities*[m] of which one can take *advantage* when one knows how to *seize the moment* by transforming fate into luck. As von Mises writes, "Those eager to make profits are always looking for an opportunity. . . . He who wants to make profits must be always on the watch for new opportunities" (1944, 28).

The discovery of new goods that take on reality during a market test transforms insignificant items into clearly identifiable valuables. The sudden and unpredictable emergence of such new objects offers an opportunity favorable to the compromise of a *creative market*.

The fact remains that the possibility of taking advantage of chance opens the way to compromises that can be denounced if the world of origin of the beings that have been seized by a stroke of luck is specified. Here we shall have to distinguish between an inspired opportunity, which marks a being and raises him to a place among the elect (a creator will attribute to "grace" an encounter that others might have understood as a chance event), and a market opportunity, the chance of the century, in which someone grasps the possibility of a convergence of desires on a particular object.

Do something crazy

If the unexpected arrival of a new item on the market can be associated with the sudden break that the creative gesture institutes, the rise of an irrepressible desire for appropriation may also be related to the irresistible passion to which the inspired person yields. Examples include the passion that drives someone toward the market to "go on a spending spree," or the frenzy to start a business, or the strength of the "burning desire" that leads to *success*[m] in *making deals*.

The sublime is priceless

Maintaining that beauty has no price is a way of instituting a compromise between the market world and the world of inspiration by attributing a price, paradoxically (a very high one, to be sure), to an inspired being. In the work on which we based our depiction of the market world, we find two particularly significant examples of this compromise. In the first, the author offers a motto that is troubling from the standpoint of either of the two natures from which the beings engaged may stem: "Take Advantage of a Setting Sun" (McCormack 1984, p. 103). The author describes the negotiation in which such *sublime*[i] beings were engaged in a *business deal*[m] that was satisfactorily concluded. Another example cited, this one quite well known, is the story of the woman who accosted Picasso in a restaurant and asked him to scribble something on a napkin, claiming to be prepared to pay whatever he asked. Picasso did as she requested and then said: "That will be $10,000" (169).

With the Industrial World. The energy that is the specification of human dignity in the industrial world, the *potential* for *activity* that nourishes the human *machine* in its work[u], can enter into a compromise with inspired *passion*[i], when bodily *effort*[u] is linked to an expression of *affect*[i]. The compromise developed is a "capacity for creation": "Man is *intuitive*[i], *affective*[i], . . . and the *efficiency*[u] of the *organization* is a *function* of man." Such a compromise is expressed in the figure of the "*person in charge*" demonstrating "*efficiency* along with *passion*[i] for his *activity*[u]" and drawing from the "astonishing goad of *creativity*" a "guarantee of a higher level of participation on the part of the staff."

The passion for hard work

In the effort to reconcile *efficiency* and *passion*, one can work with a repertory of compromises that have already been consolidated in arrangements offered by psychology, the science of affects. Thus the work we examined refers to a "satisfactory psychological atmosphere" that "favors the mobilization of *creative*[i] and *productive*[u] energy"; "*production* defects" are associated with defective *energy*." In the industrial world, the *atmosphere* or *environment* is viewed as a reservoir of *factors* that can *affect* productive *activity*. Depending on whether it is "hierarchical" or "psychologically satisfactory," the *atmosphere* is inscribed either in a coherent assemblage or in a compromise.

Creative techniques

Compared to *creative techniques* that "teach people to dream" and offer methods to help people "stop thinking all the time about being useful, efficient, logical, and rational," techniques for energizing groups work out more complex compromises with other worlds. To understand their use without crediting them with magical powers or reducing them to ideological discourses, it is helpful to analyze the compromises that they instrument. The *spontaneous outpouring*[i] of *free expression*, in "*brainstorming*" sessions, is extended by a *collective*[c] *dialogue*, in the *group*, which presupposes attentive *listening* on the part of each member. This *common*[c] *experience*[i] leads to *questioning*[i-c] that is sanctioned sooner or later by a *voting*[c] procedure: "The group leader enables all members to *express* themselves, to engage in *dialogue* and *questioning*; this in turn gives him a better grasp of the *reality* he is expected to *change*. A *common experience* is forged in the process." In "quality circles," any original ideas that emerge are subjected to a debate that helps forge a general will, and they are then systematically organized and *diagrammed*[c] in terms of *cause* and *effect* in order to be tested, frequently through recourse to statistical methods.

Inventors More generally, the scenario of "discovery" that requires the transformation of an *unexpected intuition*[i] into an *effective innovation*[u] includes such a compromise. The *open-mindedness* that is the source of *creative*[i] *acts* thus merges, in the figure of the inventor, with the *innovative*[u] *evolution* that characterizes the *dynamics* of the industrial world. However, the radical break caused by an inspired gesture threatens to shatter the compromise with the assurance of a predictable future: "It is thus not a good idea to provoke an abrupt change, but it is absolutely necessary to lay out the major axes of tomorrow's organization."

Compromises Involving the Domestic World

Maintain good contacts *With the World of Fame.* Compromises between the domestic world and the world of fame are established when arrangements destined to attract the attention of the public need to be associated with arrangements intended to foster the development of personal relationships. For example, a *reception*[d], a purely domestic event when it is held in order to solidify bonds of friendship, tilts toward the world of fame as soon as it is a question of *connections* and *who people know*. This compromise is strengthened when a *reception* is given as a way to make *connections*[f] by *rubbing shoulders* with important people: "The advantage of stand-up as opposed to sit-down *receptions* is that you can *rub shoulders* with far more people than just your *neighbors*[d] at the dinner table." Receptions facilitate the shift into the world of fame more readily than do banquets, which are highly stabilized in the domestic world. At a reception, where guests are free to move around as they like, they can make contact with one another in turn, while the other attendees can always see who is giving and who is receiving signs of recognition.

But this unstable compromise lends itself to a decisive shift into the world of fame, as we see from the passages devoted to it in the public relations guide we used to identify objects of this nature. The reception given on the occasion of an *inauguration*[c], for example, is described in our manual only as a means to bring *well-known people*[f] together, people qualified by their *celebrity*[f] along with selected, important *audience members*[f] and also *journalists*[f], so that the event that one is seeking to highlight will have "maximum *exposure*[f]." Conversely, a banquet is a more suitable arrangement for the formation of a compromise between the civic and the domestic worlds. The fact of *gathering* around a single table for a meal taken in *common* destined to celebrate a common *cause* ensures the presence of the civic world, whereas the inscription of the *hierarchy*[d] in the way people are seated (at the head or foot of the table, in places of honor, and so on) and in the order of precedence that presides over the meal service favors the reactivation of domestic worths. This compromise arrangement is especially clear in banquets that bring already constituted groups together (alumni dinners, for example), events celebrating the persistence of ties established in the past, or in the banquets described in detail by Antoine Prost that brought First World War veterans together in every commune in France in the 1920s and 1930s (1992).

A reference to *opinion* can also bring about the passage from the world of fame to the domestic world, where opinion is inscribed in the chain of personal relations: for example, a hierarchical superior may have a "good opinion" of his subordinate. Thus compromises with beings of the domestic world are sketched out whenever an *opinion*[f] is connected to a *personal relationship*[d], to the *maintenance* of a *contact* or a "network": "Where public relations are concerned, we try to weave a network of good relationships." "The best approach is to phone the journalists you want to invite, a couple of weeks before the scheduled date; the press agent—if he is any good—ought to know most of these journalists personally." The worth of fame is stabilized by this sort of compromise, in which a "positive *image*[f]" is connected with *trust*[d]. Similarly, *consideration* or *reputation* may shift from an economy of fame toward a domestic nature, depending on the configuration in which they appear, and especially if the *number*[f] of such people is a more important factor than the hierarchical position of those who can give consideration and make reputations. We see an instance of this shift in the following example: "Women, in particular, are in a sense the ambassadors of the home. From the way they behave at the butcher shop, the post office, or the hairdresser's, certain deductions will be made that will end up establishing the reputation of the home. 'I met Mrs. So-and-So this morning, at the grocery store, she's terribly nice . . .'; this is enough to establish a reputation, on the basis of an attitude that very often reflects reality."

Behave properly toward civil servants

With the Civic World. A compromise can be initiated between the domestic world and the civic world by using the register of personal relations, that of *good manners* and *polite behavior*, to address situations that bring citizens and representatives of the State into direct contact in public settings. One must thus "be *polite*[d] to *agents of law and order*[c], who are only applying *rules*[c] for which they are not *responsible*[d]." Similarly, being kept waiting, which is an offense against domestic politeness ("punctuality is the *politeness*[d] of *kings*[d]"), must not rule out *common courtesy* in the office of a public official: "whether it is in the Governor's office or the Mayor's, the post office or Social Security, waiting is the rule. . . . Nevertheless, courtesy is called for, as it is everywhere else." When someone in the civic world talks about "humanizing public services" (for example by putting a name plate on the desk of a public employee in contact with the public), a civic-domestic compromise is involved.

The need to show oneself to be "human" (instead of acting in a "rigid" fashion like a "machine") is also often invoked to support the compromise between the domestic world and the civic world that consists in demonstrating *good sense*[d] in the application of a *rule*[c] (Corcuff and Lafaye 1989). Thus in the municipal services of a medium-sized town, a city councilor asks the supervisor of city streets and the official in charge of public gardens to demonstrate *good sense* in an effort to collaborate (in the interest of all the inhabitants) on the maintenance of contiguous spaces that do not technically fall under their control (Lafaye 1987). Compromises like these, made in order to circumvent obstacles by people who are "flexible" enough not to apply a rule "literally" and who *trust*[d] one another, appear as *scandals*[d/c], private arrangements that do not conform to the *law*[c], when they are denounced in the civic world. In the same way, someone may appeal to people's *good sense* in an effort to apply a law or enforce a rule without destroying *good relations*[d] among the people involved. The tension between forms of domestic judgment and civic arrangements for dealing with conflicts can thus be overcome by compromise formulas, as when parties seek reconciliation through the mediation of an arbiter. Such compromises can be observed in certain arrangements for dealing with professional mistakes and clashes, for example, labor relations boards or, in France, the Conseil des *prud'hommes*[1]; because groups like these seek conciliation, they can be denounced as paternalistic[d/c] (Cam 1981). Arbiters, well-known people whose *authority* is *respected*[d], try to reach a just verdict by making flexible use of the *law*[c] in order to promote agreement while taking into account the singularity of particular cases and personalities. A compromise of this nature is reached, for example, when a school's disciplinary council meets to pass judgment on some unruly students. People who know one another, parents or teachers, have to set up a tribunal to pass judgment on their own children or students; they have to turn themselves into judges for a day. The change of state, often incomplete, requires lengthy preparations designed to attenuate the hold of domestic bonds; council members may study legal texts that establish the council's legitimacy or may research specific points of law. Still, their domestic bonds

Use good sense in applying rules

must also remain present, so that a humane solution acceptable to everyone can be reached (Derouet 1984).

A similar effort to reduce domestic bonds in order to open up the possibility of support from a civic form can be witnessed during certain conflicts in a business context which are based, at least initially, on disagreements between persons, for example between office workers and their supervisor. This effort may accompany the work of unions as they take up the conflict. Unions must in fact suppress all traces of personal bonds in order to transform contentions that can be described in the register of the domestic world into *collective*[c] conflicts that can be addressed as labor-management disputes. For this, the qualifications of the persons involved have to be changed and, more profoundly, the list of pertinent beings must be transformed. The protagonists are no longer designated by their first names (as when the contention is reported on a one-to-one basis in conversation among colleagues, or passed along as gossip), or by family names (as they would be, for example, in the transcript of a court case), or even by title (for example, "head supervisor"), as when the case is written up formally in management records, but by forces of which they are "agents" (capitalism, the state as employer, and so on). The particular dispute that opposed Tom to Harry (assuming they are on a first-name basis), Ms. X to Ms. Y, the administrative assistant to the bureau chief, is redefined with reference to a much broader struggle between salaried workers and management, of which it constitutes just one example among others. Each of the persons involved is treated as a member of a category, in such a way that for each of the actors any other member of the same category could be substituted without introducing any modification into the conflictual relation, which has been reduced to its *structure*[c-u].

We can see this work of transformation in progress if we observe the way clashes that have arisen locally in the form of contentions between persons (within a particular office or shop, for example) extend to the company and to the outside, by taking on conventional forms (Thévenot 1986) that link production units to other companies in the same region or in the same sector, thus giving them the status of *work conflicts*[c-u]. The work of

a union—and more precisely the work of union officials—
consists at least to a large extent in selecting from among
the many daily clashes those that can be the object of
civic engagements and that can thus be described as *collective demands*[c]. This work of clarification transforms the
situation from a personal contention in which people are
engaged in a personal struggle against one another into a
conflict between categories. This clarification in the civic
world is necessary so that a denunciation can be formulated publicly without seeming awkward, abnormal, or
even "crazy," as would be the case if it took the form of
"personal grievances" or an "*ad hominem* attack"—an
"airing of dirty linen," in a phrase often used to designate and condemn the public exhibition of domestic
contentions. In relation to *collective* conflicts, which are
"clean" in the sense that they do not directly involve personal interests, disagreements between persons have
something dirty and impure about them. They are often
qualified as petty, a characterization suggesting that they
are motivated by hidden and shameful interests. They are
the object of gossip[d] and *rumor*, and it is inappropriate to mention them in situations in which the participants are presenting themselves as belonging to collectives and in terms of general interests, such as *general
assemblies*[c], *representative commissions*, public works councils, and so on. Similarly, conflicts that have great *causes*[c]
as their object must disregard persons: their reference is
to the common interest, and each of the parties must
consider only the general good. The people involved,
who are not personally implicated and who may not be
on familiar terms, indeed may not even know one another, understand that they are opposed to one another
only inasmuch as they "personify" *objective*[u] *social*[c] *forces*[u]
rather like those that operate in the industrial world. In
order to be seen as normal (rather than as a pathological
manifestation of some psychic imbalance), the public expression of a disagreement must be taken up by an
agency declared competent to act in the *public interest*[c]
toward *collective* ends: a union, an association, or some
other organization capable of *desingularizing* the relation
between the different parties involved. This agency must
be able to deal with the clash by using the equipment of
the civic world (legal forms, collective conventions, and

so on) and by formulating the disagreement in terms that are general in the civic world, so its expression will be acceptable to the public (Boltanski 1990a).

The extension of civil rights

What is called the *extension of civil rights* thus consists in constructing legal instruments and establishing collective persons in ways that allow clashes previously treated as stemming from people's private lives to be brought into the public sphere. We see this process at work in the appearance of new *causes* connected with sex, family relations, age: these and other *conditions*[c-u] (the condition of being a woman, a father, a child, a senior citizen, and so on) for the defense of whose rights there are associations (National Organization for Women, American Association of Retired Persons) and statutes, laws, or legal demands. Thus a "female condition" had to be instituted as such before the outrages committed against women, in particular sexual harassment in the workplace, could begin to become objects of public denunciations and legal pursuit. The civic world recognizes women only as *citizens* or *workers*[u-c]: in situations set up according to a principle of civic work, women must either suspend any reference to their sex or espouse it in the categorical form of a collective identity tied to a *cause*.

The public school community

Public schools in France, when they are apprehended concretely in the study of a particular establishment (Derouet 1989), are often the object of relations establishing a compromise that dissolves the tension between two countervailing pedagogic models. The first is the civic model worked out during the French Revolution and more fully developed under the Third Republic. Based on the principle of equality of instruction, it leads to the institution of impersonal relations between teachers, between students, and especially between teachers and students; any infringement of this imperative is denounced as favoritism. This principle emphasizes impersonal forms of transmission and evaluation of knowledge: national diplomas, statutes, and grades, and a national curriculum based on universal values. In the same way, in this model, each educational unit, which is not supposed to possess its own distinct identity, is treated as a projection of that national model. The second pedagogic model, predominant under the Old Regime but still very present in France, emphasizes the continuity between children's education at home and their education at school. It finds its justification not in conformity to the principle of equality but in a search for "cohesion" and "happiness" around a "small, warm community rooted in its particularities." In compromise formulas, the public school system appears indissociably as an educational community whose value depends on the quality of the persons who compose it and the quality of their relationships on the one hand and as a public service justified by the application of national rules on the other.

With the Market World. The question of a possible link between market coordination and coordination by way of trust was a central issue for political economics before it came to occupy an important place in anthropological literature on exchange. We have recalled the texts in which Jansenist thinkers suggested that the market helps simulate the effects of a faltering charity. In contrast, philosophers in the Lockean tradition treat trust as a necessary condition for contractual transactions, thus establishing a hierarchical structure between the domestic and the market orders. However, as we have pointed out, for Adam Smith, the sympathy that makes human nature favorable to exchange is not the same thing as benevolence. Questions about the relative place of benevolence in the market order—questions about its necessity, its complementary role tempering the harshness of laissez-faire practices or the disturbances that this harshness provokes—run throughout discussions of free-market liberalism. The debates over whether the market should be defined in "substantive" or "formal" terms, debates triggered by an anthropological approach to the study of actual markets, shed light on the critical relations and the possibilities of compromise between the domestic and the market worlds.

The classic economic theory of general equilibrium did not take the domestic order into account. This order—in particular via the question of trust—has returned to the heart of recent economic debates, in particular debates over contracts and transactions that cannot be interpreted according to the classic definitions of the market because they involve specific goods, bring durable relations into play, or rely on asymmetric information.

References to *reputation*[d], or less explicit recourse to effects of *memory*[d] in approaches based on repetitive game models, presuppose the elaboration of a compromise with this market order.

Trust in business   Domestic relations are sometimes inserted into a market situation in compromise figures. In such cases a "gesture" is recommended: "Business gestures are acts made on behalf of or at the request of someone *for the purpose of obligating that person in some way*" (McCormack 1984, 37). This shift may even lead to a critique of a market calculation that would strip the gesture of its disinterested nature: "I have dealt with executives who seem to keep a running tab of favors owed and given" (38). The "personalizing" of relations with clients and the sale of "made-to-order" goods and services operate through such compromises, as do the "domesticated" or "concerted" markets described in economic literature as challenging the classic approach to marketing. Thus the commercial activities of businesses imply arrangements that help ensure client loyalty, in addition to the compromises with the industrial world that are worked out in sales methods. More fundamentally still, the "trust" that makes it possible to inscribe time in market relations, along with the guarantee of promises, presupposes an accommodation with domestic reputation.

According to John Maynard Keynes in *The General Theory of Employment, Interest, and Money*, businessmen also rely on a "state of confidence" in order to set up a market arrangement and ensure that it will have a certain stability through a convergence of expectations (1936, p. 148).

The transformation of the homogeneous global market space into a domestic space that has the physiognomy of a territory leads to a similar compromise with the domestic world: "Even if you have a tiny office, it is better for you to hold meetings on your own territory." Let us note that in neoclassical economic literature, the qualification "specific" ("specific investment," "specific information" [Eymard-Duvernay 1986]) serves to work out a compromise of this sort in order to deal with a space that lacks the homogeneity of industrial or market space. Similarly, the concept of an "internal labor market" (Doeringer and Piore 1985) has made clear the place of customs and relations of authority alongside an industrial instrumentation in work relations, which then become quite different from market transactions and indeed actually replace them (Favereau 1982, 1986). The approach in terms of "transaction costs" also gives an important place to durable relations by showing their coherence with local specificities (Williamson 1985).

The term "service," understood as an extension of the goods attached to the market world, entails a compromise with the domestic world from the outset, since it includes a personal relation that is difficult to separate from specific, durable ties, as we see particularly clearly when the service is said to be "personalized."

Personalized service

Despite the need we have already pointed out to *free oneself from personal relations* in the market world and to dismiss *patrimonial*[d] objects in favor of *market*[m] objects, the appropriation of goods tends to lead to compromises between these two worlds. The notion of *property* and often that of goods themselves make it possible to shift from the result of a market transaction, which has neither past nor future and is entirely open to cancellation, to a durable attachment that is inscribed in relations of responsibility and trust.

Alienable property

With the Industrial World.   Because the industrial and domestic worlds allow everyone to play on displacements in space and time, compromises designed to go beyond the topographies and temporalities relative to each of these two worlds can also be worked out. Moreover, the two corresponding worths are evaluated in terms of scales of states that are highly differentiated in each case, and compromises may also be sought by associating the two hierarchies.

Compromises constructed between an industrial *company* and a domestic *home* seek to transcend the differences in the way space and personal relations are qualified, differences that manifest the incompatibility between the two natures. In the industrial world, space is *homogeneous, governed* by *axes* and *dimensions* that define coordinates, whereas in the domestic world space is determined by *domains* that mark an *outside*, distances, or neighborhoods. Thus we encounter many formulas that associate domestic qualities with objects from the indus-

The spirit and know-how of the home

trial world and thereby make it possible to slip from one nature to another: for example, *offices*[u] that are *welcoming*[d], or *factories*[u] surrounded by *gardens*[d], features that are supposed to ensure the "harmony of individual relations." Whenever the company is treated as a *territory*[d] rather than as a *functional*[u] *unit*, compromises with the domestic world are initiated, as when reference is made to the "spirit" or "reputation" of the "house," or to the "company spirit." Thus the division of a company into independent production units entails a compromise with the domestic world: "Each 'independent' production unit must occupy its own space and be supplied with all the human and material means it requires."

Private arrangements regarding the nature of space go hand in hand with propriety in relations among persons: "The world of work is a form of society in which there is no excuse for being rude"; "professional life and family life are so interdependent that when problems come up at work they have repercussions at home, and vice versa." Thus a person of *higher* rank "may invite a middle-level *manager*[u] to *lunch*[d], so he can see how [his subordinate] behaves." The compromise is fragile, for, profiting from an "atmosphere of *trust*[d]," the higher-ranking colleague may well "take advantage of the situation." The collaboration of a "trustworthy person" is particularly precious in special circumstances, as in emergencies where one has to "go the extra mile." The same sort of compromise is sought when people are expected to dress appropriately for work, especially in the recruitment process, and when rule-governed selection procedures based on formal criteria are supplemented by evaluations stemming from the domestic world (cordiality, style, physical appearance, and so on). This formula for compromise between the domestic and industrial worlds sets aside legal relations and treats professional relations in a personal mode. In the civic world, such a compromise is denounced as a form of *paternalism*.

Another compromise of this sort comes with attention to the notion of "local-ness," which may be manifested by company directors eager to become "implanted" in a "traditional fabric"; they may refer to a form of common good that presupposes the development of a region or a locality (Pharo 1985, 144–45).

A domestic-industrial compromise is also at issue in efforts to transcend the differences between the perpetuation of a deeply rooted custom and the predictability of a well-honed tool by promoting the effectiveness of good habits. Domestic forms of coordination have long been taken into account by industrial sociology. Indeed, this approach has sought to show that industrial arrangements are more complex than production functions, and it has even relied on "local practices" and real "know-how" to denounce the illusory advantages of "formal procedures."

The effectiveness of good habits

Today, even economic literature on technological change is attentive to the sorts of objects and relations whose coherence we have sought to restore within the domestic world. The evolutionary approach seeks to go beyond the figure of "head engineer" adjusted to a *technical capacity* that can be *formalized* in *manuals* and *instructions* ("blueprints" [Nelson and Winter 1982]). Taking its cues from Michael Polanyi's analyses of "tacit knowledge (1962), this approach stresses the specific character of skills, and their rootedness, which is an obstacle to their transferability. *Habits*[d] ("routines"), transmitted through apprenticeship, are the *memory* of skills (one can best "remember by doing" [Nelson and Winter 1982, 99]).

The work of compromise is particularly intense in efforts to *modernize*[u] that seek to retain a *traditional*[d] art and quality while attempting to *automatize*[u] the *personal touch*[d] (Boisard and Letablier 1989). This work has become routine in industry, where companies' everyday operations are based on the presupposition that industrial and domestic forms can be made compatible and where these operations rely on mediation carried out by "domestic experts" (Thévenot 1989a, 184). Even government statisticians, the most industrial of experts, have ended up seeking such compromises, trying to "straighten up" an "equilibrium that they do not like," that they "do not recognize." Thus they construct industrial measures, figures, and ratios that appear on charts, with evaluations of a domestic nature concerning what persons and things can produce, evaluations obtained on the basis of durable bonds that make it possible over time to assess the trust that one may place in beings of a domestic nature (Kramarz 1989).

The competence of the
professional

The figure of the *skilled artisan*, the *professional*, produces a similar compromise by conflating technical skill
with experience acquired over time and by uncovering
forms of apprenticeship and transmission of knowledge
in the most advanced technologies that are related to the
domestic arrangements of artisanal trades. Since domestic authority is ordered by *generations*[d], *older persons*—
persons with *seniority* in the *house*—are more worthy than
the *young*. The compromise with industrial authority
thus credits the most senior people with aptitudes associated with their *professional experience*[u-d]: "The most important sector of the factory is entrusted to the highly
conscientious senior staff." This compromise, made concrete by the figure of the employee who has "thirty years
with the house," is obviously threatened by the need to
face an industrial test, for such tests recognize as conclusive only standardized technical capacities. The quality
of self-taught engineer or "house engineer" is subject to
this tension, and the manual we examined, which is especially well adapted to this public, is designed to teach
"managers coming up from the ranks" how to become
worthy of inclusion among the "engineers" with "fancy
degrees." The latter have *diplomas*[u-c] based on general
knowledge; the former have *baggage*[d] that "must at least
include the ABCs of etiquette." The compromise is built
around "continuing education": "Ultimately, 'etiquette'
today has to fall within the framework of a continuing
education that evolves over time [and allows one] to succeed with or without a degree."

The procedures for ratifying degrees in technology
that lead, for example, to equating someone who has
earned the title "best worker in France" with a holder of
the baccalaureate degree (equivalent to one to two years
of university study in the United States) presuppose a
similar compromise (Affichard 1986, 155–56).

Traditional quality

The type of compromise devised in order to overcome
the critical tension between seniority and technical skill
in the qualification of persons can also be sought in order
to define the quality of products. One of the benefits of
the approach adopted here, indeed, is the possibility of
addressing the qualification of persons and that of things
within a single framework.

The supervisor's
responsibility

Industrial and domestic worths have in common the
fact that they are deployed over a broad gamut of states,

and the scale of these states can be expressed as a *hierarchy*[d-u] established on the basis of *authority*[d-u]. This ambiguous *authority* depicts a supervisor as possessing both the authority of a *father*[d] over his *children*[d] and that of a *director*[u] over his *staff*[u]. Through this compromise, "the *head* of the *unit*, with his *support* team, becomes a real little boss." The same ambiguity is at issue in the denunciation of the "little boss" whose domestic authority (*respectability*) is undone in the face of his weak industrial authority (*competence*).

More clearly engaged in the industrial world, arrangements of *human relations* tend to reconcile standards of *efficiency*[u] and good *interpersonal relations*[d]. *Human relations* are thus associated with relations qualified as *traditional*[d], or natural, in the domestic world: "Human relations, which are the object of so much attention today . . . are in fact only the rules of traditional good manners in an updated form."

Human resources

Compromises Involving the World of Fame

With the Civic World. The *public*, an ambiguous being, facilitates passages between the civic world and the world of fame. Arrangements that take numbers into account are often common to the two worlds, although they are the object of different specifications in each world. This is the case for *demonstrations*, associated with protests in the civic world (*demonstrations in favor of a cause*[c]), and with spectacles in the world of fame (*public relations campaigns*[f]). But it is equally true for actions of *mobilization*, which signify enrollment in a cause in the civic world ("the conscious and active *mobilization* of the *majority* of *workers*[c]"), and an effort to capture the public eye in the world of fame ("find new subjects capable of *mobilizing* the interest of the *public*[f]"). Abolishing the ambiguity would lead to denouncing the compromise, but one can point it out by putting the ambiguous term in quotation marks so as to suggest that the reference points toward another nature. Thus, in the manual we used to analyze the civic world, the term "public" appears in quotes when it brings a worth of fame into play: "The *information*[f-c] of a union *chapter*[c] is a *tool*[u] at the service of

Touching public opinion

action[c]. It must therefore be *organized*[u]. . . . So you have to study the '*public*[f-c]' if you want to address (all the workers in the company, or certain categories . . .), the forms of transmission (*tracts, posters, meetings*[c], and so on), their frequency, and their specific objectives."

Information, which is not foreign to the civic world, as we have seen (the "people" must be "adequately informed" in order to "deliberate"), and which is often invoked in brochures describing this world, also makes it possible to sustain a compromise with the world of fame, as when the author of the public relations manual we used invokes the necessity of *informing public opinion*. "Today a company can no longer allow itself to neglect public opinion," especially when the use of information is an opportunity for *participation*[c] by *leaders*[c-u] and *representatives*[c]: "Prior to any demonstration, you should undertake an internal *public relations*[f] campaign so you can *inform*[f-u] the staff about your goals and the solution you are contemplating and can ask for ideas, suggestions, and help. This way, later on, you can *present*[f] a given action as arising from the suggestions collected (even if this is not entirely true). Above all, without going too far, you can hold so-called coordination *meetings*[c] every once in a while and invite *leaders*[f-u] from other *departments*[c] and *representatives*[u] of the staff at various *levels*[u] to attend." But, as we can see from the parenthesis the author introduces into his text, which is intended not for union members but for public relations managers, this compromise may easily be denounced from the civic world as cynical, instrumental, and manipulative.

Among the compromises that build bridges from the world of fame to the civic world, there is also *company sponsorship*, which can associate *national interest*[c] with a *public relations*[f] action: "*Conscious*[c] of its *civic* and *social*[c-u] *responsibilities* toward the *national collectivity*[c], the *Singer Company* has set the goal[u] of *attracting the attention*[f] of the *public*[f] in relation to a *duty*[c] in the *national*[c] *interest*, via "*Singer Sponsorship Day*"; "a *campaign*[f-u] in the *national interest*[c] (highway safety, hunger, and so on), can be an ideal opportunity for the company to exploit its *participation*[c] skillfully and to *appear*[f] before *public opinion* with a very appealing, very *human*[c] *image*[f]." But here again, as in the previous example, the author almost invites denunciation of the compromise he is promoting by introducing a reference to a strategic activity ("exploit skillfully").

Compromises between civic worth and the worth of fame will be sustained by objects, persons, or arrangements that are at once *famous*[f] and at the service of the *common good*[c]. Thus in *petitions*[f-c], the presence of persons is ensured by their *names*. It is because they have made *names*[f] for themselves that they deserve to figure on the list of signers, a list that may also have been put together, moreover, on the basis of *personal relations*[d]. The *opinion* that has made these persons *famous*[f] is the principle of equivalence on which the list is based: presented in alphabetical order or in the order in which the signatures have been gathered, such a list brings into association persons who lack any common measure from the standpoint of other ways of establishing worth. The same thing holds true in other arrangements, such as biographical dictionaries of celebrities (*Who's Who*) in which persons exercising different *professions*[u] or *functions* are presented as equivalent from the standpoint of *renown*[f]. But in petitions, as in meetings or organizing committees, well-known individuals are brought together in the service of a *cause*[c]. They bear witness in the face of opinion, which they embody owing to the very fact that they are *famous*, and the better they are *known*, the fewer of them are needed.

Putting one's name at the service of a cause

When the number of signatures increases but the celebrity of each signer decreases, a petition inclines toward the civic world or, as in *gestures*[c-i], toward an inspired-civic compromise, if it is presented as a *spontaneous*[i] manifestation of the *general will*[c]. As we have already seen in the case of gestures, which have to be visible in order to bring people together, the media are necessary instruments for the establishment of a compromise between the worth of fame and civic worth. The history of this compromise merges with the history of *public opinion*, especially in its relations with the press, and its elaboration is linked to the appearance of major legal "*affairs.*" In France, the Dreyfus Affair in particular brought compromises and tensions between worlds into play, especially a tension between the judicial system and public opinion.

Official sanction

In the world of fame, *appearance* and *reality* are conflated. But when compromises are directed toward other worlds, the concessions that ensue may desecrate the purest expressions of worth in this world. This occurs, as we see from examples in our manual, whenever the reality of appearances is called even partially into question: measures intended to bring attention or recognition are treated as instrumental aims undergirded by a manipulative intent. Writing for public relations specialists, the author sometimes advises his readers to *present*[f] something in a certain fashion even "if it is not completely true." In other passages, he brings up the possibility of "creating an event out of whole cloth," which presupposes an implicit reference to a reality distinct from the one that the framework of public relations brings to light by "skillful exploitation" of the resources at its disposal: "When an event does not exist naturally, you can always create one . . . organize a demonstration at an open house, call a meeting, create an exhibit." For example, the usefulness of inviting a cabinet minister in the context of a public relations operation depends not only on how well known the minister is (the only reality that counts in the world of fame) but also on his status as a *public*[c] figure: by his presence, he brings the company *official*[c] sanction. *Officials* who can sanction a company event may be *representatives* or high-ranking *civil servants*[c]; more generally, they are *big names, people in the news*[f] envisaged in situations that connect them with the *general*[c] *interest.*

The sanction effect also comes up in the context of *displays*[f-c], and especially *inaugurations*. In its canonic form, an inauguration consists in taking an object—a product of industry, a bridge, a building, a ship—and detaching it from the industrial world to dedicate it to the general interest, offer it to everyone and make it public. During the ceremony itself, it is treated as an object in the civic world. Thus when a *minister*[c], a representative of the civic world, is present "for the "*inauguration* of a new *factory*[u] or for the *launching*[f] of a new *product*[u]," "his remarks are are translated by *public opinion* as *official*[c] approval."

In a world in which fame establishes equivalences, sanctioning is an operation that allows one being to increase its power by making an ally of another being, one whose credit brings the first an extra measure of power (Latour 1988). But the act of sanctioning also makes reference to the worth from which beings that are worthy in the world of fame may benefit in other worlds. This tension between the principle of equivalence proper to fame and other principles is expressed through marks of awkwardness ("as it were") or in the distance with which sanctioning is handled when market beings (*merchandise* or *products*) or civic beings (*minister*) are implicated. Through the intermediary of a competent authority, the State certifies what is presented as true ("this is definite, it's official").

Similarly, *polls*, compromise objects facilitating multiple passages since they constitute an industrial instrumentation of opinion[f-u], on which they confer an *objective*[u] character while also allowing slippages toward civic consultation and the principle of the majority[f-c], are said to sanction *opinion*: "The increasingly frequent recourse to opinion polls has made it possible to highlight the following fact: the publication of results indicating that a *majority*[c] of persons have a given *opinion*[f] reinforces the opinions of these persons, sanctions them, as it were, and *influences*[f] the opinions of others." In a parallel fashion, "for his readers, the journalist represents a sanction": "He has found a piece of information interesting, has verified it and in all *objectivity*[u] has reproduced it in his columns on the assumption that it might be of use to those who read the newspaper. The difference between an article signed by a journalist and an advertisement or a piece of information presented for advertising purposes is obvious."

Arrangements stemming from the world of fame are introduced into situations of a civic nature when operations intended to arouse the expression of the *general will*[c] are accompanied by measures designed to gain people's *support*. *Propaganda* is denounced in the world of fame, where it indicates a concession to political interests ("it is appropriate to emphasize that public relations are not synonymous with *propaganda* or 'brain-washing' "); in the civic world, however, it is a point through which a compromise with fame may be worked out. Thus, in the manual we used to depict the civic world in business, we

Campaign for support

read that "the [union] *chapter* will always make a *collective*[c] determination of the sectors to which it will regularly direct its *propaganda*[c-f] efforts." The intent to compromise with the civic world is particularly clear in the case of *campaigns* (an arrangement that is common to the world of fame—media campaigns—and to the civic world— electoral campaigns): during campaigns, "in order to create a *climate*[f] favorable to gaining support," instruments foreign to the civic world are called up along with *mobilizing themes* evaluated according to the degree to which they are *captivating*[f] and *attention getting*. For since the *aspirations*[c] of *all*[c] cannot be expressed directly, they must be *translated* by an organization that is charged with spreading them[f] and thus stimulating *awareness* in people. In this case, *influence*[f] will be at issue ("what are the 'strategic' sectors of the factory, those in which it would be useful to have a strong influence?"), along with *audience*[f] and *impact*[f]: "This distribution [of the union newsletter] is very important. It will allow the chapter to measure its audience and help it evaluate its impact."

Brand image　　　**With the Market World.** Attempts at compromise between the worth of fame (*celebrity*[f]) and market worth (*price*[m]) reinforce one another owing to their common versatility, the continuous scale of their states, and the homogeneity of the spaces across which they are valued. In the world of fame, the worth of a market item, which is at the heart of marketing or advertising activities, is the key to one such compromise between these two worths.

As we indicated earlier, the manual we chose to depict the market world is particularly rich in examples of this type of compromise, since the author's own profession involves selling famous beings, *representing*[f] the brand of well-known persons ("big names in sports": tennis players or golfers) or organizations known worldwide (the Nobel Foundation, the Vatican, the Catholic Church in England). The author thus sets about to *make deals*[m] with *famous names*[f], taking charge of their "marketing and management" and thereby combining a worth of fame with a market worth. When one client, a company head, thinks he is being asked to pay too high a price to associate the name of his product with that of a famous sports figure, the author explains that "what he was buying was instant brand name identification, and compared to the tens of millions of dollars it would cost to develop a comparable degree of brand recognition, the guarantees were indeed reasonable" (McCormack 1984, 116).

More generally, in a company, the "climate favorable to sales" that is sought by public relations activities stems from a similar compromise conceived to draw public attention to a product. However, the overall set of public relations arrangements is not constructed with such a compromise in mind, as we see when the purification of the world of fame leads to critiques of the dependence of a public relations department on the *commercial* leadership[m], *commercial* "ways of reasoning," or when it leads to distinctions between the *company image*[f], which stems from this world, and the *brand image*[o-m], which presupposes a compromise with the market world: "*Image* problems can be contradictory. If the general policy behind the *company image* has not been clearly defined, the public relations office will always be caught between two tendencies: promote the brand image, promote the company image. Yet in the short run, the actions taken to promote a company image may very well be of no interest whatsoever to the key figures in the marketing department, who for their part would prefer to act on the brand image." Stock market arrangements may also be involved in such compromises ("a good image . . . stimulates the price of the stock"), with the risk of ending up with speculative movements and a breakdown of the market.

It is rare for compromises of this sort not to be extended to a third world (industrial or domestic) that contributes to stabilizing a product's "brand image" or its reputation (Eymard-Duvernay 1986). In the first case, this constancy is ensured by a shift into the industrial world. The stability of a brand's reputation then depends on the stability of equipment and production methods as well as on the durability of the product's *effectiveness*[u] from the consumer's standpoint. In the second case, it is because the company exists as a *house*[d] with a reputation to uphold, and because it *maintains*[d] domestic bonds of mutual *trust*[d] with its clientele (marketing theorists talk about "domestic markets"), that the consumption of its products is not subject to the rapid fluctuation of natural evaluations in the market world.

Methods for
implanting an image

With the Industrial World. The worth of fame is inconstant. "All you have to do is follow the press carefully for a month to be persuaded of this: events that galvanize public opinion in a country for several days running are totally forgotten from one day to the next because they have dropped out of the newspapers. Yet if a journalist doesn't come back to the subject, it's because he's decided that public opinion is no longer receptive, that 'it's already had enough,' and that other information is more important." Attempts to make this worth less changeable pass through compromises, either with the domestic world (when *opinion*[f] becomes *confident*[d]), or with the industrial world. In the first case, we again find the "state of confidence" that stabilizes opinion and that Keynes put forward as a restraint on speculative dealings (1936, 148, 152). In the second case, the anchorage in tools of an industrial nature is the key factor in stabilization: *means*[u], *methods*, and *organization* ensure more *predictability*[u] and *stability*.

When the author of the manual we chose to depict the world of fame speaks of "public relations," he is referring specifically to the *professional capacity*[u] of *company experts* who work out compromises such as those we have described, using *tools* and *techniques* for *controlling* opinion. Our material is thus very rich in illustrations. For example, "a *campaign* seeks to *implant*[u] an *image*[f]" the way one *installs*[u] a piece of industrial equipment. And public relations tools, like those *put to work*[u] in the wake of industrial *investments*[u], have to be *maintained*[u] if they are to last: "An image that is not systematically maintained gradually fades away from public opinion, and all the capital invested in that image disappears."

The measure of
opinion

Compromises between the world of fame and the industrial world are also manifested in the fabrication of instruments for *measuring*[u] the *audience*[f] won by a campaign, especially *polls*[f-u] based on *representative sampling*.

An objective opinion

Figures referring to a reality that is not solely based on opinion also stem from compromises with the industrial world, as when someone says that an opinion is "well founded" or not, or when someone distinguishes "objective" from "subjective" elements: "The *product* itself may be good or of questionable *quality*[u], *useful or useless*[u], *expensive or inexpensive*[m], and so on: it entails, *ipso facto*, a largely *objective*[u] judgment on the part of consumers and a *subjective* judgment on the part of nonconsumers, who refer solely to the *opinions of others*[f]."

Compromises Involving the Civic World

With the Market World.   In the work we examined, we did not come across any compromises between these two worths.

With the Industrial World.   In spite of everything that separates an order in which work derives more efficiency from an order in which worth derives from a more general will, industrial and civic worths are the objects of intense compromise efforts, especially in French society, as we have seen in our examination of Durkheim's political philosophy. The figure of the *worker*, supported by the arrangements of unionism and by the equipment of labor laws, has its origin in this work of compromise. In French, the label *social* often suffices to bridge the gap between dignity exercised in the creation of a collective will inscribed in groups and dignity expressed in work. *Groupes sociaux* are thus groups made up of people who tend to merge in a single collective will and who all play the same role in the context of a division of labor.

The central compromise, which we shall call "workers' rights," is complemented by less symmetrical figures in which one of the two worths reinforces the other in a more or less instrumental fashion. Thus, in a labor union, one can seek to consolidate the civic relation of solidarity by "effective methods of mobilization," at the risk of triggering a denunciation of the union bureaucracy. Similarly, in people's aspirations to be part of a collective, to work in teams and groups, managers can find means for "increasing the productivity of motivated workers" and enhancing the benefits derived from "group work."

The compromise between civic and industrial worths that is evidenced in labor laws has been the object of intense efforts of construction and reinforcement. This task, illuminated by Ewald's *L'État providence* (1986), gives some idea of the elaborations that would be required prior to the emergence of a new polity. That goal has not

Workers' rights

been achieved, however, for want of a systematization that would presuppose the formulation of a new principle of equivalence and equilibrium on which a test of justification could be based. The incomplete character of the movement that might lead to the creation of a new polity becomes obvious when we see that clashes involving beings from the industrial and civic worlds cannot be resolved without an agreement recalling the need to come to terms with different requirements. The impossibility of carrying a single test through to the end, for want of a higher common principle—an impossibility observed in particular in the application of labor laws or right-to-work laws—precisely defines the compromise that seeks to move beyond the two available principles but cannot do so.

This compromise is instrumented by the *labor union movement* and, still more broadly, by all the arrangements that can be qualified as related to work or the *welfare state* (labor laws, social work, welfare policies). It refers both to the *unity of all*[c], the group, *collective solidarity*, and to a function of *utility*, *productive capacities*[u]. This compromise, which highlights the *dignity of workers*, is marked by the substitution of the term *"workers"* for terms used to designate civic worth, such as *"citizens*[c]*"* or *"men"* in general. Often invoked by Saint-Simon, where they are contrasted with *inactive* persons, *workers* no longer appear as such in an industrial context today unless this context also includes a civic element. "Confronted with the politics of exploitation practiced by all bosses," workers are qualified by their common *condition as workers*, which has to be "improved," and which can include a capacity for political expression as well as technical competence at work. The situation of the "unemployed" themselves (as opposed to the strictly industrial situation of the "idle") is included in an arrangement of indemnization that entails a similar compromise with the civic world (Salais, Bavarez, and Reynaud 1986).

The intermingling of civic and industrial common goods is also accomplished in situations that aim to be conclusive, such as *strikes*, which "show, by the capacity to mobilize the population, that a latent 'dissatisfaction' exists." Similarly, workplace *inspectors* participate actively in this compromise when, in situations of disagreement, they moderate the requirements of production[u] or the constraints of the market[m] by an *appeal* to *solidarity*[c] or by recourse to the *law*[c] (Dodier 1989). Efforts to reinforce the civic-industrial compromise are apparent in the many arrangements that are used precisely to establish a *convention* or a *collective agreement*, by a *contractual negotiation*, or to permit *concessions—compromises*, in the ordinary sense of the term—"in which workers' organizations have had input but also management and the state," or to put a *labor policy* in place by means of *equal representation* at *meetings* with *counterparts* and *delegates from the staff*. These compromises move the situation away from "classic productivist methods that may lead to bitter setbacks and that almost always develop antagonisms between the 'company's interest' and the 'workers' interest,' with lasting negative consequences."

Compromises with industrial worth may also bear upon the very way the civic bond is conceived. In such cases, they are worked out in relation to *organizing efforts* by tying together instruments of stabilization that are based on *routines*[u] and on manifestations of the *general will*[c] in a single configuration. They are often associated with denunciations of inspiration. They crystallize around technological objects, instruments for measuring or forecasting, skills or capacities qualified as *technical*: "If the problems faced by workers and union chapters require, for their resolution, a *will to act*[c], they also require a minimum of *technical capacity*[u]." Civic persons, represented here by the union *chapter*[c], are characterized by their *potential for action*[u] and thus treated like machines, as if they were subject to an evaluation in terms of *efficiency* or *output* that could be the object of a *measurement* and a *forecast*. This applies for example to the *work plan*, the development of which "represents a peak moment for the chapter": "Union activists cannot let themselves be carried along by events. They have to seize opportunities. They have to be able to face reality on a daily basis, in order to use all the instruments that allow them to confront what they cannot foresee." Thus the chapter has to develop a work plan that will lead to the introduction of a whole set of objects and arrangements deriving from the industrial world: *tasks* to be carried out, *objectives* useful to the membership so that they will "know

Effective methods of mobilization

where things stand and what needs to be done," *programs*, *charts* "indicating the progress of spreading information," *censuses* ("for example, if 70 percent of the people in the establishment are workers and only 10 percent of the union members in the chapter are workers, that must pose a problem for the chapter,"[2] *charts* ("a chart of the company indicating the distribution of the staff, the number of union members and the names of activists in each office, shop, and department, will be a useful instrument for refining the recruitment plan; it will allow you to visualize what needs to be done"), and a *budget* ("which makes it imperative to raise the question of the relation between action and financial resources").

The increased productivity of motivated workers

The search for ways to "interest people in their work," to "motivate" them and make them "responsible," is implemented through the construction of an arrangement that is not purely industrial, one in which the dignity of persons is not anchored exclusively in their work, one in which work is not, as the saying goes, an end in itself. "Increased motivation, a better atmosphere, and greater interest in one's work will lead to an increased commitment of energy and thus to an increased production capacity." The compromises worked out in this case associate *technological evolution*[u], a harmonious figure of the natural order in the industrial world (another way to characterize *progress*[u]), with *people's aspirations*[c], an expression of the dignity of persons in the civic world. "To define the future of the company while taking into account both its technological evolution and the aspirations of its people is to bring elements of a response to an industrial society whose members are less and less tolerant of their industries and yet cannot get along without them."

The humanitarian character of the work accomplished may reinforce an arrangement supporting a similar compromise. Thus in the Mutuelle Générale de l'Éducation Nationale (MGEN, roughly equivalent to a health maintenance organization in the public sphere), the French Minister of Education inaugurates a national office during a scene that presents an industrial character (a tour of the premises, technologically advanced hospital equipment, a big budget, high standards of hospital management, and so on), but that also includes civic beings, in the presentation of the humanitarian and disinterested character of the psychiatric activity of this Center and the agreement that ties it to the Ministry of Education: "Alongside its health care services, the MGEN has sought to create favorable conditions for readapting patients to their workplaces and to society. While for some people this goal may have a utilitarian value, if the employee is considered strictly as an element of production, for MGEN members it has a human value that goes beyond economic criteria and seeks to give the patient back his place, his independence, and his dignity—in a word, to put him back on the path to human freedom thanks to a collective effort of solidarity" (*MGEN Actualité*, June 1985).

Compromises between these two worths thus seek to reconcile an *increase* in *productivity*[u] and the *satisfaction* of *aspirations*[c], for "there are solutions that optimize both the costs and the satisfaction of all categories of the personnel" and that are based on the "combined apprehension of technical problems and human problems." Thus a "work group" puts an "expert" and a "particularly motivated staff member" side by side, on the same scale, in a private arrangement whose incoherence would not stand up to a purely industrial (or purely civic) test.

An identification of "working conditions" and an assessment of "job security" are also involved in compromises of this type. To be sure, even while remaining in the industrial world, one may bring to light the *factors*[u] in the *workplace environment* that have a *negative* or *harmful* impact on workplace *efficiency*. But private arrangements of working conditions presuppose a tension between two principles of worth, as we see clearly in denunciations of poor working conditions and environmental "pollution," or in compromises through which management "isolates the solutions that optimize productivity and working conditions." It is by shifting into civic worth that one can appeal to a human dignity that transcends the context of a person's work: "A company's human investment is probably at once the most difficult and the most fruitful of investments—profitable, yes, but with a profitability that extends beyond the company."

The shift toward a civic world may be based not on the civic dignity of persons ("people's aspirations") but on a reference to the civic higher common principle and its

Working in groups

form of worth (*all*[c], *together*, in a group, *collective*): "*All*[c] together, to *produce* better[u]." Through this shift, the state of worthiness is no longer the *expert*[u] state, but the *group*[c] state: "Already, it's no longer the expert who's speaking, but the group: 'Yes, we quite agree, it's unhealthy to work at these temperatures. How can anyone expect to work properly under these conditions?'" From truth established by *measurement*[u], *mathematical* truth, we shift toward truth established by *public opinion*[c], by group consensus. "Since it is so hard to assess what cannot be measured, this guide has adopted the approach of codifying norms and assigning grades . . . and compiling them nonmathematically, synthesizing them in a way that can be presumed to give us a sense of the . . . confrontation of opinions. . . . While our approach is not mathematical, the large number of grades allows us to arrive at an overall evaluation representing the opinion of the group and giving a direction to action."

The *mobilization*[c] of this *collective energy*[u] works through compromises like those that support post-Taylorian methods of work organization such as the "autonomous team," "in which a set of workers carries out a set of tasks without the institution of a biunivocal relation between a person and a task." More generally, shifts like these take place when "problems are treated in a participatory mode" that "makes it possible to reach consensus."

As implementations of this kind of compromise, we can also cite arrangements in which inequalities in workload can be compensated through solidarity within a work team—arrangements set up by workers rather than by management (Dodier 1986).

Certifying competency

The certification of skills presupposes a compromise between the civic and industrial worlds that has taken hold to such an extent in our day that we have to go back to a state prior to its consolidation in order to analyze its elements. For example, in comparing the way two French schools of higher education—Centrale and Polytechnique—functioned in the early-nineteenth century, John Hubbel Weiss has shown that the predegree dropout rates were higher at Centrale (60 percent, compared to 10 percent at Polytechnique) because industrialists sent their children there so that they could acquire strictly industrial skills without attaching any importance to the diploma itself; conversely, the diplomas (rather than the skills) were relevant for people going on to careers in government (Weiss 1982, 183–85).

Another form of civic-industrial compromise can be supported by a reference to a requirement of safety, as we can see in the case of a major public transportation company in France, the Société Nationale des Chemins de Fer (Corcuff 1989). This organization encompasses a large number of situations of an industrial nature (machines, workshops, and so on); as a state-owned company, it has to maintain strong ties with the civic world. Unlike American railroad companies, which have been strongly marked since the beginning by commercial concerns, French railroads, although they were managed as private companies until the Second World War, have been associated with the construction of a civic-industrial compromise whose stability has largely relied on arrangements set up to ensure safety in transportation. Defined as "public services," the railroads are obliged to give priority to the common good and thus to public safety; the stress on this imperative increases the importance of engineers in company management and facilitates the introduction of psychotechnology, defined as an effort to extend to human beings the same concern shown for the reliability of the rolling stock, along with an effort to ensure the appropriateness and predictability of human behaviors by equally scientific means.

The imperative of safety

Public services offer another example of compromise between the civic world and the industrial world when measures intended to increase work efficiency are justified, especially to the staff, by a concern for the common good of the users. This is the case, for example, in the municipal services of a medium-size city in the north of France, studied by Claudette Lafaye (1989). In an organization such as this one, which is roughly equivalent in scope to a large company and which has responsibility for very diverse tasks, compromise arrangements between the civic world and the industrial world are particularly numerous. Indeed, the legitimacy of a municipal action relies first of all on a civic principle, supported by a set of legal texts and rulings that embody the general will, of which the administration is the executive agency. Thus the mayor and the city council, elected by universal

The efficiency of public service

suffrage, have a mission of general interest and must guarantee, among other things, the equality of citizens as recipients of public services. However, in order to carry out their mission, they have to rely on a large number of technical arrangements of very different orders whose implementation rests on the possession of specific competencies and whose evaluation appeals to a principle of industrial legitimacy. The tension between the civic polity and the industrial polity is inscribed in the very arrangement that presides over the implementation of each activity. The responsibility for these activities rests—in a way that can easily become conflictual—on a city councilor elected by the citizens without regard for competence in the field in question, and on a department head who has no legitimacy of a civic nature but who can claim to have the skills and knowledge necessary to carry out the task that falls to his department. Thus both from the residents' standpoint and from that of city officials, an investment in technical equipment can never be justified through reference to the single principle of industrial efficiency alone, as we see for example in the case of a new system for collecting household wastes, a system justified both in terms of "profitability" ("rapid amortization," "efficiency," and so on), and in terms of the common good ("a clean city," but also "better working conditions for the personnel").

Compromises Involving the Market World

With the Industrial World. Our decision to draw all our practical arguments from manuals intended for business use clearly reflects the fact that a business enterprise is a complex arrangement composed of elements stemming from all the natures examined here. Given the plurality of registers of action identified in this chapter, we can hope to increase our understanding of this type of organization by analyzing it as a *composite* arrangement calling on several forms of justification.

The need to work out a compromise between an order governed by the market and an order based on efficiency lies at the very heart of a business enterprise. Without this requirement, a company has no reason to exist. In a market world, the requirement is only a source of rigidity, owing to the routines it presupposes. In an industrial world, the need to compromise is a source of inefficiency owing to the unpredictability of clients' desires, a factor that is prejudicial to the rigorous organization of technical arrangements. The traditional institutionalist economic literature that focuses on organizations and companies (Coase 1987) highlights the necessity for compromises between these two worths, making clear that the transactions on the basis of which business enterprises operate are more complex than market exchanges (Williamson 1975, 1985), and stressing the role of Alfred Dupont Chandler's "visible hand" (1977).

Products are the most common points of passage between the industrial and market worlds. Products may be the output of the *operation*^{u} of an *efficient production unit*, or they may consist in more or less *rare market goods*^{m} coveted by *competing desires*.

A salable product

So-called Fordian or mass production systems are compromise arrangements that seek to reconcile the demands of efficient production, characterized by high productivity, with the need to satisfy a demand in the marketplace. These arrangements are based on economies of scale implying that the price of merchandise goes down when the number of buyers who express the desire to own it goes up—a relation that is not natural in the market world. What is called the size of the market, then, is not strictly an indicator of market worth, since it signals a concentration that interferes with competition (Eymard-Duvernay 1989b, 128). Ford's advice is to ignore the spirit of competition and specialize; the byword "specialization" indicates clearly that the division of labor is a functional requirement having nothing in common with the market world. The arrangement underlying Ford's system is made up of elements ensuring industrial efficiency and a "flourishing market"; standardization of the product and the mode of remuneration are supposed to ensure a compromise between objects that stem from two different worlds. With the constitution of a mass market, the lowering of the cost price is supposed to be accompanied by a stabilization of demand that presupposes the reconciliation of the market's fluidity with the

Control of demand

predictability characteristic of the industrial world; it implies that the instability of market worths can be *controlled*[u] (in particular through "marketing").

More generally, an investment decision and the economic calculation behind it presuppose a compromise between the industrial requirement that is encountered when one tests the technological efficiency of new equipment and the constraint of a financial market that could be expressed by short-term interest. The compromise is based on a reference to a growth rate and to a timetable for decision making associated with an interest rate, in the search for compatibility between the two requirements (Favereau and Thévenot 1996).

Methods for doing business

Compromises between the market world and the industrial world are relatively rare in the American manual we examined, especially in comparison with French works of the same sort; the latter, even when they are chiefly devoted to business deals and sales, all present a highly instrumented panoply of methods that borrow significantly from the industrial world. These French manuals are not addressed to *businessmen*[m], but rather to company sales managers, representatives, salesmen, technical and/or commercial engineers, marketing directors, or product developers. The approach is chiefly industrial, since the goal is to *increase* the *efficiency* and the *productivity* of the sales force through the use of *rational methods*[u].

In the American manual, the industrial world is much less present, although it does appear when the author addresses himself to entrepreneurs, who must "hold to a steady course." Such borrowings as there are mainly involve the *instruments*[u] for recording and *measuring* that allow *stabilization* and *forecasting*: "notes" ("Writing something down is a commitment" [McCormack 1984, 214]), "yellow pads," "itineraries," "agendas" that have to be respected, *planning* and *timing* to which one has to adhere and that allow one to "*manage*[u] time" with "military punctuality." Similarly, a CEO has worth owing to his long-term vision as well as his business sense and his sense of opportunities to be seized: "I have yet to meet a chairman[u] or a CEO[u] of a major corporation who didn't pride himself on his powers of persuasion—in other words, his *salesmanship*[m]" (McCormack 1984, 90).

In the complex arrangement we call a company, just as products allow passages between the market world and the industrial world, the notion of utility—when it does not correspond strictly to the satisfaction of a desire—often makes it possible to work out a compromise with the requirement of functionality that is specific to the industrial world. This compromise tends to blend together elements that motivate people who are prey to subjective *desires*[m] and elements that drive people for *functional*[u] reasons.

Utility, between desire and need

Eleven

RELATIVIZATION

Private Arrangements

THE PRESUPPOSITION OF a common good is required in order to establish a compromise. But the compromise will not hold up if the parties involved try to move ahead toward clarification, since there is no higher-ranking polity in which the incompatible worlds associated in the compromise can converge. An attempt to stabilize a compromise by giving it a solid foundation thus tends to have the opposite effect. An effort to define the common good that is supposed to sustain a compromise may actually shatter the compromise and shift it back into discord. For an exploration of the grounds for agreement shows the compromise up as a simple assemblage without any foundation at all, and this is tantamount to denouncing it. The compromise will no longer look like an agreement among all parties in view of a common good, but like a circumstantial agreement among people who get along well together. The thrust toward a general interest is indeed what raises compromises above the level of "local," "friendly," "person-to-person" agreements, in which people make concessions to one another and come to terms for the time being on the definition of a good that is common to them in the situation.

We shall call the latter sort of transaction, which benefits the people involved, a *private arrangement* (Rousseau used the term "intrigues" to designate such associations oriented toward private interests). A private arrangement is a contingent agreement between two parties that refers to their mutual satisfaction rather than to a general good ("you do this, which is good for me; I do that, which is good for you"). The bond that brings persons together in the situation cannot be generalized to everyone. For example, in one department of a city administration, the director allows the assistant director, who is very helpful in the office and with whom he has a good relationship, to keep a car assigned to the department for weekend use; this is a *private arrangement*, a friendly understanding between the two of them. It is not the object of any specific agreement, it cannot be justified publicly, and it can be challenged at any moment—for example, it can be denounced as unjustifiable favoritism by other department employees or by hierarchical superiors. The suppression of the privilege from which certain employees "arrange" to benefit on a personal basis does not lead to public protest, and the interested parties express their discontent freely only in the form of grumbling and gossip. In contrast, the suppression of a grade-related bonus, which affects them as members of a defined category, may lead to collective action, even a strike.

This sort of arrangement is often what people have in mind when they say that a relationship, a situation, or an agreement is "private" or when they speak in similar contexts of a "coalition." The term "private," in its ordinary usage, has more than one meaning. It can be used to qualify what stems from the domestic or market worlds in contrast with other worlds: the civic world, for example (respect for private life), or the world of fame (the private life of a star). But it also serves to contrast arrangements people make privately with arrangements whose justifiable character can be made manifest by going back to the principle that supports them. This is the sense in which we are using the term here. In this sense, the term "private" designates something that ignores the common good, implies benefits only to the parties involved, and does not aim at justification. We may say, for example, that a coalition has a private character in the sense that it cannot be justified in relation to a polity. These two senses are often confused, especially when the term "private" is used to qualify situations involving friends or family members. But they must be separated if we are to bring the domestic world to light in its generality and distinguish domestic arrangements presented in a justifiable form, such as family reunions on the occasion of a marriage or a death, from situations that bring together persons who are inclined to make private arrangements among themselves while setting aside the constraint of having to justify their agreement in a broader context.

To be "among ourselves" is thus to suspend the goal of the common good and to establish bonds that are no longer supported by a requirement of justice and cannot be universalized: "among ourselves, I'd be inclined to say that . . ." Among ourselves, we can say anything we like; we understand one another. It is precisely the setting aside of the others, and in some cases the attendant secrecy, that helps shape a coalition whose members will be said to be in a relation of "complicity." When two people make jokes about a third party, jokes that would be unacceptable not only in that person's presence but in the presence of others who are not directly involved, we denounce the connivance that links them by saying that they are "bonding" at the expense of a third party and making that person their scapegoat. Jokes that are made "among ourselves" but that would be considered in bad taste if they were made in broad daylight, that is, exposed to a requirement of justification—"dubious" irony, asides, and more generally any expression of complicity—lead into the sphere of private arrangements.

We needed to analyze private arrangements in order to understand how a compromise can be denounced. In a denunciation, a compromise is reduced to a private arrangement that benefits the parties involved. The unspecified common good at which a compromise is aimed is reduced to an *interest*, that is, to a quality that can be used to establish equivalences among persons and to rank them without any possibility of justifying the ranking in its full generality, because it is not based on a principle of equivalence that respects the parties' membership in a common humanity. Private arrangements in fact rest on shared interests that, once they are put into play to qualify other persons, are engaged in a process of generalization that has no legitimacy. But we still have to distinguish between associations that would simply be called "arbitrary" in the sense that they have not been confronted with the constraints of a polity and associations that are unacceptable because they are not compatible with the polity model, which we have used to formalize the competencies that persons bring into play in their judgments. This is the case, for example, when someone establishes equivalences of the eugenic type that subordinate worth to the possession of a biological quality inscribed once and for all in the body.

Insinuation

During a dispute, when one of the parties accuses the other of making insinuations and thus attaches a negative value to that operation (this is not the only form intimation can take, of course), the accuser is seeking to unveil hidden secrets. The adversary is accused of making, in the secrecy of his own heart, unacceptable associations that are betrayed—without his knowledge or, worse still, intentionally—by the ambiguity of his utterances. Intimation is a form of concealment that by definition cannot be presented as such by the speaker when it is identified in a polemical figure. Consequently, to bring intimation into play in a test, one must offer an interpretation whose validity can in turn be challenged. Pointing out an insinuation is thus a form of unveiling. The accuser, seizing on an utterance judged ambiguous in order to allege the presence of an implication, challenges the adversary to make his intentions explicit. The accusation of insinuation presupposes in fact that the ambiguity cannot be lifted, because clarification would entail explicit reference to unjustifiable forms of equivalence. In this process, the demand for clarification may be sustained. The person challenged then recognizes that there is indeed a subtext, but she defends herself by claiming that she did not want to make matters worse. The clarification then leads her to involve herself further in the process of justification by directly presenting the valid argument to which she was alluding; the reference to a legitimate principle then results in aggravating the clash.

When insinuations are identified and the speaker is challenged to justify them (in the case of a racist or sexist allusion, this would cause the situation to tilt into a civic test), these intimations can also be shoved aside by way of an escape hatch. In this case, the incident will be described as having been brought back "into proportion" ("let's not make a big deal out of this; I was only joking"). For example, let us suppose that during an altercation with colleagues over work schedules, someone says to a radiologist: "You'd be better off in Saint-Germain than in a hospital." The radiologist interprets this utterance as a reference to his homosexuality, by association with a frivolous artistic world. When he asks for clarification ("What do you mean by that?"), he is told: "I don't mean anything in particular, just that you live in Saint-Germain-des-Près." As this example shows, the accusation of making insinuations in a situation subject to an imperative of justification may be associated with the denunciation of a hidden coalition, a conspiracy, one that includes scenes in which unjustifiable judgments have been able to solidify an understanding (someone says, for example, that people have been talking behind his back, there have been rumors, people have been gossiping, and so on).

Flight from Justification

The analysis of the way people stop supporting a private arrangement or refuse to clarify an insinuation leads us to examine another way of exiting from a dispute. However, unlike the solutions we have examined up to now, denunciation and compromise, the way out that we are going to explore here makes it possible to escape the rigors of a dispute only by suspending the constraint of justification, yet without yielding to the sort of constraint that opens up the possibility of pardon—a type of constraint that cannot be analyzed in the framework we are developing in this book (see the afterword).

To get out of a test and escape from a clash over what matters in reality, persons may in fact agree that nothing matters. Disagreement is pointless if nothing matters. We shall call this figure *relativization*. In relativization, the reality test is abandoned in favor of a return to the circumstances. The situation is treated as if it were inconsequential and purely local, and the beings it contains are treated as if they were unranked and unimportant, so that it would be both useless and impossible to seek to establish a general relation among them. The relief that relativization brings depends precisely on the pacification that is procured by a return to relaxed situations in which the question of agreement is suspended. Relativization may in this way constitute a response to the fear of facing an examination (as when schoolchildren stir up a commotion on a test day). But relativization may also be a way of working out a smooth passage toward another world by avoiding the discord that cannot fail to arise when an alternative principle of justice is introduced by a denunciation.

To relativize, it is not enough to let oneself go. Relativization presupposes active complicity among persons, a tacit agreement to interest themselves in contingency and bring it into the foreground. The return toward the circumstances demands efforts to suspend the question of justice by setting aside or ignoring beings that would, were their importance to be highlighted, once again draw the situation in the direction of a test. It is necessary to limit associations in order to avoid all generalizations that would threaten to reintroduce tension among incompatible principles, and in order to make it clear than nothing matters, nothing deserves special attention: "it's nothing"; "no problem"; "never mind"; "it's OK"; "whatever." When spatial or temporal proximity imposes associations that are difficult to ignore, they can be circumvented by being treated apart from justification, in the mode of metaphoric comparisons, temporary and fortuitous associations "that prove nothing." As a result, one has to stay at the level of the trivial, and—as we see in regressions toward childish behavior— enjoy the happiness of being "small," that is, unworthy.

Children do not have access to all these forms of denunciation because they do not have access to generality in all worlds. In the civic world, for instance, children remain on the margins of humanity, since they are relevant only as future citizens and thus only insofar as they can be the object of instruction in civics. Consequently, they are equipped to dismantle moments that are heavily inclined toward a given worth by their shouts and untimely games, their disarming laughter, their childish expressions. Relativization, which ignores worth, is one of the states into which children can easily slip. But the temptation to return to circumstances in which they are at ease because everything in them is "small" enters into tension, in the case of children, with the desire to "grow up," that is, to "get big," to "become worthy"—to accede to the possibility of a generality that defines the adult state.

The foregrounding of contingency confers an eminently unstable character on relativization. If everything has the same value because no common measure exists, the polity falls apart. To be sure, clashes are suspended, but only to the extent that all judgment becomes impossible. This is why relativization is often a figure of passage between tests of different natures.

Relativism

Relativization constitutes a moment in a particularly unstable dispute, a moment that suspends a clash, but only in order to work out a passage toward another world once the danger has been set aside. Persons cannot in fact remain for very long in insignificance before the bond of identity that unites them begins to unravel, before they begin to exit from the political state and regress toward self-love, toward a self-satisfaction that is no longer concerned about establishing agreement with others. To seat relativization in a more stable position and thus move on toward *relativism*— as an explicit attitude toward life—one must thus go a step further: one must put the constraints of the polity into parentheses and adopt a position of externality on the basis of which what goes on in the world can be subordinated to a general equivalent that is not a common good. In our day, this general equivalent is most often qualified as a force, power, interest, or strength, and treated as if it were naturally attached to all beings. All beings find themselves mixed together in a single cosmos that tends to abolish distinctions among the various registers of justification and even between human persons and nonhuman beings. The worths proper to each of the worlds we have analyzed can be treated through relativism as disguised manifestations of a primordial force.[1]

Relativism is thus distinguished from relativization by its capacity to denounce the common good from a general viewpoint. Nevertheless, it does not bring us back to denunciation. Relativism takes what is important in the situation and diminishes it without relying on an alternative principle: the wealthy make deals because they love money, just as public officials or delegates, worthy beings in a democratic polity, rule because they love power. The same will to power, a will to be without limits, is exemplified in the passion for money, the desire to dominate, strength of character, inspired disinterest treated as interest when a debt is created in order to secure an attachment, the obscure persistence of instinct, the blind obstinacy of the unconscious—in all these undefined, mutually convertible or translatable forces, an unbridled impulse is limited only by the obstacle of a superior force. Thus while, in a denunciation, a challenge to the validity of a given principle is made by relying on a different one that is brought to light as a result, critical relativism allows someone to formulate a denunciation without making explicit the position from which the denunciation is issued, because relativism aims at abolishing not a particular form of the common good but the very possibility of the existence of a common good. Interest drives the world, and all human beings in the world, dominated by the forces that inhabit them, are "all wrapped up in themselves." The reduction to interests is one of the preferred instruments of relativism. But the meaning of the term "interest" has to be distinguished here from the one it may have with reference to a market polity, in which it constitutes the property that allows beings to accede, by the sacrifice of a singular attachment, to the generality of worth. Conversely, in critical relativism, the reduction to interests serves to suspend the reference to worth and to challenge the reality of all forms of sacrifice.

The social sciences today are often called upon by people seeking a grounding for relativist positions, when such people are in a position to have access to this resource. This detour is not entirely unfounded. We find the most systematic expression of the questions raised by the possibility of relativizing in the critical stance adopted by Nietzsche and transported, in particular by Max Weber's work (Fleischmann 1964), into the practice of the social sciences. The theme of "nihilism" can serve to reveal the abject state to which a world deprived of values is reduced—a state that presupposes, at least implicitly, the hope of a restoration of values ("The aim is lacking; 'why' finds no answer" [Nietzsche 1968 [1901], 9), and at the same time it can be used as a critical procedure to establish itself in a position of freedom from the tyranny of values, by turning values against one another: "All ends are abolished; value judgments are turned against one another" (Nietzsche 1948 [1901], 51). This figure would be similar to denunciation if the reference to each particular value were not subordinated to a critical project that seeks to surpass them all. Values are rendered relative by the association of contrary denunciations whose collection in a single corpus of texts is designed to reduce all worths to abjection and to unveil the vanity of a common good, whatever it may be. Every sacrifice is only an interest in disguise: "We follow our *taste*, and that is what we call in noble terms duty, virtue, and sacrifice" (121). Once equivalence is established through the will to persist in being, it is then possible to outline a general economy of the forms of reconversion of this common appetite for power:

> In reality people act 'disinterestedly' because it is on this *sole* condition that they can still exist; they have gotten into the habit of thinking about the existence of others rather than their own (for example, the prince thinking about the existence of his people, a mother about her child's, because without that the prince would no longer exist as a prince, nor the mother as a mother); what they all want is to keep their feeling of power, even if it requires constant attention and countless sacrifices in favor of their subordinates. (120–21)

The recourse to a general equivalent is necessary because the most consistent relativism cannot exempt itself from the constraints that weigh on relativization without falling into a radical and self-destructive nihilism, since it would be condemning itself to silence, and this is never completely achieved in philosophical or political nihilism. Once the critical perspective on all values has been established, relativism is summoned in turn to found and justify itself; this requirement leads it to exit from its own logic, either by regressing toward denunciation, which will seek another principle of worth, or else (and the two operations are not incompatible) by orienting itself toward the search for a new principle. Critical relativism can thus shift into the indignation that relies on a worth to denounce the abjection of illusory vanities. In Nietzsche, the worth of fame is often criticized by inspired worth: "In our day, events take on 'greatness' only by their echo—their echo in the press" (1948 [1901], 63). Relativism can also be oriented toward the reconstruction of a polity through the transformation of power, as an underlying general equivalent, an absolute master freed of the burden of justification and purely affirmative, into a true worth destined to achieve recognition for its universal vocation to order beings in the most just fashion, thus reinstituting the horizon of a common good: "What determines rank, sets off rank, is only quanta of power, and nothing else" (1968 [1901], 457). The foundation of this polity, in which justice will be "the vitality of life itself," is not achieved in Nietzsche's writings, no doubt partly owing to a reluctance to acknowledge the principle of common humanity (a principle associated with Judaism and Christianity and treated both as an expression of the morality of *ressentiment* and as a means by which the weak oppress the strong), and a resultant tendency to congeal persons in states of worth (an obstacle we have already encountered in connection with attempts to establish a hygienic polity on the basis of biological equivalence).

Violence and Justification

But a third possibility remains. If it cannot fall back on a common good, relativism may still seek to ally itself with science, as is suggested in the fragment cited above by the reference to the quantity of power. Either power is not measurable, and this first possibility introduces a contradiction in terms, or else someone can give its measure, and this second possibility is consistent with the project of making force a general equivalent; in the latter case, methodological rules have to be established that will allow this measured force to be detached from persons and therefore objectifiable.[2] The reduction to interests thus constitutes the critical moment in positivism, the moment when science becomes autonomous with respect to values. But it cannot constitute the totality of scientific activity, which, to demonstrate its own validity, has to be able to grasp reality, make predictions, and surpass the reductionism of singular interest. If every being is dominated by its own interest, these multiple interests are incommensurable, and the result is a chaotic order about which we can say nothing at all. Science is thus obliged to specify interest by introducing a supplementary constraint and subjecting it to a determination that spells out its direction. This constraint differs from the principles of political philosophy in that it is treated as a determination acting on individuals without requiring the intervention of their will. We find the same distinction when we compare Durkheim's collective consciousness to Rousseau's general will, for example, or when we compare determination via the market in economics to the market as the principle of agreement in Adam Smith.

This distinction is particularly pronounced when it can be shown that the constraint to which science submits interest is distinct from the values to which persons refer in order to justify their own behavior. The social sciences have profited from this alliance and have leaned on relativism in order to free themselves from the authority of values (and in particular to detach themselves from legalistic disciplines). But beyond the fact that they cannot ensure their own foundation, a criticism that has often been addressed to them,[3] the social sciences can no longer recognize the need for human beings to base their agreement on a common good and to found the legitimacy of this good on a metaphysics. What is most specific in their object thus tends to escape them. Not that they can close their eyes to the metaphysics of agreement that support the justifications of persons. But, floundering in the attempt to develop these metaphysics as sciences, they externalize them as illusory indigenous forms of knowledge. They can no longer recapture the imperative of justification except in an unveiling, and in the form of an illusion or a deception, as is shown for example by the most frequent uses of the term "ideology." By the same token (and Max Weber himself is always ambiguous on this point), the study of the constraint of legitimacy gives way to an analysis of legitimation, no longer as a necessary foundation but as a rationalization, in the psychoanalytic sense, as an enterprise of a posteriori legitimizing, a transformation of what is into what ought to be, a validation via a normative retranslation of the way things are. Legitimation thus helps bring consistency to the sociological conception of the social order both as a product of unconscious regulations and as an expression of the domination of the weak by the strong. This legitimation is unveiled as arbitrary and thus, at least implicitly, as unjust, although the absence of reference to a common good presents an obstacle to a clarification of the injustice at issue. For such a clarification would logically presuppose the possibility of relying on a principle of worth that would found a legitimate order and thus offer a way out of relativism.

Taking up on its own terms the question of the possibility conditions of a political order without relying on contract theories, which it opposes, classical sociology constructs models aimed at detaching the factors of order and stability from the motives and causes invoked by the actors. These models presuppose the existence of an *unconscious* (Nisbet 1966, 82–83), although this schema, often left more or less implicit, does not take on the status of a theory properly speaking, as will be the case for psychology at the end of the century, starting from partially different traditions and grounded in biology (Sulloway 1981). These models, in their most fully developed forms, integrate contributions drawn from Durkheim's work and from Marxism, contributions whose most obvious divergences—consensus versus conflict—blur the deep links between them that are attributable in particular, as Pierre Ansart (1969) has noted, to the common influence of Saint-Simon. Persons are presented as inconsistent (and thus as unworthy) because they offer rational justifications for their behavior in the name of superficial and fallacious motives (prenotions or ideologies), whereas their behavior is actually determined by hidden but objective forces. Order is maintained by some form of deception (alienation, belief) that, without being imposed by the force of arms, nevertheless stems from violence. This deception guarantees the stability of the social order, which is self-evident and is only rarely called into question. The sociologist does the work of a scientist insofar as he himself is not fooled and is able to unveil what is hidden under false appearances, in keeping with the axiom according to which "all science would be superfluous if the appearance and the essence of things were one and the same" (Marx 1959 [1867–94], bk. 3, p. 96). The schema of the unconscious offers an original solution to the question of ordering, because it makes it possible to conceive of constraint as a power that is at once and inextricably external and internal to persons, as an internalized externality: a force that would manifest itself as violence if it were to be imposed from the outside comes to inhabit persons, constrains them from within, and determines their behavior by espousing the contours of their will. It tends to blur the difference between physical violence and other forms of constraint, and in the extreme case it tends to treat all determinations as equal, whether they are justifiable or not. The general explanation by way of "power relations," an eminently ambiguous expression because it associates recourse to violence with a reference to a principle of equivalence that is necessary to establish "relations," no longer leaves room for the justifications people give for their actions. However, the fallacious character of the interpretations that people produce for themselves cannot be explained by their inability to know the hidden nature of phenomena—a natural blindness—since, in the cases studied by the social sciences, the systems that ensure the regularity of causes are of the same order as the motives invoked by persons themselves (the value of work, family upbringing, collective solidarity, and so on). Moreover, theories that subordinate the scientific enterprise to a principle of nonawareness credit persons with the capacity to shed their illusions and become aware of reality when it is revealed to them by science.

A rigorous social science must take seriously the justifications of persons and the metaphysics of agreement on which these justifications are based, because this requirement brings a constraint to bear on interpretation. Yet interpretation is threatened with arbitrariness when it treats all appreciations in the same way, and when it thereby gives itself as its object an infinite universe of "representations" or "values," or when it yields to the spontaneity of practice, to the anarchic character of reality, or to the unpredictability of associations given over to the randomness of encounters between forces. By positing the constraint of an imperative of justification, the model we are presenting here obviously does not aim to turn a blind eye to the fact that persons can exempt themselves from this imperative by violence and deception; on the contrary, it allows us to identify those very shifts into violence or regressions back toward insignificance; it allows us to discriminate between situations oriented toward justification and situations of domination or contingency; and, by drawing out the general constraints that a principle must satisfy in order to be put to work in a judgment, it allows us to distinguish acceptable justifications from unacceptable associations. The model thus offers a way of taking into account the competence put into play by persons themselves in order to ground their harmony or conduct their disputes. It is precisely the capacity of the model to limit and specify the objects to be dealt with, and above all its focus on test situations to the detriment of contingent circumstances, that opens up the possibility of taking into account new facts whose relevance cannot be identified on the basis of analytic frameworks centered on violence, and of describing operations of justification, denunciation, or compromise while escaping from a perpetual shuttle between disillusioned relativism and caricatural accusations. It is in fact in test situations, or in situations prepared for tests, that persons put their faculty of judgment to work, because these situations must be coherent so that agreement on the result of the test can be reached.

AFTERWORD: TOWARD A PRAGMATICS

OF REFLECTION

THE MODEL OF JUSTIFICATION we have presented here in its broad outlines does not claim to account for the behavior of actors in any and all situations they may encounter. A number of empirical studies have used this model (Boltanski and Thévenot 1989), and they have shown its relevance for analysis of the operations of justification that are at the heart of disputes, while at the same time they have made clear the need to broaden the framework so it can encompass behaviors that are less directly confronted by an imperative of justification. Moments of dispute constitute interruptions in actions being carried out with other persons; they must thus be resituated within a course of action that unfolds, both before and after the moment of judgment, apart from the powerful constraints of reflection and justification that we have examined. In our current work, undertaken in continuation and extension of the program described in this book, we have focused on configurations in which the weight of justification does not make itself felt in the same way, either because the actor does not have to confront a critique and a requirement that he develop arguments about what he is doing or because the requirement of justification would run the risk of tilting pacified relations into discord.

The Place of Justifications in the Gamut of Actions

In a first phase, our investigation consisted in exploring the limits of the framework by seeking out situations quite different from those on the basis of which it had been established; we brought the model of justification to bear on cases that did not meet all the criteria of a critique (Thévenot 1989b). We found that requirements similar to those of justification may weigh upon an individual's behavior, apart from any controversy with others, when constraints of coherence and control come into play. The effect of resistance encountered in the action undertaken, comparable to that of an objection requiring a response, is reminiscent in this respect of the cycle of critique and justification. Actions that do not imply the participation of other persons, and that therefore do not seem to face constraints of agreement, still cannot be described without reference to tests of coordination between the different states in which persons find themselves. Although it does not include a justification in the sense in which we have used the term up to now, the coordination of the actions of a single individual thus implies that the actor looks back on his action and faces a test of coherence (Thévenot 1990a). The same research showed, moreover, that several persons can coordinate their actions without any requirements governing agreement reaching comparable to those we had described as imperatives of justification. Finally, field observations brought to light situations in which disputes had been abandoned but in which we were unable to identify a return to agreement that relied on general arguments and on operations that established equivalences and supplied solid bases for judgment.

The strategy we adopted was not to set aside the results of earlier work in approaching these new configurations, but to try to discover to what extent these configurations accommodated the constraints we had specified, in the model presented in this book, on the basis of situations of justification. Analysis of the actions surrounding justification led us to study moments of the action in which no disagreement was declared, in the prejudgment phases, even though the people involved could not be said to be in agreement, because there had been no judgment. As we examined the process of moving toward judgment, we paid particular attention to the way in which gaps with respect to people's expectations were gradually filled in, even though the parties involved did not enter into a dispute that would have interrupted the course of the action, and thus did not experience a rise in the level of generality that would have called attention to the equivalences (Thévenot 1990a). This analysis also led us to look closely at the other end of the process, at the aftermath of judgment and the ways in which a conflict could be pacified and a critique abandoned so that a dispute could be brought to an end (Boltanski 1990a).

Below the Level of Public Judgment: Determining the Appropriate Action in Light of a Snag

As a pragmatics of reflection is the object of research in progress, we shall not develop it in detail here. Still, we can suggest some of its principal configurations: we shall begin with the less reflective moments that fall short of public judgment, then return to the tension that surrounds the moment of judgment, and finally examine the possibility that actors may reduce that tension by engaging in less reflective regimes of action.

To study the way in which actors orient themselves toward judgment in a course of action, we adopt an approach to action that privileges the moment when one looks back to reflect on what has happened or to interpret what is happening. We limit our investigation of intentions and beliefs to the analysis of the quest undertaken by the persons themselves, especially when they begin to question intentions. We thus retain the methodological position we adopted to study justifications in disputes, a position that consists in following the actors' movements as closely as possible without assuming the privilege of a bird's-eye view and thus without adding anything to the operations being undertaken. Our interest in judgment was not inscribed in a critical reflection about categories of knowledge; it started from an analysis of disputes and thus led to a pragmatics. Similarly, our attention to the moment of reflective return has to focus on the way in which actors themselves reach the point of making this return.

The decision to begin our analysis with the moment of interpretive return was not distorted by the importance we attached to justification in earlier stages of our research. It constitutes a reasonable point of entry, to the extent that it takes into account the limits to which actors are subjected in identifying their own actions and those of others. Now, the actors' own knowledge can be shaped only through an experience of failure, that is, in the discovery of a snag, in an encounter with something that is "a bit off." To gain access to the moment of reflective return, then, we have to focus first of all on the snags that lead actors, even outside the presence of other human beings, but a fortiori if they are engaged in a common action with others, to spell out their expectations concerning the other things or persons involved. Thus we find ourselves facing a relation that recalls the relation of judgment, a relation between an unsatisfied expectation and the need to identify beings according to the capacity on which one has to be able to count in order to carry out an appropriate action.

Nevertheless, a reflective return in a course of action is not based on the use of language that is at work in judgment, for judgment presupposes that a state of affairs will be set forth in a report. Unlike a report, a reflective return is not constrained by the requirement of concentrating the state of affairs in a transportable form that has been abstracted from the train of circumstances toward which it would point. In a reflective return, the designations of beings can remain vague and local, so long as they can be used here and now to grasp the snag. They are weakly controlled in relation to their referents and amply supported by acts of pointing out. The question of a common qualification does not arise, nor does the necessity of passing through legitimate worths to apprehend persons. The course of action can be modified by any of the actors involved in it without any requirement that the parties must agree about and draw consequences from the incident. In this configuration, the actors have no way of ensuring the consistency of the interpretations made by the various protagonists. It is precisely when divergences of interpretation are made explicit that the way to other possibilities—some of which we shall now examine—is opened up.

From Anger to Crisis

When a snag is not repaired, someone may seek to minimize it by forcefully setting the action back on course, without examining the circumstances, at the risk of betraying anger. In the urgency of a midcourse intervention, the moment of deliberation that would precede the formation of a common judgment is sidestepped. In its place, an option is selected but not made explicit; thus it cannot be the object of a shared qualification. Expressed in anger, it may burst forth in invective. The outburst characteristic of this moment is a response to the tension created by the impossibility of deliberating. It grips the actor in an impulsive gesture that is accomplished without any possibility of reflecting or turning back.

If efforts to repair a snag fail, that is, if they do not succeed in silencing the divergent interpretations, the actors can escape violence only by involving themselves in the formation of a common judgment. Resembling neither repair work nor anger, the operation of judgment presupposes suspension of the course of action and commitment to a deliberative process. In order to understand the tendency to display anger, we have had to measure the cost of the reduction of divergent interpretations through deliberation, a possibility that we have examined in this book and to which we shall return in a moment. The move to debate in fact entails a profound upheaval, because access to the space of deliberation, whether internal or public, presupposes an interruption of the action under way, an action that by definition engages the future inasmuch as it is directed toward a change in the state of the world.

With the shift to debate, the discord that the tensions in the course of the action did not suffice to bring into view—since divergent judgments were not expressed—comes to light. The result is a crisis that accompanies the halt in the action. In the concept of crisis, we have chosen to retain not a moment of chaos created by actors following their own separate paths with no attempt to coordinate their actions, but moments in which the partners agree on the need to define the reality that they have to take into account. Only then can one speak of uncertainty, a notion that would not have a place in the confusion of chaotic actions. A common effort to reduce uncertainty regarding a given reality leads to qualifications that convey assurances as to the future. It requires that the actors refrain from engaging immediately in an intervention that, carried out in isolation, would look like recourse to violence. The crisis is thus a paradoxical moment in which, unlike the moment of action, the question of agreement about reality occupies everyone's mind but in which, in the absence of realization in a present filled with commitments and expectations, the sense of reality is lacking. In a moment of agreement, reality takes the form of a picture of objects endowed with general capacities, whereas in a moment of realization, it consists in facing up to things that are present. In a crisis situation, both of these modalities are suspended. The persons involved are no longer confronted with the localized presence of things to be done without delay, and they cannot yet lean on the reality of a common judgment. They are thus led to lend their own support to judgments purporting to be of general validity. In so doing, the actors run the risk of getting dragged down into a sort of unrealism in which the difference between the local or the personal, on the one hand, and the general or the universal, on the other, is abolished. The pathological lack of realism encountered in delusions of grandeur or paranoid delirium appears in particular when the actors indefinitely prolong the moment of crisis by continually introducing new interpretations that prevent the actors themselves from agreeing on what is real. In fact, interruption of the action in a crisis is acceptable only if the actors manifest good will in the search for convergence. If it is not to be pathological, the deliberation has to be oriented toward closure in the form of a coherent decision based on the arguments brought into play.

The Moment of Truth in Judgment

Deliberation oriented toward judgment is subjected simultaneously to argumentative constraints associated with official records of proceedings and to the obligation of basing arguments on proofs by proceeding to observations that seek to reestablish the reality that has been shaken by the crisis. The status of language in a judgment is adapted to the rhetorical requirements of argumentation and to those of a scientific quest for truth. When we take the argumentative operations into account, we are led to examine the constraints of legitimacy and coherence that a judgment must satisfy in order to be concluded and inscribed in a report. This argumentative dimension of justification is rationalized by political philosophy, by theories of justice, and by rhetoric, when the latter remains tied to normative disciplines such as ethics. From this perspective, what counts is the establishment of a decision, not merely by adapting it to the circumstances but by giving it a general import that allows its validity to be transported to other times and other places. The closing of the decision-making process and the agreed-upon termination of the inquiry matter more in the moment of judgment than the way the decision will be implemented when the action starts up again. By closing off the action on a decision, one places oneself in a space of deliberation where the logical coherence of the arguments exchanged is the only thing at issue.

But a judgment includes more than the argumentative aspects of communication. It is also the moment of truth in which the actors, in order to advance their own positions, have to qualify the beings present, have to make their nature explicit and move from argumentative coherence to the test of facts. Operations of proof entail an obligation to be attentive to the relation that the report entertains with reality and to privilege a referential use of language. Reality has to be represented in a report that produces a verifiable account of the facts and records them in a form detached from local contingencies so that they can be transported beyond the limits of the situation, without regard to the quality of the person who is uttering or transmitting the judgment. Now, this shared delimitation of what is involved does not impose itself in all forms of action. It is only when it is at work that configurations corresponding to the concept of situation come to light. The dynamic of the process, with its critiques, its tests, and its relaunchings of the investigation, shapes situations and contributes to the objectivity of the beings that have been engaged as proofs. In order to refer to facts, a judgment has to apprehend those elements that transcend the immediate action and ensure their subsistence. That is why the identification of the situation requires a halt in the action, so that its pertinence can be discovered.

The Tension of Judgment and the
Qualification of Ungraspable Persons

By problematizing the halt in the judgment process, we bring to light the internal tension that weighs on the sense of fairness when we pass from a construction subject to the constraint of a well-formed judgment to the integration of a judgment into a course of action. To encounter this tension, we must look closely at the pragmatic aftereffects of judgment and anticipate the coming back together of persons involved in a common action. This tension is not visible in situations where the basis for judgment is a report on a test and thus on the general qualifications of the persons involved.

The tension can be described schematically in the following way. The resolution of a dispute in a test presupposes a qualification of the capacities of persons from a determined standpoint, that is, within a given world, and in a state of worth that permits the convergence of expectations. The judgment thus fixes the relation between a person's capacity and an action. But as our elaboration of the polity model has shown, the sense of fairness can be qualified only with the restriction that worths must not be attached to persons. As we have seen, this model seeks to reconcile two requirements that are not easily made compatible: a requirement of order, without which actions with others that are not disputes cannot take place, and a requirement of common humanity. The reference to a fundamental equality among human beings precludes their definitive hierarchization by a qualification, whatever it might be, that would block the establishment of a common humanity by setting up a continuum of the more and less human. Properties attached permanently to beings do indeed allow the construction of expectations. But they are obstacles to the conception of a common humanity, as well as to the recognition of an uncertainty that is inherent in the action of human persons.

When we reinsert judgment into a series of actions, one of the consequences of the requirement of nonattachment is expressed in the need always to leave open the possibility of a new attribution of worth, by means of a new test in which the association between person-states and thing-states can be reconfigured. Indeed, it is by meeting the test of things that the capacities of persons are revealed. But this possibility also presupposes that person-states cannot be confused with persons themselves. We thus pass from an approach to common humanity centered on the impossibility of an essential hierarchy and on equality—an approach shared by political philosophies of the common good and theories of justice—to an approach oriented toward the ungraspable character of persons and the impossibility of enclosing them in a qualification summing up the knowledge of their capacities. The tension between the two requirements of the polity model (order and common humanity) is thus at the heart of the relation between the act of reaching a judgment and what follows.

When we plunge from judgment back into action, the problems of compatibility between the two requirements—order and common humanity—reappear, in a tension that the formal construction of the common good makes it possible to assuage. The requirement of qualification has to be integrated into an ontology of personhood that recognizes both the subsistence of a being between acts (which presupposes a power making qualification in judgment possible) and the inexhaustible (and thus not fully knowable) character of the powers of a person; this considerably limits the possibility of relying on a judgment to establish the way in which one can behave with others. The passing of a judgment results from a retrospective work of investigation to qualify what has happened and is oriented toward stabilization of mutual expectations, since it describes capacities for the future. It thereby faces the potential accusation of seeking to absorb inexhaustible persons completely in the qualification of their state.

It is the possibility—always open—of this accusation and the common knowledge of the impossibility of interrupting the investigation once and for all that confer a conventional character on the moment of reaching a judgment, in the sense in which everyone knows that the qualifications proposed can neither sum up the totality of past actions nor embrace all the potentialities of actions to come.

Judgment between Power and Oblivion

A judgment that has been implemented risks being denounced as perpetuating a past state of a test in an unacceptable manner by reducing the persons involved to their qualification and enclosing them within the limits of established relations of worth. The term "power" (or "abuse of power") is frequently used to denounce a judgment that has been implemented once and for all. To inscribe a judgment definitively into reality is to presuppose that persons can be identified with the capacities that the judgment has qualified, and thus that their actions can be controlled, either directly, by force and violence, or indirectly, by the arrangement of objects that surrounds them. The denunciation of power is not limited to the confinement of persons within an arrangement of objects lacking any margin of tolerance, an arrangement in which their actions are reduced to those of passive agents. Power can also be denounced in more insidious forms. For example, even if an action is confronted with tests, the deficiency of the available objects may prevent the manifestation of the worth of persons, thus indefinitely prolonging the consequences of a past test. In such cases, the inferiority ascribed to a person is no longer clearly the result of a disciplinary arbitrariness. Quite to the contrary, it is inscribed in a common judgment from which the person himself cannot escape, because it is the object of continual verification. The behaviors of human beings in this state no longer correspond to the language of action but can be readily described in the language of forces. The equivalences needed in order to generalize the description in terms of laws are thus ensured.

Pardoning offers a figure at the opposite pole from the halting of a dispute: here, the qualification of capacities is abandoned. Whereas evaluation presupposes the implementation of equivalences in order to focus on a singular approach to persons, in pardoning, attention is directed elsewhere. The movement of pardoning opens the possibility of consigning past actions to oblivion rather than undertaking to totalize past actions in order to reach a judgment. Unlike judging, pardoning interrupts a dispute without establishing expectations referring to qualified capacities and thus to equivalences. More surely than a judgment, a pardon brings the investigation to a decisive halt by disqualifying it. Pardoning undoes the operations of association that are necessary for judging, and it gives up all attempts to put past actions into perspective and to totalize them. An emotional granting of pardon allows the pardoner to avoid using language in ways that might relaunch the dispute by reintroducing qualifications—especially the sort of language that characterizes formal reports prepared in view of a test of truth. Reference to objects is not called for here, since it would entail the equivalences implied in the identification of objects and the test for highlighting them. Finally, pardoning can only be carried out face to face; consequently, it cannot be generalized. The action that has been halted resumes after a pardon, although the consequences of the crisis have not been drawn and the lessons of the investigation—and of the judgment, if any—have not been put to use.

The Humane Use of Judgment and Tolerance in Action

People manifesting a humane attitude with respect to public judgment do not limit themselves to a characterization of persons based on the judgment rendered. As they carry on with a course of action after a judgment has been made, the concerned parties accept the tension between the qualification of person-states and the construction of the notion of a person as a being irreducible to his or her qualifications. Evidence of this acceptance can be found in the fact that the people involved do not treat every action as a test; in other words, they remain within a course of action without constantly worrying about how well it conforms to the judgment reached. This demands tolerance toward deviations, which must be treated as if they were inconsequential. Tolerance is thus not approached here as a moral attitude but as a pragmatic requirement. Without it, the return to action is thwarted. Either one remains in a permanent posture of judgment manifested by suspicion—and by preventing the actor from taking part in the ongoing action, this posture rejoins the paranoid anxiety mentioned above—or one engages in the action and seeks to set up an arrangement of objects that is in rigorous conformity with the judgment, by making every action a test. The latter situation is exemplified in an assembly line. Here, coordination is so dependent on instruments with rigorously defined capacities that every deviation is immediately and publicly visible as a failure, and its consequences for others cannot be repaired by corrections. From the standpoint of morality, in relation to the figure of pardon, this pragmatic tolerance is included in patience. Postponing the moment of testing, tolerance shunts aside the will to know that impels investigation and leads to judgment.

Tolerance makes it possible to understand the position in which actors bear the weight of correction separately, without bringing it to light by a remark or an excuse. Only when the efforts to associate incidents are revived, and when someone loses patience in the face of a succession of incidents configured as a series, does that person associate a new failure with earlier ones and shift toward an interrogation—initially in private—about the capacities of persons ("this can't go on; he's incompetent"). The model of action toward which we are heading, which associates the requirements of pragmatics with those of ethics, allows us to avoid reducing ethics to the question of judgment by focusing attention on the way people deal with the tension between the requirement of a well-formed judgment, which will absorb persons in person-states, and the requirements of persons demanding that their field of action be left open. A human action that would renounce testing and do without judgment may be considered utopian, but a course of action constantly controlled and generalized in the mode of a test would be totally inhuman. A pragmatics of reflection has to account for the passage between moments of involvement in the action when reflection is reduced—moments that are manifested in tolerance or local accommodations and that can go as far as the oblivion of pardoning—and moments in which the action turns back on itself in crisis and in which reality is pinned down in a report.

Knowledge about Actions

Crises and their closure in reports, which have served as our entry point for the construction of a model of justification, offer a way to analyze actions that allows us to avoid the problems posed by introspection when the object is to unveil nonmanifest intentions and the problems posed by a mechanistic objectification of human actors. In fact, moments of crisis and judgment are occasions in which actors exhibit their action and unfold it verbally. On such occasions, they seek to generalize and to constitute facts by means of language, and as they do so they use language in a way that approaches that of the sciences. When actors are involved in crisis or judgment, they take on the task of investigating and imputing intentions, a task that brings the categories of analysis of action into play. That is why a research strategy focused on moments of testing and explicitation seemed to us particularly opportune. In asking questions about reality and conducting tests to find out what holds together, actors set aside contingent phenomena in favor of phenomena to which general validity can be ascribed, by bringing to light the bonds that connect local and global phenomena. Considering the action from an objective distance and trying to discover truth, these actors use descriptive languages that offer a handhold to the social sciences. It is thus in a moment of anxiety oriented toward judgment, when several realities are in confrontation, or in the moment of truth of a judgment that gives body to reality once again, that the actors' practice can be transposed into a scientific exposé with the least risk of distortion. But by stopping at justification, are we not running the risk of distancing ourselves, like persons who embark on the process of judgment, from the constraints of action?

Whatever the risk, our detour is nevertheless necessary, for it is only by concentrating on the moment of justification that one can approach a course of action in a way that takes into account the place occupied in it by the moment of reflective return. To extend our program in this way toward a pragmatics of reflection, we turned our attention in particular to moments in the course of an action that are characterized by corrections. These corrections come in the wake of resistance offered by some other being, one that no longer corresponds to expectations and thus takes on a relief that makes it stand out against the background of the action under way. The study of such moments may benefit from the preliminary analysis of justification because they have in common with judgment the presupposition of a return—even if the loop is only a short one—to what has taken place. These moments of return require taking into account bumps in the road whose nature has not yet been determined. In contrast, these moments are distinguished from the judgments studied in this book in that they are not subject to the other constraints of explicitation and common knowledge. In these moments, the actors are obliged neither to agree as to the object of their concern nor even to experience a shared uneasiness. This difference in posture is the supporting point that allows us to gain access to the analysis of moments of oblivion and of pardon— moments that are in fact indiscernible when the persons involved are all in the same frame of mind, for in that case the question of what frame of mind they are in is undecidable. In contrast, these two moments are distinct and offer a handhold to analysis when the actors are in different frames of mind. The dividing line between the behavior of those who are preoccupied with an investigation and the attitude of those who reject the investigation makes it possible to identify the work of oblivion and to analyze the operations that are required either to exit from the test or to eradicate the traces of judgment.

By extending the examination of justification toward a more general analysis of the relation between reflection and action, the approach we have taken provides a way out of a classic alternative in the social sciences. In this alternative, approaches concerned with human behaviors only insofar as these can be connected with rational decisions—treated as the only objects allowing access to truth—are opposed to approaches that associate reflection with an illusory rationalization and seek direct access to the reality of practices whose motives are unknown to their agents. In order to surmount this opposition, we have had to extricate it from the space of doctrinal quarrels in which incompatible anthropologies are in conflict and include it in the course of the human activities in which it is at work. In fact, in order to face the world, people have to shuttle continually back and forth between reflection and action, shifting constantly between moments of conscious control and moments in which the appeal of the present launches them into the course of events. To be sure, the study of the faculty of judging and of the structure of well-formed judgments is indispensable to the analysis of the sense of fairness. But it does not exhaust this analysis, for it does not account for the tension that weighs on the sense of fairness whenever it is called upon. To continue to study the sense of fairness, we have to follow it in the operations that form the weft of daily life. The elaboration of a dynamic model ought to make it possible to include sequences that have escaped analysis up to now, because the ruptures that they imply confer a chaotic appearance on the movement of persons, from reparation to crisis, from tolerance to dispute, from judgment to oblivion.

January 15, 1991

NOTES

1. In an extension of the common usage, we use the verb "qualify" to designate the operation by means of which (*a*) one identifies a particular being by putting it into an equivalency class; (*b*) one designates the being by a conventional epithet, a process that corresponds fairly closely to what English speakers mean by "categorize" or "label," except that the term "qualify" makes it possible to specify, as in French legal usage (when a judge decrees that the situation calls for the application of the law), that (*c*) one is inscribing the being within a performative code. The qualifications that we study in this book also have an evaluative dimension which presupposes that (*d*) one is referring to a common good.

2. The process of representation assumes both a cognitive operation (to represent a category to oneself) and a political process through which representatives are designated as spokespersons.

3. The notion of "investment of form" stresses the treatment of persons and things in forms or formats that help maintain them at a certain level of generality by establishing equivalences. In such cases, general characterizations, classifications, and standards are envisaged in material terms on the basis of costly operations that give form to persons and things and that facilitate—for a price—subsequent coordinations that rely on these beings "in good form." On the model of a productive investment, the actors expect to receive a benefit in exchange consisting in ease of coordination. Investments of form are differentiated according to the extension of the scope of validity, in time or space, of the establishment of equivalence, and also according to the consistency of the material support by which the equivalence is sustained.

4. We use the term "affair" to designate processes of mobilization in the public sphere that revolve around the case of a person or persons constituting the object of an accusation and potentially subject to legal charges. In this sense an affair is defined first of all by a system of slots that include a victim (unjustly accused), an offender, an accuser, a denouncer (the person who takes it upon himself or herself to exonerate the accused), a judge (whose role is played most often today by the sovereign people, public opinion, or humanity in general). An affair constitutes a moment of uncertainty as to the identity of the empirical persons who are to occupy the various slots in this system. The presentation of proofs, which are subject to tension in a debate, must make it possible to remove this uncertainty and to qualify the events and the states of the persons involved with respect to various forms of worth. The "Dreyfus Affair" in France, which developed at the end of the nineteenth century and gradually affected all aspects of the nation's political and social life, is a paradigmatic example.

5. In such cases, persons can coordinate with one another on the basis of phenomena rooted in subjective experience, because they all implicitly refer to the same external source of worth.

6. The idea of a test is a central one in this book; taken in a broad sense, the term designates procedures that are capable of reducing the uncertainty of a situation through the achievement of agreement as to the qualification of the beings involved. In this sense, a test encompasses both an evaluation according to a moral standard and an assessment according to the standard of truth (see n. 1, above).

CHAPTER TWO: THE FOUNDATION OF AGREEMENT IN POLITICAL PHILOSOPHY

1. The verb "comprehend" (French *comprendre*) is used here to refer to an operation of representation in which more worthy beings are presumed to *encompass* less worthy ones; the former are thus best able to *understand* and express the aspirations of the latter.

2. To qualify the virtues he attributes to systems, Smith uses terms that express not only their capacity for articulation and their performance equal to that of machines, but also the grace that would result if they measured up to a defined goal: "Systems in many respects resemble machines. . . . A system is an imaginary machine invented to connect together in the fancy those different movements and effects which are already in reality performed" (Smith 1880, 352). "That the fitness of any system or machine to produce the end for which it was intended, bestows a certain propriety and beauty upon the whole, and renders the very thought and contemplation of it agreeable, is so very obvious that nobody has overlooked it" (Smith 1976 [1759], 178).

3. We have chosen to translate the French *grandeur* as "worth" in order to avoid the archaic effects introduced by the term "greatness." Still, as we see in the translation of Pascal's text, the latter term constitutes one of the ways to express the orders we are analyzing.

4. For an examination of the notions of "sympathy" and "impartial spectator" that clarifies the relation between *Theory of Moral Sentiments* and *The Wealth of Nations* while stressing the role of sympathy as the "self-regulator of social harmony," see Dupuy 1987.

CHAPTER THREE: POLITICAL ORDERS AND A MODEL OF JUSTICE

1. The acceptance or rejection of a mix or composition made up of different political principles is a classic question in political philosophy. Thus Jean Bodin, confronting different types of republics in *The Six Books of a Common-weale* (a translation of *La République*), examines the possibility of combining the benefits of the "aristocratic State" with those of the "popular State." Projecting the opposition of these two principles of sovereignty onto Aristotle's distinction (*Nicomachean Ethics*, 5) between distributive justice (which becomes geometric proportion in the aristocratic State) and corrective justice (arithmetic proportion in the popular State), Bodin (1606) demonstrates the merits of an intermediate situation characterized by what he calls harmonic proportion and exemplified by the popular seigneury of Venice. However, as Pierre Mesnard points out, "a mix is (from this perspective) not a principle, a flag that one can fly boldly over institutions. It is much more an inscription of a fact that emerges from the *prudence* of the governing agents" (1977,

516–17). Samuel Pufendorf speaks out, moreover, referring to Bodin, against the sense of persons that results from this harmonic proportion and owing to which "the same Punishment doth not affect all Persons alike" (1749 [1672], 790). The author of *Abrégé de la République* (1755) offers a fine example of the opposite position with respect to the question of mixes. Setting aside as a "pure question of grammar" the identification of different types of republics, he stresses that "the interesting question for political law is whether assembling two or three (sorts of republics) can be advantageous, and can merit the name of well-governed republic" as a "composite or mixed republic."

2. Let us note that ordering principles that do not satisfy the axioms of the polity model may nevertheless include a formula for sacrifice and the possibility of achieving equilibrium over several lifetimes. In our study, we have not included such ordering principles, which presuppose reincarnation, nor have we dealt with the theological constructs that carry over into an afterlife the reward or punishment for acts committed during a person's lifetime.

3. In France, demography—in particular "qualitative demography—and, secondarily, administrative statistics—have been sites of an intense effort to reconcile the eugenic value with industrial, civic, and domestic worths, an effort whose stages can be traced in the genealogy of investigations dealing with the quality of persons, ranging from the attempt to take a "census of defective children in France," or surveys of the "qualitative state" of the population, undertaken by the French Foundation for the Study of Human Problems, to surveys of professional orientation and professional training and qualification carried out by the Institut national d'études démographiques and the Institut national de la statistique et des études économiques (Thévenot 1990b).

4. As Francis Galton puts it, "the improvement of the natural gifts of future generations of the human race is largely, although indirectly, under our control" (1972 [1869], 41). Lucien March, a eugenicist and the director of General Statistics of France summarizes the claim in a formula that even more clearly evokes the common good: "Belief in eugenics extends the function of philanthropy to future generations" (Desrosières 1985).

CHAPTER FOUR: POLITICAL FORMS OF WORTH

1. Translator's note: In keeping with the standard English translations of Augustine, the French word *cité* is translated here as "city" when it refers to the Augustinian concept. When the term is used in the broader sense the authors give it in this book, *cité* is rendered as "polity."

2. Augustine 1984, 471 (12.1). The following abbreviations are used hereafter for the works of St. Augustine: *CG*, *The City of God* (1984); *LMG*, *The Literal Meaning of Genesis* (1982); *CO*, *Confessions* (1998).

3. The *City of God* was written between 410 and 420. It followed *The Literal Meaning of Genesis*, written between 400 and 410, and thus it is roughly contemporary with the works on grace that were published in connection with the polemic with Pelagius (see Marrou 1957, 48).

4. Domestic worth, denounced in order to emphasize detachment toward grace, is the object of a compromise when St. Augustine sets out to justify slavery ("the

slavery caused by sin," *CG* 875–876 [19.15–16]), which cannot be encompassed within the framework of the model of the city of God. After bringing slaves back into common humanity by noting that Isaac, in prescribing circumcision for all, not only of all the sons, but of the house-born slaves and the purchased slaves as well, attests "that this grace pertains to all men" (687 [16.26]), Augustine establishes a compromise between inspired worth and domestic worth:

> That being so, even though our righteous fathers had slaves, they so managed the peace of their households as to make a distinction between the situation of children and the condition of slaves in respect of the temporal goods of this life; and yet in the matter of the worship of God—in whom we must place our hope of everlasting goods—they were concerned, with equal affection, for all the members of their household. This is what the order of nature prescribes, so that this is the source of the name *paterfamilias*, a name that has become so generally used that even those who exercise unjust rule rejoice to be called by this title (*CG* 876 [19.16]).

5. The sacrifice of the inspired body is the object of a domestic compromise in the institution of patronage and in the cult of the relics of the *local* holy protector of a city or a community (see Chiavaro 1987).

6. In order to account for a state of society prior to the constructions of jurisconsults, which begin "with the latest times of the civilized nations (and thus of men enlightened by fully developed natural reason)" (Vico 1984 [1725], 124), Vico describes two other ways to build a bond among human beings, which he connects with the "ages" of humanity. The second, corresponding to the "age of the heroes" (20), encompasses elements that we shall designate further on as the domestic polity. The first form Vico presents includes many features that we shall attribute to inspired worth. Associated with the divine age, the form is supported by what Vico calls "a poetic metaphysics in which the theological poets imagined bodies to be for the most part divine substances," crediting them with "senses and passions" (127–28). And Vico describes the forms of generality of what he himself calls a "sensory topic, by which [the first founders of humanity] brought together [the] properties or qualities or relations of individuals and species" (166). Always attaching crucial importance to language, Vico presents synecdoche as the privileged instrument for reaching a greater degree of generality: "*Synecdoche* developed into metaphor as particulars were elevated into universals or parts united with the other parts together with which they make up their wholes" (130).

7. We shall return later on to the way in which the market is distorted in belief (see chapter 8, the section titled "The Damaging Effects of Speculation"). However, let us note here that this slippage from market value to fame fosters a great deal of sociological literature based on the notions of "credit" or "market," used with reference to the opinion of others.

8. Hobbes himself speaks of "vain-glory," which can only be distinguished from fame by a subtle distinction between "flattery" and "esteem."

> *Joy*, arising from imagination of a mans own power and ability, is that exultation of the mind which is called GLORYING: which if grounded upon the experience of his own former actions, is the same with *Confidence*: but if grounded on the flattery of others;

or onely supposed by himself, for delight in the consequences of it, is called VAINE-
GLORY: which name is properly given; because a well grounded *Confidence* begetteth
Attempt; whereas the supposing of power does not, and is therefore rightly called
Vaine. (Hobbes 1997 [1651], 34)

9. The following abbreviations are used for Rousseau's political works: *SC* for
the *Social Contract* (1994 [1762]); *FD* for the "Discourse on the Sciences and Arts"
("First Discourse," 1997 [1750]); *SD* for the "Discourse on the Origin and Foundation of Inequality among Men" (Second Discourse, 1997c [1754]); *CF* for the
Confessions (1995 [1782, 1789]); *EM* for *Emile, or On Education* (1974 [1762]); *NH*
for *Julie; or, the New Heloise* (1997b [1761]).

10. Honor makes all the parts of the body politic move; its very action binds them, and
each person works for the common good, believing he works for his individual interests. Speaking philosophically, it is true that the honor that guides all the parts of the
state is a false honor, but this false honor is as useful to the public as the true one
would be to the individuals who could have it. And is it not impressive that one can
oblige men to do all the difficult actions and which require force, with no reward
other than the renown of these actions? (Montesquieu 1989 [1748], 27)

(On the tradition to which this argument belongs, see Hirschman 1977.)

11. The relation between the general will in Rousseau and theories of grace is
analyzed by Patrick Riley in his history of the idea of "general will" (1986). Riley
shows how the idea of general will developed during the seventeenth century
through discussions of grace. The general will, which is first and foremost a theological notion, designates the type of will attributed to God when He decides
who is to receive the grace that suffices for salvation. The question comes up in
connection with the interpretation of St. Paul's assertion that "God wants
all men to be saved." The Jansenists interpret this divine will as follows: the
reference to "all" does not refer to "all men" taken each in his particularity; it
designates a will to salvation that can bear upon any sort of man, whatever his
qualities, Jew or Gentile, slave or free, and so on. The term "general" is thus associated with the idea of "man in general," detached from any particular qualities, and this opens the way to a slippage toward the use of the term in political
theory to designate a citizen in general (as opposed to membership in corporate
bodies and the hierarchical dependencies that qualify persons in the domestic
polity) (4–13).

12. In an earlier work devoted to the analysis of the concept of will in contractualist political philosophies, Riley emphasizes the paradoxical character of will in
Rousseau's writings. In keeping with the tradition of contracts, Rousseau makes
consent the condition for the legitimacy of a political order. But this voluntarism is
clouded by the ambiguous character of the general will. The general will is sometimes identified with the will that emanates from the political body as a whole,
sometimes with the will of an individual to the extent that this individual is willing
to give up his or her own will and personal appetites in order to reach the general
state. Riley explains this ambiguity as deriving from Rousseau's intention to reconcile contractualist individualism as a principle of legitimacy with nostalgia for the
immediate cohesiveness and unity of the ancient city-states (especially Sparta and

Rome during the Republic), conditions conceived as "non-individualist" or "pre-individualist" forms of solidarity (1982, 99–100).

13. Saint-Simon's influence on Marx, which Pierre Ansart analyzed in *Marx et l'anarchisme* (especially in the chapter titled "Une critique saint-simonienne de la philosophie" (1969, 329–58), is emphasized by Georges Gurvitch in his introduction to a selection of works by Saint-Simon: "Gans, one of the rare professors whose courses Marx took at the University of Berlin, was the first Hegelian to attempt to correct Hegel's *Philosophy of Law* by invoking the Saint-Simonian idea that economic society (so-called civil society) is much more important than the State, determining the latter's operation and its very fate" (Saint-Simon 1965 [1808], 36).

14. The following abbreviations are used for works by Saint-Simon, cited in *Oeuvres* (1869 [1817]): *Syst.* for *Le système industriel; Org.* for *L'organisateur; Ind.* for *L'industrie*.

CHAPTER FIVE: JUDGMENT PUT TO THE TEST

1. Amelot de la Houssaye translated Gracian's *El oraculo manual y arte de prudence* into French under the title *L'homme de cour,* manifestly inspired by Castiglione's *Il libro del cortegiano,* as Alain Pons remarked in his introduction to his own translation of the latter work (1987, p. ii). Amelot justifies his choice of title by arguing that this book is "a sort of primer for Court and the political code" (Gracian 1685 [1647], preface). Let us note that in these works, the art of prudence is governed chiefly by fame, since the assessment of worths is carried out under the gaze of others. Worthy occupations are the ones that are "universally applauded," the ones that "win common favor because they are exercised in front of everyone" (85). Antoine de Courtin's French civility (1671) is, in comparison, more clearly oriented by a domestic hierarchy; as Jacques Revel notes, "the first lesson is to recognize one's place in society and one's precise distance from people of every other rank" (1989, 198).

CHAPTER SIX: THE SIX WORLDS

1. The italicized terms in chapters 6, 8, and 10 come from the corpus of manuals to which we are referring.

2. Desecration is a gesture that proposes an internal critique by pointing out the inhumanity of people who go too far, a critique that opens up a path to externality and prepares the way for a compromise. The term has been used because desecration and blasphemy take on their full force only when the person formulating a critique recognizes the value of the beings he is criticizing. This distancing figure often operates by a shift from letter to spirit, from the literal to the figurative.

CHAPTER SEVEN: WORLDS IN CONFLICT, JUDGMENTS IN QUESTION

1. Rousseau uses this figure in many passages of the *Confessions,* especially to denounce fame and wealth. This is the case, for example, in the story of the "illumination of Vincennes," which belongs to the register of inspiration, as attested not

only by the sudden emotion that inspired the drafting of the *Second Discourse* but also by the description of the way it was written: "I worked on this discourse in a very peculiar manner and one which I have almost always followed in my other works. I dedicated the insomnias of my nights to it. I meditated in my bed with my eyes closed, and I shaped and reshaped my passages in my head with unbelievable difficulty; then when I had succeeded in being satisfied with them, I deposited them in my memory until I could put them on paper: but the time it took to get up and get dressed made me lose everything, and when I had applied myself to my paper, almost nothing of what I had composed came to me any more" (Rousseau 1995 [1782, 1789], 295). To situate this particularly inspired scene, Rousseau sets aside alternative worths and lays claim, not without pride, to solitude and poverty: "hardly in a condition to pay for cabs," he is in the habit of traveling from Paris to Vincennes "on foot," "alone," "exhausted from the heat" (294).

2. These translations, which make an association between the common good of one polity and what in another can only be identified as a particular good, without generality or worth, are made easier if they can follow the path opened up by an association deposited in language. Thus, to return to the previous example, the reference to a common form by means of which it is possible to express, in different terms, on the one hand an outpouring of inspired worth (bubbling up) and on the other hand an outbreak of chaos in families (boiling over), the reference to something that boils, blends, and becomes agitated in a disorderly way under the influence of an external cause and, by association, the reference to something that goes too far, carries away and disturbs, allows an inversion of worths that would not impose themselves with the same self-evidence if we were for example to pass from "boiling over" to "being resourceful" or "operational." Nothing, in the latter case, would orient the work of denunciation, which may on the contrary follow, in the previous example, a path already traced in the words: "What you describe pejoratively as boiling over is actually the bubbling up of genius."

What is called ordinary language already contains, in its own flesh, as it were, in the play of semantic networks, traces of natural relations and also of denunciations or compromises among natures. Synonyms and especially derogatory or denunciatory word pairs often seem linked to the need to reformulate the qualities of worths in a given nature, by disqualifying them in such a way that they can be applied to the unworthy in another nature. But these transformations are easier to bring about when they can be based on a common root, that is, on what might be called domestic relations among words. When the derogatory element is backed by a common root, a whole family of words is disgraced or put under suspicion. However, semantic networks as such do not suffice to support a denunciation, because they do not contain the principle that could justify it. To exclaim that someone is "at the boiling point" is nothing but an insult unless one can connect the exclamation to the order of worths that prevails in the situation—for example, the person in question is participating in a democratic debate where dispassionate speech is the rule. But the networks can help sustain and orient the justifying impulse as it moves back up toward a founding principle. An exception has to be made, however, for the inspired world, in which the correspondences and associations embedded in language can be unveiled and read as inscriptions drawn by the Creator's hand, or as expressions of an authenticity originating deep in the unconscious mind. They are proofs par excellence, for in this world the inexhaustible multiplicities of meaning that language harbors, a stratum whose treasures are unveiled by poetry or mysticism, constitute the highest form of generality.

3. In May 1968, in France, it was possible to "turn" a theater audience, get it to shift from the world of fame to the civic world, because people were preoccupied with current events and could not detach themselves from their concerns as citizens, concerns of which they were constantly reminded by the noise of the crowds in the streets. This very arrangement is often used in theatrical works in order to create a depth allowing the actors' onstage activity to be denounced as artificial and cut off from "reality." Thus for example in Genet's *The Balcony*, the sounds of the riot taking place outside the closed shutters denounce the closed universe, the snug perversity of the bordello in which the worthy act out their worth, and thus unveil its vanity, in sketches that are disrupted by the reality of the shouting outside.

4. Thus under the most extreme conditions of servitude, as, for example in the Nazi concentration camps (Pollak 1986, 1990), the masters exhibit sadistic behaviors with respect to the inmates' behaviors that would be highly incongruous if their power were exercised over things, or even over animals; this demonstrates that they recognize the humanity of their victims. In the testimony of Jewish deportees, we often find narratives of moments presented as particularly disturbing in which the torturers forget, the way one commits a lapsus, to deny the humanity of the subhumans (for example, a German doctor at Auschwitz steps into a room where a female deportee assigned to work in the hospital unit is getting undressed and quickly backs out, saying "Excuse me"). These memories are colored with the shame that accompanies a compromise, when the victim has acknowledged this recognition (for example by making eye contact) and has drawn some advantage from it, or saved her own life.

CHAPTER EIGHT: THE CRITICAL MATRIX

1. The italicized terms come from the corpus of manuals on which we relied and are attached to a common world. The superscript letters that follow indicate the world of reference: ^{i} = inspired, ^{d} = domestic, ^{f} = fame, ^{c} = civic, ^{m} = market, ^{u} = industrial. The notation $^{f/d}$ indicates a *critique* addressed to the world of fame from the domestic world. The notation $^{d\text{-}u}$ indicates a *compromise* initiated in the domestic world and involving the industrial world.

CHAPTER NINE: COMPROMISING FOR THE COMMON GOOD

1. The Economic and Social Council, created after the war, is an arrangement allowing the institution of a representation of professional interests in the French State. Such representation was excluded from the model of political representation established during the Revolution, and the need to represent professional interests lay behind a number of social struggles in the second half of the nineteenth century and the first half of the twentieth. The Council considers and proposes economic or social adjustments necessitated by new technological developments.

2. This passage can be associated with maxim 3: "In one thing great men have an immense advantage over others; they may enjoy their sumptuous banquets, their costly furniture, their dogs, horses, monkeys, dwarfs, fools, and flatterers; but I envy them the happiness of having in their service their equals, and sometimes even their superiors, in feelings and intelligence" (La Bruyère 1929 [1688], 222).

3. La Bruyère sketches out a response in a number of passages in his *Characters* that open up onto other worths, with special emphasis on skill and competence. For example, in maxim 19: "The great believe themselves the only persons who are the pink of perfection, and will hardly allow any sound judgment, ability, or refined feelings in any of a meaner rank; but they arrogate to themselves those qualities by virtue of their birth. However, they are greatly in error in entertaining such absurd prejudices, for the best thoughts, the best discourses, the best writings, and perhaps the most refined behaviour, have not always been found among them" (1929 [1688], 226). On the crisis of legitimacy, especially in Pascal's discourse on the condition of the great, see Louis Marin (1988), especially the last chapter, "The Legitimate Usurper, or the Shipwrecked Man as King" (215–38).

4. Durkheim 1993, 64–65. This text is largely devoted to a critique of utilitarianism:

> For the Manchester School, political economy consists of the satisfaction of the needs of the individual, especially his or her material needs. In this conception the individual is the unique goal of economic relations; it is both by and for the individual that everything is done. Society, on the other hand, is an abstraction, a metaphysical entity, which the scientist can and should ignore. What one refers to by this term is only the interrelationships of individual actions; it is a whole which is nothing more than the sum of its parts. (63)

"Society," Durkheim declares in the same text, "is a real being"; it has "its own nature and personality. Current expressions such as 'social conscience,' 'collective spirit,' 'the body of the nation,' do not have simply a linguistic value; they express facts that are eminently concrete. It is false to say that the whole is equal to the sum of its parts." The social being has "special properties" and it may "under certain conditions even be conscious of itself. Society is not, therefore, reducible to a blurred mass of citizens" (64), and "the social organism" cannot be reduced to "a collection of individuals" (66). The totality to which Durkheim refers when he speaks about "society" is equated here with a "nation" or a "State." "In other words, the great laws of economics would have been exactly the same even if there had never been nations or states in the world; these laws presuppose only the presence of individuals who exchange their products" (63).

5. "Doubtless, individuals who are busy in the same trade are in contact with one another by the very fact that their activities are similar. *Competition* with one another engenders mutual relationships. But these are *in no way regular*; depending upon chance meetings, they are very often entirely of an *individual* nature. One industrialist finds himself in contact with another, but the body of industrialists in some particular specialty do not meet to act in concert" (Durkheim 1997 [1893], xxxv, emphasis added).

6. In the course of this book, on a number of occasions we emphasize the state of legal and moral anomie in which economic life exists at the present time. . . . Those actions most blameworthy are so often excused by success that the boundary between the permissible and the prohibited, between what is *just* and what is unjust, is no longer fixed in any way, but seems capable of being shifted by individuals in an almost *arbitrary* fashion. . . . It is to this state of *anomie* that, as we shall show, must be attributed the continually recurring *conflicts* and *disorders* of every kind of which the economic world affords so sorry a spectacle. For, since nothing restrains the forces present from reacting together, or prescribes limits for them that they are obliged to respect, they tend to grow beyond all bounds, each clashing with the other, each warding off and weakening the other. To be sure, those forces that are the most vigorous succeed in crushing the weakest or subjecting them to their will. Yet, although the vanquished can for a while resign themselves to an enforced domination, they do not concur in it, and consequently such a state can provide no stable equilibrium. . . . That such *anarchy* is an unhealthy phenomenon is clearly very evident, since it runs counter to the very purpose of society, which is to eliminate or at least to moderate warfare among men, by subjecting *the physical law of the strongest* to a higher law. (Durkheim 1997 [1893], xxxi–xxxiii, emphasis added)

7. Durkheim distinguishes the "social question" from the question of the working class, the issue of "social justice," and the problem of doing away with poverty. These distinctions are clearly visible in the passages in which Durkheim distinguishes socialism, characterized by the preponderant role granted to economic functions (1958, 64–65), from communism (with which he associates Rousseau [196]), which seeks only to neutralize their effects. "What [communism] questions are the moral consequences of private property in general and not—as does socialism—the expediency of a specific economic organization appearing at a particular time in history" (37).

8. For Saint-Simon, "the way to realize social peace is to free economic appetites of all restraint on the one hand, and on the other to satisfy them by fulfilling them. But such an enterprise is contradictory. For such appetites cannot be appeased unless they are limited and they cannot be limited except by something other than themselves" (Durkheim 1958 [1928], 199). Hence it follows that "[t]hey cannot be regarded as the only purpose of society since they must be subordinated to some end which surpasses them, and it is only on this condition that they are capable of being really satisfied. Picture the most productive economic organization possible and a distribution of wealth which assures abundance to even the humblest—perhaps such a transformation, at the very moment it was constituted, would produce an instant of gratification. But this gratification could only be temporary. For desires, though calmed for an instant, will quickly acquire new exigencies" (199).

9. What is needed if social order is to reign is that the mass of men be content with their lot. But what is needed for them to be content, is not that they have more or less but that they be convinced that they have no right to more. And for this, it is absolutely essential that there be an authority whose superiority they acknowledge and which tells them what is right. For an individual committed only to the pressure of his needs

will never admit he has reached the extreme limits of his rightful portion. If he is not conscious of a force above him which he respects, which stops him and tells him with authority that the compensation due him is fulfilled, then inevitably he will expect as due him all that his needs demand. And since in our hypothesis these needs are limitless, their exigency is necessarily without limit. For it to be otherwise, a moral power is required whose superiority he recognizes, and which cries out, "You must go no further" (Durkheim 1958 [1928], 200).

10. [T]he subordination of private utility to a common utility, whatever that may be, has always a moral character, for it necessarily implies some spirit of sacrifice and abnegation.... [T]his attachment to something that transcends the individual, this subordination of the particular to the general interest, is the very well-spring of all moral activity.... A life lived in common is attractive, yet at the same time it exerts a coercion.... That is why, when individuals discover they have interests in common and come together, it is not only to defend those interests, but also so as to associate with one another and not feel isolated in the midst of their adversaries, so as to enjoy the pleasure of communicating with one another, to feel at one with several others, which in the end means to lead the same moral life together. (Durkheim 1997 [1893], xli–xliv)

Let us note the similarity between this last argument, which evokes civic worth, and the argument developed by Albert Hirschman (1982b, 77–91) in his critique of Mancur Olson's hypothesis of the "free ride" (Olson 1965): according to Hirschman, collective action is sought for itself, so that "the benefit of collective action for an individual is not the difference between the hoped-for result and the effort furnished by him or her, but the *sum* of these two magnitudes" (Hirschman 1982b, 86).

11. Durkheim criticizes the artificialism, voluntarism, and individualism of contract theories in numerous passages, often associating Rousseau's political works with his critiques: for example, in the fourth lecture on sociology devoted to "civic morality" (Durkheim 1992 [1950], 51), in the introduction to the study on Montesquieu (Durkheim 1960a, 3–4), and also in "La leçon d'ouverture du Cours de sciences sociales de la Faculté de Bordeaux" (published in 1888 in the Annales de la Faculté des lettres de Bordeaux and republished in Durkheim 1970 [1888], 77–110). Such passages have tended to obscure the similarities between construction and totality in Rousseau and in Durkheim (see for example Lacroix 1981, 73; or Boudon and Bourricaud 1989, 189). In the same way, the critique of political philosophy to which Durkheim often turns to emphasize the specificity and the novelty of social science has relegated to the background the aspects of his work that take up the old questions of classical political philosophy. These questions reappear clearly in the texts in which Durkheim undertakes to define the institutions that are the most apt to ensure happiness and justice in society.

12. Society is

a moral Being with qualities of its own and distinct from those of the particular Beings constituting it, more or less as chemical compounds have properties which they owe to none of the components that make them up.... [T]here would be a sort of common sensorium which would make for the concert of all the parts; the public good or evil would not only be the sum of particular goods or evils as in a mere aggregate, but would reside in the connectedness between them, it would be greater than that sum, and the public felicity, far from being based on the happiness of individuals, would be its source. (Rousseau 1997a [1762], 155, cited in a different translation in Durkheim 1960a, 82)

13. In Durkheim, this disembodied reason is realized by science, a "social and impersonal thing first and foremost," as the "highest" form of collective consciousness. "In the sphere of morality, as in the other spheres of nature, *individual* reason has no particular prestige as such. The only reason for which one can claim the right of intervention, and of rising above historical moral reality in order to reform it, is not my reason nor yours; it is the impersonal human reason, only truly realized in science" (1965 [1898], 65, author's emphasis).

14. The importance Durkheim grants to the reinternalization of supraindividual rules is manifested in particular in his interest in the educational process. His pedagogical preoccupations bring him back once again to Rousseau, as we see from the outline of the course devoted to Rousseau's pedagogy and published in 1919 in the *Revue de métaphysique et de morale* (reprinted in Durkheim 1975, 3: 371–401). As Philippe Besnard emphasizes, this text brings out the parallelisms between Rousseauist anthropology and Durkheimian anthropology with particularly clarity: "Durkheim reads in *Émile* that 'the road to true happiness' consists in 'diminishing the excess of desires on the faculties'" (Besnard 1987, 28–29).

15. To be shot of anomie a group must thus exist or be formed within which can be drawn up the system of rules that is now lacking. Political society as a whole, or the state, clearly cannot discharge this function. Economic life, because it is very special and is daily becoming increasingly specialized, lies outside their authority and sphere of action. Activity within a profession can only be effectively regulated through a group close enough to that profession to be thoroughly cognizant of how it functions, capable of perceiving all its needs and following every fluctuation in them. (Durkheim 1997 [1893], xxxv)

16. "A society made up of an extremely large mass of unorganized individuals, which an overgrown state attempts to limit and restrain, constitutes a veritable sociological monstrosity. . . . A nation cannot be maintained unless, between the state and individuals, a whole range of secondary groups are interposed" (Durkheim 1997 [1893], liv).

17. The sole group that meets these conditions is that constituted by all those working in the same industry, assembled together and organized in a single body. This is what is termed a corporation, or professional group. . . . Since the last century, when, *not without reason*, the ancient corporations were dissolved, hardly more than fragmentary or incomplete attempts have been made to reconstitute them on a different basis. . . . For a professional morality and code of law to become established within the various professions in the economy, instead of the corporation remaining a conglomerate body lacking unity, it must become, or rather become once more, a well-defined, organized group—in short, a public institution. (Durkheim 1997 [1893], xxxv–xxxvi, author's emphasis)

18. We like to believe that in blood kinship there exists an extraordinarily powerful reason for moral identification with others. But, as we have often had occasion to show, blood kinship has in no way the extraordinary effectiveness attributed to it. The proof of this is that in a large number of societies relations not linked by the blood tie are very numerous in a family. . . . Conversely, very frequently those closely knit by ties of blood are morally and legally strangers to one another. . . . The family does not derive its whole strength from unity of descent. Quite simply, it is a group of individuals who have drawn close to one another within the body politic through a very specially close community of ideas, feelings and interests." (Durkheim 1997 [1893], xliv)

19. For decades, the Commissariat Général du Plan has been the site where the economic and social policies of the French state are worked out and organized. Proposed by various political interests in the 1930s in the wake of the economic crisis and set up in 1945 by de Gaulle after the Liberation, the French planning system may be compared to the New Deal. In a country such as France, where democracy had been perceived as incompatible with the political representation of interests, economic and professional interests in particular, the establishment of a planning system went hand in hand with a recognition of the need to provide for representation of the socioprofessional groups whose existence was semiinstitutionalized through labor unions, collective bargaining agreements, and right-to-work legislation.

CHAPTER TEN: FIGURES OF COMPROMISE

1. The French Conseils des prud'hommes, closer to the workplace than ordinary courts, address situations in which salaried workers or apprentices are involved in a controversy with employers over some aspect of a work contract (its execution, violation, or termination). The procedures followed by these Councils call for an initial effort at reconciliation; if this first phase fails, then the Council passes a judgment oriented toward equity, in the sense that it seeks to be particularly attentive to the circumstances. These Councils are sharply differentiated from other agencies of the French judicial system: they are organized according to sectors of professional activity, and the members who serve as judges, called "councilors," are not professional jurists but members elected in equal numbers by salaried workers and employers.

2. In France, a single labor union (for example the Confédération Générale du Travail) may include not only blue-collar workers but also white-collar workers, technicians, professionals, and so on.

CHAPTER ELEVEN: RELATIVIZATION

1. Constructions that define beings according to the degree to which they are inhabited by a force, and that consequently treat this primordial force as a general equivalent, are not the exclusive property of the social sciences. People often take recourse to this type of interpretation when they have to account for behavior

that seems to escape the imperative of justification, and for the repetition of tests whose outcome is always judged unjust, as if this behavior offered abnormal resistance to the rules of equity on which the possibility of reaching agreement is based. For example, the model of sorcery that Jeanne Favret studied in Mayenne, a model that rests on a theory of power (a sorcerer is a powerful person who succeeds at everything and whose worth increases unjustifiably and incomprehensibly [1977]), constitutes one of the forms in which the competence put to work by persons can be schematized in order to account for actions that are successfully repeated even though they do not fall under the rules of equivalence and equity that are obeyed by just or at least contestable tests (what Favret calls "ordinary mediations").

The possibility of increasing in worth at the expense of others owing to an essential excess of strengths, which is at the heart of the model of competence that makes it possible to generate interpretations in terms of sorcery (Augé 1975), is taken seriously by some people because they themselves are familiar with states in which they feel strong enough to exempt themselves from the outcome of an adverse test by drawing on their weakness to reverse it, by a pure act of will without justification or foundation. This formula of reversal—beneath your worth lies abjection, beneath my abjection lies power—describes the way in which absent worths stir around the edges and come knocking at the door. Power is manifested in such cases (as it is in early childhood) in the form of a desire for omnipotence, in the raw state, at once unlimited and imprecise. But in a model of justified action, an outburst of power like the one on which sorcery constructs its own theory of worth must transform itself as soon as it meets the obstacle of criticism in the form of a requirement of clarification, from which persons cannot exempt themselves without their pretensions being disqualified by the accusation of madness. If it is to be expressible and justifiable, the increase in power has to be specified with reference to a grounded worth, which shifts the situation into another worth including new tests (often, when the instrumentation is reduced to the body alone, into the inspired world).

2. On the project of basing values on scientifically measurable forces and, more generally, on the delicate problem of measuring forces in Nietzsche, see Gilles Deleuze, who writes, in *Nietzsche and Philosophy*: "Nietzsche always believed that forces were quantitative and had to be defined quantitatively" (1983, 43). In support of his thesis, he cites the following passage, excerpted from *The Will to Power*, in which there is a clear expression of the intent to make force a new general equivalent that allows true worth to be distinguished from illusory values: "Our knowledge . . . has become scientific to the extent that it is able to employ number and measurement. The attempt should be made to see whether a scientific order of values could be constructed simply on a numerical and quantitative scale— All other 'values' are prejudices, naiveties and misunderstandings. They are everywhere reducible to this numerical and quantitative scale of force" (Nietzsche 1968 [1901], cited in Deleuze 1983, 43). But this project is made ambiguous by the price attached to what "cannot be reduced to equality," in other words, "that aspect of quantity that cannot be equalized" inasmuch as *"quantity itself is . . . inseparable from difference in quantity"* [author's emphasis]. If "[d]ifference in quantity is the

essence of force and of the relation of force to force," forces then exist only in "encounters of forces." They thus depend on chance encounters and remain "as such, alien to every law" (43–44)—a proposition that runs singularly counter to the industrial principle of stabilizing measurements, a principle that is inherent in the scientific enterprise.

3. See, for example, Leo Strauss's critique of Max Weber (1953, 36–78).

WORKS CITED

Adorno, Theodor W. 1973 [1949]. *Philosophy of Modern Music*. Trans. Anne G. Mitchell and Wesley V. Blomster. New York: Seabury Press.

Affichard, Joëlle. 1986. "L'homologation des titres et diplômes de l'enseignement technologique, une transformation pour donner valeur d'État à des formations spécifiques." In Salais and Thévenot 1986, 139–59.

———. ed., 1987. *Pour une histoire de la statistique*. 2 vols. Paris: INSEE-Economica.

Aglietta, Michel, and André Orléan. 1982. *La violence de la monnaie*. Paris: Presses Universitaires de France.

Akrich, Madeleine. 1989. "De la position relative des localités: Systèmes électriques et réseaux socio-politiques." In Eymard-Duvernet 1989, 117–66.

Angenot, Marc, 1983. *La parole pamphlétaire: Typologie des discours modernes*. Paris: Payot.

Ansart, Pierre. 1969. *Marx et l'anarchisme*. Paris: Presses Universitaires de France.

———. 1970. *Sociologie de Saint-Simon*. Paris: Presses Universitaires de France.

Aristotle. *The Nicomachean Ethics*. Trans. H. Rackham. Loeb Classical Library.

———. *Politics*. Trans. H. Rackham. Loeb Classical Library.

———. *Rhetoric*. Trans. John Henry Freese. Loeb Classical Library.

———. *Topica*. Trans. E. S. Forster. In *Posterior Analytics and Topica*. Loeb Classical Library.

———. 1967. *Rhétorique*. Ed. Médéric Dufour. Paris: Les belles lettres.

———. 1997. *Topics: Books I and VIII with Excerpts from Related Texts*. Trans. with commentary by Robin Smith. Oxford: Clarendon Press. In French: 1984. *Organon*. Vol. 5: *Les topiques*, ed. and trans. Jean Tricot. Paris: Vrin.

Arnauld d'Andilly, Antoine. 1736 [1647–53]. *Les vies des saints pères des déserts et de quelques saintes écrites par des pères de l'église et autres anciens auteurs ecclésiastiques grecs et latins*. Paris: Josse et Delespine.

Arnauld d'Andilly, Antoine, and Pierre Nicole. 1996 [1683]. *Logic or The Art of Thinking: Containing, besides Common Rules, Several New Observations Appropriate for Forming Judgment*. Ed. Jill Vance Buroker. Cambridge: Cambridge University Press.

Aron, Raymond. 1998 [1967]. *Main Currents in Sociological Thought*. New Brunswick, N.J.: Transaction Publishers.

Aubenque, Pierre. 1976 [1963]. *La prudence chez Aristote*. Paris: Presses Universitaires de France.

Auerbach, Erich. 1953. *Mimesis: The Representation of Reality in Western Literature*. Trans. Willard Trask. Garden City, N.Y.: Doubleday.

Augé, Marc. 1975. *Théorie des pouvoirs et idéologie*. Paris: Hermann.

Augustine, St. 1963. *The Trinity [by] St. Augustine*. Trans. Stephen McKenna. Washington, D.C.: Catholic University of America Press.

———. 1982. *The Literal Meaning of Genesis*. Trans. and annotated by John Hammond Taylor. New York: Newman Press.

————. 1984. *Concerning the City of God against the Pagans.* Trans. Henry Betten-son. London: Penguin Books.

————. 1990a [414–15]. "Letter 157" (to Hilary). In *Letters 156–210 (Epistulae)*, in *The Works of Saint Augustine: A Translation for the Twenty-first Century*, pt. 2, 3:16–39. Hyde Park, N.Y.: New City Press.

————. 1990b [415]. "Nature and Grace." In *Answer to the Pelagians*, in *The Works of Saint Augustine: A Translation for the Twenty-first Century*, pt. 1, 23:225–75.

————. 1998. *Confessions.* Trans. and ed. Henry Chadwick. Oxford: Oxford University Press.

Baker, Keith Michael, 1975. *Condorcet: From Natural Philosophy to Social Mathematics.* Chicago: University of Chicago Press.

Bastid, Paul. 1970 [1939]. *Sièyes et sa pensée.* Paris: Hachette.

Baumgartner, Charles, ed. 1966. "Grâce." In *Dictionnaire de spiritualité*, vol. 6, col. 701–63. Paris: Beauchesne.

Bénichou, Paul. 1971 [1948]. *Man and Ethics. Studies in French Classicism.* Trans. Elizabeth Hughes. Garden City, N.Y.: Anchor Books.

Benjamin, Walter. 1969. "The Work of Art in the Age of Mechanical Reproduction." In *Illuminations*, trans. Harry Zohn, 229–30. New York: Schocken Books.

Berger, Suzanne, and Michael J. Piore. 1980. *Dualism and Discontinuity in Industrial Societies.* Cambridge: Cambridge University Press.

Berman, Marshall. 1970. *The Politics of Authenticity.* New York: Atheneum.

Besnard, Philippe. 1973. "Durkheim et les femmes ou le *suicide* inachevé." *Revue française de sociologie* 14:27–61.

————. 1987. *L'anomie, ses usages et ses fonctions dans la discipline sociologique depuis Durkheim.* Paris: Presses Universitaires de France.

Bloch, Maurice. 1986. *From Blessing to Violence. History and Ideology in the Circumcision Ritual of the Merina of Madagascar.* Cambridge: Cambridge University Press.

Bodin, Jean. 1606 [1576]. *The Six Books of a Common-weale.* Trans. Richard Knolles. London: G. Bishop.

————. 1755. *Abrégé de la République* (adaptation). London: Jean Nourse.

Böhm-Bawerk, Eugen von. 1959. *Capital and Interest.* Trans. George D. Huncke and Hans F. Sennholz. 3 vols. South Holland: Libertarian Press.

Boisard, Pierre, and Marie-Thérèse Letablier. 1987. "Le camembert: Normand ou normé; Deux modèles de production dans l'industrie fromagère." In François Eymard-Duvernet, *Entreprise et produits*, 1–29. Paris: CEE-Presses Universitaires de France.

————. 1989. "Un compromis d'innovation entre tradition et standardisation dans l'industrie laitière." In Boltanski and Thévenot 1989, 209–18.

Boltanski, Luc. 1987 [1982]. *The Making of a Class: Cadres in French Society.* Trans. Arthur Goldhammer. Cambridge: Cambridge University Press.

————. 1990a. *L'amour et la justice comme compétences.* Paris: Métailié.

————. 1990b. "La dénonciation publique." In *L'Amour et la Justice comme compétences: Trois essais de sociologie de l'action*, 255–366. Paris: Métailié.

Boltanski, Luc, and Laurent Thévenot. 1983. "Finding One's Way in Social Space: A Study Based on Games." *Social Science Information* 22 (4–5): 631–80.

————. eds. 1989. *Justesse et justice dans le travail.* Paris: CEE-Presses Universitaires de France.

Bonald, Louis Gabriel Antoine, vicomte de. 1985 [1830]. *Démonstration philosophique du principe constitutif de la société*. Intro. François Azouvi. Paris: Vrin.

Booth, Charles. 1886. "On Occupations of the People of the United Kingdom, 1808–1881." *Journal of the Royal Statistical Society* 49:314–445.

Bossuet, Jacques Bénigne. 1686 [3d ed. 1700]. *A Discourse on the History of the Whole World*. Trans. from the French. London: Matthew Turner.

———. 1990 [1709]. *Politics Drawn from the Very Words of Holy Scripture*. Trans. and ed. Patrick Riley. Cambridge: Cambridge University Press.

Boudon, Raymond, and François Bourricaud. 1989 [1982]. *A Critical Dictionary of Sociology: Selections*. Ed. and trans. Peter Hamilton. Chicago: University of Chicago Press.

Bourdieu, Pierre. 1977 [1972]. *Outline of a Theory of Practice*. Trans. Richard Nice. Cambridge: Cambridge University Press.

———. 1990 [1980]. *Logic of Practice*. Trans. Richard Nice. Stanford, Calif.: Stanford University Press.

———. 1991 [1982]. *Language and Symbolic Power*. Trans. Gino Raymond and Matthew Adamson. Cambridge: Cambridge University Press.

Brown, Peter. 1978. *The Making of Late Antiquity*. Cambridge: Harvard University Press.

———. 1981. *Cult of the Saints: Its Rise and Function in Latin Christianity*. Chicago: University of Chicago Press, 1981.

———. 2000 [1967]. *Augustine of Hippo: A Biography*. Berkeley and Los Angeles: University of California Press.

Cabanis, Pierre Jean Georges, 1981 [1802]. *On the Relations between the Physical and Moral Aspects of Man*. Ed. George Mora, trans. Margaret Duggan Saidi. 2 vols. Baltimore: Johns Hopkins University Press.

Cairnes, John Elliott. 1874. *Political Economy*. New York: Harper.

Callon, Michel, and Bruno Latour. 1981. "Unscrewing the Big Leviathan: How Actors Macrostructure Reality and How Sociologists Help Them to Do So." In Karin Knorr-Cetina and Aaron Victor Cicourel, eds., *Advances in Social Theory: Toward an Integration of Micro- and Macro-sociologies*, 277–303. London: Routledge.

Callon, Michel, and John Law. 1989. "La proto-histoire d'un laboratoire ou le difficile mariage de la science et de l'économie." In Eymard-Duvernet 1989, 1–34.

Cam, Pierre. 1981. *Les prud'hommes, juges ou arbitres*. Paris: Presses de la Fondation nationale des sciences politiques.

Camusat, Pierre. 1970. *Savoir-vivre et promotion*. Paris: Éditions d'Organisation.

Carrel, Alexis. 1935. *Man the Unknown*. New York: Harper and Brothers.

Castiglione, Baldassare. 1929 [1580]. *The Book of the Courtier*. Trans. Leonard Eckstein Opdycke. New York: H. Liveright.

———. 1987. *Le livre du courtisan*. 1987. Ed. and trans. Alain Pons, based on 1580 translation by Gabriel Chappuis. Paris: G. Lebovici.

Certeau, Michel de, Dominique Julia, and Jacques Revel. 1975. *Une politique de la langue*. Paris: Gallimard.

Chamboredon, Jean-Claude. 1984. "Émile Durkheim: Le social, objet de science; Du moral au politique?" *Critique* 40:460–531.

Chandler, Alfred Dupont. 1977. *The Visible Hand. The Managerial Revolution in American Business*. Cambridge: Harvard University Press, Belknap Press.

Charlety, Sébastien. 1931. *Histoire du saint-simonisme (1825–1864)*. Paris: Gonthier.

Chateauraynaud, Francis. 1986. "Formes de justice, épreuves de normalité et traduction psychiatrique dans la construction des affaires." 2 vols. DEA in sociology. Paris: EHESS.

———. 1989a. "La faute professionnelle." In Boltanski and Thévenot 1989, 247–80.

———. 1989b. "Les affaires de faute professionnelle: Des figures de défaillance et des formes de jugement dans les situations de travail et devant les tribunaux." Doctoral thesis, Paris, EHESS.

Chiavaro, Francesco. 1987. *Les saints dans l'histoire du christianisme: Anthologie de la sainteté*. Vol. 1. Paris: Hachette.

Cicero. *De officiis*. Trans. Walter Miller. Loeb Classical Library.

———. *De oratore*. Trans. E. W. Sutton and H. Rackham. 2 vols. Loeb Classical Library.

———. *Topica*. Trans. H. M. Hubbell. Loeb Classical Library.

Clausewitz, Carl von. 1984 [1832]. *On War*. Ed. and trans. Michael Howard and Peter Paret. Princeton: Princeton University Press.

Claverie, Élisabeth. 1984. "De la difficulté de faire un citoyen: Les 'acquittements scandaleux' du jury dans la France provinciale du début du XIXe siècle." *Études rurales* 95–96:143–66.

Claverie, Élisabeth, and Pierre Lamaison. 1982. *L'impossible mariage: Violence et parenté en Gévaudan, XVIIe, XVIIIe, et XIXe siècles*. Paris: Hachette.

Coase, Ronald H., 1987 [1937]. "The Nature of the Firm." *Economica* 4 (Nov.): 386–405.

Condorcet, Jean-Antoine Nicolas de Caritat. 1986 [1788]. *Essai sur la constitution et les fonctions des assemblées provinciales*. In *Sur les élections et autres textes*. Paris: Fayard, Corpus des oeuvres philosophiques en langue française.

Confédération française démocratique du travail., 1981. *La section syndicale*. Paris: CFDT.

———. 1983. *Pour élire ou désigner les délégués*. Paris: CFDT.

Corcuff, Philippe. 1989. "Sécurité et expertise psychologique dans les chemins de fer." In Boltanski and Thévenot 1989, 307–32.

Corcuff, Philippe, and Claudette Lafaye. 1989. "Une relecture critique du *Pouvoir périphérique*—du fonctionnalisme au constructivisme." *Politix* 7–8:35–45.

Courtin, Antoine de. 1671. *The Rules of Civility, or, Certain Ways of Deportment Observed in France amongst All Persons of Quality upon Several Occasions*. London: J. Martyn and John Starkey, 1671.

Croce, Benedetto. 1913 [1911]. *The Philosophy of Giambattista Vico*. Trans. R. G. Collingwood. New York: Macmillan.

Cropsey, Joseph. 1975. "Adam Smith and Political Philosophy." In Skinner and Wilson 1975, 132–53.

Darré, Jean-Pierre. 1986. "La fonction de production de la vache." In Thévenot 1986, 115–27.

Delamourd, Vinoli. 1988. " 'Monsieur le Président . . . ': Les formes de justification de l'état de chômeur." DEA in sociology. Paris, EHESS.

Deleule, Didier. 1979. *Hume et la naissance du libéralisme économique*. Paris: Aubier-Montaigne.

Deleuze, Gilles. 1983 [1962]. *Nietzsche and Philosophy*. Trans. Hugh Tomlinson. New York: Columbia University Press.

Demory, Bernard. 1974. *La créativité en pratique*. Paris: Chotard et associés.

Derathé, Robert. 1970 [1950]. *Jean-Jacques Rousseau et la science politique de son temps*. Paris: Vrin.

Derouet, Jean-Louis. 1984. *Pour une sociologie de l'établissement scolaire*. Paris: Institut national de la recherche pédagogique.

———. 1989. "L'établissement scolaire comme entreprise composite: Programme pour une sociologie des établissements scolaires." In Boltanski and Thévenot 1989, 11–42.

Descartes, René. 1993 [1637]. *Discourse on Method; and, Meditations on First Philosophy*. Trans. Donald A. Cress. Indianapolis, Ind.: Hackett Publishing Company.

Desrosières, Alain. 1985. "Histoire de formes: Statistiques et sciences sociales avant 1940." *Revue française de sociologie* 26 (no. 2): 277–310.

———. 1986. "L'íngénieur d'État et le père de famille." *Annales des Mines*. Série "Gérer et comprendre" 2:66–80.

———. 1987 [1977]. "Éléments pour l'histoire des nomenclatures socio-professionnelles." In Affichard 1987, 1:155–231.

———. 1989. "L'opposition entre deux formes d'enquête: Monographie et statistique." In Boltanski and Thévenot 1989, 1–9.

Desrosières, Alain, and Laurent Thévenot. 1988. *Les catégories socioprofessionnelles*. Paris: La Découverte.

Di Bella, Maria Pia. 1981. "Implications et conséquences du code de l'honneur dans l'*Orestie* d'Eschyle." In *Atti del Convegno Internazionale "Letterature classiche e narratologia,"* 131–43. Perugia: Istituto di Filologia Latina dell'Università di Perugia.

Dodier, Nicolas, 1986. "Corps et accords: Les événements corporels individuels dans l'organisation collective des ouvriers." In Thévenot 1986, 91–114.

———. 1989. "Le travail d'accommodation des inspecteurs du travail en matière de sécurité." In Boltanski and Thévenot 1989, 281–306.

———. 1990. "Représenter ses actions: Le cas des inspecteurs et des médecins du travail." In Patrick Pharo and Louis Quéré, eds. *Les formes de l'action*, 115–48. Paris: EHESS.

Doeringer, Peter B., and Michael J. Piore. 1985 [1971]. *Internal Labor Markets and Manpower Analysis*. Armonk, N.Y.: Sharpe.

Domat, Jean. 1828 [1689]. *Oeuvres complètes*. Paris: F. Didot.

Duby, Georges. 1964. "Les jeunes dans la société aristocratique dans la France du Nord-Ouest au XIIe siècle." *Annales: E.S.C.* 19 (5): 835–46.

Dumont, Louis. 1970 [1966]. *Homo Hierarchicus: An Essay on the Caste System*. Trans. Mark Sainsbury. Chicago: University of Chicago Press.

———. 1986 [1983]. *Essays on Individualism: Modern Ideology in Anthropological Perspective*. Chicago: University of Chicago Press.

———. 1994 [1977]. *German Ideology: From France to Germany and Back*. Chicago: University of Chicago Press.

Dupuy, Jean-Pierre. 1987. "De l'émancipation de l'économie: Retour sur 'le problème d'Adam Smith.' " *L'Année sociologique* 37:311–42.

Durkheim, Emile. 1958 [1928]. *Socialism and Saint-Simon*. Ed. Alvin W. Gouldner, trans. Charlotte Sattler. Yellow Springs, Ohio: Antioch Press.

————. 1960a [1953]. *Montesquieu and Rousseau: Forerunners of Sociology.* Trans. Ralph Manheim. Ann Arbor: University of Michigan Press.

————. 1960b. "Sociology." Trans. Jerome D. Folkman. In *Emile Durkheim, 1858–1917: A Collection of Essays, with Translations and a Bibliography,* ed. Kurt H. Wolff, 376–85. Columbus: Ohio State University Press.

————. 1965 [1898]. *Sociology and Philosophy.* Trans. D. F. Pocock. London: Cohen and West.

————. 1970 [1888]. "Leçon d'ouverture." In *La science sociale et l'action,* intro. Jean-Claude Filloux, 77–110. Paris: Presses Universitaires de France.

————. 1975. *Textes.* Ed. Victor Karady. 3 vols. Paris: Minuit.

————. 1992 [1950]. *Professional Ethics and Civic Morals.* Trans. Cornelia Brookfield. London: Routledge.

————. 1993 [1887]. *Ethics and the Sociology of Morals.* Trans. Robert T. Hall. Buffalo, N.Y.: Prometheus Books.

————. 1995 [1912]. *The Elementary Forms of Religious Life.* Trans. Karen E. Fields. New York: Free Press.

————. 1997 [1893]. *The Division of Labor in Society.* Trans. W. D. Halls. New York: Free Press.

Elias, Norbert. 1983 [1974]. *Court Society.* Trans. Edmund Jephcott. New York: Pantheon Books.

Elster, Jon, 1979. *Ulysses and the Syrens. Studies in Rationality and Irrationality.* Cambridge: Cambridge University Press; Paris: Maison des Sciences de l'Homme.

Ewald, François, 1986. *L'État providence.* Paris: Grasset.

Eymard-Duvernay, François, 1986. "La qualification des produits." In Salais and Thévenot 1986, 239–47.

————. 1989a. "Coopération et concurrence dans les relations d'entreprises." In Boltanski and Thévenot 1989, 121–33.

————. 1989b. "Conventions de qualité et pluralité des formes de coordination." *Revue économique* 2 (March): 329–59.

———— ed., 1989c. *Innovation et ressources locales.* Paris: CEE-Presses Universitaires de France.

Faccarello, Gilbert, 1984. "Quelques réflexions sur l'équilibre économique chez P. de Boisguilbert." *Œconomia,* Cahiers de l'ISMEA, series P.E. (no. 1): 35–62.

————. 1999 [1986]. *The Foundations of Laissez-Faire: The Economics of Pierre de Boisguilbert.* New York: Routledge.

Farge, Arlette, and Michel Foucault. 1982. *Le désordre des familles.* Paris: Gallimard.

Fasso, Guido. 1972. *Vico e Grozio.* Naples: Guida Editori.

Faucci, Dario. 1969. "Vico and Grotius: Jurisconsults of Mankind." In Tagliacozzo and White 1969, 61–76.

Favereau, Olivier. 1982. "Le niveau de l'emploi dans une économie en croissance." 2 vols. State doctoral thesis, University of Paris I.

————. 1986. "La formalisation du rôle des conventions dans l'allocation de ressources." In Salais and Thévenot 1986, 249–67.

————. 1989a. "Marchés internes, marchés externes." *Revue économique* 2 (March): 273–327.

————. 1989b. "Valeur d'option et flexibilité: De la rationalité substantielle à la rationalité procédurale." In Patrick Cohendet and Patrick Llerena, eds. *Flexibilité, information et décision*, 121–82. Paris: Economica.

Favereau, Olivier, and Laurent Thévenot. 1996. "Réflexions sur la notion d'équilibre utilisable dans une économie de marchés et d'organisations." In Gérard Ballot, ed., *Les marchés internes du travail: De la microéconomie à la macroéconomie*, 273–313. Paris: Presses Universitaires de France.

Favret, Jeanne. 1968. "Relations de dépendance et manipulation de la violence en Kabylie." *L'Homme* 8 (4) (Oct.–Dec.): 18–44.

————. 1977. *Les mots, la mort, les sorts*. Paris: Gallimard.

Fleischmann, Eugène. 1964. "De Weber à Nietzsche." *Archives européennes de sociologie* 5:100–238.

Foucault, Michel. 1973 [1966]. *The Order of Things: An Archaeology of the Human Sciences*. New York: Vintage Books.

————. 1990 [1984]. *The History of Sexuality*. Vol. 3, *The Care of the Self*. Trans. Robert Hurley. New York: Pantheon Books.

Furet, François. 1981a [1978]. *Interpreting the French Revolution*. Cambridge: Cambridge University Press; Paris: Editions de la Maison des Sciences de l'Homme.

————. 1981b. Préface to Alexis de Tocqueville, *De la démocratie en Amérique* [1835], 2 vols, 7–46. Paris: Garnier-Flammarion.

Furet, François, and Jacques Ozouf. 1982 [1977]. *Reading and Writing: Literacy in France from Calvin to Jules Ferry*. Cambridge: Cambridge University Press.

Galton, Francis. 1972 [1869]. *Hereditary Genius*. Intro. C. D. Darlington. Gloucester, Mass.: Peter Smith.

Geertz, Clifford. 1978. "The Bazaar Economy: Information and Search in Peasant Marketing." *American Economic Review* 68 (2): 28–32.

————. 1983. *Local Knowledge*. New York: Basic Books.

Ginzburg, Carlo. 1980. "Signes, traces, pistes: Racines d'un paradigme de l'indice." *Le Débat* 7:3–44.

Girard, René. 1977 [1972]. *Violence and the Sacred*. Trans. Patrick Gregory. Baltimore: Johns Hopkins University Press.

Godard, Olivier. 1989. "Jeux de natures: Quand le débat sur l'efficacité des politiques publiques contient la question de leur légitimité." In Nicole Mathieu and Marcel Jollivet, eds., *Du rural à l'environnement: La question de la nature aujourd'hui*, 303–42. Paris: L'Harmattan.

————. 1990. "Environnement, modes de coordination et systèmes de légitimité: Analyse de la catégorie de patrimoine naturel." *Revue économique* 2 (March): 215–42.

Goffman, Erving. *The Presentation of Self in Everyday Life*. Garden City, N.Y.: Doubleday, 1959.

Goldschmidt, Victor. 1974. *Anthropologie et politique: Les principes du système de Rousseau*. Paris: Vrin.

Gouhier, Henri. 1970 [1941]. *La jeunesse d'Auguste Comte et la formation du positivisme*. Vol. 3, *Auguste Comte et Saint-Simon*. 2d ed. Paris: Vrin.

Gracian y Morales, Baltasar. 1685 [1647]. *The Courtiers' Manual Oracle: or, The Art of Prudence*. Trans. from the Spanish. London: Printed by M. Flesher, for Abel Swalle.

Grassi, Ernesto. 1969. "Critical Philosophy or Topical Philosophy? Meditations on the *De nostri temporis studiorum ratione*." In Tagliacozzo and White 1969, 39–50.

Guy, Jean-Claude. 1976. *Paroles des anciens: Apophtegmes des pères du désert*. Paris: Seuil.

Habermas, Jürgen. 1984–87 [1981]. *The Theory of Communication Action*. Trans. Thomas McCarthy. Boston: Beacon Press.

Hacking, Ian. 1975. *The Emergence of Probability*. Cambridge: Cambridge University Press.

Halbwachs, Maurice., 1976 [1943]. "Introduction, notes, commentaires." In Jean-Jacques Rousseau, *Du contrat social*. Paris: Aubier-Montaigne.

Hayek, Friedrich A. von. 1944. *Scientism and the Study of Society*. London: London School of Economics and Political Science.

———. 1952. *The Counter-Revolution of Science: Studies on the Abuse of Reason*. Glencoe, Ill.: Free Press, 1952.

Héran, François. 1984. "L'assise statistique de la sociologie." *Économie et statistique* 169:23–26.

Hirschman, Albert O. 1970. *Exit, Voice, and Loyalty*. Cambridge: Harvard University Press.

———. 1977. *The Passions and the Interests*. Princeton: Princeton University Press.

———. 1982a. "Rival Interpretations of Market Society: Civilizing, Destructive, or Feeble?" *Journal of Economic Literature* 20:1463–84.

———. 1982b. *Shifting Involvements: Private Interest and Public Action*. Princeton: Princeton University Press.

Hobbes, Thomas. 1969 [1640]. *The Elements of Law: Natural and Politic*. Ed. Ferdinand Tönnies. London: Frank Cass and Co.

———. 1997 [1651]. *Leviathan*. Ed. Richard E. Flathman and David Johnston. New York: W. W. Norton and Co.

Hollander, Samuel. 1975. "On the Role of Utility and Demand in *The Wealth of Nations*." In Skinner and Wilson 1975, 313–23.

Hume, David. 1978 [1739–40]. *A Treatise of Human Nature*. Ed. L. A. Selby-Bigge. Oxford: Clarendon Press; New York: Oxford University Press.

Jamous, Raymond. 1977. *Honneur et baraka*. Paris: Éditions de la Maison des Sciences de l'Homme.

Jaume, Lucien. 1983. "La théorie de la 'personne fictive' dans le *Leviathan* de Hobbes." *Revue française de sciences politiques* 33 (6): 1009–35.

Julia, Dominique. 1981. *Les trois couleurs du tableau noir: La Révolution*. Paris: Belin.

Kantorowicz, Ernst. 1957. *The King's Two Bodies: A Study in Medieval Political Theology*. Princeton: Princeton University Press.

Kaplan, Steven L. 1976. *Bread, Politics, and Political Economy in the Reign of Louis XV*. The Hague: Martinus Nijhoff.

———. 1982. *The Famine Plot: Persuasion in Eighteenth-Century France*. Philadelphia: American Philosophical Society.

———. 1984. *Provisioning Paris: Merchants and Millers in the Grain and Flour Trade during the Eighteenth Century*. Ithaca: Cornell University Press.

Kauder, Emil. 1953. "The Retarded Acceptance of the Marginal Utility Theory." *Quarterly Journal of Economics* 67 (4): 564–75.

Keohane, Nannerl. 1980. *Philosophy and the State in France: The Renaissance to the Enlightenment*. Princeton: Princeton University Press.

Kerr, Clark. 1954. "The Balkanisation of Labor Markets." In Edward Wight Bakke et al., *Labor Mobility and Economic Opportunity*, 92–110 New York: MIT Press.

Keynes, John Maynard. 1936. *The General Theory of Employment, Interest, and Money*. New York: Harcourt, Brace and Co.

Koselleck, Reinhart. 1988 [1959]. *Critique and Crisis: Enlightenment and the Pathogenesis of Modern Society*. Cambridge: MIT Press.

Kramarz, F. 1989. "La comptabilité nationale à la maison." In Boltanski and Thévenot 1989, 219–45.

La Bruyère, Jean de. 1929 [1688]. *The Characters of Jean de la Bruyère*. Trans. Henri van Laun. New York: Brentano's.

Lacan, Jacques. 1980 [1932]. *De la psychose paranoïaque dans ses rapports avec la personnalité*. Paris: Seuil.

Lacroix, Bernard. 1981. *Durkheim et le politique*. Paris: Presses de la fondation nationale des sciences politiques.

Lafaye, Claudette. 1987. "La cohérence des services municipaux et la pluralité des logiques d'action." Mimeo. Paris, Groupe de Sociologie politique et morale.

———. 1989. "Réorganisation industrielle d'une municipalité de gauche." In Boltanski and Thévenot 1989, 43–66.

———. 1990. "Situations tendues et sens ordinaire de la justice au sein d'une administration municipale." *Revue française de sociologie* 31–32 (April–June): 199–223.

Lagarde, Georges de. 1956. *La naissance de l'esprit laïque au déclin du Moyen Âge*. Louvain: Nauwelaerts.

Langlois, Charles Victor, and Charles Seignebos. 1926 [1898]. *Introduction to the Study of History*. Trans. G. G. Berry. New York: H. Holt.

Lapierre, Jean-Pie., 1982. *Règles des moines*. Paris: Seuil.

Latour, Bruno. 1988. *The Pasteurization of France*. Trans. Alan Sheridan and John Law. Cambridge: Harvard University Press.

———. 1989. *La science en action*. Paris: La Découverte.

———. 1994. "Une sociologie sans objet? Remarques sur l'interobjectivité." *Sociologie du travail* 36 (4): 587–617.

Latour, Bruno, and Shirley Strum. 1986. "Human Social Origins: Oh, Please, Tell Us Another Origin Story." *Journal of Social and Biological Structures* 9:169–87.

Latour, Bruno, and Steve Woolgar. 1988. *La vie de laboratoire*. Paris: La Découverte.

Le Bon, Gustave. 1977 [1895]. *The Crowd*. Ed. Robert Nye. New Brunswick, N.J.: Transaction Publishers.

Lévy-Bruhl, Henri. 1964. *La preuve judiciaire*. Paris: Marcel Rivière.

Lewis, Andrew W. 1986 [1981]. *Royal Succession in Capetian France: Studies on Familial Order and the State*. Cambridge: Harvard University Press.

Lida de Malkiel, Maria Rosa. 1968. *L'idée de la gloire dans la tradition occidentale*. Paris: Klincksieck.

Locke, John. 1966 [1690]. *The Second Treatise of Government (An Essay Concerning the True and Original Extent and End of Civil Government) and a Letter Concerning Toleration*. Ed. J. W. Gough. Oxford: Blackwell.

Lombroso, Gina. 1931. *La rançon du machinisme*. Trans. H. Winckler. Paris: Payot.

Lukes, Steven. 1973. *Émile Durkheim, His Life and Work: A Historical and Critical Study*. London: Allen Lane.

Luedtke, Alfred. 1986. "Cash, Coffee-breaks, Horse-play: '*Eigensinn*' and Politics among Factory Workers in Germany around 1900." In Michael Hanagan and Charles Stephenson, eds., *Confrontation, Class Consciousness, and the Labor Process: Studies in Proletarian Class Formation*. New York: Greenwood Press.

Mackenzie, Donald A. 1981. *Statistics in Britain, 1865–1930*. Edinburgh: Edinburgh University Press.

Macpherson, Crawford Borough. 1964 [1962]. *The Political Theory of Possessive Individualism: Hobbes to Locke*. Oxford: Oxford University Press.

Mandeville, Bernard. 1924 [1714]. *The Fable of the Bees; or, Private Vices, Publick Benefits*. Ed. F. B. Kaye. Oxford: Clarendon Press.

Marin, Louis. 1988 [1981]. *Portrait of the King*. Trans. Martha M. Houle. Minneapolis: University of Minnesota Press.

Marrou, Henri Irénée. 1957. *Saint Augustin et l'augustinisme*. Paris: Seuil.

Marx, Karl. 1959 [1867–94]. *Capital, The Communist Manifesto, and Other Writings*. Intro. Max Eastman. New York: Modern Library.

Mauss, Marcel. 1990 [1923]. *The Gift: The Form and Reason for Exchange in Archaic Societies*. Trans. W. D. Halls. London: Routledge.

McCormack, Mark H. 1984. *What They Don't Teach You at Harvard Business School*. Toronto: Bantam.

Mead, George Herbert. 1962 [1934]. *Mind, Self, and Society from the Standpoint of a Social Behaviorist*. Ed. Charles W. Morris. Chicago: University of Chicago Press.

Mesnard, Pierre. 1977 [1969]. *L'essor de la philosophie politique au XVIe siècle*. Paris: Vrin.

Montesquieu, Charles de Secondat, Baron de. 1989 [1748]. *The Spirit of the Laws*. Trans. Anne M. Cohler, Basia C. Miller, and Harold Stone. Cambridge: Cambridge University Press.

Morin, Edgar. 1972. *Les stars*. Paris: Seuil.

Moscovici, Serge. 1985 [1981]. *The Age of the Crowd: A Historical Treatise on Mass Psychology*. Trans. J. C. Whitehouse. Cambridge: Cambridge University Press; Paris: Editions de la Maison des Sciences de l'Homme.

Mousnier, Roland. 1979–84 [1974]. *The Institutions of France under the Absolute Monarch, 1598–1789: Society and the State*. 2 vols. Trans. Brian Pearce. Chicago: University of Chicago Press.

Nelson, Richard R., and Sidney G. Winter. 1982. *An Evolutionary Theory of Economic Change*. Cambridge: Harvard University Press.

Nicole, Pierre. 1696 [1671]. *Moral Essayes, Contain'd in Several Treatises on Many Important Duties*. 2d ed., 4 vols. London: Sam Manship.

Nietzsche, Friedrich. 1948 [1901]. *La volonté de puissance*. Trans. Geneviève Bianquis. Paris: Gallimard.

———. 1968 [1901]. *The Will to Power*. Trans. Walter Kaufmann and R. J. Hollingdale, ed. Walter Kaufmann. New York: Vintage Books.

———. 1971 (1887). *La généalogie de la morale*. Ed. Giorgio Colli and Mazzino, trans. Cornélius Heim, Isabelle Hildenbrand, and Jean Gratien. In *Oeuvres philosophiques complètes*, vol. 7, Paris: Gallimard.

———. 1974 [1883–87]. *The Gay Science.* Trans. Walter Kaufmann. New York: Vintage Books.

———. 2001. *The Gay Science.* Ed. Bernard Williams, trans. Josephine Nauckhoff. Cambridge: Cambridge University Press.

Nisbet, Robert A. 1966. *The Sociological Tradition.* New York: Basic Books.

Nozick, Robert. 1974. *Anarchy, State, and Utopia.* Oxford: Basil Blackwell.

Olson, Mancur. 1965. *The Logic of Collective Action.* Cambridge: Harvard University Press.

Palladius. 1965. *The Lausiac History.* Westminster, Md.: Newman Press.

Pappas, John N. 1982. "La campagne des philosophes contre l'honneur." *Studies on Voltaire and the Eighteenth Century* 205:31–44.

Pareto, Vilfredo. 1968 [1917]. *Traité de sociologie générale.* Pref. Raymond Aron. Geneva: Droz.

Parrot, Jean-Philippe. 1974. *La représentation des intérêts dans le mouvement des idées politiques.* Paris: Presses Universitaires de France.

Pascal, Blaise. 1696. "Three Discourses of Monsieur Pascal, Lately Deceas'd: Touching the Condition of the Great." In *Moral Essayes, Contain'd in Several Treatises on Many Important Duties,* 2nd ed., 4 vols. London: Sam Manship.

———. 1954. *Oeuvres complètes.* Paris: Gallimard, coll. Pléiade.

———. 1966. *Pensées.* Trans. A. J. Krailsheimer. Harmondsworth: Penguin, 1966.

———. 1995 [1670]. *Pensées and Other Writings.* Trans. Honor Levi. Oxford: Oxford University Press.

Pharo, Patrick. 1985. *Le civisme ordinaire.* Paris: Librairie des Méridiens.

Pierrot, Maurice. 1980. *Productivité et conditions de travail: Un guide diagnostic pour entrer dans l'action.* Paris: Entreprise moderne d'édition.

Pizzorno, Alessandro. 1990. "On Rationality and Democratic Choice." In Pierre Birnbaum and Jean Leca, eds., *Individualism: Theories and Methods,* trans. John Gaffney, 295–331. Oxford: Clarendon Press; New York: Oxford University Press. 295–331.

Plato. *Gorgias.* Trans. W.R.M. Lamb. Loeb Classical Library.

———. *Phaedrus.* Trans. Harold North Fowler. Loeb Classical Library.

———. 1950. *Oeuvres complètes.* Ed. Léon Robin with M.-J. Moreau, 2:431–524. Paris: Gallimard, coll. Pléiade.

Polanyi, Michael. 1962. *Personal Knowledge: Toward a Post-Critical Philosophy.* Chicago: University of Chicago Press.

Pollak, Michael. 1986. "La gestion de l'indicible." *Actes de la recherche en sciences sociales* 62–63:3–53.

———. 1990. *L'expérience concentrationnaire: Essai sur le maintien de l'identité sociale.* Paris: Métailié.

Prost, Antoine. 1992 [1977]. *In the Wake of War: 'Les anciens combattants' and French Society.* Trans. Helen McPhail. Providence: Bery.

Pufendorf, Samuel. 1749 [1672]. *Of the Law of Nature and Nations.* 5th ed. Trans. Basil Kennet. London: R. Sare.

Raphael, D. D. 1975. "The Impartial Spectator." In Skinner and Wilson 1975, 83–99.

Rawls, John. 1973 [1972]. *A Theory of Justice.* Oxford: Oxford University Press.

Revel, Jacques. 1989 [1986]. "The Uses of Civility." In Philippe Ariès and Georges Duby, eds., *A History of Private Life*, 3:167–205. Cambridge, Mass.: Harvard University Press, Belknap Press.

Reynolds, Lloyd George. 1951. *The Structure of Labor Markets*. New York: Harper.

Ricoeur, Paul. 1970 [1965]. *Freud and Philosophy: An Essay on Interpretation*. Trans. Denis Savage. New Haven: Yale University Press.

———. 1974 [1969]. *The Conflict of Interpretations: Essays in Hermeneutics*. Ed. Don Ihde. Evanston, Ill.: Northwestern University Press.

———. 1991 [1979]. "Practical Reason." Trans. Kathleen Blamey. In *From Text to Action: Essays in Hermeneutics*. vol. 2, trans. Kathleen Blamey and John B. Thompson, 188–207. Evanston, Ill.: Northwestern University Press.

Richards, Alfred Bate, and Adam Kuper, eds. 1971. *Councils in Action*. Cambridge: Cambridge University Press.

Riley, Patrick. 1982. *Will and Political Legitimacy*. Cambridge: Harvard University Press.

———. 1986. *The General Will before Rousseau*. Princeton: Princeton University Press.

Robertson, H. M., and W. L. Taylor. 1957. "Adam Smith's Approach to the Theory of Value." *Economic Journal* 67 (266): 181–98.

Roover, Raymond de. 1955. "Scholastic Economics: Survival and Lasting Influence from the Sixteenth Century to Adam Smith." *Quarterly Journal of Economics* 69 (2) (May 1955): 161–90.

———. 1971. *La pensée économique des scolastiques, doctrines et méthodes*. Montréal: Institut d'études médiévales; Paris: Vrin.

Rosanvallon, Pierre. 1985. *Le moment Guizot*. Paris: Gallimard.

Rosch, Eleanor, and B. B. Lloyd. 1978. *Cognition and Categorization*. New York: Erlbaum.

Rousseau, Jean-Jacques. 1964 [1762]. *Du contract social, ou principes du droit politique*. Ed. Robert Derathé. In Rousseau, *Oeuvres complètes*, 3:349–470. Paris: Gallimard.

———. 1968 [1758]. *Politics and the Arts: Letter to M. D'Alembert on the Theatre*. Trans. Allan Bloom. Ithaca, N.Y.: Cornell University Press.

———. 1974 [1762]. *Emile*. Trans. Barbara Foxley. London: Dent; New York: Dutton.

———. 1994 [1762]. *The Social Contract*. In *Discourse on Political Economy and The Social Contract*. Trans. Christopher Betts. Oxford: Oxford University Press.

———. 1995 [1782, 1789]. *The Confessions; and, Correspondence, including the Letters to Malesherbes*. Ed. Christopher Kelly, Roger D. Masters, and Peter G. Stillman, trans. Christopher Kelly. Hanover, N.H.: University Press of New England.

———. 1997a. "Geneva Manuscript" (*The Social Contract*, first version, 1762). In *The Discourses and Other Early Political Writings*, ed. and trans. Victor Gourevitch. Cambridge: Cambridge University Press.

———. 1997b [1761]. *Julie; or, The New Heloise: Letters of Two Lovers Who Live in a Small Town at the Foot of the Alps*. Trans. Philip Stewart and Jean Vaché, ed. Roger D. Masters and Christopher Kelly. Hanover, N.H.: University Press of New England.

————. 1997c. "Discourse on The Origin and the Foundations of Inequality among Men" ("Second Discourse," 1754). In *The Social Contract and Other Later Political Writings*. ed. and trans. Victor Gourevitch, 113–228. Cambridge: Cambridge University Press.

————. 1997d. "Discourse on the Sciences and Arts" ("First Discourse," 1750). In *The Social Contract and Other Later Political Writings*, ed. and trans. Victor Gourevitch, 1–112. Cambridge: Cambridge University Press.

Sabel, Charles. 1982. *Work and Politics*. Cambridge: Cambridge University Press.

Sacco, Nicola, and Bartolomeo Vanzetti. 1928. *The Letters of Sacco and Vanzetti*. Ed. Marion Denman Frankfurther and Gardner Jackson. New York: Viking Press.

Sahlins, Marshall. 1976. *The Use and Abuse of Biology: An Anthropological Critique of Sociobiology*. Ann Arbor: University of Michigan Press.

Saint-Simon, Claude-Henri de. 1869 [1817]. *L'industrie*. In *Oeuvres complètes*, vol. 2. Paris: E. Dentu.

————. *L'organisateur* (1819). In *Oeuvres complètes*, Paris: E. Dentu.

————. *Du système industriel* (1819). In *Oeuvres complètes*, Paris: E. Dentu.

————. 1965 [1808]. "Introduction aux travaux scientifiques du XIXe siècle." In *La physiologie sociale: Oeuvres choisies*. Ed. Georges Gurvitch. Paris: Presses Universitaires de France.

Salais, Robert, Nicolas Bavarez, and Bénédicte Reynaud, 1986. *L'invention du chômage*. Paris: Presses Universitaires de France.

Salais, Robert, and Laurent Thévenot, eds. 1986. *Le travail: Marchés, règles, conventions*. Paris: INSEE-Economica.

Sartre, Jean-Paul. 1956 [1943]. *Being and Nothingness: An Essay on Phenomenological Ontology*. Trans. Hazel E. Barnes. New York: Philosophical Library.

Schneider, Christian. 1970. *Principes et techniques des relations publiques*. Paris: Delmas.

Schumpeter, Joseph Alois. 1954. *History of Economic Analysis*. Ed. Elizabeth Boody Schumpeter. New York: Oxford University Press.

Seneca. "De vita beata" (On the happy life). Trans. John Basore. In *Moral Essays*, 2:98–179. Cambridge: Harvard University Press (Loeb Classical Library).

Sewell, William Hamilton. 1980. *Work and Revolution in France: The Language of Labor from the Old Regime to 1848*. Cambridge: Cambridge University Press.

Sieyès, Emmanuel Joseph. 1970 [1789]. *Qu'est-ce que le Tiers-État?* Ed. Roberto Zepperi. Geneva: Droz.

Silver, Alan. 1989. "Friendship and Trust as Moral Ideal: An Historical Approach." *Journal européen de sociologie* 30:274–97.

Skinner, Andrew S., and Thomas Wilson, eds. 1975. *Essays on Adam Smith*. Oxford: Clarendon Press.

Skinner, Quentin. 1978. *The Foundations of Modern Political Thought*. 2 vols. Cambridge: Cambridge University Press.

Smith, Adam. 1880 [1795]. *Essays Philosophical and Literary*. London: Ward, Lock and Co.

————. 1976 [1759]. *The Theory of Moral Sentiments*. Ed. D. D. Raphael and A. L. Macfie. Oxford: Clarendon.

————. 1977. *Correspondence of Adam Smith*. Ed. Ernest Campbell Mossner and Ian Simpson Ross. Oxford: Clarendon.

————. 1991 [1776]. *The Wealth of Nations*. Books 1–3. Intro. Andrew S. Skinner. Harmondsworth: Penguin Books.

Starobinski, Jean. 1988 [1971]. *Jean-Jacques Rousseau, Transparency and Obstruction*. Trans. Arthur Goldhammer. Chicago: University of Chicago Press.

Steuart, James. 1767. *Inquiry into the Principles of Political Oeconomy, Being an Essay on the Science of Domestic Policy in Free Nations*. London: A. Millar and T. Cadell.

Strauss, Leo. 1953. *Natural Right and History*. Chicago: University of Chicago Press.

Sulloway, Frank J. 1979. *Freud, Biologist of the Mind: Beyond the Psychoanalytic Legend*. New York: Basic Books.

Tagliacozzo, Giorgio, and Hayden V. White, eds. 1969. *Giambattista Vico, an International Symposium*. Baltimore: Johns Hopkins University Press.

Thévenot, Laurent. 1979. "Une jeunesse difficile: Les fonctions sociales du flou et de la rigueur dans les classements." *Actes de la recherche en sciences sociales* 26–27:3–18.

————. 1983. "Les économies du codage social." *Critiques de l'Économie politique* 23–24:188–222.

————. 1984. "Rules and Implements: Investment in Forms." *Social Science Information* 23 (no. 1): 1–45.

————. ed., 1986. *Conventions économiques*. Paris: CEE-Presses Universitaires de France.

————. 1987. "Les enquêtes: Formation et qualification professionnelle et leurs ancêtres français." In Affichard 1987, 2:117–65.

————. 1989a. "Économie et politique de l'entreprise: Économies de l'efficacité et de la confiance." In Boltanski and Thévenot 1989, 135–207.

————. 1989b. "Équilibre et rationalité dans un univers complexe." *Revue économique* 2 (March): 147–97.

————. 1990a. "L'action qui convient." In Patrick Pharo and Louis Quéré, eds., *Les formes de l'action*, 39–69. Paris: EHESS.

————. 1990b. "L'origine sociale des enquêtes de mobilité sociale." *Annales E.S.C.* 6 (Nov.–Dec.): 1275–1300.

Thomas Aquinas, St. 1949 [1265–73]. *Somme Théologique*, 2a–2ae, questions 47–56. Ed. and trans. T.-H. Deman. Paris: Desclée de Brouwer.

————. 1981 [1265–73]. *Summa Theologica*. Vol. 3. Westminster, Md.: Christian Classics.

Tocqueville, Alexis de. 1988 [1835]. *Democracy in America*. Ed. J. P. Mayer, trans. George Lawrence. New York: Harper & Row.

Turgot, Anne-Robert-Jacques. 1970 [1776]. *Les édits de Turgot*. Pref. Maurice Garden. Paris: Imprimerie Nationale.

————. 1977. *The Economics of A.R.J. Turgot*. Ed. P. D. Groenewegen. The Hague: Martinus Hijhoff.

Turner, Victor. 1967. *The Forest of Symbols: Aspects of Ndembu Ritual*. Ithaca: Cornell University Press.

Vaughan, Charles Edwin. 1971 [1915]. *The Political Writings of Jean-Jacques Rousseau*. 2 vols. New York: Burt Franklin.

Veblen, Thorstein. 1953 [1899]. *The Theory of the Leisure Class: An Economic Study of Institutions*. Intro. C. Wright Mills. New York: New American Library.

Vernant, Jean-Pierre, ed. 1974. *Divination et rationalité.* Paris: Seuil.

Vico, Giambattista, 1963 [1744]. *The Autobiography of Giambattista Vico.* Trans. Max Harold Flesch and Thomas Goddard Bergin. Ithaca: Great Seal Books.

———. 1981 [1744]. *Vie de Giambattista Vico écrite par lui-même.* Intro. and notes by Alain Pons. Paris: Grasset.

———. 1984 [1725]. *The New Science of Giambattista Vico.* Ithaca: Cornell University Press.

———. 1990 [1709]. *On the Study Methods of Our Time.* Trans Elio Gianturco. Ithaca: Cornell University Press.

Villey, Michel. 1983. *Le droit et les droits de l'homme.* Paris: Presses Universitaires de France.

von Mises, Ludwig. 1944. *Bureaucracy.* New Haven: Yale University Press.

Walliser, Bernard. 1985. *Anticipations, équilibres, et rationalité économique,* Paris: Calmann-Lévy.

Walras, Léon. 1954 [1874]. *Elements of Pure Economics; or, The Theory of Social Wealth.* Trans. William Jaffé. Homewood, Ill.: Richard D. Irwin.

Walzer, Michael. 1974. *Regicide and Revolution. Speeches at the Trial of Louis XVI.* Cambridge: Cambridge University Press.

———. 1983. *Spheres of Justice. A Defense of Pluralism and Equality.* New York: Basic Books.

Ward, Benedicta, ed. and trans. 1967. *The Sayings of the Desert Fathers: The Alphabetical Collection.* London: A. R. Mowbray; Kalamazoo, Mich.: Cistercian Publications.

Weber, Max. 1968 [1922]. *Economy and Society: An Outline of Interpretive Sociology.* Ed. Guenther Roth and Claus Wittich, trans. Ephraim Fischoff et al. New York: Bedminster Press.

Weiss, John Hubbel. 1982. *The Making of Technological Man: The Social Origins of French Engineering Education.* Cambridge: MIT Press.

Williamson, Oliver E. 1975. *Markets and Hierarchies: Analysis and Antitrust Implications; A Study in the Economics of Internal Organization.* New York: Free Press.

———. 1985. *The Economic Institutions of Capitalism: Firms, Market, Relational Contracting.* New York: Macmillan.

Wissler, André. 1987. "Cohésion de l'entreprise et pluralité des logiques d'action." Mimeo. Paris: Groupe de Sociologie politique et morale.

———. 1989a. "Les jugements dans l'octroi de crédit." In Boltanski and Thévenot 1989, 67–119.

———. 1989b. "Prudence bancaire et incertitude." In Eymard-Duvernet 1989, 201–37.

PRINCETON STUDIES IN CULTURAL SOCIOLOGY